Hello and welcome aboard my dear fellow *"Living on Earth Game"* Co-Traveler. It is my soul's utmost pleasure to connect with yours right here in this very *"Now Moment"*. Thank you SO much for having picked UP this "magical", emPowering and somewhat as "difFeRent" interpreted reading adventure exercise. Happily, I would love to introduce to you the probably first ever, a 100% A-Z Swiss made accepted book Artwork creation challenge, that guided by a LOT of "Doing Me" purpose ends up presenting itself into your awareness as *Authentic, Real, Pure* and *Truthful* to my own, in Switzerland started out soul as possible. Throughout our travels, you therefore will be finding yourself *"ongRowingly"* being exposed to my own, within the past 11 1/2 years adapted "AmericanSwiss" developed "accent", of which reasons you will be able to collect One-by-One as we keep on moving forward. Furthermore, I would love to point out to you that this entire *"the DOiNG ME PROjECT"* storyline solely has been approached and guided by my *Heart's*, my *"little Linda's"* and by my *Soul's* Own internal appeared interpretation perspectives. Any head "logic" therefore thrillingly has been banned out of this liberating and *"Self-stDream"* opening exercise at hand. YAY. Please also know, that this entire *"Finding back Home again"* writing journey did take place over a magical, though *"NeverEnding"* seemingly duration period of EXACTLY 2 years and 5 months, which time span in retrospective therefore enabled for the wonderful Universe to support my "assigned" mission in its uncompleted "real time" considered perspective from *"Moment-to-Moment"*, Day in Day out, alongside with YOU and for the two of US. The countless reasons as of WHY, I guided by my inner voice in a way got "forced" to share this entire *"Living on Earth Game"* Linda Wartenweiler "AutoBiography" with you, lie within all the many UPcoming, with *Positivity, Music Tunes, Quotes* and with a LOT moRE *"FuN Facts"* packed lines and within your own *"Head Cinema"* interpretation creation experience. Now, as this excursion ahead intentionally has been created for our two own unique and precious *"True little Self's"*, *"little Linda"* therefore very much so feels prompted, to encourage your soul to direct ALL of your attention towards your Own *Co-Traveling "inner Child's"* existence, who with No Doubt from the get-go will be enriching Your daily *"Living on Earth Game"* adventures in an Abundance of sparkly new ways. iF you allow it to. BOOM. That's right. Alrighty then. That's it for NOW. Let's Do this! *"Get Ready Steady to Jump my Darling. Just take my hand. jUMP!"* ABRACADABRA.

Chapter iNdex

SWiTZERLAND or "Let the Games Begin"

"Whoomp! There she is."	1
"This is How we Did it"	10
"Dream a little Dream for Me"	16
"Don't Stop Believin'. Hold On to Your Dreamin'."	24
"The Only way is UP"	36
"One way or Another, I'm gonna Find Ya' and Get Ya'. Watch Out."	48
"Get Ready Steady to Jump my Darling. Just take my hand. jUMP!"	62
"STOP! In the name of LOVE."	83

NEW YORK CITY or "Don't Dream your Life. Live your Dream."

"Let's Get really ROCKED. Yeah. Let's go ALL the way."	94
"Put your hands UP in the Air. Put your hands UP in the Air."	111
"Step-by-Step. Oh yeah. I really know it's just a Matter of Time."	117
"I got the Poison and the Remedy. I got the Pulsating Rhythmical remedy."	134
"Here we Go again with total Dedication."	147
"Get UP my Darling and Get Your Dreamin' before your Chance is over."	160
"Keep on Movin' my Darling. Ooh ooh-ooh ooh."	176

LOS ANGELES or "Finding back Home again"

"Love and Devotion, my "True little Self". Please come back into my Life."	188
"Time to say Goodbye"	200
"My Way. I'll do iT MY way."	214
"Hit Me, baby, One More time."	222
"Rising UP, Back on my Feet. Have the Guts, to Chase my Glory."	235
"So this is What "The Truth About self-Love" Feels Like. 'Cause I'm Feeling it. Oh yeah I'm Feeling it."	246
"WOW. I truly was re-Born in the U.S.A. Yeah."	267

P.S.   275

the DOiNG ME PROjECT
by linda wartenweiler

* * *

"Think of this random Universe where EVERYTHiNG iS Possible. The Organizational Skills belong to Law of Attraction. If you will Relax and Allow Law of Attraction to Do the Organization and the Managing, then YOU can Spend your Time Doing the Things that Please YOU." - Abraham-Hicks

* * *

"Don't EVER let ANYTHiNG Stand in the Way of YOUR Dreams. Catch the Star that Holds YOUR Destiny, the One that FOREVER Twinkles within Your Heart. Take Advantage of Precious Opportunities while they still Sparkle before you. ALWAYS Believe that your Ultimate Goal iS Attainable as long as you Commit yourSelf to it. Though Barriers May Sometimes Stand in The Way of Your Dreams. Remember that Destiny is Hiding Behind Them. The Greatest Gifts in Life are NOT Purchased but Acquired through Hard Work and Determination. Find the Star that Twinkles in YOUR Heart for You are Capable of Making YOUR Brightest Dreams Come True. Give Your Everything You've Got and You WiLL Catch the Star that Holds YOUR Destiny." - Shannon M. Lester

* * *

"You Can't Connect the Dots Looking Forward, you can ONLY Connect them Looking Backwards. So you HAVE to Trust that the Dots Will Somehow Connect in Your Future. You Have to Trust in Something — Your Gut, Destiny, Life, Karma, Whatever. This Approach has NEVER Let Me Down, and it has Made ALL The difFeRence in my Life." - Steve Jobs

* * *

Copyright © 2018 by *Linda Wartenweiler*

First Paperback Edition *May 2018*

Published by *Linda Wartenweiler, Encinitas, CA*

www.TheDoingMeProject.com

All rights reserved. No part of this book may be reproduced or transmitted in any form or any means, electronic or mechanical, including photocopying, recording, or by any information storage and retrieval system without the written permission of the author, except in the case of brief quotations embodied in critical reviews and certain other non-commercial uses permitted by law.

Photograph of the Author by *Bettina Perler-Sutter*
Instagram *@be.pe.su*

Cover Design and Layout by *Linda Wartenweiler*

Library of Congress Control Number 2018905929

iSBN13 978-0692119938
iSBN-10 0692119930

uncredited *"Head Cinema"* Soundtrack Reference iNdex
in chronological order

Please note that the complete, throughout our travels appearing "Head Cinema" soundtrack collection finds itself within one CLiCK accessible via a on www.TheDoingMeProject.com HOME placed Spotify and YouTube link. Enjoy!

"Whoomp! There she is."
based on Tag Team's *"Whoomp! There it is."* (1993)

"This is How we Did it"
based on Montell Jordan's *"This is How We Do it"* (1995)

"Dream a little Dream for Me"
based on The Mamas & Papas' *"Dream A Little Dream Of Me"* (1968)

"Don't Stop Believin'. Hold On to Your Dreamin'."
based on Journey's *"Don't Stop Believin'"* (1981)

"The Only way is UP"
by Yazz & The Plastic Population (1988)

"One way or Another, I'm gonna Find Ya' and Get Ya'. Watch Out."
based on Blondie's *"One Way or Another"* (1979)

"Coo-coo-cool. Yeah, yeah. I know You're Cool."
based on Gwen Stefanie's *"Cool"* (2004)

"Get Ready Steady to Jump my Darling. Just take my hand. jUMP!"
based on Madonna's *"Jump"* (2005)

"Destiny's Path"
by DJ Kai Tracid (1999)

"STOP! In the name of LOVE"
by The Supremes (1965)

"Girls just wanna have FuN"
by Cyndi Lauper (1983)

"Rebel Yell"
by Billy Idol (1983)

"High on Emotion"
by Chris De Burgh (1984)

"Dancing On The Ceiling"
by Lionel Richie (1986)

"Maniac"
by Michael Sambello (1983)

"Smooth Criminal"
by Michael Jackson (1987)

"Hello? Is it me you're looking for?"
by Lionel Richie *"Hello" (1983)*

"Love is a Battlefield"
by Pat Benatar *(1983)*

"I've had the Time of My Life and I Owe it All to You"
by Jennifer Warnes and Bill Medley *"The Time Of My Life" (1987)*

"Let's Get really ROCKED. Yeah. Let's go ALL the way."
based on Def Leppard's *"Let's Get Rocked" (1992)*

"Getting into the exploration Groove"
based on Madonna's *"Get into The Groove" (1984)*

"Empire State of Mind"
by Alicia Keys *(2009)*

"Eye of the Tiger"
by Survivor *(1982)*

"Put your hands UP in the Air. Put your hands UP in the Air."
by DJ Tonka *"Put Your Hands Up" (1998)*

"Step-by-Step. Oh yeah. I really know it's just a Matter of Time."
based on New Kids on The Block's *"Step By Step" (1990)*

"All night long. All night. OOH YEAH."
by Lionel Richie *"All Night Long" (1983)*

"Smooth as an Operator"
based on Sade's *"Smooth Operator" (1984)*

"Let's Go Crazy"
by Prince & The Revolution *(1984)*

"Because we are your friends, you'll never be alone again. Oh, come oooon"
by Justice *"We Are Your Friends" (2006)*

"Alive and Kick-in'"
by Simple Minds *(1985)*

"Knock, Knock, Knockin' on her "I Want to Break Free" door"
fusion of Guns N' Roses' *"Knockin' On Heaven's Door" (1991)* and Queen *(1984)*

"I got the Poison and the Remedy. I got the Pulsating Rhythmical remedy."
based on The Prodigy's *"Poison" (1994)*

"Here we Go again with total Dedication."
based on Stakka Bo's *"Here We Go Again" (1993)*

"Buffalo Stance"
by Neneh Cherry *(1988)*

"Ah. Push it. P-Push it REAL GOOD."
by Salt-N-Pepa *"Push It" (1986)*

"Get UP my Darling and Get Your Dreamin' before your Chance is over."
based on Technotronic's *"Get Up" (1989)*

"Seriously?!?"
by Joan Jett & The Blackhearts *"Seriously" (2013)*

"Enjoy the Silence"
by Depeche Mode *(1990)*

"Hitting with its Best Shot"
based on Pat Benatar's *"Hit Me With Your Best Shot" (1980)*

"Keep on Movin' my Darling. Ooh ooh-ooh ooh."
based on Milli Vanilli's *"Keep On Running" (1990)*

"Irgendwie/Anyhow. Irgendwo/Anywhere. Igendwann/Anytime."
by NENA *(1984)*

"With or Without You"
by U2 *(1987)*

"Somewhere over the Rainbow"
by Marusha *(1994)*

"SHOUT"
by Tears for Fears *(1984)*

"Just Hangin tough. Oh. Oh. Oh. Oh. Oh."
by New Kids on The Block *"Hangin Tough" (1988)*

"All Fired UP"
by Pat Benatar *(1988)*

"Back, Back, Forth and Forth"
by Aaliyah *"Back & Forth" (1994)*

"Eye-to-Eye"
by Joan Jett & The Blackhearts *(1994)*

"Oops. I did it again."
by Britney Spears *(2000)*

"Love and Devotion, my "True little Self". Please come back into my Life."
based on Real McCoy's *"Love And Devotion" (1995)*

"CALiFORNiA LOVE"
by 2pac ft. Dr. Dre and Roger Troutman *(1995)*

"You must be my Lucky Star"
by Madonna *"Lucky Star" (1983)*

"The Truth About self-Love"
based on P!NK's *"The Truth About Love" (2012)*

"Strike it UP"
by Black Box *(1990)*

"Help! I need Somebody."
by The Beatles *"Help!" (1965)*

"jump, jUMP A little HiGHer"
by Rotterdam Termination Source *"Poing" (1992)*

"Get the Balance Right. Get the Balance Right."
by Depeche Mode *"Get The Balance Right" (1983)*

"On and On and On and On"
by Zhane *"Hey Mr. D.J." (1993)*

"Time to say Goodbye"
by Andrea Bocelli *(1995)*

"We Come 1"
by Faithless *(2001)*

"Californication"
by Red Hot Chili Peppers *(1999)*

"Final Countdown"
by Europe *"The Final Countdown" (1986)*

"Hit that Road Jack"
by Ray Charles *"Hit The Road Jack" (1961)*

"My Way. I'll do iT MY way."
by Frank Sinatra *"My Way" (1969)*

"Should I Stay OR should I Go now"
by The Clash *"Should I Stay Or Should I Go" (1982)*

"Last Resort"
by Papa Roach *(2000)*

"Hit Me, baby, One more Time."
by Britney Spears *"...Baby One More Time" (1998)*

"Yeah, Oh Yeah, Oh Yeah"
by Joan Jett & The Blackhearts *"Do You Wanna Touch Me (Oh Yeah)" (1981)*

"And there upon a Rainbow is the Answer to a "NeverEnding" Story. Ah. Ah. Ah."
by Limahl *"The NeverEnding Story" (1984)*

"Watch and Learn, baby. It's Hot, it Burns, so I Drop it."
by Fergie ft. Nicki Minaj *"You Already Know" (2017)*

"Get this Party Started"
by P!NK *(2001)*

"That's why we have to say Goodbye."
by Madonna *"Bye Bye Baby" (1992)*

"Rising UP, Back on my Feet. Have the Guts, to Chase my Glory."
based on Survivor's *"Eye of the Tiger" (1982)*

"I Don't wanna Lose You"
by Tina Turner *(1989)*

"Shooting at the Walls of jUstice. BANG. BANG."
based on Scandal's and Patty Smyth's *"The Warrior" (1984)*

"So this is What "The Truth About self-Love" Feels Like. 'Cause I'm Feeling it. Oh yeah I'm Feeling it."
fusion of Gwen Stefani's *"Truth" (2017)* and P!NK's *"The Truth About Love" (2012)*

"Leave Me ALONE. Leave Me AlooHoHone"
by Michael Jackson *"Leave Me Alone" (1987)*

"Do the Thing that Keeps the Smile on your Faces"
by Jens *"Loops & Tings" (1993)*

"I want it ALL. I want it BACK. And I want it NOW!"
based on Queen's *"I Want it All" (1989)*

"Hilfe. Rette mich. Bitte Hilf mir so wie früher. Rette mich./ Help. Rescue me. Please Assist me as you did prior. Rescue me."
based on NENA's *"Rette Mich" (1984)*

"Simply safe THE BEST"
based on Tina Turner's *"Simply The Best" (1991)*

"WHAM. BAM."
by Wham! *"Wham Rap!" (1983)*

"Wunder Gescheh'n/ Miracles DO happen"
by NENA *(1989)*

"Do you Remember the Time"
by Michael Jackson *(1991)*

"'Cause We go Way Back, Way Back, Way Back"
by TLC ft. Snoop Dogg *"Way Back" (2017)*

"WOW. I truly was re-Born in the U.S.A. Yeah."
based on Bruce Springsteen's *"Born in The U.S.A." (1984)*

"Gotcha. Where I wanted Ya'."
based on Joan Jett & The Blackheart's *"Gotcha" (1985)*

"Starting to make that CHANGE with the Soul in the Mirror"
based on Michael Jackson's *"Man in the Mirror" (1987)*

Most significant used Quotes iNdex
In chronological Order

"The Power of Words"

"Spread your Wings my Child and Fly HiGH"

"Always follow your Hearts Desires as Radiant as possible by ensuring to Keep On Pushing Any presented Boundaries with a Living Life to its Fullest possible Approach and to therefore absolutely NEVER take NO for an answer, No Matter what, as Not even the Sky is the Limit."

"Life is Good"

"Thoughts become Things"

"Empty your Mind and become Water my Friend"   -   Bruce Lee

"Everything at its Perfect Time"

"Where there is a Will there ALWAYS is a Way"

"Everything happens for a Reason"

"The Key to your Success is to KEEP your Dream in Focus and to have the Courage to do things Other's WON'T do."

"Ask and You shall Receive at its PERFCT Time"

"Don't Dream your Life. Live your Dream."

"One can Only Know the Outcome of Anything by Giving it its Fair Shot."

"Follow your Hearts Desires. It will Lead you Towards your Destiny."
  - Oprah Winfrey

"Your Time is Limited. Don't Waste it Living Someone Else's Life. Don't be Trapped by Dogma, which is Living the Result of Other people's Thinking. Don't let the Noise of Other Opinions Drown your Own inner Voice. And Most Importantly, have the Courage to Follow YOUR Heart and Intuition, they somehow already Know What You TRULY Want to Become. Everything else is Secondary." - Steve Jobs

"Nothing is impossible. The word itself says it I'M POSSiBLE."
  - Audrey Hepburn

"All Beginnings are Hard"

"One Thing ALWAYS leads to Another in its magical Cause and eFFecT unfolding truth."

"The ONLY Person standing in Your Way is YOU" - "Black Swan"

"Where there is a Way iN, there Always is a Way OUT."

"You Always Are what you Thinkest"

"sHe, who looks OUTside DREAMS. sHe, who looks iNside AWAKENS."
- Carl Jung

"Change the way you Look At Things and the Things you Look At Change."
- Wayne W. Dyer

"When the Student is Ready, the Teacher will Appear." - Buddha

"The Key to your Own inner Happiness lies in your attempt to Bravely Embrace and Look those possibly within YourSelf existing Dragons with LOTS of LOVE and COMPASSiON into the eyes by simultaneously Surrendering Yourself with all of your Heart and Trust into the whirlwind appearing Chaos, knowing that this is HOW Your beautiful Caterpillar successfully metamorphoses itself into the so-called magical Butterfly. Abracadabra."

"Energy Flows where ones Attention Goes" - Michael Beckwith

"Patience is a Virtue"

"Less is More" - Ludwig Mies van der Rohe

"Eventually all Things Fall into Place. Until then Laugh at the Confusion. Live for the Moments. And Know that Everything happens for a Reason."
- Albert Einstein

"The TWO Most important Days in your Life are THE Day when You were Born and THE Day when you Figure Out Why."
- Mark Twain

"Action holds the Key to your Freedom"

"Good Things take Time"

"Like Attracts Like" - Ernest Holmes

"One Door Always MUST get closed First, before MANY others thereafter will be able to Burst Wide Open by rewarding THE Daring Soul with many UPgrading and more Suitable Blessings instead."

"tHinK BiG. thiNk difFeRent. Do YoU."

"Everything you Desire lies on the Other Side of Resistance."

"All the World's a Stage" - William Shakespeare

"Turn your Attention To the Desire. Think about Where you are Going and Never Mind where you have been. It Doesn't Matter." - Abraham-Hicks

"Whatever the Mind can Conceive and Believe it can Achieve."
- Napoleon Hill

"Living The Art Life means a Dedication to it, a COMPLETE Dedication, and therefore Anything that Distracts from that Path is NOT part of The Art Life." - David Lynch

"All is Good. All is Well."

* * *

"Der Anfang vom Ende/The Beginning of the End"

Let's GO
LOVE
*

SWiTZERLAND or *"Let the Games Begin"*

"Whoomp! There she is."

It all started on an early Wednesday May morning back in the mid 1970ies, in a Swiss hospital located right at the Lake Constance in the beautiful canton of Thurgau (TG). This also turned out to be the day, during which my soul after a *"NeverEnding"* and boring developing, growing and floating around journey of a total amount of 8 months came to the conclusion that *"Enough was Enough"* and that therefore it officially was at the time to finally get this *"Living on Earth Game"* adventure started. Anew. Now. As soon as my very first workout, which contained a LOT of grabbing, squeezing and willpower, successfully got completed, my soul then happily ever after reentered this sphere on earth through the only available exit door leading out of my mother's womb, wrapped around a newly designed vessel called *Linda Wartenweiler. "Hooray. And. Hello world. It is nice seeing you again."* turned out to be my instant thoughts and simultaneously found myself quite overwhelmed by this sudden and fast transition from this small bubble into this BiG earthy one, which as a result had me fall into an outburst of many happy salty teardrops. Then, the second that my freshly built lungs found themselves able to inhale their very first own breath towards my independence reality creation, I to my surprise immediately came to realize that I must have forgotten to read a very important fine print in the manual of this whole "Being in the womb Process" exercise. What? Yes. Only a few minutes after spending some more overwhelming and precious moments with my newly met parents Heidi and Urs, we all got informed by someone called *Doctor*, that with my decision of starting this adventure for once 4 weeks earlier than suggested, my weight of 2.170 kilograms or 4.7 pounds was not considered *A 100% of a safe ride yet.* What?! pOops. Immediately my vessel therefore got taken away from my parents and instead I found myself being relocated into my new temporary home called *The Incubator*, which put my next physical contact to my parents out of safety reasons on hold for the time being. Ufff. My carrying mother, as a consequence out of this early bird decision of mine, kindly got asked to daily deliver her milk to the nurse so that I properly could get fed during my very first vacation alone. Then, after an additional added *"NeverEnding"* and boring developing, growing and laying around ride of another approximately 2 weeks, this doctor finally found it safe enough to release my vessel permanently into my parents' arms with a now weight of 2.5 kg or 5.5 lbs. YES. Happy, proud and excited about my first taste of how to overcome an obstacle, I arrived at my parents' apartment safe and sound, which happened to be located in *Sulgen* TG. *"Home Sweet Home"*. Even though I experienced a LOT of FuN with Heidi and Urs, my craving for some more action, diversity and exploration kept *"ongRowing"* all along and 7 days into this new reality check of mine had me decide that it officially was time for a new challenge. Yeeha! Now, as my mother happened to be dealing with an inguinal hernia about 1 month prior to my arrival, my soul therefore felt quite prompted to give this scenario a trial as well, as I after all felt very lucky to have been able to witness everything closely from my first-row seat. With a *"Thy Wish is my Command"* attitude, I thankfully found the generous Universe instantly agreeing with my request by sending me my own inguinal hernia experience my way as a next step. Hooray! My parents for some reason though seemed a LOT less excited about my happy choice then I felt and immediately drove me back to the hospital, where my brand-new vessel ended up experiencing its very first surgery, followed by its proper needed attention instead. What?! And back I found myself anew in this boring and rather cold environment, away from those slowly and surely on me growing friendly souls, Heidi and Urs. Bummer. Then, after another *"NeverEnding"* *"Wait-a-While"* round of about 7 days, my patient parents finally ended up being able to keep my vessel close to theirs and this time for good, which I very much so made sure of. Oh yeah. Thrilled about this new success at hand, I as a result found my soul completely motivated and driven to continue this already quite action filled *"Living on Earth Game"* journey as *"little Linda"*, now lastly outside of the womb and as far away from this boring hospital environment as possible. *"Let's Rock 'n Roll!"* I therefore ended up screaming out LOUD and clear into my parent's ears as a heads up. Ha! According to my mother *"little Linda"* happened to be a very happy and pleasant soul to be around with, which certainly had a LOT to do with the supporting intent of my parents to experience their tiny baby girl that way. Yup. Whenever I apparently found myself about to dive into a puddle of salty teardrop state of mind reality, she and my dad therefore simply would jump ahead and safe the situation with some FuNNy grimaces, accompanied by some interesting sounding tunes exiting from their hysterical looking faces, which as a result had me giggle away very well entertained instead. Giggle. Giggle. Giggle. Well and that scenario leaves myself wondering right now if *"little Linda"* actually loved Heidi's and Urs' super amusing performances so much that she, whenever she caught herself being bored or in the mood for some giggles, exactly knew how to put those comedians into action. Ha! One never knows after all, right? Well, this behavior certainly would be matching my sense of humor. Oops. Wink. Some further *"FuN Facts"* that my lovely mom and I quickly ended up developing turned out to be 1) The dressing *"little Linda"* up activity and the rule of 2) Creating and experiencing as much FuN as possible. Well and here I am finding myself guessing that all those many exciting activities surely must have ignited my love for the magical world of Entertainment, from which my soul and heart further alongside of my travels the most got enticed by the fascinating elements of 1) Acting and 2) Music. Oh yeah! Certainly, you shall get to read a LOT more about those two *"FuN Fact"* passions of mine along of our both' journey together, my dear *Co-Traveler*. Yup. That is a sure "thang". Another very wonderful lesson, that I quite quickly picked up on from those many uplifting interaction experiences sides my parents, was that *Being Happy, Open Minded, Positive, Kind, Adventurous, Loving* and this all performed with an as much FuN as possible attitude, appeared to be very helpful, effective and amazing *"Life Toolbox"* ingredients to apply in ones

"Living on Earth Game" travels. Great. Got it. Shall be done. Thanks. The results out of those very early on practiced good mood exercises definitely must have influenced my, with time developed trademarks of having 1) A LOT of HiGH vibrating energy and 2) Many *"NeverEnding"* laughing attacks. LOL. Yup. True fact. Very vividly I do recall those many moments, during which *"little Linda"* got asked to please sit or stand still. Uiii. And right then I always got presented with a new quite challenging task, as *to Explore, to Experience, to Achieve and Being in Action* always played a BiG part in my daily Keeping myself happy and Radiant activities. In regards of my laughter, I assume that this muscle must have gotten its very proper workout with all those many giggling opportunities throughout my early on upbringing. Ha! The older my vessel grew, the longer those "attacks" actually would last along with it, as soon as someone or something triggered my *"Head Cinema"* successfully. *"You have such a wiLD imagination"* probably used to be the most heard of comment, delivered by those souls with whom mine shared these upcoming and hysterical images or short stories with and the *"Your laughter is so contagious and heart felt"* one from those who simply happened to be in my presence during one of those *"little Linda"* moments. Smile. Yes, and those many in my head looping scenarios with possible added FuNNy lines used to be the main reason why *"little Linda"* still found herself giggling or cracking up for another "little" while, even though everyone else already seemed to have been over the joke. LOL. Later on, during my travels, I then actually came to realize that this laughing quality gene of mine definitely must have been transmitted to my vessel sides my FuNNy mother's and from my "Oma" Wartenweiler's. Yup. With both ladies, my soul actually always found "herself" in a laughing rally and sometimes even their attacks outlasted mine. Ha! Love. This *"NeverEnding"* laughing attack trademark of mine actually ended up traveling so closely with me throughout my youth, that with time everyone in my circle instantly kept on recognizing *"little Linda"* from afar already as soon as I got put into "action". Yup. When my vessel used to be in its teenager growth state for example, I recall a friend shouting throughout the entire Movie theater *"Linda, be quite!"*, whilst I found myself busy cracking up over a scene in which "Crocodile Dundee" in part II got forced to make a very urgent phone call within Australia's desert. Well and as by the end of the 1980ies the invention of cell phones happened to be in its baby shoes still, Crocodile Dundee ended up using his own quickest available method in order to do so, which turned out to be a fast-circular swinging move of a wooden string with a stone attached to it, whilst standing on top of a huge rock. What?! This to me very abstract interpreted Acting choice definitely hit my spot instantly and "Gone with the Wind" I was by even overlapping the further appearing dialogue of the following scene or maybe even sceneS. Oops. LOL. My friends "silence" efforts though ended up helping as far as of having my face blush within the following seconds and for my soul to crack up even more so. Ha! Thank God that The Dark Room perfectly well assisted my attempt of covering my by then out of embarrassment *"Tomato-Red like"*

glowing head. Of course, I then instantly tried my very best, to bring my apparently "interrupting" actions down to an "as quiet as possible" level, which then as another result had *"little Linda"* almost burst out anew. Oh boy. The to me even FuNNier part of this story actually turned out to be the fact, that this particular friend's vessel found itself sitting on a balcony seat, mine on a parterre one and both of our two souls happened to remain unaware of each other's presence, until he recognized my *"NeverEnding"* solo laughing performance and I his voice. LOL! Yes, and this very FuN, freeing and uplifting trademark hobby of mine I ended up practicing very passionately up unto this point in my 20ies, during which those attacks suddenly started to get "re-attacked" by comments like *"Oh no, here she goes again"* or *"You laugh at everything"* resulting from newer and probably more "grownUP" minded connections. Hmmm. And that was then, when *"little Linda"* suddenly came to realize that this very first *"FuN Fact"* love choice of hers also contained a to her rather disturbing "truth" of it being "wrong", "unwanted" and of "bother", which as a result quickly led my soul to repress the length and intensity of my performances or to even end them right away, along with the just in front of my eyes popping FuN bubble. SLAM. Lost and still on the lookout for it I am to this day. Thank you. *"The Power of Words."* When my vessel counted 4 1/2 years, my parents decided to relocate from our 2nd home base in *Romanshorn* TG to a more central and a tiny bit "bigger" small town called *Amriswil* TG, in which my soul spent the following 21 years in. Yup. And therefore, Amriswil is THE place that I proudly call my hometown and where my roots happily are anchored in. Oh yeah! Shortly after we moved into our new apartment, which was located right next to a wonderful small pond with 2 white swans, many ducks, coots and a beautiful park with a great playground in it, my soul got quite fortunate to already have been introduced to my very first BFF and this during a sledding and exploring adventure on a close by hill called *Müllerhalde*. Yay! On this particular day, my mom and dad as so often allowed *"little Linda"* to explore the outdoors world on her own, as thankfully words like crime and violence rarely got used in those hippie ending days, especially in this safe small town with its then approximately 11'000 inhabitants. Now, whilst I found myself being busy with sledding down and walking up the hill over and over again, a very lovely blond and blue-eyed boy and his mother all over sudden came to my attention, which quickly had me decide to spend some time with them. As my soul ended up loving to sled, play and interact with this friendly and FuN playmate so much, I therefore instantly decided to simply follow those two vessels as soon as they started to walk off, so that we all could spend some more magical moments together as a unit. Ha! Yes, welcome to the "innocent" late 1970ies. Wink. Then, on our way back to their apartment, this blond boy's mom apparently kept on wondering and asking my soul to whom I belonged to and where I would live. Well and all that she received as a probably rather unhelpful response from *"little Linda"* turned out to be a continuous smiley and happy face accompanied with some giggles. LOL. Luckily, shortly after the three of our vessels arrived in their home space, one of their neighbors happened to appear in the hallway, who ended up being able to reveal "my" secret to Rita's question with a *"Oh, this is Linda. She is from the Wartenweiler's, who recently moved into an apartment on the 3rd floor."* response. Ufff. And this information instantly calmed my new friends mother down and ever since that day, her son Danny and I bonded on a sibling level and started to spend more and more time together, until the day my "brotherly" BFF relocated its vessel to Zurich at the count of 19. Yup. My favorite *"FuN Facts"* about the two of us will always remain that 1) We both happened to be only children born on a Wednesday and that 2) Danny's vessel counts exactly 8 weeks more than mine. Ha! Well, and throughout this "grownUP" process of ours, we probably ended up spending so much time together that as a result 1) One of our souls at some point started to say exactly what the other just happened to be thinking of at the same time and that 2) Strangers would perceive us as blood siblings and then leave us with a *"Oh you are not siblings? Well, then you two most likely will end up getting married one day."* reaction. Ah, what?! LOL. And this fortune cookie message Danny and I always ended up dismissing instantly, as our both souls from the get-go knew that our love for each other would remain purely platonic and that we are meant for each other as the wonderful *"Extended Family Member"* BFF's that we turned into, ever since that particular sledding Winter day somewhere in 1979. Yup. And so it is. And shall remain. Always. Then, a few months after my connection with Danny, 3 months before my 5th anniversary to be exact, *"little Linda"* as a next awareness *"Life Toolbox"* ingredient for the first time got introduced to a *"Time to say Goodbye"* moment, which showed her that any vessel in our sphere on earth can permanently disappear from one second to the other. Boah. What? Well and this reality check definitely left a "little" mark on my soul, as the vanished vessel turned out to be my beloved fathers', who ended up departing on his own terms after a for him rather difficult *"Living on Earth Game"* ride experience. Blessings. Love. Always. Of course, his sudden "disappearance" added a quite unexpected twist to my mom's and to my own inner and outer journeys here on mother earth and the whole from others called *Tragedy* had me take until very recently to fully grasp, "understand" and embrace. Yup. The one thing that my soul instinctively knew though, as soon as I learned from my mother that my father instantly started to live with the angels was, that this new "set-up" happened to be the best for everyone involved, as the marriage between my parents had been inharmonious for quite some time. Out of my child's eye perspective this solution therefore simply felt "right" and had me prefer it over a rather complicated and dramatic seeming divorcing occasion, which most likely would have taken place along of our travels as a Wartenweiler unit instead. In addition to this sudden separation option, my soul further instinctively knew, and still does to this very day, that my father never actually "left" and that "his" soul still remains amongst us. That's right. Which "truth" further meant to *"little Linda"* that he now would be able to accompany my *"Living on Earth Game"* journey tirelessly from a first-row seat, Day in, Day out and watch over me from his nonphysical realm existence. Yay. And so it is. Love. And therefore, accompanied by this instant inner knowledge of mine, I never caught myself shedding a tear over this "tragedy" at hand, until some circumstances in my late 30ies triggered *"little Linda"* to do so, which I will happily share with you, my dear *Co-Traveler*, at its "perfect" arising moment. Oh yeah. Now, finding one parent on the "other side" to me always brought along the advantage of having the most loving and protecting guide possible around at all times, No Matter what. Ha! This transformed father version, I therefore quickly adapted and accepted as my new reality, including "normality" and made me forget quite fast how it felt like to have "Urs" around me as he used to. To this day, I therefore always find myself very happy, whenever certain elements spontaneously are able to trigger his physical existence back into my *"Head Cinema"*, when only for a few seconds. A Walnut, a Bolognese Omelet, a Ducati Motorcycle, a Sidecar Motorcycle, a light blue Gauloise Caporal Cigarette Package and a 70ies Oldsmobile were some of his own so called *"FuN Facts"* items and proudly *"little Linda"* finds herself sharing some of them with him. Yay! In regards of my father's "early" disappearance, I therefore ever since experience quite interesting reactions sides my opposites, as soon as they learn about his passing. Comments like *"Oh, I am sorry for your loss Linda"* or *"I am sorry to hear that"* are the most common ones, especially during the first two decades of my travels, as my "normality" seemed to be an "abnormality" for others. Hmmm. Even though my soul always *"ongRowingly"* appreciates this very nice reaction gesture, I ever since that day instantly catch myself jumping ahead assuring that there is nothing to be sorry about and that things are perfect the way they are and always will be. Well, for *"little Linda"* at least. Yup. To me being raised by a female parent and to therefore having a mom "only" equals the exact same reality as of being an only child. The thought of having a "real" sibling for instance causes a weird eFFecT to my awareness and the same way I do meanwhile also feel towards having a father existing in a vessel in this physical realm of ours. Surely my curiosity at times gets triggered, during which I would love to experience both versions as a sneak peek SpeCial eFFecT option, especially now in my adulthood. Well and this adventure of course shall remain a mystery of its own in this, my *"Living on Earth Game"* ride and therefore am finding my soul very grateful to have been given the opportunity to connected with my Danny's and with some few others so early on instead, who ended up filling those so called "sibling spots" perfectly well. Love. Alongside with my father's "sudden" disappearance there of course instant further changes welcomed themselves into our world, especially for my brave and strong mother. With her then only 25 years young vessel, she certainly got introduced to a LOT of inner and outer appearing pressure and with an intense reality shift on her end. Looking back, I must admit that my mom did perform an incredible job managing both of our lives all on her own under the given circumstances. Right here, I want to express my BiG Respect, Admiration and Gratitude for all that she has achieved for the both of us. Danke Mami. Blessings. Always. Now, as my parents at that time owned a taxi company in Amriswil, my mom of course had to take care of this business even more so, now that there "only" were the two of our vessels left. With that naturally the question came up of how to the best way possible take care of *"little Linda"*, whilst she found herself being busy making a living for the both of us, by simultaneously also trying to find a way of dealing and adjusting her quite shaken inner world with the very limited available helping resources at hand. Uiii. In regards of my care taking, our building luckily occupied this great and loving family, which included 3 girls in my age range, who were willing to become my daycare foster family, whenever my mom found herself busy experiencing all her many taxi adventures. Interestingly the mother of this family turned out to be this nice neighbor, who ended up revealing "my" secret to Rita, after this wonderful sledding adventure from a few months prior. Ha! Even though my soul liked spending time with my newly gained "siblings" and "family members" quite a lot, I recall that those Morning handing Over transitions presented themselves from a rather dramatic challenging side at first, as only the thought of being separated from my beloved mother as well awoke a LOT of resistance within my vessel. Sometimes it bothered me so much that I almost gave her no choice as to bring me along to her many taxi driving adventures. Of course, that decision always made me the happiest girl on this planet and the world immediately turned into a magical place again. Yay! During these taxi driving days, I always would keep myself busy with solving children's crossword puzzles, with studying all her many traveling guests and with enjoying my mother's presence and our random rides to the fullest. "Educational" those days definitely constantly ended up being. Wink. Even though I got introduced to this initial handing over resistance of mine, I at some point came to realize that this new reality check of being exposed to another family interpretation actually brought along quite some great advantages. These 5 days per week adventures within my daycare foster family's lifestyle, granted me my very first opportunity to experience how it feels like to be part of an "intact" and harmonious family, as it is perceived from society. Yup. Ruth to me very much represented the perfect housewife and mother and always seemed to be very happy of taking care of the entire household, the grocery shopping, the cooking, in assisting each one of us with our homework if needed and to also look after her father, who used to live in a tiny, tiny neighbor village called *Hefenhofen* TG, and who for years joined us daily for lunch as well. The father Koni I usually would only experience during lunch time and then again at the end of his workday. Out of my perspective he always played his father part perfectly well too. Early on I actually established a LOT of respect towards his mostly calm floating soul, as he had this ability to raise his voice to a very strong and LOUD level, whenever there appeared a need for him to bring his boundaries and points across for us young ladies. Uiii. Thankfully this to me rather frightening outburst only happened here and there and I certainly made triple sure to stick to my foster parents' boundaries and rules as much as possible, while my vessel found itself amongst theirs. At this point *"little*

Linda" definitely happened to be WAY out of practice of being confronted by a LOUD male voice indeed. Smile. Another plus factor that this foster family opportunity brought along turned out for me to experience a reality, in which my Linda vessel actually would be having 3 siblings, another set of parents and a 3rd "Opa". Ha! Welcome to the magical world of Acting. Yay. Besides finding myself mostly exposed to Koni's and Ruth's upbringing style, my mom definitely made sure to continuously and simultaneously also pass me along the proper guidance and rules from our Wartenweiler home, whenever the both of our souls spent time with one another. LOT's of freedom, within its strict attached boundaries and its clear given roadmap of how to approach and complete certain things in this *"Living on Earth Game"* ride, I definitely had been given from the get-go. *To Work Hard, to Be Committed, Respectful, Disciplined, Grateful, Honest, Punctual, Responsible, "Correct" and Reliable* are amongst those many further useful *"Life Toolbox"* ingredients that my dear mom passed her *"little Linda"* along throughout our 2 decades of living as a unit. Thank you. Another to me very useful parenting choice turned out to be that, even though I am an only child, she would still remain as quite strict whenever it came to buying me "things". Yup. As soon as my soul picked up on her saving and down to earth spending attitude, I as a result quickly came to learn about my boundaries as of how far I could be traveling with any of my wishes. Of course, on certain occasions I would test my luck on how far I would be able to stretch those "limits", especially whenever my requests happened to be of utmost importance for my own soul. Wink. And yes, on those glorious days, my mom mostly would grant me my extended wishes after the successful application of my SpeCial trick convincing techniques, as she by then became to understand how important those wishes were for *"little Linda"*. Love. Now, in regards for me to get in touch with my own money and its value experience, my mom early on started to hand me a 5 Swiss Franc coin, which equals about 5 US Dollars, that features our folk hero William Tell on it, each Saturday and then it was up to me what I made out of this just given treasure. Now guess, where I ended up with this silver coin lesson? Ha! Each week, I actually found myself able to keep some Rappen/cents in my *"Red and White Saving Sock"*, which I knitted in my 2nd grade crafting class. Yay! This tactic very much turned out to be a success formula for me to see what it takes to actually own the money first in order for it to then be spent on any of my equivalent appearing desires afterwards. This lesson definitely convinced my soul as a very glorious choice and to this day *"little Linda"* finds herself practicing the exact same saving and spending habit to her fullest satisfaction. Hooray! What I further loved about my given freedom from my hard-working mother was that whenever she found herself either busy making a living for the two of us, with the completion of our household or simply felt the need to physically rest after a long day or week, she would always allow for my vessel to be part of my friendly neighbors' adventures when requested from my end. Meaning, that whenever one of my, with time further *"Extended Family Members"* invited me over to their house, to one of their family trips, excursions or for some other FuN activities, my mom instantly would allow *"little Linda"* to be part of this just presented opportunity so that my *"inner Adventuress"* could explore more of this *"BiG Wide World"* out there. A *"Spread your Wings my Child and Fly HiGH"* attitude definitely was and still happened to be her overall encouraging and loving attitude towards our relationship, ever since our two souls first connected on that early May morning in the mid 197Oies. Yup! Happily, *"little Linda"* therefore finds herself stating that her beloved mother always made triple sure that she played her two-in-one inherited MotherFather part perfectly well. And so she did. To me. Always. Thank you! As soon as I felt ready to accept this new Wartenweiler set-up for what it was, my *"inner Adventuress"* as a result instantly felt prompted to continue her many explorations in my still fairly new neighborhood. Quickly, I therefore came to learn that there happened to be four more girls and another blond-blue eyed boy living in our street called *Parkweg*. Manuela and Nicole built one set of sisters, Simone and Maya another, which all turned out to be residing in each a difFeRent house right next to my apartment building and the boy Marco conveniently vacated the apartment right across from my door on the 3rd floor, before he and his mom moved into another house across the street right next to Simone's and Maya's a few months later. Interestingly all the girls' families ended up having both sets of parents intact living as a unit as I already experienced it with my foster family and Marco's family portrait appeared exactly in the same divorced kind as Danny's. In Marco, who's vessel counts 3 years more than mine, I quickly found another very FuN and definitely quite courageous, daring and with life filled playmate, who my soul instantly felt drawn to spend time with as well. His soul certainly left a, from mine just now realized, quite impressive impact on mine and actually ended up unknowingly introducing *"little Linda"* to a to her quite inspiring way of interpretation of how this *"Living on Earth Game"* ride can be approached as well. A *"Always follow your Hearts Desires as Radiant as possible by ensuring to Keep On Pushing Any presented Boundaries with a Living Life to its Fullest possible Approach and to therefore absolutely NEVER take NO for an answer, No Matter what, as Not even the Sky is the Limit"* attitude is definitely what Marco's soul always communicated to mine and certainly still does to this day. Boom! Genius. Thank you, Marco for sharing and know, that *"little Linda"* definitely ended up applying your wise wisdom on and off up until today. Yeeha! A few years down the road though, all my many other found playmates and I unfortunately had to let go of his "wiLD" soul, as Marco's mother decided to relocate their vessels closer to the Lake Constance, which left me with a new opportunity to practice this at times as rather sad and uncomfortable appearing *"Time to say Goodbye"* moment exercise. Bye-Bye. Ufff. A FuNNy twist that this early on bonding took though turned out to be that in our 20ies the two of our vessels unknowingly ended up being neighbors anew in my future home called *Bottighofen* TG, which certainly had this "coincidence" unfold itself into a wonderful mini Parkweg flashback reunion, only now as almost "adults". Ha! My soul certainly felt very happy to have been given one of my very first collected friendly and inspiring *"Extended Family Member's"* so close by again, at least for some time. *"Life is Good."* Smile. Synchronically, while finding myself busy making friends with my dear Danny, Marco, Helene, Andrea and Cornelia, *"little Linda"* of course also kept on exploring all those many other presented playmates, including their families in order to *"To Grow and to Prosper"* as fast as possible. Very soon those four other souls grew on mine as well quite a LOT and together each one of us Parkweg kiddies transformed our street into a quite FuN, magical, LOUD and adventurous playground. Ha! With time *"little Linda"* therefore found herself able to even broaden her *"Extended Family Member"* experience into an additional two set of families located within a very close by radius, which provided me with many more valuable insights into the world of how an "intact" and loving family further can feel and look like. Over those many magical two Parkweg decades, I therefore found myself able to attract an unexpected amount of total 2 brothers, 7 sisters, 4 more moms, 3 dads and 1 more Opa into my, this Linda *"Living on Earth Game"* adventure. Boah! Who would have thought?! Yay! Very grateful and bonded my soul and heart therefore always will remain feeling towards each one of them, as every member kept treating me as if I would be one of "theirs". Love. Later on, throughout my travels, *"little Linda"* then with LOTS of joy actually came to learn that some of those wonderful neighbor "parents" happened to have known my father even before my arrival into this earthy sphere and this information flow instantly explained to me, why they integrated my vessel even more so well into their own world. Gratitude. Looking back, I must admit that this quite diverse parenting upbringing of mine definitely caused a wonderful shift in regards of my whole world perspective, which still serves my many travels wonderfully well to this very day. Yup. With this game starting out set-up, I early on received the opportunity to practice my adaptability and flexibility to each family's environment as the "good" sister and daughter character and to further establish my ability of using and developing my charm and learning skills to a to my experience most eFFecTive way possible. Ha! As soon as *"little Linda"* trusted a to her new "thrown in" situation full on, her Actress within then quickly began to study all the many new appearing rules, lifestyle, talk and behaviors around those presented "strangers" to in order then fit in as smoothly as possible, which results left me with a *"Linda feels and is at home everywhere"* remark, delivered from other souls. Smile. And so it was and still is to this day. Yup. Wherever my vessel is traveling to, my soul usually seems to seamlessly melt in within a heartbeat and therefore Linda Wartenweiler found herself throughout these past few decades able to extend her family member collection onto other countries and even to this magical *"The Other Planet"* formation. Woohoo! And thank you.

"This is How we Did it"
After some more exploring, growing and after getting to know all my

neighbor playmates better and better, Danny, Maya, Cornelia, Manuela, Nicole and my vessel as of our close birth years rather quickly instinctively transformed ourselves into a solid and very tight gang, who ended up ruling our street of its "finest" for many years. Oh yeah! While doing so, my perfectly gained playmates and I would spend as much time together as possible and always found ourselves busy giving birth to many adventures, games and priceless memories into our own BiG and magical created universe throughout the following decade. What I really loved about our gang happened to be that we all showed each other the needed respect, honored one another's opinions and feelings for the most part and therefore got along pretty well. Of course, we experienced disagreements and some small fights here and there, as it simply occurs whenever souls spend so much time together. Smile. Thankfully, we always found ourselves able to swiftly find a peaceful solution towards a mutual happy ending, which then allowed us to create some further FuN memories as a unit. Ufff. The only somewhat "unfortunate" soul turned out to be the youngest, Nicole, who certainly got a liiiittle bit bullied by our gang. Oops. With youngest, I am referring to her 5 years less count then to our oldest member Danny, which reality check very often happened to play against her and in our five favors instead. Her from everyone at that time perceived BiG age gap "truth" certainly turned out to be the reason, why Nici naturally got picked to play pranks with, to get cheated on during any game at hand or to simply have her make do things that her soul very much so disagreed with. Then, as soon as her vessel turned old enough to figure out what really was going on behind the scenes, she as a "revenge" act suddenly started to get smart on us in return. Ha! Whenever Nici picked up on our pranks, this little one's soul then instantly would come to the conclusion that *"Enough was Enough"*, which reality update then led her to disengage from our group with a *"Hey guys, I need to use the bathroom. I'll be right back"* action move. Her vessel then immediately walked itself home and kept us waiting and waiting and waiting until one of us lost its patience. We then as a next step would send Manuela after our "missed" playmate in order to find out why it would take her sister so long to return. Manu then either would ring the doorbell or walk into her house and from either chosen option we always were given the exact same *"Nicole is watching TV and decided to stay in for today"* result, which got provided by either their mother via the window or through Manuela after her vessel's return. Boom. Yup, she learned from the best and made those payback time moments appear in its perfect light. Ha! Good for her. My probably meanest prank on Nici that my soul recalls, is the one on that day, during which some street workers finished fixing and smoothing out a few street wholes on our beloved Parkweg. As this day blessed us all with warm summer temperatures, my gang and I therefore as usual enjoyed our escapes into our own magical universe in bare feet, as this "naked" touch simply enhanced our whole outdoors experience. Smile. Now, as soon as my eyes espied a still quite moist tar spot from those street workers on the ground, a wonderful idea immediately popped into my head. Kindly, I therefore found myself asking Nicole to close her eyes with the instructions that I needed to show her something REALLY amazing. After some stubborn convincing undertaken attempts from my end, that she could "truly" trust me on this one and that I had good intentions only, Nici then hesitantly gave in, by probably only granting me half of her trust, if even. LOL. My lovely playmate then allowed my hand to cover her eyes, whilst my vessel began leading hers towards my espied tar spot. What?! Yes. And as soon as her right foot stepped into the chosen "trap", I quickly came to realize that my eyes oversaw her mom observing the whole scenario from a first-row seat, placed within the open kitchen window right next to our vessels. pOops. Of course, Anita immediately started scolding *"little Linda"*, the second that she picked up on what I was doing to her daughter. Unhappy about my deed, Nicole's mom then ordered for my soul to clean the tar off the little one's foot. Ok. You got it. Kindly, I of course obeyed, apologized by the two ladies and asked Nicole to follow me to our laundry room, which was located in the basement of our apartment building. All the other gang members certainly followed the two of us well entertained and everyone, except for my "victim", kept on giggling over the whole established spectacle. Once our vessels arrived in the laundry room, I then of course continued my prank on my friend and ordered her to have a seat on the now as "oldschool" considered spin dryer right next to the sink. Equipped with a small brush and with some detergent powder, my hand then as directed by her mother rubbed the tar off her naked foot and found myself quite surprised about this little one's complaint of my apparently "too rough" cleaning approach. What?! Wink. While Nicole kept herself busy with cursing at us, we all eventually received what we were looking for and some more laughter resulted from our ends. LOL. Poor soul. We definitely granted our Nici some tough moments during those days, this I am certain of. My apologies. Wink. Another "Nici procedure" that we always had to perform as a Must Do game plan was to have her vessel sit secluded in the dining room, whilst the rest of us enjoyed ourselves with watching Horror Movies at Danny's house. My BFF therefore simply would go ahead and mark our sacred space by closing the curtain in front of her face, which wonderfully was able to divide the living room area from the dining room one. Snap. This "protection" definitely happened to be a necessity, as the little one with time developed a tendency to call us out to our parents, whenever we did something "forbidden" or "wrong". Go figure. LOL. Often times though Nicole got so tired of our mean behaviors that she instead silently would call in her famous "pee breaks" on us and simply sneak home without us noticing. Ha! Well done. Yes, I am sure that especially Danny and *"little Linda"* gave our beloved soul sister quite some challenging moments at times. Thankfully though, we both always owned the wonderful skill of being "nice and charming" bullies and this approach certainly must have added to the fact that Nicole kept on loving the both of us all along very much. Yup. It actually always astounded my soul of how attached we found our "youngest" gang member towards especially Danny and my own *"Self"*, despite our "mean" kindness. True fact. Even after the two of our vessels embarked onto our High School journey, followed by our job education chapter, my BFF and I always experienced our dear Nicole quite eager to stay in touch with both of our two souls, which leaves me assured that the little one's certainly must have known all along "herself" about our priceless Parkweg sibling connection. Ha! Well and the fact that the three of our souls, even though my vessel currently finds itself enjoying many magical adventures miles away from theirs on an even entirely difFeRent "planet" and "universe", have continuously been sharing a close and trusting bond throughout each one's own *"Living on Earth Game"* ride experience to this very *"Now Moment"*, finds *"little Linda"* very blessed. Yay! And this reality check definitely proves to me that my BFF and I after all still found ourselves able to appear as kind and "fair" playmates and that our beloved gang member only got some "minor" marks out of our FuN bully play days. Ufff. Love. Always. As all of this took place throughout my favorite decade the 80ies, the general fear factors thankfully found themselves sleeping on a much, much lower scale of things, which allowed each one of us to explore the world with LOTS more Peace, Freedom and Possibilities than how my soul keeps on noticing it to be for the younger generations at hand. Yup. Almost anything did go and out of my perspective *"Not even the Sky was the Limit"* and so I still do believe to this day. And so you do too Marco, I am certain of. Ha! The one thing that I am finding myself very grateful for, is the reality that we all were granted to fully explore our childhood, including teenager years in, without being too much exposed to any technology devices as of yet. Danny owned the very first released Nintendo edition, when our vessels counted about 12 years. Prior to that historical event, I recall him owning a Commodore computer, on which we used to play the game called *Larry* directly from a floppy disc. Yes, a floppy disc. Do you remember those days? LOL. And prior to that experience, he owned this amazing Atari spaceship shooting game monitor, which movements we had to maneuver with a red joystick in order to survive. The latter definitely thus far is my favorite computer game of all times and I actually believe that along with this Atari box *"little Linda"* also got exposed to an actual computer for the very first time. Boah! Yup. Speaking of technology. The only 3 mainstream electronic items that all my many friends and I had access to at first were 1) A home phone with a wired landline 2) A color or black n' white TV with 8 channels to start out with, which hopefully already came with a convenient remote control in addition to the buttons located on the actual device and to 3) Maybe a VHS recorder, if one already decided to be that "modern". That was about it. Boom. And those moments btw also happened to be the times, during which MTV still appeared what its abbreviation actually stands for, a Music TeleVision Channel. Yes. This used to be the place on which the wonderful Art of Music videos got celebrated 24/7 as the only channel of its kind in Europe. YouTube is the platform into which this genius 24/7 Music video streaming access idea from 1981 evolved itself into, with its enhanced opportunity to create one's own selected song and video playlist or by simply clicking on already existing ones created by other users. Ha. And if one really feels a sense of experiencing a retro flashback, then this lovely homepage even finds itself offering many links to numerous uploaded original MTV aired recordings. Wow. The magical wonders of this *"ongRowing"* technology rEvolution. Namaste. Looking back to those quite groundbreaking days actually made me notice that alongside with the transformation of our own vessels into teenager ones, the electronic world literally grew simultaneously with us. True fact. This realization actually delights *"little Linda"* very much, as I believe that my generation happened to be the last one of its kind, whom I consider to have been "fortunate" for the last time to experience the opportunity to connect with nature, our fellow human and animal souls in its purest and very minimized distractive ways. Yup. Our outdoor toys therefore mainly consisted Wood, Stones, Sand, Water, Dirt, Trees, Bugs, Bushes, Leaves and whatever else nature provided. Then every soul added each ones very own and unique skills and imagination to the given circumstances and off our creativity mix led us into a magical world that we as a collective decided to experience at that very *"Now Moment"*. Boom. *"Thoughts become Things."* Further we also started to invent our own games, which carried names like Sennsenmann/Reaper, Bruce Lee, Chräbslis/Little Crab, Tabea or Schwanger mit 9/Pregnant with 9, which was based on a shocking newspaper article that we heard of and lastly, we created our own houses in a very long fence like bush located in "our" park, which "spaces" apparently still exist today. Cool! Bruce Lee btw turned out to be *"little Linda's"* very first collected Hero and the invention of his name-based game travels back to the day, on which one of my classmates in 1st or 2nd grade introduced me to one of his Movies, which her parents recorded on a VHS tape. Wow. How mesmerized my soul instantly felt, the second that I witnessed all of his many amazing and incredible vessel movement skills and his FuNNy *"Oo-wah!"* sounding fighting noises. The latter certainly must have reminded *"little Linda"* of those precious Heidi and Urs Entertaining days. LOL. Well and from that moment on, my vessel very often followed this particular classmate right back to her house after school, which luckily was located only one block away from my house, so that I could experience more of this fascinating and difFeRent looking men. Thankfully, her parents owned all the few Movies that Bruce Lee ended up recording, during his exact same amount of years, including months *"Living on Earth Game"* experience as my father's, which opportunity therefore allowed me to enjoy all his many to me outstanding talents in a range of difFeRent scenarios. Oo-wah! That's right. Wink. At some point my fascination with Bruce Lee actually grew so strong that I wanted to be like him and in order to accomplish that, *"little Linda"* simply came up with the solution of inventing a game based on his name and character. Oo-WAH! Of course, the most important part of its rules turned out to be that ONLY my vessel was allowed to "be" Bruce Lee and my lovely Parkweg gang members therefore ended up being predestined to play my all-time "victims". Over and over anew. Boom. Charming bully, here we go. Wink. My fellow playmates though loved and hated this game in one breath, especially Manuela and for some reason though we still kept on playing it for the longest period of time. LOL. *"Empty your Mind and become Water my Friend"* remains as one of his many wise teachings and thank you for all your incredible inspirational "moves". R.I.P. Oo-wah. Now, whenever my gang members and I felt the urge to explore our playground beyond our street and park area, our vessels then as a next step simply would take off with our bikes or by our feet only and start heading towards our chosen direction, with hardly ever informing our families about our possible whereabouts. Quite often, none of us happened to have a real end destination idea anyway and therefore our souls simply allowed for our many adventures to unfold from *"Moment-to-Moment"*. This form of us vanishing for a couple of hours used to be everyone's normality and therefore our trusting parents always knew that we would return for lunch and dinner just in time safe and sound and that each playmate would always look out for the other as an honor code. Always. And so we did. Yup. Right Nici? Wink. One of my favorite adventures happened to take place on the day, on which our gang decided to follow our close by creek called *Aach*, which is about a 10 min walk away from our Parkweg homes. It must have been on a Wednesday afternoon, our weekly half off day, during which I believe, Danny came up with the idea that we could follow it all the way to where it merges with the Lake Constance in *Salmsach* TG, by adding that this excursion probably would turn into a super FuN adventure. The walking distance counted about 6 kilometers/4 miles from where we started and of course everyone instantly agreed to be part of his proposed adventure. Yeeha! And off my friends and *"little Linda"* took towards our fantastic "ride", which ended up being filled with nature, fresh air and some walking obstacles here and there. One particular moment actually turned into a quite scary one for all of us. Yes! As the Aach at some point ran by next to a small farm, our vessels got forced to cross the farmer's private ground in order to continue our mission smoothly. By doing so, we all over sudden found ourselves being chased by the farmer's barking dog. Instantly, my friends and I ran off screaming as fast as we could and the next thing I knew was that this pet decided to pick *"little Linda"* as his next scare target. Oh my. Help! My wonderful intuition then quickly guided me to jump up on a small wall located right behind my back. Yeeha! Hold on. What was I thinking? A small wall behind me I intuitively picked to "safe" myself from this very property protective animal? What?! He easily could have jumped on it in a snap as well Linda. Oh. LOL. Well, my instinct thankfully turned out to have been spot on, as this seemingly dangerous pet right after decided that his scaring off job successfully got completed and that it was time for us to leave already. And so we did. Instantly. Equipped with a rush of adrenaline kicks, LOTS of laughter and with some scary emotions. Ufff. How relieved my dear friends and I found ourselves about this dog's abrupt mood change. To this day, my dear Parkweg "siblings" and I actually are still reacting quite amused about this "impulsive" way of saving myself from this "dangerous" creature. LOL. Well it helped, somehow, and that was all that mattered. Once our vessels finally arrived at our planned merging spot in Salmsach an hour or two later, we all found ourselves quite thrilled and happy about this, with our own two feet only successfully completed adventure. Yeeha! This spontaneous "on the road" experience definitely left my soul with a little "Stand by Me" feel. You know, the Movie with River Phoenix and Corey Feldman. Ha! How cool this "little" trip simply revealed itself as. Then, as each one of us always carried some change in our pockets, we then happily headed towards the closest train station in Romanshorn TG and jumped on the next departing train right back home to Amriswil, which is only a 5 minutes ride away. Yes, these days absolutely are missed by each one of us, that is a given. Sometimes, my gang members and I simply wished to beam ourselves right back to those magical and carefree days with a Time Machine, just as Marty McFly does it in "Back to the Future". Oh yeah. Well, thankfully each one of our souls carries an Abundance of these precious adventures and memories within our hearts and therefore we always kind of end up achieving our goal, whenever my gang members and *"little Linda"* reunite. Ha! Yup. Right in those very rare moments, we then actually with guarantee instantly succeed in bringing the magic alive again and the next thing our souls then know is that we "somehow" managed to transmute our then *"Now Moment"* right into a "real time" 80ies experience instead, during which we then end up recreating our BiG and magical universe all anew as a unit. Oo-WAH! That's right. Much LOVE and many thanXOXO for everything, my magical Parkweg gang. Much LOVE.

"*Dream a little Dream for Me*"
As already established, my soul early on into this *"Living on Earth Game"* adventure as Linda Wartenweiler found "herself" able to get in touch with "her" two main Music and Movies passions, which my beloved mother's thankfully shares alongside with mine. Yay! Well, and I am actually quite certain that, besides our internal shared loves for *Positivity, FuN and Uplifting Vibes,* those two-outer existing enhancing medias must be one of my favorite reasons, as of why my soul chose "Heidi" as my birthmother. Yup! And this fact therefore made it super easy for *"little Linda"* to be exposed to them both a LOT, whenever our two vessels spent time together. Strike. As soon as our color TV was on for example, she then either would pick a great classic Movie, a Comedy or a mutually liked Cartoon. The only genre that I always found myself really bored with ended up being those animal Documentaries, which she on the other hand truly loved and still does to this very day. *"One gotta stay True to OneSelf"* after all, right? Ha! Way to go. Even though that I am a BiG animal lover myself, my soul on the contrary to hers actually always preferred to interact with all the friendly ones on a One-on-One basis and the same way I do feel about my fellow human travelers as well. Yup. Whenever our TV set was off, then our apartment or car mostly got filled with some FuN melodies, which always kept our both vibrations and moods quite elevated. These to me precious early on provided *"Life Toolbox"* ingredients must have been the igniter, why my soul to this day feels the MOST drawn towards UPlifting, Deep and Touching Music vibes

and this formula a 100% finds itself also applying to any further available Entertainment tools, like *Interactions, Thoughts, Pictures, Activities,* etc. with one exception at hand. Yup. As everything exists in its duality, my soul therefore does love to get in touch with those from my end as "darker" perceived areas of life through the magical world of Movies and during my own Acting excursions. Ha! That's right! And these therefore remain as The Only occasions, during which I allow myself to fully dive into the opposite direction, in order to explore those lower existing vibrations and actions a little bit further, as I know that I can snap myself right back into the "actual" and "safe" reality at any desired second. Snap. In general, my soul carries this reflex that whenever something or someone has the ability to lower my own energy level, that I then instantly feel the need to however quickly possible find a way to adjust those sudden to me unpleasant appearing elements into a from my end as much happier and comfortable interpreted solution. Yup. And this is why *"little Linda"* in general tries to stay away from these kinds of situations as much as possible, as life is simply too short and magical in order to pay those "forces" too much attention, focus and one's precious own "powers". Been there. Done that. Yup. In a later chapter of my many *"Living on Earth Game"* explorations, my *"inner Adventuress"* actually got enticed by her curiosity to give a lower vibrating reality for a few years its fair trial, though then at some point came to the conclusion, that this chosen "new" lifestyle simply ended up interfering a little bit too much with *"little Linda's"* all-time daily desired Keeping myself happy and Radiant task at hand. Oops. Hey, it certainly was worth its one time ever "shot" for so many uncountable discovered reasons. You shall see, my beloved *Co-Traveler*. You shall see. Bang. One state of mind reality that I for quite some time found my soul driven to understand, turned out to be the reason as of WHY an already sad and low vibrating soul would choose to stay in those "darker" areas by enhancing these feelings with, from my end as depressing perceived Music tunes for example or with putting themselves into situations, which are the opposite of "healthy" for their overall well-being and reality experience. Hmmm. Meanwhile, I do believe to have found myself able to crack this code and came to the understanding that some souls simply choose to explore their *"Living on Earth Game"* ride mostly in the "darker" area of things and others in its "lighter" opponent one, which then as an eFFecT creates difFeRent kinds of *"Emotional Comfort Zone"* realities and results in this perfectly existing interacting equation of the magical *"Yin and Yang"* duality. Ha! Truly very grateful I feel by now, that my soul decided to pick a "HiGH vibrating experience" quest as the main ingredient for "her" travels as Linda Wartenweiler from the available palette at hand. Oh yeah. Thank you, my soul! Thank you. And this leaves *"little Linda"* wondering, my fellow *Co-Traveler*, what *"Emotional Comfort Zone"* explorer your soul with all of its heart chose back then and where it these days finds itself floating in. Hmmm?! Hmmm. Love. Now, as my mom started her own *"Living on Earth Game"* journey back in the 1950ies, she therefore used to own and play many records of Led Zeppelin, The Doors, Uriah Heep, The Beatles, The

Who, Deep Purple and Jimmy Hendricks from our get-go and with time, she then further also ended up developing a passion for Italian songs and for any other FuN vibes that the radio had to offer. For my own taste though, those from her end chosen melodies mostly sounded a little bit too abstract to my still rather "brand new" ears, which therefore made my soul decide to simply go ahead and start my own Music taste discovery mission instead. Ha! Let's Go. During this new and very FuN quest of mine, *"little Linda"* as a result very soon came in touch with her very first star love, who's vessel turned out to be the leading voice of Kajagoogoo aka Limahl. Oh, how my soul instantly "fell in love" with this handsome *"Too Shy"* singer, as soon as "she" set eyes on his angel like face, which was surrounded by an amazing looking blonde and dark brown "halo" mullet on a page in the German trend teen magazine BRAVO. LOL. Yes. And this ended up being the very moment, in which I instantly decided to become his fan by giving Limahl my heart, along with its next beat. Beat. That's right. At around that time, my vessel must have counted about 8 years, when he just happened to also release his first solo album *"Don't Suppose"* and my kind mom instantly purchased this yellow colored tape for her daughter, right after my loving wish got expressed. Yay. From its many recorded songs though, *"Only for Love"* and *"Too Much Trouble"* ended up being the tracks that instantly lit my fire and with all the others my soul continued connecting on a rather unimpressed level, however finding Limahl's face on the tape cover, which shows his very handsome vessel with a stubble beard, an ear piercing on his left hand side, his by now iconic two-toned mullet, dressed in a black leather jacket and a white t-shirt, turned out to be the ultimate needed experience in order to feel even closer to my chosen star love. Oh yes. LOL. And *"little Linda"* actually still happens to love that shot quite a LOT to this very day. Blush. Then, a few months later, Limahl happened to be releasing his probably most famous solo single ever, which is the opening soundtrack to one of my all-time favorite Movies "The *NeverEnding* Story", that then shortly after its amazing in 1984 celebrated success instantly found itself even being added to the newer *"Don't Suppose"* produced playlist. Ha! And this magical soundtrack combination indeed revealed itself as a genius formula for my "loving" soul. Wink. My first female inspiration that I recall, belongs to the German *"99 Luftballons/99 Red Balloons"* singer NENA, whom I still adore to this very day with all of my heart and soul and always will. Guaranteed. About NENA's existence I learned at my foster family's home, as their oldest daughter Helene used to be a BiG fan and therefore ended up decorating her two bedside walls with many NENA posters. Soon after, Danny then happened to own this German Musician's very first vinyl record titled *"Nena"* and as for so many of her fans, I instantly found myself connecting with her Music and energy on a soul level, the second that *"little Linda"* got exposed to this *"99 Luftballons"* star's first few songs. Very grateful I therefore feel towards her kind and loving soul to have stayed active over the past more than 3 decades by now. Yay! Go NENA gO! My second female inspiration turned out to reside within the

United States and happens to keep leading the charts to this very day herself. Wow. And this "winner's" vessel goes by the name *Madonna*. Yeah! Very clearly, I do recall that moment, in which the then famous German Top 10 Music video countdown TV show "Formel Eins" aired *"Like a Virgin"* for the *"VERY FiRST time"*. And yes, this certainly WAS the VERY FiRST time, as this show happened to be part of my weekly MUST DO rituals. Ha! Seeing that cool lady with her unique, "crazy" and somewhat provoking style cruising in a gondola throughout Venice's canals, definitely also caused another very mesmerizing eFFecT onto my soul. Madonna is another Artist, who *"little Linda"* kept in her inspirational *"Life Toolbox"* repertoire to this day, especially when it comes to her provoking "Warrior Spirit" expressions. Oh yeah. With "the Madgesty's" many powerful creations though, my soul finds "herself" more gravitating towards her earlier decades developed "babies". Well, for now at least. Maybe this will change with time, alongside with my taste and own creative expansion journey. We shall see. *"Everything at its Perfect Time."* Smile. During this own Music taste discovery quest of mine, my soul then soon came to detect, that 1) Australia's Kylie Minogue appeared as the first person ever into my reality, who happens to share the EXACT same birthday May date with *"little Linda"*, which to this day makes me sing *"I should feel so Lucky, Lucky, Lucky, Lucky. I should feel so Lucky. Yeah!"* and that 2) My soul the most felt drawn towards those Synth-Pop, Pop and Freestyle described beats, which I with time came to learn therefore unknowingly turned me into a "popper". What?! LOL. One of my favorite Music activities always occurred on Sundays and got marked as another VERY important ritual on my weekly MUST DO list. As the Swiss German radio station DRS 3, now called SRF, since January 2nd 1968 keeps on playing all the weekly best-selling single hits, this "Hitparade" titled Music celebration opportunity for that reason definitely needed to be attended by my soul. Back in the 80ies they ran down all the weekly Top 30y hits "only" and made these afternoons for that reason turn into a very sacred occasion. Ha! Each Sunday, *"little Linda"* therefore anxiously would be waiting for her Music hunting mission to continue and this very well equipped with a specific selected tape sitting ready in its PLAY, RECORD and PAUSE holing position, located in her precious red and black tape recorder. Yup. Then, as soon as some desired tunes would be released through its LOUDspeakers, my only next step therefore resulted in simply hitting the PAUSE button anew at its perfect moment and "on air" the recording was. Yeah! The "Hitparade" always started at 2pm and ended somewhere between 6pm and 6:30pm. During this timeframe, my mom very much so found herself aware of the fact to ONLY disturb my doings in an emergency situation, as this quite finicky mission needed my fullest attention. Yes. It was of utmost importance to my existence to catch my desired song from A-Z and any other result would have been reason enough for another trial. So any possible interruptions therefore could have interfered with this very delicate process and waiting for another week in order to try my luck anew, happened to be what *"little Linda"* tried to avoid as good as she could. Yup. Well and then there always existed this 50/50 added chance for this particular song to remain in the Top 30ies for another week. Uiii. What if not?! That of course would have been a disaster. LOL. One uncontrollable challenge that my soul got exposed to all along though turned out to be this secret race with the moderator. Yes, with the moderator. Sometimes he truly dared talking before the song even ended and that to me with "No Doubt" happened to be an absolutely unacceptable move. How dare he interrupting "my" song by further screwing up my workflow? Common. All I then as a next step found myself able to do in order to "save" this disaster at hand, ended up having me decide to let go of my frustration and to shift my focus on all the perfectly caught recordings instead. And this *"Positivity Card"* trick always worked its magic. Oh yeah! Let me tell ya'. Then, after the completion of another adventurous Music hunting afternoon, *"little Linda"* therefore happily would go ahead and enjoy all her many tunes throughout the following week, by further starting to learn them all by heart. Ha! One week later, whenever I found myself succeeding to add any open and missing piece/s onto my collection, *"little Linda"* then finally ended up being a super happy camper. Victory! And now I am actually finding myself curiously wondering if those precious tapes are still existing somewhere in a box at my mom's house. Hmmm. This priceless treasure would be amazing to "stumble upon" one day in the future. Fingers crossed. One of my many wonderful discoveries over the past few decades is that Music and Movies in general are providing my soul with the probably thus far best existing Time Machine eFFecT experience ever at hand. True fact. Any 80ies tunes or visuals for instance that my vessel gets exposed to, seem to somehow contain this magical dust, as it perfectly well gets demonstrated in this amazing and enchanting "13 Going 30" production, starring my so called "look alike" Jennifer Garner, that possesses the ability to instantly push all my senses into a HiGH gear mode activity by further zoOMing my soul and *"Head Cinema"* right back to its then experienced moments and emotions in a to me quite powerful way. Boah! Yes, about in the same way as it occurs during those magical and to me SpeCial Parkweg gang member reunions. Ha! Love. Now, whenever my auricles on top of it all get enticed by a soundtrack of any 80ies Movie that *"little Linda"* truly loves, then my soul even more so finds "herself" getting lost somewhere in space and time. Oops. Ha! Well, and some of those favorite 80ies flicks of mine include "The Goonies", "Dirty Dancing", "Rocky", "Top Gun", "Pretty in Pink", "Footloose", "Big Business" and as already established "The *NeverEnding* Story", to name a few. Wink. Besides this wonderful, from any to my soul meaningful connected Music tunes or screen experiences evoked "Back to the Future" flashback eFFecT, I further very much love what amazing Movies and TV shows in general awake within my vessel, once they are able to lure me in. Oh yeah. As soon as my soul finds "herself" connecting with its world, material and with its characters, then this very pleasant feeling suddenly starts to arise within me, which immediately has my reality melt into the one created behind its projected screen. Yes. A sense of unity right then awakens as part of my reality state of mind creation, which as a next step allows for my soul to become one with "them" or with even a certain character and that always turns into the moment, during which *"little Linda"* completely starts forgetting about everything else that is happening around her. Smile. Danny and his mom most likely have experienced this spectacle the most thus far. LOL. Whenever my BFF and I would entertain ourselves with watching all those many "dark" and thrilling "Nightmare on Elm Street", "Friday the 13th", "The Exorcist", "Poltergeist" or "The Shining" Horror Movies for example, then my soul eventually got "sucked in" so much that my vessel at some point actually began to climb up their couch and other furniture available in the living room in order to deal with my own internal experiences. That then always turned into the moment, when Danny and his mom found themselves cracking up quite well entertained by *"little Linda's"* LiVE performance held in their own living room. LOL. My soul though happened to be way too preoccupied with chasing others or with escaping from a heated situation myself along with the Actors and Actresses behind the screens, which kept me from being able to pay them any proper attention. "Survival" was the key action plan at that very moment. Ha! Then, as soon as something thrilling would occur in a scene, my vessel as a reflex immediately would jUMP UP all scared or excited along with the characters. Yup. This actually reminds me of my "Crocodile Dundee" story and of the fact that experiencing an engaging Movie in the Movie theatre always turns out to be a torture for my soul, as my instincts constantly find themselves getting triggered to reproduce these action moves, which I used to express *"wiLD & Freely"* at Danny's house. Wink. Meanwhile, I of course developed my own technique on how to control myself "better" in regards of expressing those intense emotions without being a too BiG of a distraction to others. All that I now am allowing my vessel to perform, during a whatever to me heated and amazing interpreted scene, is to transform itself into a small package position placed on my seat, which allows those tensions and many emotions to remain safely contained within, until the kind Universe sends me a chance to release them all out of my system in one burst. Splash! And. Hooray! Whoever has experienced these "Linda spectacles" before knows exactly what I am talking about. Wink. "Game of Thrones" definitely causes a battlefield of those SpeCial eFFecTs on *"little Linda"* in my current reality and thankfully I usually find myself able to watch this TV show with "her" undisturbed on my computer. *"Winter is coming."* Ha! Well, and all these many Music and Movie experiences must have been my collected key moments, which successfully found themselves triggering and possibly even remembering my soul's love for Acting and for the world of Entertainment. Yay. And therefore, Acting revealed itself as one of my BiGGEST loves and passions in this, my *"Living on Earth Game"* ride thus far. Oh yeah! It is THE ideal place for *"little Linda"* to *Play*, to *Explore*, to *Experience*, to have *FuN* and to simply *Create any Magic* available by surrendering to this inner provided freedom state of mind reality of expressing my own and personal interpretation to others as *"wiLD & Free"* as my soul desires to be. Anything goes and *"Not even the Sky is the*

Limit." That's right! Ha! Now, whilst I found myself busy indulging and experiencing all those wonderful and inspiring 80ies flicks, which so perfectly well got orchestrated by some amazing and powerful soundtracks, my urge to REALLY becoming part of "their world" started to grow stronger by the day as well and that must have been When and How my so called *"Childhood Dream"* introduced itself with a friendly *"You should be Acting as a Leading Lady in a Hollywood Motion Picture"* suggestion into my awareness. Wow! What?! Yeah. YEs. YES LET'S! This sounds amazing! And that thought, including its right then mentally presented vision, within a snap even more so started to entice my soul and *"little Linda"* by further having my *"Head Cinema"* taking off in a rocket ship, whilst I simultaneously also kept reminding myself that this *"Dream come True"* experience happened to be granted mainly to those lucky ones only, who decided to start their *"Living on Earth Game"* adventure on this *"Other Planet"*, called The United States. Bummer. Oh well, it's a dream for another lifetime to come then, always ended up being my consolation in this repeating parenting approach of mine. Sniff. And yes, this reality check of knowing that being an Artist in my "own" home country would remain an impossible "profession" to pursue, especially when a soul chooses to start out in the canton of Thurgau, the countryside, is exactly as how realistic *"little Linda"* perceived "our" dream as for a very long time. Then, on top of this perception, I alongside with the growth of my own vessel further gained the understanding via my Swiss surrounding that any activities that involve Art, FuN and Sports are considered "hobbies" and that they therefore remained accessible "only" to those very, very few truly talented and fortunate souls in order to actually officially getting paid for what they feel PASSiONATE about doing and that for everyone else these activities remained as a spare-time or as a retirement option, just as I witnessed the latter happening with my quite talented painter grandfather Ernst Wartenweiler, while his soul thereafter *"ongRowingly"* found "himself" being led by its mission in bringing all the many empty, within "his" workspace placed canvases with the help of the *"NeverEnding"* over time collected magical oil color tricks to live. Abracadabra. An additional existing believe that *"little Linda"* took on in that matter happened to be the "fact" that a soul must learn a from society considered "normal" profession as a "grownUP", one that gets practiced by everyone else, one that "guarantees" a steady income in order to "survive" and that this was the ONLY existing way for us all to choose a career path later on throughout our travels. Boom. "Stability. Security. Certainty" therefore appeared to be the ultimate and "typical" Swiss developed safe *"Swimming ALONG WiTH the Current"* thinking pattern and the more risky and laughed at *"Swimming AGAiNST it"* approach to a rather rare and rebellious seemingly lifestyle choice. Further, *"little Linda"* then even started witnessing that whenever a soul actually DiD choose to bravely *"Swim AGAiNST this Stream"* by following "its" *"Own Artistic Calling"* for instance, that this vessel then most certainly ended up facing comments like *"Ah, she/he is an Artist? That is something for lazy people. There is*

"No Way" that she/he will succeed. Who does she/he think she/he is?" followed by some laughter. Yes. This happens to be a true Snapple fact indeed. Been there. Heard it. Live. Yup. Thank God though that rules are created with the wonderful opportunity to get broken by any soul that desires and dares to explore what hidden treasures and possibilities DO exist beyond them. Ha! And this topic we certainly shall be exploring into further depth at some point as well, my beloved fellow *Co-Traveler*. We certainly will. Yay! During these exciting and magical *"little Linda"* days, I therefore kept on admiring all those "lucky ones" from my audience seat and chose to continue practicing this *"FuN Fact"* of mine, whenever an opportunity for it arose in my own reality instead. Some of those happy Entertaining moments definitely always got sparked, whenever the end of a school year approached, especially during my travels from 1st to 5th grade. That time period then usually transformed itself into the one, when our teachers had my classmates and I prepare a play for our parents, which rehearsals and preparation process always excited *"little Linda"* quite a LOT. Well and this *"FuN Fact"* procedure for some whatever reason found itself out of nowhere getting interrupted by a super boring bee documentary decision from my all-time favorite teacher at the end of our 6th grade journey. What?! b*zZZ*. b*zZZ*. Bummer. Hmmm. Maybe his well-meaning soul secretly intended to "properly" prepare ours for those in front of the door standing High School "teenage days" as part of a "smooth" transitioning plan by introducing our souls to the "bees" for now and by deciding to leave the "bird" chapter to our soon biology teacher to be? LOL. Who knows, right? Well, at least my mom must have felt quite excited about this sudden twist of "ending". Wink. My favorite 3 Acting *"FuN Fact"* projects from my 9 years school adventure definitely remain as 1) *2nd grade* Max & Moritz, in which I got cast as "Onkel/Uncle Fritze" 2) *3rd grade* A fantasy city built with letters and native Americans and 3) *High School* A with our 3 parallel graduate classmates *"Self"* compensated decade period flashback piece, that transported our parents in our especially for them "built" Time Machine all the way from the 1930ies into the then present 1991 year count *"Now Moment"* and this perfectly expressed by an *"ongRowing"* fashion show, Music interpretations, several dance Acts and a *"Self"* written storyline, which had this spectacle appear as a Musical of its own kind. Ha! How much FuN this experience turned out to be for *"little Linda"* of getting this magical opportunity to step into these difFeRent characters and time elapses within a short period of time. Wow. Well, and therefore this "Back to the Future" enhanced Musical definitely will always remain as my favorite piece of them all. Sure thang! Luckily one of our teachers happened to record this "gem" on a then very modern VHS tape, which genius gesture therefore ever since allows *"little Linda"* with her own meanwhile UPgraded DVD copy, to travel right back to this with *"FuN Facts"* packed giggling event very well entertained, whenever desired. Hooray! Speaking of school. This all-time favorite teachers' vessel of mine got called *Toni Keller*, who I consider myself very fortunate to have encountered during my 4th to 6th grade *"Living on Earth Game"* adventures, as his very kind soul kept us creative as often as he found himself able to. Those 3 remarkable "Herr Keller" years actually caused my own soul so much FuN that I ended up preferring school over any breaks, which apparently quite "odd" considered SpeCial eFFecT often times left my mom in a puzzled and joyful state of mind reality about her *"little Linda's"* education attitude. Smile. Our most creative hour, my 23 classmates and I were granted every Wednesday at around 11am in 4th grade. This hour then would turn into the magical moment, during which Herr Keller allowed each one of us to present anything creative to our classmates if we felt like it. Yeah! "Freestyling" he ended up setting as the only game rule at hand, which therefore left every Entertainment genre door, like a Skit, a Scene, a Reading, a Song, a Poem or anything else accessible to each soul to choose from or to come up with. Of course, *"little Linda"* ended up taking advantage of these creative opportunities as much as she could and therefore always chose her BFF classmate Danny as so often as the "blessed" guinea pig to be. Wink. Usually, we would shortly after meet-up in his apartment, invent some FuN creations and already experience quite a blast whilst doing so. LOL. My BFF's open and willingness to try out most of my at times somewhat as *"wiLD & Free"* considered ideas definitely belongs amongst my favorite Danny traits. This blond blue-eyed sledding buddy from 1979 simply proofed "himself" to be as THE best playmate to have and horses our souls would have stolen together, if we needed to. Ha! Now, whenever THE *"Now Moment"* arose for us to present our original and well-prepared masterpieces to everyone else on those Wednesdays, then the both of us usually ended up cracking up before our performances even started. LOL. As a reminder, back then I still explored my famous *"NeverEnding"* laughing attack trademark to its fullest potential, which combined with my Danny's laughing support would usually last even longer. Oops. Therefore, only the thought of what was about to be happening had us go on and on and on and on giggling and in addition to this "unplanned" prelude, my face would as a next step start highlighting this blooper with its usual *"Tomato-Red like"* glowing added SpeCial eFFecT. UiUiUi. One can probably only imagine, right? LOL. Meanwhile, the two of our souls of course found all of our classmates already laughing along very well entertained and this opening Act always transformed itself into THE most perfect and glorious warm up "accident" choice as an introduction for what was "really" in store for them all. Action.

"Don't Stop Believin'. Hold On to Your Dreamin'."
As soon as my High School chapter began to run its course, all those to me many creative *"FuN Facts"* somewhat sneakily seemed to fade away in order to instead create enough room to an apparently somewhat more "serious" required lifestyle. Hmmm. Within the first few months, my new classmates' and my soul therefore all over sudden got confronted with the "urgent" question from our teachers, of what professional path we intended to walk upon after everyone's graduation in 2 ½ years. What?! In 2 ½ years? Why do I have to know NOW what *"little Linda"* intends to do for the rest of her *"Living on Earth Game"* ride, starting THEN?! Ufff.

Well, and as this task, in this my 13 years count by then, seemed to be of utmost importance to our teachers to get solved for our own sake as soon as possible, I therefore very much so tried my best to come up with the required solution in order to complete this homework at hand, sooner than later. Secretly *"little Linda's"* heart and soul of course all along kept on dreaming of putting this wonderful *"Acting as a Leading Lady in a Hollywood Motion Picture"* vision into action. Somehow. One day. Maybe. Ufff. Which bubble usually shortly after got popped by my oh so parenting and "well-meaning" head voice, which 1) Kindly kept reminding my soul, where my vessel chose to start out at and still existed in and by 2) Furthermore underlining its "concerns" with its successful *"Stay reasonable Linda. Stay reasonable"* snapping out narration. POOF. Bye-Bye. You are right. With that, the search for my "truly" desired Swiss "grownUP" profession path continued its course and as *"little Linda's"* earlier on created ideas of "one day" possibly becoming a Kindergarten or an Elementary School teacher meanwhile vanished from her interest list, I therefore needed to dig a little bit deeper into mySelf in order to get "there" in time. Now, while I kept myself busy trying to solve this given homework task at hand, I thankfully soon after found myself connecting with an already pre-created Plan B solution, which instantly solved this "mainstream" education puzzle at hand within a SNAP. Yay! And this more "reasonable" alternative revealed itself as a *Swiss Banking Career*. That's right. And this is how this Plan B got "born". As my mom early on decided to teach *"little Linda"* the importance of this *"Life Tool"* instrument called *Money*, I therefore rather soon ended up discovering that this valuable paper certainly looked like an important and powerful ingredient to add to my already very preciously growing *"Life Toolbox"* collection and that the knowledge of its proper use and of the to it attached potentials certainly would be enhancing my overall *"Living on Earth Game"* experience ahead. A further, very enticing reality check that this money instrument introduced itself to me as, revealed itself through my observation that if one uses it in a "smart" way, that it then as a result transforms itself into this magical key, which instantaneously contains the needed "combination" in order to swing open any desired doorway, during ones *"Living on Earth Game"* ride, whenever applied. Wow! And this SpeCial eFFecT opportunity certainly very much appealed to my adventurous and curious soul as well and had this Plan B option therefore introduce itself into my awareness with another inner *"Head Cinema"* vision, that I suddenly recalled as well. Ready? Good. Do you remember those days, during which *"little Linda"* would safe as many coins as possible from her weekly 5.00 Swiss Francs given treasure? Well, as my *"Red and White Saving Sock"* at some point found itself getting quite heavy and stuffed, my mom as a next step then would be accompanying my vessel to our house bank in order to safely deposit my fortune into my own savings account. Yay! During one of those depositing missions, my vessel must have counted about 11 years, my mom's and mine found themselves waiting in line for the next available teller clerk in order to take care of our "wish". Whilst doing so on this particular day, I recall how I kept myself busy with observing my surrounding by taking everything in a little bit more attentively than usual. This activity then led my soul to this one moment, during which I very vividly ended up deciding that I really liked their banking lobby, the atmosphere and their employees so much, that this workspace needed to become my "grownUP" activity, in order to *"Swim along With"* everyone else. Sweet! And further, I also instantly loved the fact, that my beloved and hard-working mom actually happened to be part of this banks construction. True fact. Besides being a cab driver, she actually also used to work as a crane driver on and off for many years, which at times even had Koni and Anita's husband end up as her coworkers on certain projects. Ha! The world is a small place after all. Yup. Well, and this "realistic" future workspace wish *"little Linda"* then clearly sent out to the beloved Universe knowing that this would end up being the perfect "Plan B" alternative. So shall be it. My *"Head Cinema"* then kept on traveling even further by suddenly presenting me this vision of seeing my "grownUP" vessel working for a Swiss bank branch located on this *"Other Planet"*. Genius. At least this making a living option would provide my soul with the opportunity to get transferred to my dream destination in its "reasonable and responsible" way, whenever educated fully. Woohoo. Deal. Now guess how this chosen professional path plan took its course a few years later? Correct. After mailing out an application to my house bank, the Thurgauer Kantonalbank/Bank of the canton of Thurgau (TKB) in Amriswil for their 3 years apprenticeship education program and after the successful completion of their required psychological entry test, *"little Linda"* then indeed found herself getting hired by her then envisioned bank EXACTLY as order by the magical Universe on that particular day. *"Thy Wish is my Command"*. Boom. And. Yay. Soon though, I came to realize that my order came along with a "tiny" problem. What?! As this reasonable future workspace wish of mine happened to be a local bank, their many branches therefore ended up being spread throughout the wonderful canton of Thurgau ONLY and that was about it. Oops. Hmmm. An adjustment in regards of my *"The Other Planet"* exploration dream therefore urgently revealed itself as a necessity and the Doing it on My Own option by the time my vessel would be hitting the magical American 21 count therefore got born as part of my Plan C creation instead. Perfect. And so this venture turned out to be. You shall see. Wink. This 3 years TKB education adventure as hoped ended up being a super FuN and very helpful *"Living on Earth Game"* experience and definitely revealed itself as THE perfect choice for starters. Yup! This chapter also happens to mark the time, during which those computer machines and technology in general made themselves shine in a quite popular light and inventions like the World Wide Web aka "www.", Windows, Apple, Linux, Outlook and Centralization Centers suddenly started to assist our daily tasks with *"ongRowing"* speed as a faster and in a way also more distractedly option. Hmmm. Slowly, many of those manual and mechanical helping tools therefore entered onto their own vanishing journeys, which made these once as "modern" considered typewriters, physical archives and stacks of preprinted formularies move into a mostly "memorial" experience. The wonderful outcome out of this *"ongRowing"* technological UPgrade truly revealed itself as the "faster" and more productive work option. As glorious this computer invention and its provided program called *Windows 3.1* certainly ended up getting praised from my end, as they suddenly transformed those annoying typo experiences into very pleasant "mistakes". Sweet. How happy *"little Linda"* felt about this newly provided magical button called *Delete*, which allowed her to correct and erase ANYTHiNG as seamlessly as it can be. All day long. If needed. Yay. This SpeCial eFFecT treat definitely revealed itself as such a wonderful lifesaver compared to my previous only available starting from scratch option, which always forced me to reload a new preprinted formulary with its many attached see through copies into my typewriter. Ufff. Life and work surely transformed themselves instantly into such a more pleasant and convenient flow, as suddenly less focus and discipline got required in order to receive even more compliments resulting from my happy bosses. Yay. And. Strike! Yes, those nostalgia days surely carry a SpeCial place in my heart as well and with them all the many wonderful (ex)-coworkers, including these daily guaranteed *"FuN Facts"* and the overall magic that we as a unit found ourselves able to create in this, to *"little Linda"* perceived mundane world of *"Swimming ALONG WiTH the Current"* reality. Yup. To *Laugh*, to *Play Pranks*, to *Support One Another* and to complete the designated jobs while doing so, marks what made this *"Living on Earth Game"* chapter absolutely a pleasant one to travel in, which probably explains why my vessel ended up "working" for this bank on and off for 10 years in total. Wow. With some of those to my soul dearly grown coworker ones I happily stayed in touch over the past decades and very grateful *"little Linda"* feels about these extra gained precious *"Extended Family Members"*. Yay. Thank y'all. Before my quite FuN banking adventure began its course though, my mom thought that it would do me good, to spend 1 year in the French part of Switzerland, as she did when her vessel counted 17 years. Hmmm. Reluctantly, I therefore agreed to this to me undesired experience and chose Geneva as my home destination in order to absolve this from her end suggested 1-year Housekeeping Apprenticeship. Ufff. Yes. Housekeeping. So it was and as expected, this journey ended up unfolding itself into a quite challenging ride. Yup. First of all, my love for American English happened to be far BiGGER than my soul felt it for this French language and secondly, I imagined my life to be a little bit more thrilling than spending it for 10 months straight with those FuN stopping b*zZZ* activities like Cooking, Sewing, Washing, Ironing and with other Housekeeping tasks at hand and this on the opposite Swiss side from my beloved Thurgau. Ufff. Of course, *"little Linda"* did as suggested and instantly decided to stay as positive as possible with the hopes, that maybe it would turn out cooler than expected. The family that I ended up picking presented itself as another added challenge, which therefore had me right away draw my *"Positivity Card"* from my thus far collected *"Life Toolbox"* as its adjusting ingredient, in order to make this new *"Living on*

Earth Game" experience work for the time being. *"Where there is a Will there ALWAYS is a Way."* And this my soul keeps on believing for it to be truer than true. Yup. Wink. Now, as my soul basically from the get-go remained very eager for this chapter to pass by as quickly as possible, I therefore decided to create a countdown sheet taped on a piece of paper with the remaining days at hand. Every morning, my vessel for that reason, right after my hand turned off the alarm, as a next step would straight ahead be relocating itself towards that sheet on my wall and found itself with LOTS of joy crossing this new day ahead off with a red sharpie, which list btw started somewhere in the late 200's. LOL. A long journey certainly happened to be waiting ahead for me, which therefore unexpectedly also brought along a wonderful opportunity for *"little Linda"* to practice and to further develop her with time more and more needed persistence and willpower muscles even more so. Ok. Let's then. Thank God that the magical Universe ended up sending another amazing soul my way, who got placed in the exact same reality as I found myself in: Same birth year, Swiss-German roots, Positive Attitude, Loves Pranks, is super FuN and UP for Anything, same school and felt the same way about her family as I did about mine. Yay. Very easy it therefore felt for our two souls to connect, once we got introduced to one another on this first day of our delightful Housekeeping School Adventure. Boom. And starting from that moment on, the two of our vessels basically kept on spending every single day together throughout the following 10 months to come. Love. The way of HOW the kind Universe brought Monika to my attention, actually still amuses *"little Linda"* to this very day quite a LOT. As our boring school found itself located in this tiny village called *Morges* VD, right next to Lausanne, all of my about twelve classmates therefore were obliged to travel from their host family homes to Morges by train. Now, whilst I happened to be busy waiting on my seat for the vehicles departure, my eyes all over sudden spotted a girl running towards the wagon in which my vessel was placed in. And let me tell you, this girl really ran FAST. She actually ended up running so fast that the doors immediately closed themselves right in front of her nose, the second that her vessel reached its desired wagon by further "deciding" to roll off without her aboard. Oops. Understandably, this girl as a result ended up cursing and stomping her feet in a quite agitated way, as I knew it from my dear friend Nicole, which spectacle therefore instantly found itself triggering *"little Linda's"* giggling buttons full on. LOL. Poor girl. About 1 hour later, I actually found myself pretty amazed about her vessels sudden appearance at the train station in Morges and then even more so, when my soul learned that the two of us would be classmates for the following "year" to come. Ha! The Universe definitely has its own very FuNNy and unique ways of introducing certain important souls into one's reality. Well done. Thanks to my newly gained *"Extended Family Member"*, this Geneva chapter unexpectedly turned itself into an absolute memorable and FuN adventure, which her soul with "No Doubt" ended up transforming into a more than worthwhile ride. Ha! Merci. Every day the two of our vessels would meet up at the Bel-Air bus station during our lunch breaks from 1pm – 4pm, and on Fridays we found ourselves in b*zZZ* school learning all these from my end as super boring interpreted tasks. Sunday used to be our off day and those days got reserved for our mutual adventures as well. Thank God. Wink. Too my surprise though, my soul at some point came to realize that *"little Linda"* actually experienced a LOT more FuN during those sewing, cooking and cleaning classes then whenever she found herself preoccupied with completing all these many weekly "nonsense" tasks noted on the given To Do list at her new *"Home Sweet Home"* base. Yup. Let me tell you, my dear *Co-Traveler*, living with this host family definitely turned into another very "interesting" ride. LOL. Luckily, my mid-aged Madame and Monsieur mostly happened to be gone all day long and so was their teenaged daughter. The only time that I really got to see them all, occurred during lunch and dinnertime and that was about it. Yay! Very quickly, I therefore came to the understanding that my "existence" simply resulted in a somewhat prestige choice from their ends and that this weekly task sheet turned into a "pro forma" gesture. All that my vessel really got called in for, happened to be to take care of the cooking, the cleaning, the laundry, the grocery shopping and for the ironing of their HUGE pile of clothes task, which even grew BiGGER by the weekly added and mainly containing bottom down shirt drop off loads from their adult lawyer son. Ufff. Besides these recurring "responsibilities", I also got asked to weekly SpeCial clean their many unused silverware and silver dishes on Mondays and all their about 20 pair of shoes on Thursdays, which basically remained untouched all along as well. Ha! What?! Exactly. My two very favorite disasters ended up being 1) Their kitchen, that presented the once with bright white painted walls and originally white installed "Chuchichästlis/kitchen cupboards" in a throughout the years into a yellow and greasy transmuted "coat" and 2) The with time so used up carpet, that allowed for the underneath existing concrete floor to at certain spots scream *"HELLO!"*, whenever my vessel passed by. True fact. Right Danny?! LOL. Well, and as soon as my awareness picked up on their tidiness interpretation, I therefore instantly started to develop my own cleaning and short cut methods in order to be more "efficient". Ha! My Madame actually seemed to have noticed only one of my many skipping actions throughout those *"NeverEnding"* 10 months and innocent *"little Linda"* of course talked her way effortlessly out of the situation within a snap. SNAP. During this remarkable time period, filled with many more rather interesting collected episodes resulting sides this lovely host family, I joyfully also found myself able to finally send in my application for my envisioned Plan B TKB banking education journey and certainly turned into a very happy camper, the second that my acceptance letter flew into my mailbox. Strike. This reality shift therefore instantly transformed the rest of my stay into a so much more enjoyable ride, as I now got to see this exciting bright light at the end of that cleaning tunnel. Yeeha! This year away from "home" also revealed itself as the one, during which my soul for the first time ever got introduced to some new Music beats, called *Tekno*. Yeah. As Monika and I early on into our Geneva adventure felt the mutual urge to get our dancing shoes out on an upcoming Saturday night, I as a starting point suggested the from another Geneva Swiss German friend recommended club *Jacque-Fille,* which at that time was supposed to play amazing Tekno tracks. Tekno, what?! Technotronic? *"Pump up the Jam"*? Ahhhm. Not quite. Smile. Well, and this Music genre definitely ended up revealing itself as a brand new one to *"little Linda's"* ears and also remained as a BiG secret for a little bit longer. Hmmm. Certainly, I eagerly tried my luck to find out more from this particular friend, the second that she shared her Jacque-Fille discovery a few days prior. After my first attempt of getting a possible Music description, my soul got instructed that it would be too hard for her to explain what Tekno exactly was or sounded like, as it differed very much from "regular" Music. "Regular" Music? Hmmm. Cool! Then, my second trial of getting a possible singing sample, in order for me to get a better idea of how this interesting sounding new genre sounded like, got dismissed with a polite *"Linda, they don't sing in Tekno Music and I definitely can't give you a sample of how it sounds like. It is a new style made up with many electro elements only. Just go and experience it for yourself. You might like it."* reaction. Boom! Baffled and quite enticed in one shot, *"little Linda"* then decided to accept this closing answer and immediately found herself adding this mysterious Music adventure onto her mental To Do list. This overall genre description certainly sounded very intriguing to my ears, as *difFeRent* and *Electro Beats* appear amongst those magical expressions that easily awaken my *"inner Adventuress'"* attention within a heartbeat when presented. BEAT. As Möne happens to be a trooper like my beloved BFF, she immediately jUMPed aboard on this "difFeRent" dancing adventure proposal of mine as soon as I shared my newly gained discovery with her. Yay! On the following Saturday, our vessels therefore found themselves hopping into a bus, which vehicle then ended up dropping us off a few blocks from our desired destination. The second that the two of our curious souls entered through the club's doors, our ears and senses immediately got exposed to some very to me interesting and weird sounding noise elements. LOUD Electronic beats and sound waves, that here and there dropped some words, was what my auricles picked up on first, accompanied by LOTS of strobo light and many magical colorful lasers, which furthermore stimulated my eyeballs in a curious way. Hmmm. Somewhat puzzled about this unexpected VERY difFeRent and unusual scenario, the two of us at first only found ourselves able to exchange some skeptical looks and remained for quite some time unsure as of what to think of this whole new presented world as of yet. Then, while I kept taking everything within that active room in, my eyes further started to notice a very interesting behavior and dance style amongst the other club goers. Some of them wore white gloves and had a whistle sitting in between their lips and besides their attention grabbing and in a way fascinating moves, I then actually caught them blowing their whistles at times along with the beat, whilst simultaneously fiddling with their arms and hands in wavy and floating movements in front of their bodies and faces, which scenario then suddenly began to remind me of Madonna's very Artistic, in 1990 released *"Vogue"* video. Hmmm! Awkward this new experience truly felt for these two Swiss German countryside chicks indeed. LOL. Then, the next thing that our souls acknowledged turned out to be that the magical Universe went ahead and sent us a really handsome guy our way, who all over sudden began his eye-catching dancing journey on a pedestal right in front of our vessels. AHHH. And. Ha! As our two souls very much so found themselves enjoying this newly presented view, Möne and I therefore instantly decided that this "Mister Attractive" actually happened to be more than reason enough for us to extend our stay for a tiny bit longer. Wink. His topless and perfectly trained Adonis vessel definitely did a fantastic job in at least having our teenage female senses satisfied for the night. BiGSMiLE. On our way back home, we then actually found ourselves quite happy about this first Tekno excursion and decided to definitely give it another trial soon. And so we did. And that is how my soul slowly began to develop its love and passion for this to me quite magical Tekno/Techno/Trance/House/Acid House/Deep House Music genre experience, which on top of it all also offers so many of these amazing synthesizer elements that *"little Linda"* already fell in love with during her own Music taste discovery years. Yeah! The first Tekno song that found itself able to catch my like attention, originates from L.A. Style and is called *"James Brown is Dead."* LOL. Yes, I know. This title appeared as quite a macabre one at that time, as Mister Brown happened to be still *"Living in America"* for another 15 years. Oops. The more that *"little Linda"* then found herself *"ongRowingly"* cruising in this Electro beat discovery quest, the more her knowledge about this genre developed itself along with it as well and therefore she soon came to learn that there actually existed 3 difFeRent levels of Tekno Music. What?! 3 difFeRent levels? Boah! Yes. #1 teKno, #2 teKKno and #3 teKKKno. Ha! The more K's a producer would add to his creation, the more intense and "aggressive" the overall experience therefore would appear. Wow. My soul therefore found "herself" tremendously enjoying all these many beats up to 2 K's and after that it got a little bit too messy for my taste. Smile. By the time that my vessel returned back to Amriswil, my soul ended up resonating with TeKKno so much, that I desired to continue this venture with my "old" girl friends for a change. Sadly, *"little Linda"* quickly came to learn though that those wonderful Tekno beats still sounded quite foreign to her Swiss-German Confederates and that their "in" Music instead happened to be this Neue Deutsche Welle/New German Wave Oktoberfest sounding like genre, which got played at this recently opened *"Villa Wahnsinn/Villa Madness"* location hit all night long. Villa what?! Wahnsinn? That truly sounded like madness to my ears indeed. Wink. A *"Oh boy. Really?"* outburst therefore resulted as my immediate reaction toward this surprising Thurgau *"FuN Fact"* UPdate and all I found myself left with ended up to either stay in, which definitely remained as a NO option, or to obey into entering the from this Villa Wahnsinn provided Time Machine in order to travel a few steps back into a from *"little Linda"* rather undesired vibe destination. Ufff. Thankfully my NENA remained as a loyal "guest" during those excursions and kept successfully kidnapping my emotions, including *"Head Cinema"* experience right into my happy zone, whenever her *"99 Luftballons"* showed up. Woohoo! Well, at least for a few minutes. Wink. Then, a few weeks later, the kind Universe finally sent me my desired underground news my way. Strike! One wonderful advantage that growing UP right at the boarder to Germany always brought along with was that our neighbors in Konstanz/Constance always lived one or two steps ahead in time than we did on our, from my end as somewhat "conservative" perceived Swiss borderline side. Yup. The delightful news turned out to be that 2 small clubs in this city "abroad" happened to be playing my newly discovered Music love for quite some time already. Hooray! As soon as my soul learned about this very important UPdate, I therefore immediately found myself dragging my ladies along for some FuN Konstanz/Constance Tekko adventures. Of course, they at first as well experienced quite mixed feelings towards this somewhat "abstract" Music experience and with some "practice" most of them soon started to like the TeKno version enough, which led us to repeat those excursions here and there, for starters. Smile. Then slowly, very slowly Techno, as we call it today, finally took over the German part of Switzerland as well and this just in time for the celebration of a newly invented sensation called *Redbull*. Ha! And this rEvolutionary gummy bear drink turned out to be the PERFECT Redbull-Techno marriage in order for our vessels to last even longer. At first this magical energy drink though happened to only be legal and sold in Austria, which therefore made this country our top pick in regards of satisfying our clubbing needs. Then, once it finally got legalized with its much lower caffeine and taurine content in Switzerland and Germany as well, my ladies and I therefore decided that it now was at the time to stick closer to our territories again. Wink. Good old days! In regards of my transition from my delightful Housekeeping School Adventure back into my "old" Amriswil reality, I must admit that this journey turned out to be a quite interesting experience as well. As Möne's father decided to pick his daughter up in his car on this, our last Geneva June day, they offered for my vessel to join them along to their house in the canton of *Aargau*, which is located about an additional 1 ½ hour drive away from Amriswil. Happily, I of course accepted this kind offer and its further plan for my mom to pick *"little Linda"* up at their house on the following day. Wonderful. And this first "picking up" moment at my host family's house actually turned out to be much more dramatic than ever expected. LOL. Who would have thought that after all this longing and crossing the many days off from my magical *"NeverEnding"* list, that the end of this Geneva adventure actually would be wrapped up with tears? What? Water drops?! Yes. Both, Monika and I actually began our weeping concert, the second that my vessel was placed next to hers in the car, alongside with our realization that this picking up action step also meant The End for our mutual daily adventures. Sniff. Then, once both of our souls became aware of this very contradicting and dramatic scene that we just ended up creating, my dear friend and I then immediately found ourselves cracking up and continued our ride back home with some more bittersweet giggling tears. Wink. Yes, and this quite heartfelt and emotional moment, accompanied by the many other unforgettable first time ever being away from "home" memories, still keeps us well entertained to this day. Oh yeah. Life and our at times abstract and contradictory human behaviors truly get *"little Linda"* to giggle quite hard at times. GiGGLE. GiGGLE. GiGGLE. One probably can only imagine how the two of our souls reacted once our own *"Time to say Goodbye"* moment arose. Wink. The remedy that made this departing from one another's immediate reality transition into a smoother ride, turned out to be the knowledge of our both souls, that this physical separation actually meant The Beginning for our *"Living on Earth Game"* journeys bonded as newly found "siblings". Yay. Another *"Extended Family Member"* I unexpectedly ended up gaining in this wonderful soul, which the sweet Universe introduced me to, whilst she felt the urge to stump her feet at Geneva's train station on that Friday morning. Yup. LOL. Who would have thought to where this FuN spectacle would lead its way towards to and this in an *"ongRowing"* state of mind reality? Ha! Love. Once my teenage vessel successfully got transported back into my beloved Parkweg bedroom again, everything suddenly seemed so difFeRent then *"little Linda"* used to experience it throughout the past decade at hand. Hmmm. My return from this delightful 1-year Housekeeping School spectacle definitely made me realize that a LOT had changed, including my own *"Self"*, which reality check therefore ended up requiring quite some readapting skills to my souls newly exposed Amriswil environment and to its "there" presented lifestyle. Boah. Further, I quite soon also came to experience that most of my friends meanwhile already found themselves "swimming" in this process of finding their ways from those easygoing school vibe days into the business world's by directing their main focus on this becoming "responsible" and "grownUP" task instead. Ufff. Well, and that knowledge of finding myself about to embark onto about the same "more serious" transitional journey definitely caused quite some inner resistance to *"little Linda"*, as the idea of being a "grownUP" always remained a state of mind reality that she eagerly tried to stay away from, for as long as possible. Yup! Wink. Now picture this dramatic moment, during which my benevolent mom approached her at that time 11 or 12 years vessel count daughter, with this life-changing *"Ewww, your underarms stink. It is time for you to start wearing deodorant now."* sentence. Oh yes, this well-meant statement from her end contained enough of a reason for *"little Linda"* to truly freak out and for my confused mother to therefore shake her head in disbelief. LOL. True fact. Only my *"Head Cinema"* vision of witnessing myself putting this "grownUP" stuff under my armpits had me instantly experience this WAY too early occurring transformation into the as more serious, conservative and responsible perceived adulthood period, which UPdated reality check therefore with guarantee simultaneously also would be making sure of to let all these many magical gang member days disappear into The Nothing right there, right then. What a disaster. Oh My God. Help! Soon after I more or less successfully calmed myself down from this tragic outlook, *"little Linda"* then as a next step came to the conclusion that this situation with "No Doubt" required her magical *"Positivity Card"* to the rescue. Abracadabra. Grudgingly, I therefore found myself trying to accept this new level of this unchangeable teenager growth stage of mine, by allowing myself to obey to my mom's suggestion. Once again. Ufff. She of course reacted as quick as a bunny and proudly handed me my first own owned MUM deodorant, right after her vessel purchased it on the following day. Parents. LOL. Well, and whilst I found myself about to undergo this undesired adulthood transformational procedure, *"little Linda"* very successfully vowed to herself that she would NEVER EVER grow UP, No Matter what. Boom. And this magical spell certainly kept on working its powers wonderfully up, until this very day. Ha! Oops. It actually keeps on working so well, that I quite often keep on forgetting that "my vehicle" meanwhile physically turned into an "adult" considered one and that my whole package actually would contain so much more authority and "powers" than *"little Linda"* at times ends up making use of. Ha! What?! The good news is though, that she just recently decided that *"Enough was Enough"* and that therefore it was at the time for her to start taking advantage of this rather interesting seemingly new *"Life Toolbox"* ingredient discovery. Yup. To my surprise, I must admit that this experiencing the adult world through the eyes of *"little Linda's"* trial transformed itself into a quite FuN *"FuN Fact"*. Yay! This new Acting like an adult approach, whatever that means anyway, I am finding can be a pretty cool force to apply into so many difFeRent *"Living on Earth Game"* situations. At first though, it required my soul quite some effort in order to develop my own and personal rhythm with this new way of floating through my reality. Meanwhile, I thankfully became very good at this adult skill at hand and successfully created this very convenient On and Off switch for whenever needed. Hooray! Now, as soon as I found myself Ready, Steady, Go to dive into this upcoming business "aquarium" at hand, I actually ended up being quite surprised about how quickly those rather FuN educational 3 years "swam" by. Yup. And as *"little Linda"* dared on taking an even closer look at all the many, during this time frame outer and inner occurred metamorphosis's, she even more so felt quite impressed about how much the emerging world of technology began its own and *"ongRowing"* melting journey with her daily banking tasks, by adding its "UPgrading" magical spell to it, whilst she on the other end found herself witnessing her own inner "growth" expansion, which wonderfully got enhanced by the further exploration task of this *"BiG Wide World's"* many adventurous offerings at grasp. Ha! My all-time favorite department during those educational 3 years, turned out to be the mortgage one, as being part of the whole process from a client's decision of purchasing or building a property with our help until the very end of things, made my soul the happiest. Oh yeah. As this chapter took its course just a little while before the invention of Department Centralizations and Call Centers, my job therefore resulted in literally processing and completing everything on my own for our clients. Once the first meeting successfully got completed in the TKB's favor, my next

steps then resulted in starting the whole financing process from A – Z and therefore ended with the last payment transition, which included the pay out of the entire determined mortgage amount. Yeah! And that financial approach is part of why this diverse office job remains as my very favorite position throughout my entire banking career of an overall 10 years and if actually someone would offer the EXACT same position with the EXACT same team to me anew, then *"little Linda"* might even feel quite tempted to consider it. At least. Ha! Then, once I successfully graduated from my studies, I shortly after found my vessel sitting in a meeting with another one named *Frau Marzoli* from the Human Resources Department in order for us to discuss my desired future plans and visions at hand. Sweet. One of her first questions therefore turned out to be *"Frau Wartenweiler, where are you planning on heading with your career now that you graduated? How do you envision your future?"* Well, and these questions then instantly succeeded in triggering this once so amazing *"Childhood Dream"* created vision onto my *"Head Cinema"* screen, which caused *"little Linda"* to with LOTS of excitement burst out a *"Well, honestly I would love to fly to Hollywood and appear in a Feature Film on the BiG screen one day!"* WOAH! What?! What did I just say?! What did I just do?! Are you crazy Linda? OH. MY. GOD. Now it's out! Oh NO! And right in that very second, I instantly found myself regretting my honesty and remained in disbelieve that this "unreasonable" statement truly left my mouth. Oh my. Let me tell you, my beloved *Co-Traveler*, that puzzled look on this HR woman's face *"little Linda"* will always remember that appeared right at the beginning of her Trying to make sense of the just heard Of journey. LOL. My "abstract" and somewhat out of content seemingly responds definitely hit her soul in a very unexpected way, this mine could instantly tell. Into what an embarrassing moment this one turned itself into. pOops. And. Yup. My face therefore once anew started to glow in its by then famous transmuted *"Tomato-Red like"* color, whilst my vessel furthermore decided to keep itself, during this uncomfortable and *"NeverEnding"* seemingly momentum of silence, VERY busy with the rising task of its temperature from head to toe. Help! How dare I spilling my safely kept *"Childhood Dream"* secret out aLOUD right now, to especially Frau Marzoli from the HR Department of the TKB? Oh my. As fast as I could, I therefore instantly went ahead, popped that bubble of mine as usual, landed well down on earth again and tried to save this incredibly awkward turned situation with a shy and smiling *"Ah. Well. No. Actually, I would love to stay here in Amriswil at the mortgage department if possible, as I REALLY love my team and my job very much."* Which certainly happened to be my truthful Plan B opinion and wish, as we just discovered it a few minutes earlier. Smile. Then, I further shared all my existing banking thoughts with her and quickly found myself able to gear our conversation back on track by applying some of my "hidden" Acting skills to the rescue. Ha! Once our meeting successfully got completed, my vessel then as a result ended up as the happy "owner" of my requested fulltime position in my favorite mortgage department. Yay! Very satisfied and proud *"little Linda"* therefore felt about this achievement and off she went and continued to explore her *"Living on Earth Game"* adventure, now as a TKB graduate. *"Let's Rock 'n Roll!"*

"The Only way is UP"
By now, my vessel reached a count of 20 and that was when my within lingering *"The Other Planet"* dream suddenly happily ever after started to knock on my awareness door again. Oh Hello! Yes, this United States topic seemed to remain a quite persistent one and *"little Linda"* certainly always found herself very drawn to it, whenever especially New York City or California appeared in her reality in whatever form available. During my travels through middle school for instance, I used to have this one classmate, who my soul thought happened to be such a lucky one of finding both of her brothers' vessels living in New Jersey. You know, on this *"Other Planet"*, in which everything seems to be possible. Wow! Well, and this reality check therefore meant for her, that she found herself very privileged to every summer spend 4 to 5 weeks right over there in my dream destination with her entire family. And this fact always caused a BiG WOW eFFecT on my soul and *"little Linda"* certainly found herself admiring Katja very much so for all her many *"Living on Earth Game"* adventure creations over "there". A further skill that I always loved about my dear classmate happened to be her flawless and perfectly well-trained ability to express herself in this to my soul so enticing American English language. How blessed Katja truly was out of my perspective. Ahhh. One day. One day. Now, as my dear classmate knew about my love for New York City and America in general, she therefore always made sure to yearly send me a postcard from her many Big Apple adventures my way. One probably can only imagine how thrilled *"little Linda"* felt, the second that her eyes spotted those difFeRent Manhattan postcards in her mailbox. Oh yeah. Quickly, I therefore always ended up grabbing each card and pinned it right next to the other one/s on the wall located close by my pillow, just the way I used to experience Helene doing it with all her collected NENA material. Yup. The Statue of Liberty, the Financial District and the Twin Towers therefore accompanied my journey daily for many years "already" and whenever my soul got presented that astonishing Manhattan skyline, I would instantly find my vessel covered with many goosebumps, followed by a from my *"Head Cinema"* created own US Linda trailer. Yes, and alongside with all those many inner experiences, my longing to see all of this LiVE one day with my own two eyes certainly grew stronger by the year. Ha! These 3 to me very precious postcards, I btw am still safely guarding in one of my photo albums in Switzerland. Oh yes. Thank you dear Katja for your dream nurturing support throughout those past years. Love. Now, with my achievements of being 1) Hired as a fulltime banker from a very safe employer, 2) With a to my soul satisfying monthly income and with 3) Many more added Swiss coins towards *"little Linda's"* *"Red and White Saving Sock"* account, my out of a Swiss perspective security foundation successfully got built and therefore the moment for my next *"Stepping-Stone"* jUMP upon my, this *"Living on Earth Game"* path officially emerged. Yes. *"The Other*

Planet" chapter, accompanied with my prior envisioned dream to celebrate my slowly approaching 21st birthday right over "there". Woohoo! As my bank-transferring Plan B version still remained as an out of question game plan option at hand, I therefore as a next move decided to start a collection for any of my Plan C made possibilities instead. Within a short amount of time, the *"Thoughts become Things"* reality, combined with my full on believe that *"Where there is a Will there ALWAYS is a Way"* must have worked as the magical needed formula in order for the perfect solution to appear quite randomly. Boom. And. Hooray. On the same floor that I grew UP at, my mom and I used to have an older man as our second direct neighbor, who happened to be occupying that space even before our arrival back then in 1979. Yup. That long. During one evening, I remember "running" into him in front of our building, when my friendly neighbor after some chit chatting found himself curiously wondering about my future plans, now that *"little Linda"* graduated from her banking apprenticeship. Happily, I therefore instantly let Herr Grauer in into my current accepted job situation and into my newly forged birthday plans. By now, my soul knew that this UPcoming *"The Other Planet"* adventure would occur over a duration of about 6 months, as this amount of time happened to be the previous legal visiting timeframe for any non-visa Swiss passport holders prior to 9/11. What luxurious treats those days simply used to be. Wink. Then, while Herr Grauer attentively kept on following my storyline, his soul at some point further wanted to know if mine already came up with concrete plans in regards of this US dream of mine. A *"Nope"* returned his way instantly, as *"little Linda"* truly just stepped onto this new mission of hers, a little while ago. With a smile on his face, my friendly neighbor then began to share that he happened to have two of his sons living in *Charlotte*, North Carolina, that both worked as pilots for the USAir Airways, both were the father of a very young family and that he happily would love to check in with them if one possibly would be in need of a nanny, if I would like him to. Ha! Well, that sounded like a fantastic plan to my soul und joyfully I therefore expressed my green light to Herr Grauer in order to find out more about these quite interesting sounding options at hand. *"Everything happens for a Reason"* after all. Boom. Shortly after, my friendly neighbor provided me with the wonderful feedback that one of his sons' neighbor couple turned out to show their interest in my nanny services and if I felt the same way that he therefore as a next step would provide me with their phone number. Strike. My soul of course instantly found "herself" resonating with this opportunity and had my vessel call up this American family, once their phone number was in my possession. My then English knowledge luckily turned out to be just good enough to converse the most important details with this couple on the other end of the line and quickly the three of our souls came to the agreement that my vessel would be heading to their Charlotte home, 2 weeks prior to *"little Linda's"* 21st *"Whoomp! There she is."* celebration. Woohoo! That was easy. Thank you, dear Universe. After quitting my TKB job with LOTS of excitement, I then instantly went ahead and purchased my very first flight ticket to this *"Other Planet"*, which stated *Charlotte, North Carolina*. Into what an exciting and historical moment this one truly transformed itself into. Finally, this long cherished *"Soul Childhood Dream"* of mine was about to come true after such a long *"NeverEnding"* waiting period. Boah! On May 12th 1996, my vessel therefore as planned for the first time ever set foot onto this promising *"The Other Planet"* reality of mine and entered this new *"Living on Earth Game"* phase fully energized, with LOTS of respect for the unknown at hand and with a thrilled *"Hello America. Here I am. Finally. Thank you for having me aboard for the UPcoming plus minus 6 months. Now "Let's Rock 'n Roll!" Show we what you've got."* outburst. Boom. This new adventure of mine, which this time took place many more kilometers away from my hometown Amriswil, on a now even complete difFeRent continent, certainly provided *"little Linda"* anew with many more valuable ingredients for her precious *"Life Toolbox"* collection, which mainly included more insights about difFeRent interpretations of lifestyles and cultures, and about WHO this Linda Wartenweiler soul seems to be. Hmmm. Are you as curious as I am, my fellow *Co-Traveler*, to find out what these additional discoveries where? Sweet. Let's Go! This time around, my vessel found itself set in a reality as a nanny of two little boys. One counted 1 ½ years and the other one 3. As my new host family anew turned out to be an "ok" choice, I therefore as usually decided to pull out my wonderful *"Positivity Card"* by further have it mixed with many of my thus far gained travel experiences and with the needed amount of curiosity for what magic would await *"little Linda"* this time around. Wink. Having another Herr Grauer as a direct neighbor definitely revealed itself as super help and useful on so many difFeRent levels. As Herr Grauer junior himself grew UP in Amriswil and as my Möne this time around happened to be experiencing her own adventures FAR away from where my vessel was placed at, my soul fortunately found this like-minded and fellow Thurgauer soul accessible, whenever my discouraging *Mister Loneliness* and *Misses Homesickness* friends sneaked up on me. Thankfully, *"little Linda"* remained as a welcomed guest at Grauer's home, the second we all met and instantly my soul found in "his", "his" wife's and in "his" 2 kiddies my first family abroad, which after all still halfway rooted in my beloved Amriswil. Yay. One reality check that triggered those discouraging friends of mine into my awareness surely turned out to be the fact that my new surrounding vessels either ranged from a 30y count up or 10 down, which had my 21 years one pretty much unexpectedly float around in my own "world". Ufff. Well and this gapping phenomenon just happens to be sparking this reality check into my awareness that *"little Linda"* actually all along used to experience the exact same situation with all her with time collected blood cousins at hand, which UPdate certainly reveals itself as an interesting *Dot Connection* discovery, as this Special eFFecT seems to for whatever reason cross my *"Living on Earth Game"* path repeatedly. Still. What? Yes. Even though my soul decided to experience this Linda Wartenweiler journey as an only child and with therefore many *"Extended Family Member"* exploration opportunities instead, all of my "same" blooded 9 cousins ended up starting their own journeys either somewhere in the early to mid 1960ies or in the spread out 1980ies, which left my soul as the only 1970ies reproduction aboard. Ha! Hmmm. Well, and this reality check therefore allowed *"little Linda"* to explore a world, in which those blood related family member playmate options ended up being either way "too old" or "too young" for her to really interact with during any family reunions, which therefore instead left enough room for her to even more so take advantage of this only child experience. Boom. *"Thy Will is My Command"*. Wink. So yes, and therefore this new, quiet and family oriented Charlotte experience of mine at first certainly required quite some adaptation skills on several levels from my end, as only a few months prior my soul enthusiastically started to explore Zurich's magical Rave and Techno scene with a mix of old and new friends, which included weekly Dancing until the break of Dawn adventures. Yeeha! Oh boy. And one can probably only imagine about how the world in this family-based environment at the Providence Country Club, located in a BiG quite city in the southern part of this *"The Other Planet"*, suddenly seemed to be standing still for adventurous *"little Linda"*. Help! And yes, culture shock of its finest. In every sense of the word. Yup. Truly everything seemed to move so much slower and difFeRent to where my vessel just came from, including their love for Music. Instead of any of my HiGHly beloved Electronic beats bursting out of any LOUDspeakers, my soul now got confronted with Hip-Hop, R&B and with Alternative vibes instead. What?! Help! Dune's *"I Can't Stop Raving. I Can't Stop Raving."* therefore very much so ended up beating through my head, whilst my soul found "herself" busy with this overall fitting in task at hand. To these Hip-Hop and R&B tunes though, I actually quite quickly found myself connecting with, as during my High School chapter *"little Linda"* at some point ended up considering herself a *"Hip Hop Horray. Ho. Hey. Ho."* hopper for a little while, which therefore left her with "No Doubt" with the probably most challenging task at hand, which was the Ska Punk Alternative Reggae Pop Rock band named *No Doubt*. That's right. This band's style certainly differed so much from what my auricles had been exposed to prior or better said, were used to at all, so that whenever MTV decided to air their then smashing hit *"Spiderwebs"* in an *"ongRowing"* loop, I instantly felt prompted to either quickly switch the channel or to at least mute the video for the time being. Yup. Even though *"little Linda"* found herself quite resistant towards the from her end perceived "all over the place" chosen beat combinations and by the "weird" added opera like sounding female vocal at first, she with time actually began to develop a little love for No Doubt's own and unique way of Art creation interpretation. That's right. Well, and that little love then grew into a size to where I, 5 months down the road, suddenly found myself liking this band with "No Doubt" and shortly after ended up being a proud owner of their in 1995 released *"Tragic Kingdom"* Compact Disc. Ha! And even further down the road, Gwen Stefani on top of it all somehow managed to turn herself into a secretly, from my end "followed" Artist soul of mine. Ooops! Now it's out. Well, stay tuned then for more about "us" to come, my patient *Co-Traveler*.

Gratitude. Now, as finding "playmates" in my age range revealed itself as another rather challenging task, I at some point came to the conclusion that there had to exist a point in my US itinerary stating *"The Exploration of this magical "The Other Planet" experience MUST be carried out on Your Own, as being on Your Own after all is part of your current "Living on Earth Game" agreement."* What? What?! Well, these rather unexpected "facts" definitely welcomed my reality somewhat out of the blue and my soul instantly felt very certain that "she" must have over read that part too, before "she" embarked onto this Linda Wartenweiler journey. Bummer. Of course, I followed through as suggested, after having given a suddenly appearing trip opportunity its fair trial first. As I in addition to my somewhat quite boring b*zZZ* nanny services decided to enhance my stay with a basic English course twice per week during the first 3 months, *"little Linda"* therefore was given the opportunity at the end of our program, to join her shy Japanese classmate Yoshi and his friend Hitoshi on a road trip to *Myrtle Beach,* South Carolina. Sweet! Very thrilled, I therefore instantly found myself accepting this newly on the horizon appeared adventure and this weekend away from my usual mundane nanny routine, substituted with my first real *"The Other Planet"* exploration instead, definitely turned out to be the needed trigger experience in order for me to execute some desired changes, once back in Charlotte. Smile. Alongside with the reality check of my two travel companions revealing themselves as rather quiet and difFeRent souls, I by then also understood the beloved Universe's point of having me explore this *"BiG Wide World"* on My Own more often, starting right then. Yes, and that is how this life enhancing pre-taste excursion awoke my traveling bug and my *"inner Adventuress"* even more so. Finally. Instantly, I therefore informed my host family about my further weekend getaway plans and added that the exploration of their home country after all happened to be my main reason, why *"little Linda's"* vessel found itself there. The lady of the house as expected immediately ended up expressing her concerns about my newly forged plans, as she already did prior to my Myrtle Beach adventure. Ha! Then, as she kept insisting on resisting, my soul therefore decided that the perfect moment just arose for me to *"Let Go"* of this unsatisfying nanny opportunity by making use of my already created Plan B at hand, which consisted my immediate relocation into the available empty room at Grauer's house. Boom. *"Letting go of Something that No Longer Serves One's Growth and Expansion."* Just like that. Bye-Bye. That's right. And along with this effortless dance move from one home into the other, my "truly" envisioned US dream finally found itself writing its first chapter by allowing *"little Linda"* to explore it as *"wiLD & Free",* as she desired for it to be. Woohoo! By now, my vessel spent half of my planned 6 months on this *"Other Planet"* and all that I thus far found myself able to explore happened to be Charlotte, *Raleigh* NC, Myrtle Beach and the Providence Country Club. What?! LOL. Exactly. With this new set up and with another 3 months in the pipeline, my soul therefore decided to instantly take advantage of this newly gained freedom by diving right into some further adventure creations. Yeeha! *"Let's* FiNALLY REALLY *Rock 'n Roll!"* Atlanta turned out to be my desired next pick, which I ended up exploring with the perfect travel companion, which was my very first owned car, introducing *A beautiful white Volkswagen Golf 2 convertible with white leather seats, born in 1991.* Yeeha! Now, one of the reasons why my next destination fell to Atlanta happened to be the fact, that the 100 Olympic Summer games just ended their course there a few days prior and the thought of experiencing this probably by now quite ghost town like appearing environment therefore unraveled itself as a rather rare and unique *"FuN Fact"* opportunity to explore. Atlanta definitely turned itself into a quite educational and interesting excursion choice. Besides my visit of all these remaining Olympic attractions, I to my surprise soon came to learn that Coca-Cola got invented right there in 1886 by a pharmacist called *Dr. John S. Pemberton*, who originally intended to sell this black soda drink as a patent medicine and that Martin Luther King Jr.'s soul decided to start "his" *"Living on Earth Game"* journey out there as well. Wow. Those discoveries truly threw their impressive eFFecTs on *"little Linda"* and had her especially love the many various existing Coca-Cola soda samples, which got offered in its adventurous build museum. Ha! Then, after the completion of my Atlanta mission, my vessel moved further down south with my reliable Golf friend to jazzy *New Orleans* for another few days, before we headed straight back "home" to Charlotte. Olé. One happy occasion, which allowed *"little Linda"* to even more so enjoy her long desired and remaining *"The Other Planet"* adventure, happened to be the arrival of some unexpected blessed news delivered straight from the beloved Universe. Ha! About 2 ½ months into my Charlotte ride, I to my surprise was given a to me rather random seemingly phone call from my lovely ex vis-à-vis mortgage department coworker friend Madeleine, which resulted directly from her office desk. My soul of course reacted very excited about this by then quite rare familiar voice connecting experience, before hers then after a few minutes of catching up decided that it was time to let the cat out of its bag, on this, my mid-morning. Eagerly Mady therefore suddenly started to share that my substitution right after her trial phase decided to continue her many *"Living on Earth Game"* adventures somewhere else, that "my" desk therefore happened to be available again, immediately, and that everyone in the team would LOVE to fill this spot with my vessel anew, right after my return in 3 months. Boah! What?! Then, she further added that my old direct boss and Amriswil's branch manager actually found themselves waiting right in the office next door in order to discuss any further details, if interested. Well, I must admit that by now I truly found myself very baffled and honored at the same time about this unexpected Abracadabra spectacle at hand and as this position happened to be this, my thus far favorite one, I more than happily consented to continue this conversation. Yes! After a short and crisp conversation with my soon to be anew 2 "bosses", I therefore instantly found myself accepting their offer, right after their magical *"That's absolutely ok Frau Wartenweiler. We are aware of your travels and will happily be waiting for your return."*

responds in regards of my further declared US plans at run. Wow. What?! Well, my soul by now certainly found "herself" COMPLETELY floating in a shock state of mind by simultaneously also feeling amazed about the eFFecTs of information flow that kept on traveling through my ear canal. Boah! They truly would be waiting for *"little Linda's"* return in order to fill this spot? How incredible. And just like that, I found myself out of the blue financially all set and from the TKB hired again, just as it already occurred during my delightful Housekeeping School Adventure a few years ago. Ha! Wonderful. Und. Danke. Then, right after the return from my New Orleans excursion, the magical Universe decided to brighten up my *"Living on Earth Game"* ride even more so by sending me some more exciting news my way. Hooray! As generous Herr Grauer junior happened to have access to amazing 90% off USAir Airways airfare deals, he therefore after some chit chatting went ahead and organized four "Happy Hour" tickets with my name on it, which enabled my soul to finally explore my two favorite *"The Other Planet"* dream destinations in ONE shot only. Strike. And the purchased tickets at hand said *Charlotte – JFK, JFK – Charlotte, Charlotte – LAX, LAX – Charlotte.* Super YAY! The price for this wonderful opportunity ended up being one hundred and something bucks for my *"Red and White Saving Sock"* account and instantly delivered *"little Linda"* with this joyous feeling of just having won the lottery. What a great deal this indeed was. And as one thing always leads to another, my soul then right away got presented its next opportunity in order to ensure a perfect completion for my travels to come. Ha! Ready? During that week, one of our neighbors happened to have their parents over from New Jersey for a couple of days and they instantly wondered, if I already found a place to stay, once I UPdated them about my UPcoming first New York City trip ever. After I shook my head and after we found out that the three of our vessels would be landing on the EXACT same date in JFK within a few hours difFeRence only, this lovely couple then instantly invited me to stay with them at their house in New Jersey, if interested. Yes! And. Another. Strike. Of course, my soul was and accepted their nice offer within the following second. As soon as my very "thrilled" vessel landed in JFK a few days later, I then as suggested by this friendly couple, made my way with the subway straight to the on 34th Street, Herald Square located Manhattan Mall. This spot, I was told, would offer the perfect starting out position for *"little Linda"* to dive into her very first own Big Apple adventure creation and impression collection during my wait period for them. Sweet. And so it turned out to be. Wow! How amazed my soul felt in this very impressive and legendary moment of suddenly finding "herself" LiVE amongst these many *"NeverEnding"* tall skyscrapers, accompanied by New York City's famous traffic noise and masses of other moving vessels. Hooray, I made it! Finally, One of my BiG *"Childhood Dreams"* just got materialized and *"little Linda"* found herself about to experience some of those thrilling "Katja" adventures for herself. Yay! 4 days I gifted to myself in order to explore this metropolis as a sneak peek exercise, which ended up causing enough magic for *"little Linda"* to instantly decide that she would be returning for many more *"Living on Earth Game"* adventure collections, in the hopefully near future. Deal. Once my vessel found itself safe and sound in Charlotte again, I as planned spent one night at Grauer's house, before a new airplane would be dropping *"little Linda"* off into her upcoming 6 weeks *"Cali Dreamin'"* chapter. Woohoo! Los Angeles was marked on my itinerary next and my soul reacted quite ecstatic about this additional *"Dream coming True"* event ahead. As for my City of Angels residence, I chose the right next to the ocean located Youth Hostel on 2nd Street in *Santa Monica* as the perfect fit. Ha! There, my interest in improving my English skills even more so arose with my *"ongRowing"* happiness and the lookout for a great language school turned into my next mission at hand. Now, as the Internet back then still happened to be walking around in its baby shoes, everyone's information gathering exercise therefore still needed to be approached in the "old fashioned" manner, which included a real time One-on-One interaction with other "human beings" by either using a landline phone or by "in person" visits at the actual desired resource location, by Mouth-to-Mouth propagandas, by catalogue and magazine ads or by "accidentally" stumbling over the desired answer one way or the other. Ha! Well, and as for my starting out media, I chose Santa Monica's phonebook and thankfully within a short amount of time, my eyes ended up spotting the perfect next *"Stepping Stone"* to take. Yay. A 1-month intense English course at the former ELS school, located right at the corner of Santa Monica Boulevard and 2nd Street, this new adventure introduced itself as and that is where *"little Linda"* was given her first personal inspirational quote by her favorite teacher on the last day of these very educational 4 weeks. Well, and this to me precious and wise card ever since has been a continuous dear travel companion upon my many past *"Living on Earth Game"* adventures and finds itself daily reminding my soul directly from its at times changing home wall position, that *"The Key to your Success is to keep your Dream in Focus and to have the Courage to do things Other's WON'T do."* information flow. Boom. And so I will. Thank you, Josh. The wonderful and dreamlike city of Santa Monica definitely revealed itself as the ideal English education location for various reasons. 1) It instantly filled my vessel with these lovely *"Home Sweet Home"* emotions, 2) My *"inner Adventuress"* surly got presented with many new exploration opportunities and 3) *"little Linda"* finally found herself "kind of" being part of this *"The Other Planet"* Movies reality check experience, as the scenery and its inhabitants appeared exactly as they all along did within all those many Movies and TV shows that she loved so much, which for example included "Beverly Hills 90210", "Melrose Place" and "Baywatch". Woohoo! Well and at that time, the latter thankfully still happened to be in production mode and of course I here and there organized an excursion to its *Malibu* "headquarter" set with my there purchased rollerblades in order to get my Acting fascination fed as well. Seeing Pamela Anderson and my teenage flame David Hasselhoff aka Michael Knight LiVE in Action certainly ended up marking another very inspiring experience as a further delightful presented treat from the magical Universe. Thank you.

Throughout those past few months, my BFF and I of course as usual stood in here and there mail exchanging contact as well and UPdated one another about the most important whereabouts of each one's own journeys. Now, the second that my longest friend ever learned that my vessel would be vacating in sunny Cali for 6 weeks straight, he instantaneously decided to pay me a visit during my 4th and 5th week, so that the two of our souls would be enabled to share some "actual" adventurous *"Cali Dreamin'"* moments as a unit. Yay! At the same time, I then actually found my dear "raver" and personal hairdresser friend Regu feeling about as thrilled as Danny was about my then current whereabouts, that her soul got prompted to announce "her" vessels showing up during my last 2 LA weeks. Wow. Yes, and as the kind Universe most likely thought that the three of our souls should be celebrating life together as a trio, it made sure to have them book their vacation with this overlapping week. Sweet! Of course, *"little Linda"* felt very excited to soon be surrounded by two of her dear Swiss friends as an even 1 week "Happy Hour" package, after being parted from everyone for 4 1/2 months by then. Yay! Immediately, I therefore suggested that the three of our vessels should be entering an adventurous 7 days excursion once we would be finding ourselves united as The Three Musketeers at the Youth Hostel. As both of my lovely friends instantly reacted as joyful as I felt about this suggestion, we as a result ended up picking LA, *San Francisco, Las Vegas* NV, LA for our travel route. The mixture of our three souls truly turned out to be as magical as it could have been and the fact that Danny's and Regu's first ever meeting occurred at the Youth Hostel in Santa Monica, made this whole *"Cali Dreamin'"* adventure even more so mysterious to us all. Ha! Those adventurous 7 days, we ended up filling with LOTS of laughter, FuN and priceless memory creations, which even now, 20 years later, keep the three of our souls raving about this spectacular trip with its many hysterical created moments. Even though that our dear Regu one's since the end of September 2017 finds "herself" due to an *"ongRowing"* rapid experienced production of abnormal white blood cells phenomena being forced to do so from the unseen side of sphere. SNiFF. Ufff. Yes. R.i.P. my precious friend. MUCH. LOVE. Always. Two of my personal highlights within this storyline find themselves being anchored in San Francisco, which are 1) Our hiking excursion UP to the there discovered two prominent hills named after Danny's and mine favorite early 90ies cult TV show *"Twin Peaks"* and 2) The "accidental" discovery of the famous Lombard Street on our walk back to our there booked hostel at 1:30am, which we oh so well know from the over and over watched all time hysterical Movie "What's Up, Doc?", starring Barbra Streisand and Ryan O'Neil. Oh yeah. This vacation therefore and for so many more reasons remains as one of *"little Linda's"* favorite *"FuN Fact"* experiences that she safely cherishes within her thus far collected *"Living on Earth Game"* FuNbox. Yup. Thank you, my dear friends and lovely Universe. Blessings. As soon as my vessel after a very satisfying first *"Cali Dreamin'"* glance journey returned back to Charlotte again, my further plans for the remaining 4 weeks at hand therefore were set to enjoy the Grauer's home and my *"The Other Planet"* reality "stationary" as part of a proper chapter ending, before *"little Linda"* would be anew diving back into this *"Swimming ALONG WiTH the Current"* world again, after a lovely *"wiLD & Free"* break of 6 months straight. This plan though ended up lasting for about 2 weeks, before my inner voice suddenly informed me that the time had just arrived for my vessel to continue its many *"Living on Earth Game"* travels back in Switzerland again. Alrighty. *"Thy Will is My Command"* turned out to be my instant response and therefore, I immediately went ahead and changed my Zurich flight ticket to October 24th 1996. Very happy and proud of my further achievements as Linda Wartenweiler and filled with many more valuable ingredients, stories and impressions for my, by then even more so preciously grown *"Life Toolbox"* collection, *"little Linda"* then finally found herself able to embrace her mom and all her many other dear friends, as soon as her vessel set foot back on Swiss territory again. Yay! *"Home Sweet Home"*. During the following 2 weeks, I then eagerly kept my soul busy with my by then familiar turned adaption process to my "old-new" environment, to my further transformed inner *"Self"*, with moving into my new home base in *Oberaach* TG, with meeting all my lovely missed Swiss souls and with the purchase of my first in Switzerland based car, which turned out to be a dark blue VW Polo born in 1996. Ahhh! After a successful Swiss setting up reality creation, my soul then as a next step felt the urge to be more productive and useful again, as *"little Linda"* surely enjoyed enough time to "play" during the past half year. Wink. Well and this information flow as a further impulse therefore had me instantly call up my boss wondering if it would be possible for my vessel to return to "work" on the following Monday already. Ha! Of course, my boss reacted more than happy about my earlier appearance proposal and welcomed *"little Linda"* back with open arms within a snap. SNAP. Then, 6 months into another FuN mortgage TKB revival chapter, my employer decided to UPdate "our" services to the then modern 1997 developed market trends by executing some overall restructuring strategies within the entire company. Hmmm. By now the world of technology certainly successfully started its booming process and the optimization of those many new possibilities turned into their future vision from here on instead. Oh yeah. Call Centers got invented and the Centralization strategy of a considered "most eFFecTive workflow" into one BiG modern building at the TKB headquarter in *Weinfelden* TG as its optimization result. My beloved work routine as a result of course rapidly got affected as well alongside with this modernization technique and therefore had most of my many administrational tasks relocate to this newly built building in Weinfelden. Bye-Bye. Bummer. The newly forged game plan for us souls out in the front side of things introduced itself with more provided time at hand in order to 1) Acquire a new clientele and with the further added 2) Better taking Care task of all our existing customers instead. Now, as this new reality check truly transformed my entire daily *"FuN Fact"* routine into a from *"little Linda"* as dry and mundane perceived bzZZ exercise, her love, passion and interest for this on *"The Other Planet"* appeared "blessed income opportunity" slowly started to fade away by the day and therefore left her with LOTS of boredom and inner resistance during her many *"NeverEnding"* TKB hours instead. Boom. There you go. Ha! And simultaneously to this inner and outer adjusting process in motion, my soul for the probably first time within this *"Living on Earth Game"* experience at run, found "herself" being pushed all the way to the point, which caused for "her" to question my overall thus far created reality, especially the one of my income situation. As a result, I therefore instantaneously noticed my disregarded *"Acting Dream"* screaming at me in its LOUDEST notes possible, which incidence then eFFecTively succeeded in allowing for myself to actually truly and sincerely acknowledge it for the first time with all of my heart and attention. Curious about what it had to say, I then decided to continue listening to this concerned inner voice and suddenly found *"little Linda"* wondering if there maybe DiD exist a way for her to perform this always returning dream profession, somehow, now that she had been granted access to this *"Other Planet"*. Ha! Ok. Let's find out then. With a *"Thy Will is My Command"* response, I then furthermore decided to pull this thus far quite powerful appearing *"Where there is a Will there ALWAYS is a Way"* ingredient out of my *"Life Toolbox"* collection in order to get this new mission of mine started. Let's Go! A few days later, I then suddenly caught myself flicking through Zurich's phonebook and to my amazement discovered "only" ONE *Theater Company* and ONE *Acting School* for starters and that was it. LOL. Quickly and excited, *"little Linda"* as a next step then went ahead and mailed both addresses a letter in order to gather all the details about their programs and policies for new students to enter. From the Acting School I swiftly came to learn that their maximum acceptance vessel count got set to a 23 and instantly transformed *"little Linda"* into a happy camper, as her count right then ended with a 22. Hooray! This option already presented itself as a quite promising one. Sweet. Then, a few days later, a typewriter written response from the Theater Company also fed my mailbox, which content on the other hand quickly succeeded in creating some unexpected resistance within my vessel. Oh no. Its actual, from my soul very discouraging perceived message, meanwhile thankfully found itself slipping into my subconscious memory, though what I vividly DO recall is that 1) The soul, who composed this letter with certainty must have been living in a for my taste quite conservative and old fashioned set of mind reality and that 2) All my gained courage for any further action step takings towards my just revived *"Soul Childhood Dream"*, alongside with every word that *"little Linda"* One-by-One took in, started to get pushed back into the dark again. POOF! And popped that bubble immediately got anew right in front of my eyes within the following milliseconds, whilst I simultaneously rather saddened forced myself in trying to accept the fact that this incredible and magical *"Acting as a Leading Lady in a Hollywood Motion Picture"* desire lastly found itself very soon taking off into another *"Living on Earth Game"* journey experience of mine, placed within a difFeRent vessel and generation to come. POOF. Ufff. Farewell *"Acting Dream"*. Farewell. Now that this recurring Acting question successfully got solved, I therefore decided to continue moving forward with my quest to find some further exciting and FuN oriented job options and ideas instead. During this process, my friendly inner voice then soon advised me to keep on looking for a profession, which was based on a hobby of *"little Linda"*, as those precious 42 work hours per week ideally should be spent and experienced with as many *"FuN Fact"* opportunities as possible. Ha! That sounded about right to my soul and made more than completely sense. *"Work equals FuN"*. Great. Got it. Yay! Let's. Now, the question of *"What Other Hobby, besides watching Movies and TV shows, enjoying Music, Dancing and Celebrating this "Living on Earth Game" adventure of mine as often as possible, could I possibly turn into a FuN paying profession here in Switzerland"* therefore instantly found its way into my awareness. Hmmm. After some more pondering, this supportive inner voice then furthermore approached me with a *"How about some more traveling FuN dear Linda? As you know, your "inner Adventuress" truly loves to Explore and to Experience new situations and places. Try to find an opportunity based on this genre and take it from there"* suggestion. Boom. This statement certainly sounded very appealing to *"little Linda"* and revealed a LOT of truth about my soul indeed. Thus far, my vessel after all already spent one year in Geneva and 5 ½ months on this *"The Other Planet"* and this new thought of taking this whole *"Living on Earth Game"* ride onto another exploration level felt like the perfect next move. Cool. The beloved Universe then as usual went ahead and swiftly provided me with its *"Thy Wish is my Command"* solution. As my at that time roommate in Oberaach happened to have changed her own career path from the mundane office world into the more adventurous Swissair Flight Attendant one a few months prior, I therefore found myself witnessing hands on from my first row seat what great change of lifestyle and freedom this global *"Swimming AGAiNST the Stream"* traveling choice allowed for her soul to gain out of it. The more that *"little Linda"* started to hear about her many exciting adventures from this point on, the more this reality check ended up welcoming many question marks upon her own *"Swimming ALONG WiTH the Current"* version. Hmmm. This combo of traveling the world, whilst simultaneously even getting paid seemed like the perfect *"FuN Fact"* match on the menu. Wonderful. Even though that my soul understood the kind Universe's "wink" completely, I still ended up facing some tiny resisting vibes floating within my vessel. As copycatting my roommate happened to be an out of question move, I therefore decided to start considering a staff opportunity at Zurich's airport instead. After all this solution would provide *"little Linda"* with the "almost" same experience only "located" on Swiss ground, which therefore would bring along the always remaining same time zone and coworkers. Deal. Excited about these newly forged plans, I then decided to share them with a dear fellow TKB Gemini coworker of mine, who instantly reacted with a *"Linda, if you are planning on working for Swissair then you belong UP into the air. Why would you want to stay on the ground? Then you can really stay here with us. This would end up *being about the same experience for you."* Ha! And then she winked at me with a smile on her face and my soul right away knew that my friendly coworker was "darn right". Oh yeah! Off I therefore went, ordered this thrilling Swissair Flight Attendant application kit within a SNAP and filled it out ASAP with the help of this lovely coworker, as this task happened to be one of her "specialties". Wink. After a short waiting period, my vessel then indeed got invited to their psychological and health test day in *Kloten* ZH and found myself within a few days-time happily hired as one of their new crewmembers. Yeeha! Strike. That was easy. How excited my soul truly felt about this new and UPlifting shift in my, this *"Living on Earth Game"* adventure horizon. With that additional granted opportunity in my pocket, I then promptly went ahead, quit the "same" banking position for the second time with "No Doubt", whilst *"little Linda"* simultaneously with a BiG smile on her heart kept on yelling *"Yeeha! Let's Rock 'n Roll! World here I come!"* Boom.

"One way or Another, I'm gonna Find Ya' and Get Ya'. Watch Out."
By the end of January 1999, I finally found my soul being trained into a Swissair Flight Attendant over the duration of 4 weeks straight. What a difFeRent and diverse field of expertise this job truly brought along. Wow. Besides the teachings of HOW to cater our traveling souls UP in the air and all its many required security procedures, we all additionally got educated with the basic knowledge of a Fire Fighter, a Nurse and the one of a Midwife in order to have all possible emergency situations covered while on duty. Ha! Once our education successfully got completed, my classmates and *"little Linda"* then finally got handed their first flight schedule. Now guess what flight destination turned out to be my first one? Yeeha! The City of Angels it was, followed by a "work" route to Sao Paolo as part of my long-haul training exercise, which then lead into an adventurous 3 weeks short-haul ride throughout Europe. This new journey of mine indeed started out very gloriously and ended up providing *"little Linda"* with many more unforgettable memories, cultural insights and with many more useful ingredients for her overall *"Living on Earth Game" "Life Toolbox"* collection. Thank you. During this quite impressive Exploration and Expansion chapter, my *"inner Adventuress"* certainly got as planned provided with the amazing opportunity to experience the *"BiG Wide World"* with its many shapes and forms for free by even finding herself being enabled to collect many more coins for her precious *"Red and White Saving Sock"* account for all her many further adventure creations ahead. Yay! Well and this deal to me certainly disclosed itself to be as super fair. Wink. One reality check realization that I truly liked about this profession turned out to be the "fact" that every airplane ride transformed itself into an unexpected "Theatre Company" experience, which presented its own improvised play during each take-off and landing duration. Ha! How FuNNy, right? We, the crewmembers took on the rolls of the Actors on Stage and our passengers therefore supported our individual performances as the Audience Members right from their assigned seats. LOL. Yup. With this

scenario, I am very certain of, my dear *Co-Traveler*, you are finding yourself quite familiar with as well, especially when "stranded" UP there during those long, uncomfortable and *"NeverEnding"* hours. Watching others secretly out of one's seat therefore always turns itself into this golden opportunity to kill some precious time UP in the heavens aside from watching a Movie for instance. Right? Wink. Well and back then, a long-haul flight certainly seemed to last even longer than they do these days, as the only "rEvolutionary" technology option an airplane had to offer happened to be some box monitors hanging from a few selected isle ceiling spots, which ended up screening two or three from the Maître de Cabins controlled only Movies. Boom. And that was it. Ha! The passenger's options with that set-up therefore left them with a choice of either watching those selected Movies, to follow the spectacle on "stage", to sleep, to eat, to drink, to get drunk, to read, to relax, to be, to dream, to listen to Music, to converse, to think, to wait around in the galley area or to whatever else one's creative mind came up with. Yup. My time at Swissair also provided my soul with the opportunity to be exposed to celebrities for the very first time, which turned into another very interesting and thrilling experience for *"little Linda"*. Phil Collins, Yello's Dieter Meier *"Oh Yeah"*, Marcia Grey twice and Gian Simmen, the Swiss snowboarder and gold medal winner at the 1998 Winter Olympics in men's half pipe, count as my most memorable Swissair passengers. *"Oh Yeah"*. My probably most spectacular celebrity encounter though, my soul happened to be experiencing during an overnight stay at the Swissotel in Boston. Shortly after my crewmembers and I successfully ended up checking into our each rooms, I thereafter found my vessel waiting for two of them in the lobby, as we were planning on exploring this city together as a unit. Now, whilst I kept myself busy with waiting, my eyes then suddenly noticed the receptionist, who with some waiving over gestures eagerly kept on trying to catch my attention. Driven by my natural "implanted" Gemini's curiosity, *"little Linda"* therefore slowly started to walk towards this friendly man's desk, where his soul then with a BiG SMiLE began to share that the American band No Doubt, including Gwen Stefani were on their way down to the lobby. What? Who?! LOL. Yes, and right here shall be following my already preannounced "Gwen" story for you, my dear *Co-Traveler*. Are you ready? Cool. And this also turned out to be my own responds in regards of this "gracious" insider information exchange and definitely left this lovely receptionist quite a bit more thrilled than my own soul experienced it. Cute. Surely with "No Doubt" No Doubt, their song *"Spiderwebs"*, including their entire *"Tragic Kingdom"* album will always keep on providing *"little Linda"* with the wonderful eFFecT of having her travel with her mental Time Machine right back to those very first in 1996 *"The Other Planet"* adventure creations, whenever exposed to them and this is about how far her "fan" emotions would flow towards that subject. Oh, and just now, this storyline finds itself triggering my "actual" first LiVE encounter with this band, which ended up occurring about 4 months after they appeared to me on MTV in my room in Charlotte. Ha! This almost slipped my memory. pOops.

And this is what happened. Whilst *"little Linda"* found herself busy exploring Manhattan and its many sightseeing opportunities during her magical *"Dream come True"* NYC journey, I remember how my auricles suddenly began to take notice of some LOUD blasting Music echoing through the many streets and avenues on a late afternoon. Like in Trance, my soul therefore immediately gravitated towards those unexpected vibes, as my Gemini's curiosity of finding its origin meanwhile successfully got activated. The closer my vessel approached its source, the clearer its acoustic beats therefore appeared. Then, all over sudden, I found myself close enough in order to detect what song the still out of sight playing band happened to be performing and *"Don't Speak"* by No Doubt is what I came to recognize it as. Ha! My mission then led my vessel towards the opposite sidewalk side of the main Radio City Music Hall entrance, where to my soul further came to learn that the annual MTV Music awards just happened to be taking place and that Gwen Stefani and her male band members therefore got hired to entertain the Big Apple with some of their current hits right from the above the main doorway situated balcony. Boom. Well and now 3 years later, *"little Linda"* suddenly found herself out of the blue about to be exposed to them anew, only this time in an extreme close up delivered opportunity. Odd this "LiVE" repetition certainly appeared to me at that very moment and led me to wonder WHO actually happened to be following WHOM here. LOL. Anyway, this friendly receptionist then quickly ended up handing me a notepad and a pen with the instructions for me to walk up to Gwen Stefani as soon as she would appear by then having her ask for an autograph. What?! Did this man just ask me to get Gwen's autograph? Somewhat puzzled, I then found myself starring at his face quite unsure as of HOW to react and ended up responding that I would rather prefer to respect these Artists privacy and therefore gladly would be skipping this "assigned" autograph task. This respectful behavior trait after all remains as one of the many "proper" Swiss manners and according to Tina Turner happens to be one of the reasons, why she chose Zurich as her hometown decades ago. Yup. The receptionist though stood determined with his mission and assured *"little Linda"* that this action step was an OK one for her to perform within the United States and that my vessel with "No Doubt" could go ahead and ask for this celebrity's signature. Oh boy. Then, of course along with the following second, Gwen's and two of her band member's vessels appeared as predicted right in front of our eyes. Oh no! Unsure as of what to do next, my soul therefore decided to simply keep on watching them cross the lobby towards another elevator from afar, whilst the thrilled receptionist kept on *"Go. Go! GO! NOW!"* cheering into my ears. Well, and something within his persistence then had me obey to this soul's order, which suddenly triggered my vessel to uncomfortably start approaching theirs. Once I caught up with those famous *"Spiderwebs"* Musicians in front of the still closed elevator door, *"little Linda"* instantly knew that she HAD to follow through with her *"to Grow and to Expand"* given task. Help! With all my gathered courage, I therefore slowly turned my head towards my left-hand side, to where Gwen Stefani as predicted appeared right in front of my sight. Shoot. Here she truly was and within that heartbeat at beat I knew that I had to Act NOW. Very tense and with a quite shy smile, my voice then finally delivered the "directed" *"Hello. May I please have an autograph?"* line. This moment then rapidly transformed itself into an about as embarrassing and uncomfortable encountered experience, as the one, during which Frau Marzoli from the TKB HR Department came to learn about my Hollywood *"Acting Dream"* career. Ufff. In that second, the elevator of course instantly opened up its "mouth", whilst Gwen's soul delivered "her" somewhat as annoyed interpreted *"Sure"* responds. Quickly, and now even more so uncomfortable about this entire autograph task at catch, we then all ended up stepping into the elevator box as a unit, in which Gwen's hand then swiftly started to sign the into a precious mutating front notepad page, during our ride down. Cool. As soon as the golden sparkling doors opened themselves anew on the ground level, the No Doubt members then immediately headed off towards their next adventure at hand, whilst I embarked on mine, by pushing the Lobby and Close buttons with a friendly *"Thank you"*. Once UP again, my vessel then equipped with the new treasure in my palm, walked straight towards the receptionist, tore the signed page off, placed the pad back into his hands, which finished gesture thereafter caused for *"little Linda"* to proudly present her successfully completed "dare" mission to his soul. Boom. *"Gotch Ya'."* This friendly man of course reacted very excited and proud over my deed, which feelings I meanwhile lastly ended up sharing as well. Yeah! Once I found myself back on my starting out position again, my soul then very much so kept "herself" busy with the Trying to grasp what just happened during this waiting Session at run and remained doing so, until both crewmembers finally appeared into my eye line, a little while after. Smile. Gwen's autograph in the meantime of course received its SpeCial spot within one of my photo album creations and finds itself being taped right next to my three precious Katja collected postcards. Yup. Looking back, in fact gets me to realize that Gwen Stefani's soul seems to have been glowing some sort of an *"ongRowing"* influential and inspirational vibration onto mine, ever since I spotted "her" vessel in that *"Spiderwebs"* video in 1996. Hmmm. This discovery actually finds itself resonating in a quite *"Coo-coo-cool. Yeah, yeah. I know You're Cool."* way with my soul. Ha! Besides those unplanned "LiVE" interactions with her and No Doubt, *"little Linda"* meanwhile actually finds herself being transmuted into an enthusiastic collector of Gwen's solo Artistic creations, and this ever since the releasing date of her amazing first own album *"Love. Angel. Music. Baby."* in 200 - What? Hold on! How crazy is that?! Literally right NOW, THE incredible just happened again, the second that I started to research its 2004 stated release date. WOW. As I just found myself scanning through all the many on Google appearing results, my eyes all over sudden espied on the right-hand side that Gwen currently happens to be touring "with her" on March 18th 2016 amazing new *"This Is What The Truth Feels Like"* released album within the United States. Ha! Then, once my soul took a closer look at her schedule, by furthermore wondering if she might be "close by" any time soon, since our both vessels currently happen to be residing in the Southern part of sunny Cali, my eyes truly came to spot the almost unbelievable *"Truth"*. Wow! Yes, she truly will be "around the corner" shortly, as her NEXT scheduled performance will be taking place exactly 30 minutes from my house and this in EXACTLY 2 weeks from TODAY. Ha! AHM. What?! Boah! That for sure is a VERY interesting "coincidence" and of course my hands just swiftly went ahead and purchased a ticket for May 13th 2016. Happy pre-birthday *"little Linda"*. Yay! Further, I would love to share with you, my beloved *Co-Traveler*, that Gwen Stefani actually appeared in my dream this very morning. Yes! For real! We both found ourselves conversing on a sidewalk, whilst I found myself walking her dog. Well, if Gwen happens to be a dog owner in "real" life remains an unknown fact to me. As of yet. In my dream though she did and somehow *"little Linda"* got hired from her end for this task. LOL. Dreams, right? Speaking of which. This actually seems to have been my very first dream experience that included her vessel. At least this is the only one that my brain is able to recall. Usually my NENA happens to appear here and there for some mutual dream adventures, during which my soul mostly finds "herself" enjoying one of her thrilling concerts with at times even granted One-on-One interactions. Boah. Yeeha! And yes, those moments then always turn themselves into very glorious and precious ones for my soul. Oh yeah. Wink. Anyway, Gwen's "appearance" this morning as a result found itself triggering the thought of adding my by then untold few "No Doubt/Gwen" adventures onto these past few pages, the second that I woke up a little bit after. Well and so I just followed through, by BOOM finding myself unexpectedly being enabled to enjoy her appearance LiVE "again" in 14 days count within a very close by radius, and this for the first time even kind of "planned". Ha! *"Synchronicity par Excellence"* is how my soul interprets this storyline. Wink. Thank you, dear Universe for this spontaneous treat. You are working your magic as always. Everyday. Love. And of course, *"little Linda"* now finds herself feeling quite excited about this sudden granted adventure at hand and of how it all unfolded. So cool! What the meaning of all of this is though shall remain unknown. Well, at least for now. Inspiration maybe? A *"Thoughts become Things"* SpeCial eFFecT treat? We shall see. Now let's travel back to the year 2000 in order to discover more of this *"Living on Earth Game"* ride of Linda Wartenweiler. zoOM. After an adventurous, diverse and fast speeding planet earth exploration journey of almost 2 years, I then suddenly found myself being pushed to the point again, in which my soul came to realize that *"Enough was Enough"*, that my *"inner Adventuress"* pretty much got everything possible out of this wonderful Swissair opportunity at hand and that a change therefore appeared to be the perfect next move on my path. Equipped with my with many new valuable *"Big Wide World"* impressions filled backpack of *Hiking UP and down Mount Corcovado* in *Rio de Janero*, Brazil, *Experiencing* the amazing and colorful *Cherry Blossom Season* in *Tokyo*, Japan, followed by a *Karaoke Session in* one for its therefore SpeCial created famous *Containers*,

Visiting the quite impressive 34 meters/111.5 feet high *Golden Tian Tan Buddha Statue* in *Hong Kong*, China and with the *Standing on* the still warm *Petrified Lava Flow* of the in 1999 south-flank *Mount Cameroon Volcano Eruption* located in *Cameroon*, Africa for example, I therefore quickly went ahead and handed in my 2 months' notice, which reality check right away opened the door for my reoccurring *What's Next?* question to appear. Ha! Hello again. Wink. With that, *"little Linda"* instantly decided to approach the solution of this question the same way as she did prior by anew asking herself *"What Other Hobby, besides watching Movies and TV shows, enjoying Music, Dancing and Celebrating this "Living on Earth Game" adventure of mine as often as possible, could I possibly turn into a FuN paying profession here in Switzerland."* My friendly inner voice this time around therefore drew my attention directly towards my workout love, which I found with the count of 19 years, right after my volleyball coach of 5 years introduced my team member's and my vessel to an additional weekly mandatory added workout routine at our then local fitness studio *Sportlive* in Amriswil. Yup. Now, after giving this suggested Fitness Instructor possibility some further thought, I then had to admit that this profession truly seemed to be a further pleasant and FuN way of making a living and this in a still kind of *"Swimming AGAiNST the Stream"* set reality. The more that I connected with this newly suggested outlook creation at hand, the more my soul therefore ended up finding "herself" convinced that the spending of "her" precious working hour days in an environment, in which Health, Sport, FuN and Music happened to be the core elements was what "she" wanted to explore next. *"Work* equals *FuN"*. Sweet. Got it. And these emotions then furthermore got intensified by two additional enticing collected discoveries, which introduced themselves 1) With the wonderful opportunity for me to learn more about the fascinating world of muscles, the vessel and its many functions for my own personal usage hands on and 2) With its coverage of my, from this current Swissair chapter liberating introduced "Out of The System" working reality, which as a result ever since started to leave *"little Linda"* with LOTS more personal Freedom, FuN and Trust. Oh yeah! *"Being able to Work Freely in My Own Style and Rhythm"* and *"Being Fully Trusted with No Direct Boss in my back"* therefore revealed themselves as my two most important game plan ingredients at hand. Boom. After some more reflecting and inward traveling, my soul then finally came up with the perfect seeming FuN future income earning mixture vision and therefore quickly decided to send out "her" desired order to the magical Universe, which included the 1) Finding a Fitness Instructor occupation for 2 days in a fitness studio located close by "her" vessel's then current home base in Bottighofen preference and with the further 2) Filling the remaining 3 days with a FuN office opportunity OUTSiDE of the banking world, as this profession remained as one that *"little Linda"* did NOT want to be involved in any longer added detail. YUP. Something new and exciting it had to be. That's right. And. Thank you. As usual the understanding Universe sped away with its reliable *"Your Wish is my Command"* responds and swiftly provided my soul with the desired request. Yay. Part of my upcoming next workout session therefore included the added tasks, to simply go ahead and ask the manager of my at that time home gym for advice in regards of my targeted Fitness Instructor career. *What schools he would recommend* and *How I should approach my mission of finding the desired 40% employment status* was what my soul wanted to find out directly from his "source". This manager then kindly informed me that 1) The Swiss Academy of Fitness and Sports (SAFS) in Zurich would be the best bet for my needs and that 2) He actually happened to be interested in my skills, as he currently found himself in the look-out for a new Fitness Instructor for exactly 2 days per week. Ha! What?! Really?! You anew make it that easy for me my dear Universe?! Boah. Wonderful. Of course, *"little Linda"* instantly grabbed the bull by its horns, found herself right away being hired for those 2 available days, starting in 4 weeks after her being "grounded" achieved reality check and therefore as a next step happily sent out her application for the needed Fitness Basic Training license to SAFS ASAP. Done. With my other task of attracting the remaining 60% FuN office opportunity into my reality, I decided to take it easy, as this certainly needed a little bit more time and effort. Without have given this quest too much thought yet, my soul then suddenly, during one of an always FuN, deep flowing and intense catching up evening with a dear and always supportive former TKB coworker friend of mine, felt the urge to at least share my overall future plans with her kind soul. Smile. Andrea as expected loved my new vision instantaneously and kept on wondering if I would be interested at all in returning to the TKB. A LOUD *"AHHH. NOPE!"* reaction right away popped out as my immediate response, followed by a strongly added clarification UPdate that my time in Amriswil was UP and that only MAYBE *"little Linda"* would be interested in accepting a job in a difFeRent location, for the time being, as after all she found herself quitting her job there twice already for a reason. A new challenge it had to be. Yup. That was a given. Boom. Then, a few days later, my dear friend suddenly called up my landline home phone and informed me that her soul very much so knew that my time in Amriswil "was UP", though "she" still felt the urge to share with mine that a 60% teller job opportunity just appeared in their small branch in *Erlen* TG, starting my availability date and that Amriswil's, during the in 1997 reorganization selected "new" big boss, happened to be interested in speaking with my soul about this open position at hand. What? Oh men. And a thoughtful *"Hmmm"* left my throat as a first opinion sound by adding that I would love to sleep over this proposal for one night. How FuNNy, right? Clearly and strongly I made sure to state in my order to NOT provide me with any further banking opportunities and what does come my way within the next breath? Exactly what *"little Linda"* did NOT want and "ordered". LOL. What's UP with that, right? Well, as my knowledge as of "HOW" the magical Universe interprets a soul's order happened to be at a zero at that time, I therefore found myself unaware of the "fact" that it actually ONLY focuses its attention on the during the order produced *"Head*

Cinema" created clip and that any additional NO's and DONT's added SpeCial eFFecT "specifications" remain as an insignificant detail. pOops. What?! Yup. Well and with this universal *Law of Attraction* knowledge in mind, the magical Universe actually ended up reliably delivering EXACTLY what *"little Linda"* happened to be ENViSiONiNG during her *Filling the remaining 3 days with a FuN office opportunity OUTSiDE of the banking world, as this profession remained as one that "little Linda" did NOT want to be involved in anymore* order. Ha! And. TatAAA! *"Your Wish is my Command."* Oh NO! Bummer. LOL. After giving this still kind of "matching" opportunity its promised thought, *"little Linda"* then at some point anew ended up with the conclusion that *"Everything happens for a Reason"* and that therefore she felt open to at LEAST find out more about what was traveling her way this time. *"Positivity Card"* olé. After letting my friend Andrea in on my thoughts, she then as a next step swiftly went ahead, happily organized a meeting with the vessel of the big boss's, the then responsible branch-manager's, who happened to be another ex-coworker of mine, and for my own. Boom. This getting together and reconnection exercise with these two VERY familiar TKB souls certainly ignited some wonderful *"Home Sweet Home"* feelings within, which assisted my process of accepting their friendly offer right there and then with LOTS of joy and certainty for it to be the other "right" fit. Ha! And back aboard Linda Wartenweiler therefore was for an adventurous 3rd TKB round ride ahead. Oops. With the completion of this final task, I as a result happily found myself transitioning very smoothly from the heavens back onto my earthly doings by the end of August 2000, which included my immediate fitness education start as a soon *Millennium Fitness Instructor* to be and the stepping onto my newly chosen "FuN" paths at hand. As soon as *"little Linda"* found herself as the proud owner of the Millennium Fitness Basic Instructor license, she then finally got the opportunity to enjoy her newly created lifestyle for 5 weeks straight, before the beloved Universe decided to reveal its "real" plans to her. What? Yup. On an early work morning in October, my branch-manager suddenly let me in on her 3 months pregnancy duration reality check and on the further forged game plan, that our big boss therefore chose my vessel as the ideal replacement option at hand, starting in 6 months' time. A LOUD *"WHAT?!"* instantly burst out of my mouth. What?! Our boss considered me, Linda Wartenweiler, as THE next branch-manager to come? This opportunity definitely happened to be the VERY last thing that I expected to get faced with during this current *"Living on Earth Game"* ride of mine and therefore certainly left my own reality with some shocking vibes. How was this even possible? At that time, my vessel for ONE counted "only" 25 years and on top of it all TWO just happened to be celebrating its comeback after a banking break of almost 2 years. Hmmm. Further, the image of a "boss/manager" position to *"little Linda"* also always resulted in the one of a more aged appearing version, a at least 30ies UP one, including with LOTS of more authority, with a "well" and diverse rounded educational background and with several diplomas under this defined person's belt. Well and none of these collected facts applied to my persona at all at that time. HMMM. This reality check therefore kept me wondering about my boss's thought process in regards of this to me rather "illogical" planned move on the chessboard. First of all, my further expertise grew in the works as a Flight Attendant and with exploring mother earth during the past almost 2 years, which obviously took place FAR off from my thought of needed banking track. Secondly, my last collected banking expertise occurred during my two mortgage department chapters and therefore my now needed private banking clients' advisory knowledge meanwhile surely found itself in a very rusty and moldy condition. Third and most importantly, a banking career definitely vanished from *"little Linda's"* UPdated *"Dream Catchin'"* list a LONG time ago and this current chosen *"Comfort Zone"* game plan therefore was supposed to serve as a temporary option only, up unto this point during which the beloved Universe would present her an ACTUAL desired FuN hobby income opportunity. Ha! Well and therefore this to me out of the blue appeared proposal, certainly got interpreted as a true error from my end sides my big boss's perception. Yup. During a soon One-on-One arranged meeting, his soul then happily started to share "his" thought process with *"little Linda"*, as of WHY Linda Wartenweiler happened to be THE perfect candidate for this, in 6 months opening and "UPgrading" position at hand. Hmmm. Well and my boss's reasoning's ended up presenting themselves with the delivered "facts" that out of his point of view, my soul brought along all the required human qualities and traits at this particular moment of my travels in order for "her" to successfully take over this branch as a leader and that anything bank related I therefore would be given the opportunity, to hands on rebuild a solid knowledge foundation within the following months to come. *"Ok. Help!?!"* appeared as my instant inner monologue. After having given my boss' delivered information flow a first quick though, overwhelmed *"little Linda"* then shyly began to explain that 1) She truly felt very flattered about his nice compliment and trust in her persona, including skills, though as 2) Her overall urge and interest in ANY further banking education adventures, especially the one of becoming a "real" banking expert, meanwhile very much so faded away from her wish list, that she therefore rather felt like passing. Boom. To my surprise though, I found my boss the least impressed by all of my reasoning's und simply continued his "Linda Upgrading" mission with a comforting smile and with the assurance that his soul very much respected my argument. Then, he further added that the ONLY educational journey for this outlook at hand would require the at the time popular Privatkundenberater Lehrgang/Private Client Advisory Course, which as usual would be offered and paid by the TKB and that this would be it. Hmmm. Well and this offer certainly transformed itself right away into a Quite fair and interesting enough to Consider response from my end, which granted *"little Linda"* thereafter with a 4-week Thinking and Digesting period, of this newly arisen reality check at hand. Uiii. And guess what happened next, my fellow *Co-Traveler*? Exactly. After having given this meanwhile quite enticing appearing career path some careful thought, I truly ended up finding myself accepting this "Linda UPgrading" position with a BiG LAUGH within my heart. Yes, a HUGE LAUGH to be exact, as this branch-managing opportunity to me truly felt so much out of my character and out of line. LOL. Out of my perspective, my own "growingUP" process definitely still found itself lingering in its children's shoes, which therefore had my *"wiLD & Free"* spirited beloved *"little Linda"* Act and reAct accordingly during her many FuN experienced *"Living on Earth Game"* creations. Ha! Well, and this reality check of mine certainly must have reflected itself differently to the outer world, I suppose. Smile. Some of the reasons, that convinced my soul to accept this "Linda UPgrading" opportunity at some point revealed themselves with the "facts" that this delivery 1) Seemed to be a perfect new way of feeding my still *"ongRowing" "Red and White Saving Sock"* account in a fast-tracking approach, that 2) This offer welcomed my reality as a Once in a Lifetime invitation, that 3) It actually DiD include my desired order of *"Being able to Work Freely in My Own Style and Rhythm"* by *"Being Fully Trusted with No Direct Boss in my back"* components and that at the end 4) *"Everything* after all always *happens for a Reason"*. Boom. The magical Universe therefore did wonderfully well and instantly I found myself convinced that this managing adventure certainly would provide my *"Life Toolbox"* with many more enhancing ingredients, even though this banking topic still remained somewhere towards the very end of *"little Linda's"* hobby list. Wink. Interestingly, my vessel actually ended up traveling within this newly accepted *"Swimming ALONG WiTH the Current"* reality creation over a duration of 5 ½ years. Boah! Yup. And this additional accepted puzzle piece surely revealed itself as a needed *"Stepping-Stone"* choice for my UPcoming *"Living on Earth Game"* path at hand. This *Dot Connection* result my soul meanwhile certainly found "herself" successfully able to gain. That's right. You shall see. Wink. Now, even though I decided to step back into this full-time banking agreement position, my soul very much so ended up enjoying all the freedom that "she" was able to experience throughout those 5 extra added managing years. Oh yeah! What I really loved about this new "challenge" at hand, turned out to be the many opportunities for *"little Linda"* to *Socialize*, to *Help*, to *Be of Service*, to *Create*, to *Learn*, to *Achieve*, to *Laugh*, to *Solve*, to *Listen to Music*, to *Grow*, to *Act*, to *Be*, to *have FuN* and all of this in my own style and rhythm, as previously ordered by the kind Universe. Yay! And. Thank you. Along with time, I eventually truly ended up metamorphosing into an expert in *Selling, Communicating, Educating, Managing, Observing, Leading* and in *Planning* by simultaneously paying my hidden Acting passion its desired attention as well. Oops. What? Did we just discover you again? Ha! Yes, it looks like that unconsciously I actually ended up being able to nurture this love of mine anew, only this time on a stage located on mother earth's ground. Yay. And. Smile. Now, how did my Acting get involved here as well, you might be asking yourself. Well, as *"little Linda's"* overall interest in economy and in its daily spread world "news" additionally more or less disappeared from her interest list as well, it therefore became very important for my soul to make this new engagement work successfully for all parties involved, especially for myself. Meaning, that somehow, I needed to become this new "character" that *"little Linda"* agreed upon to "play" and even well got paid for. Ha! Thankfully, my adaption skills by then already developed themselves into a quite satisfying level, which as a result had me successfully pull this magical ingredient from my thus far collected *"Life Toolbox"* whenever needed, in order for it to assist *"little Linda"* to create her own successful version of selling and being of interest. Oops. And it worked. Yup. After all I found myself being able to practice this talent all along since the count of 5 and therefore felt very pleased that it once more ended up coming in so handy. Into what a wonderful "Acting gig" this opportunity turned itself into after all. Yay! *"Empty your Mind and become Water my Friend"*. Now, as this small branch happens to be the only TKB location within Erlen's close by radius, my main job therefore contained the offering of every single existing banking service tool right out of one hand for my clients, which kept my days quite diverse. In order to do so, my knowledge of course had to be spot on in every field of money needs, which included the Investment, Teller Service, Mortgages, Payments, Leasing and Credit Cards subjects for instance. Now, as my vessel found itself about to transition from the 40% teller position into the 100% managing one, a replacement for my "old" job turned out to be our next needed step. Thankfully my boss already had a solution in mind and therefore quickly informed *"little Linda"* that his wife's soul actually found "herself" quite interested in working with mine in Erlen. Cool. Even though this option happened to be my own direct boss's wife, I as always felt open and curious in finding out HOW this opportunity would feel and look like. One after all never knows any actual results in advance. Yup. And anew I therefore found myself very happy that my Gemini's curiosity overpowered my initial resistant appearing head voice interference by instead leading me into pulling out my magical *"Positivity Card"*. Ha! The second that I got introduced to his wonderful wife Lucia, our both souls instantly clicked and knew that the two of us would form the perfect match for this Erlen ride ahead. And so it was. Lucia's first day at "my" branch dates the one on which my vessel took over on May 1st 2001 and ended with *"little Linda's"* decision to continue her many *"Living on Earth Game"* adventures "elsewhere", EXACTLY 5 years later. Ha! Well, and this quite diverse and "colorful" approaching chapter my soul very much so is looking forward to share with yours sooner than soon, my lovely *Co-Traveler*. Oh yeah! Besides Lucia's 40% position, there also happened to be another coworker hired from the previous manager period, who filled up the remaining 3 days. Those two ladies' main job resulted in taking care of all the walk-in customers in the front side of things, so that my soul was able to peacefully acquire new customers and projects and to also serve my existing customer base in the back end of things more efficiently. Soon though, we ended up losing this other employee to another small branch due to relocation purposes of her home base, which therefore required the creation of a new game plan from our end. As this change occurred at that time, during which those blossoming Call Centers and the Online Banking invention slowly started to take care of the many clients' needs from afar, my coworkers therefore as a result found themselves with a decreasing customer flow appearance at their teller spot and via the phone line, which had us decide to move forward without a replacement for this now "open" position and to instead increase Lucia's friendly and lovely presence up to 50% per week and to leave the remaining 50% exclusively to the 3 monthly rotating apprentice at hand only. Boom. And along with time, the modern computer world slowly, very slowly kept on approaching and knocking on all our doors even more so in order to ensure that the workflow would move along "faster" and "quicker" by the instant elimination of those many "inefficient" and "time consuming" manual performances. Abracadabra. And that is how the centralization optimization strategy reached its quite powerful next level, which this time found itself being located in the World Wide Web. Cheers. Besides my daily banking responsibilities, *"little Linda"* also had to ensure that those 3 monthly changing apprentices would be getting their required hands on training in the "actual" banking world. Whatever their soul got taught in school in theory, they also needed to experience and to apply parallel in the "real" working environment. Been there. Done that. Right? Wink. With specific, from the TKB provided checklists, I therefore found myself conveniently guided to fulfill this task properly, as meanwhile so much changed compared to those days during which *"little Linda"* used to walk in their shoes. Ha! What my soul probably loved the most about this managing journey of mine, was the friendly and relaxing relationship Lucia and I succeeded to establish with all our customers and amongst ourselves. As Erlen is located on the true countryside, its inhabitants therefore also ended up behaving in that manner. Meaning, that everyone knew everyone and as a result it turned out to be very easy to create a casual and still professional relationship with each one of them. Yeah! Every soul would say *"Grüezi/Hello"* to one another, while crossing one's vessel or at least symbolize its gesture by waving one's hand from afar. Yup. One friendly community this tiny village turned out to be and *"little Linda"* definitely loved this family style feeling very much. Gratitude. One particular event though, my memory will always remember for as long as my soul will be traveling in this *"Living on Earth Game"* adventure as Linda Wartenweiler. A few months after my vessel took over this branch, the magical Universe then suddenly came to decide to throw some real "Hollywood" action into our daily routine. Ready? Ok. In the morning of our last opening day in 2001, Lucia, our current apprentice and I happened to be faced with the unthought-of. A Robbery. Yes. An actual bank robbery, like the ones they show on TV, occurred in our tiny branch, on the countryside, on December 29th with a Christmas tree inside and the three of our vessels tied up on the floor. Surprise! Ufff. This event definitely changed my whole anticipation of how I imagined this last day of the year to start/end and "thankfully" the kind Universe made sure to at least send us a "good-hearted" bandit soul our way. What? A "good-hearted" bandit soul?! Yes, he indeed was. Once this man had us duct tape silenced and all tied up on the floor in the dark, his hand at some point gently started to pet my head before he asked me one of his questions, which "gesture" ended up filling my vessel with instant safeness and with the knowledge that everything would end smoothly along with our cooperation. And my intuition proofed itself to be right. Once the thief found himself in the possession of his prey, his vessel then took off, whilst the already untied Lucia immediately hit the alarm button. Parallel to the money hungry soul's escape, my apprentice and I then quickly succeeded to unleash ourselves from the strings that the robber very sloppily wrapped around our ankles and arm wrists and to then remove the duct tape. Boom. Ufff. And. Yes. Luckily, the three of our vessels remained physically unharmed and were left in an absolute shock state of mind "only". Our rational and clear-headed reaction process definitely keeps amazing *"little Linda"* to this very day anew by only thinking about this entire spectacle at hand. As with magic, everyone's subconscious mind immediately activated each souls' survival instinct reflexes, the second that our vessels found themselves absolutely unexpectedly in this quite alarming "reality check" situation. Yup. Our emotions literally got shot off within a SNAP and left there was room for reasoning actions and thoughts only. What a day already! Oh boy. As soon as the police, the TKB security boss and our big boss showed up, the three of our souls then found themselves sharing each one's own experience over and over anew, which storyline revealed itself as a quite interesting awareness "truth". Wow. The to me MOST impressive difFeRence truly remains in the description of this man's weapon, a knife. Believe it or not! Each one of us ended up describing a completely difFeRent tool and therefore the actual version of this "small knife" remains a secret to everyone involved to this day. Ha! This experience very much so proofed to me that a human brain immediately starts to work difFeRently, once put under a stressful and an even possible life-threatening situation. Boah! After the investigation and security procedures at the bank found its end, the three of us then kindly got asked to meet the police officers at their station in Sulgen. And yes, this village used to be my very first hometown, about 4 weeks after my arrival in this realm, 26 ½ years prior. That's right. Yeeha! Once our many vessels found themselves united again at the police station, my coworkers and I then each got asked to give our statement separately for one last time, in order for it to safely be typed down and kept on file, before we then finally got released into our extended "New Year's Eve weekend", which by now everyone felt more than eager to embark onto. Oh yes. Relieved about this abrupt end of this "very unique" workday, we ended up goodbye hugging each other very tightly and while doing so, it was easy to notice that none of the experienced had sunk-in in either one of us yet. Lucia, our apprentice and I found ourselves laughing all along and simply happy that everyone remained "unharmed" and safe and that the "only" damage resulted in the many gone paper bills. Yay. Once my vessel found itself back in my apartment again with my then so beloved kitty cat roommate Gina, my soul further found "herself" quite amazed about how fast news can be spread. Wow. Mind you, back then the only opportunity for information to travel happened to occur via Newspapers, the Radio, TV, "old school" Mobile Phones, Landline Phones, the Internet in its 2001 shoes and by the old-fashioned Mouth-to-Mouth propaganda. Yes, the canton of Thurgau is quite small and my vessel grew UP on the countryside, which for sure makes it more legit for news and rumors to be flying around from one mouth into another even quicker, maybe. Still, I found myself pretty baffled about the speed of word about my just experienced new *"Living on Earth Game"* adventure "action" collection from only a few hours back. Wow. Only a few minutes after my arrival at home was then, when both of my phones started ringing, while simultaneously several text massages found its way onto my Nokia screen, resulting from all sorts of friends and acquaintances. Very quickly though, I came to realize that most of those seemingly "caring" souls mainly were driven by their curiosity of finding out MORE about the How's and the How Much's than about *"little Linda's"* actual well-being. Hmmm. And so it was. "Human beings", right? During these moments, my soul then happily kept on referring to the "holy" Swiss banking secrecy rules and therefore instantly succeeded in ending those annoying phone calls and text messages without any further information flow gatherings for my nosy "audience". Ha! Then, throughout the following days, some of the TKB's big bosses decided that our branch should remain closed for an additional couple of days, so that 1) Everyone's "little" shock state of mind truly could receive its fair chance to settle and that 2) Our three vessels security would be fully granted again, once back at work. Ufff. All January 2002 the three of us therefore in addition were granted a bodyguard, who accompanied our vessels in a collective out and into our branch during closing and opening hours. Yes. And even though the TKB allowed us to take advantage of this protective service for as long as desired, Lucia and I about 1 month later decided, that it was at the time for us to find our way back into "normality" again, without these constant reminders of what happened. Certainly, *"little Linda"* got on and off faced with some still within herself lingering fear reactions, during her upcoming 4 1/2 Erlen years and this especially, whenever she found herself alone on those LONG and dark winter after hour evenings being busy catching up on paper work, with customer phone calls or with "late" meetings with old and new clients in my office. Yup. The blessing to me out of this in a way new "traumatic" experience after all results in the "luck" that the three souls of us found ourselves able to travel through it all as a unit and therefore very much ended up being able to fully support and understand one another, whenever some weird feelings arose in either one of us. Ufff. And on top of it all, I feel very grateful for this SpeCial bond that this quite unique *"Living on Earth Game"* adventure as a result tied between the three of us, especially between Lucia's and my soul, as by the end of January 2002 our apprentice's 3 months period ended and our 2 journeys' continued for another more than 4 years. Ha! Therefore, *"little Linda"* even more so will always remain thankful to have been in it together as the "Three Musketeers", instead of one by herself. Yup. Thank you. Thank you. Thank you. Yes, and furthermore, this Erlen journey kindly granted my soul with Lucia's another important and SpeCial *"Extended Family Member"*, which secretly developed itself into an unspoken "mother-daughter" bond, that is for sure. Ha! Lucia's vessel started her *"Living on Earth Game"* ride only 10 months prior to my mom's, gave birth to 3 boys and alongside with our both' individual created family picture, our two souls seemed to have enjoyed this in the room standing "mother-daughter" connection quite a LOT, even though, I was supposed to be her "boss" and she my "employee". LOL. Very grateful my soul also feels about all the many magical, personal and FuN moments that we allowed ourselves to experience together, for 5 years straight. Yeah! Our probably most memorable *"FuN Factor"* happened to be the in 2002 released Movie "Secretary", starring Maggie Gyllenhaal and James Spader, which the two of us ended up picking as part of our yearly TKB Christmas excursion activity, financed by our tip jar. Yup. Believe it or not. Our lovely customers truly left us quite often some nice cash tips for our friendly services throughout the years or decided to spoil us here and there with some yummy food. Ha! Welcome to the wonderful Thurgau world. Wink. Now, if you happen to have seen this rather "interesting" Movie, my lovely *Co-Traveler*, then you probably will understand its experienced *"FuN Fact"* level and if you happen to have "missed" it thus far, then know that this piece of Art by far is a "jewel" in the genre of *WeiRdnesS*. Oh yeah! The two of our vessels even ended up with the "honor" to experience this "X-Mas spectacle" all on our own as the only audience members amongst the many empty seats during that particular show time hour in the Movie Theatre in Konstanz/Constance. That says it all, I assume. LOL. Thank you so much for those magical years my dear Lucia. We were a Dream Team. Yes, we were indeed. LOVE.

"Get Ready Steady to Jump my Darling. Just take my hand. jUMP!"
Alongside with my many wonderful experiences throughout this Erlen chapter, I of course as well got faced with its opponent ones, which made my overall enthusiasm for my activities appear like being traded at the stock exchange. Meaning, at times I simply found *"little Linda"* in love with her many successes and on other days my soul kept on wondering what on heavens earth my vessel was doing there, still. Fact was that my current job blessed my reality in the material world on all ends with Stability, Security, wonderful Benefits, an easygoing Workflow, a great Lifestyle and a constant Growth of my longtime friend, the *"Red and White Saving Sock"* account. Ha! My inner world though on the other hand often times felt completely out of alignment and disconnected with what my soul found "herself" experiencing on the outer one. As my decision-making process in 2001 resulted on a head driven one, my neglected heart voice in those "lower" moments therefore made it very clear to me that it kept yearning for my attention as well. Whenever I found *"little Linda"* in these rather uncomfortable situations, then I either would ask her and my heart to please stay patient for a little bit longer or went ahead and organized a temporary "love" resolution for them both. Deep down my soul all along knew though, that my place was

supposed to be somewhere else then where I currently chose to travel in and until this "other" reality would appear, my heart and *"little Linda"* kindly got asked by my soul to please stay patient for a little bit longer and to make it work, somehow, with our magical *"Positivity Card"* trick. Boom. That was the deal. My overall lifestyle though truly looked wonderful out of my minds perspective and that's what mattered at that time. That's right. *"Head over Heart"*. Wink. Into quite amusing those situations usually turned themselves in, whenever the beloved Universe introduced my soul to a new one during my off-duty *"Living on Earth Game"* travels and *"little Linda"* shortly after got asked her all-time "favorite" *"Linda, what do you do for a living?"* small talk question EVER. Joyfully, she then would deliver her well-rehearsed *"Well, I am a boring banker. Actually, a bank manager of a small branch."* line and continued this moment accompanied with some GiGGLES, as this statement truly kept on sounding SO FuNNy, unbelievable and "out of character" all along. LOL. My opposite then usually would follow my assumed "joke" along very well entertained by then at some point interrupting the situation with a *"Ok. Stop kidding. Now for real. What do you do?"* follow up question. That then always ended up being the moment for me to put on my more serious face in order to be able to convince my opposite successfully with its truth factor. Smile. Simultaneously, during this Erlen ride of mine, my by now famous and also adjusted question of *"What Other Hobby, besides watching Movies and TV shows, enjoying Music, Dancing and Celebrating this "Living on Earth Game" adventure of mine as often as possible, could I possibly turn into a FuN paying profession, which would provide my daily Swiss activities with a Living, Freedom and Happiness"* of course kept on knocking on my door on and off as well. Yup! The, my thus far collected "facts" in that matter were that 1) My *"Acting Dream"* s-Express train left its station empty handed many years prior, 2) My mother earth exploration adventures offered by the in October 2001 through the to me sad circumstances grounded and shortly after ceased Swissair Airline, caused my soul a LOT of FuN at first. Right up to the point, in which "normality" started to welcome my reality, accompanied with exhausting feelings and with the appearance of my "supporting" travel buddy *Mister Loneliness*. Oh no. Here he appeared again. Yup. This constant hopping from one continent, city, time-zone to another with difFeRent souls, cultures, airplanes and impressions ended up being a little bit more challenging for my vessel, mind and health than I found myself aware off, which circumstances therefore easily allowed for my very faithful "companion" to find its way back through the unattended unlocked door. Ha! And 3) *"little Linda"* also granted her fitness passion its fair trial, which luckily got "interrupted" by this bank managing opportunity. Wink. Yes. Early into my gym journey, I actually came to discover that this challenge for ONE turned out to be much easier than assumed and that TWO most of the times, I found my soul a LOT more passionate and eager about our members workout successes than theirs turned out to be, which as a result very soon lowered my enthusiasm to share my many gained "secrets" with them. Bummer. And therefore, I found *"little Linda"* anew easily jUMPing onto her next delivered *"Comfort Zone"* opportunity by a *"Letting go of Something that No Longer Serves One's Growth and Expansion"* approach and by crossing this hobby trial off from her career list as well. Boom. And the lookout for THE ONE therefore continued with a *"What Else could I be giving a trial"* question by furthermore adding the suspicion into the discovery process that I most certainly kept on overlooking something or remained unaware of. Hmmm. And yes. So it was. What?! *"Ask and You shall Receive at its PERFCT Time"* once anew is what must have been the magical formula for my further *"Living on Earth Game"* travels at hand. Ha! Thank you. On August 14th 2004, the beloved Universe finally provided *"little Linda"* with its Three's A Charm solution, which got triggered by a friend of mine during a visit in *Lucerne* LU, my Möne's then so-called home city. Yay! As the night before, the, meanwhile into my 80ies Heroess transmuted Musician NENA, held one of her with LOTS of LOVE and ENTHUSiASM filled performances at a Festival in *Ebikon* LU, my soul of course needed to be part of it and had my dear friend Sandy join my vessel for a FuN weekend excursion. As Ebikon with its 2 hours train ride from our beautiful Thurgau is considered "far", the two of us therefore decided to extend this trip with an extra day in Lucerne, which is located right next to this tinny municipality. After a thrilling concert, Sandy and I then a few hours later woke up quite early again in a close by Youth Hostel and decided to fill this extra day with a ship ride to *Samichlausen* LU and with the added intention to then walk all the way back to the city's main train station. On our hike back, we then as so often found our two souls casually chit chatting about life, work, love, etc. You know, the things that girlfriends do and talk about, whilst they are spending some quality time together. Wink. Then, once the job topic found its turn, Sandy as so often desired to get an UPdate in regards of my "current" state of mind reality check towards my managing occupation and further kept on wondering, whether it caused my soul happiness these days or if I still caught myself being tangled in this questioning everything mode at times. And THiS innocence seemingly incidence unknowingly ended up transforming itself into THE most important key moment within my thus far *"Living on Earth Game"* experiences, which threw *"little Linda"* right back into her *"Dream Catchin'"* state of mind zone, a few days later. Abracadabra. Ha! Thank you. Thank you. Thank you, dear Sandy. Smile. Ready? Yeeha! Besides my still lasting NENA HiGH from the night before, my soul at that time actually happened to be riding a very happy wave at work as well. My friend's recurring question, I therefore easily ended up answering with a *"Yes, currently I in fact am feeling very pleased about everything. Things are going great and I am experiencing a LOT of FuN with my clients and with Lucia of course."* Sandy then looked at me with her critical eye and continued her own thought process with a *"Hmmm. Are you sure? Because you know that I don't really see you grow old in a bank. What I would totally see you in is creating soundtracks for Movies or for any other background Music existing job opportunities on the market. My coworker's boyfriend actually does something like that in

Zurich. I think that you should do some research on that topic online. There should be a school for it in Zurich. You are so not a banker Linda and you know it." remark. Boom. Spot on my dear friend was indeed and this is what she found herself referring to. A few months prior to this incidence, the beloved Universe kindly provided *"little Linda"* with the magical information that the wonderful world of the Internet now offered some websites, which provided free downloads of any desired song, if available. Wow. For real? Yes, and therefore I shortly became good friends with "LimeWire" and "FrostWire", "who" allowed me to expand my now and then Music collection in a very wallet friendly way directly onto my Sony Vaio hard drive. Woohoo! It's probably needless to say that this "Music steeling" activity, SORRY, seamlessly turned into a new BiG passion and hobby of mine, whenever my vessel reunited with my kitty cat Gina's from any outside activities and therefore right after would spend hours online hunting down all of *"little Linda's"* favorite 80ies tracks and Artists. Well, except for NENA's work. Her creations I did and always will collect in its original form. That is a MUST and an "honor code" of mine and this rule certainly always applied to any other as amazing interpreted Music tunes creators. HA. Yes indeed. Then, as soon as those desired and precious tracks found themselves safe and sound on my computer, I as a next step would go ahead and burn some of them in a from my soul perceived very smooth and specific order on CD's for some of my friends, for my mom and of course for *"little Linda"*, with the intention to enhance everyone's *"Living on Earth Game"* experience, whenever played and desired. Boom. Spreading loving vibes through UPlifting beats was my souls mission right then and probably still would be today. In a way. If I focused on it. More. Which thought actually just triggers my recurring interest of a DJ journey trial. In some sort, form and way. Oh yeah! Hmmm. Let's see. One step and the time, right? *"Music is the Answer to your Problems"* is part of a statement that my auricles heard in a song many years later in New York City on a track recorded by Danny Tenaglia feat. Celeda. That and its further written content pretty much says it all for me. Yeah! Now, even though Sandy's then suggestion welcomed my world completely out of the blue, I on the other hand found my soul instantly resonating with her words and did exactly as recommended, once my vessel got reunited with my fluffy Gina's again. PURR. By now *"little Linda"* felt quite intrigued by the thought of her MAYBE still being able to work in the Film industry in this *"Living on Earth Game"* journey, only in a difFeRent way and form than initially imagined. The Working behind the Scenes option actually never occurred my mind thus far and therefore found *"little Linda"* quite excited about the idea of possibly just have been introduced to an income stream that would combine her top two Music and Movies passions and hobbies in even one stroke. Sweet! The following week, I therefore dedicated my free evenings towards this suggested Zurich Film Sound School research task, which ended up staying in its hidden corner all along, as the magical Universe kept on insisting to distract *"little Linda"* with this intriguing and reappearing ACTiNG word. Oh no, you again. Sniff. At first, I found myself very tightly holding on to my resisting mode of even reading any of these presented Acting pages, as my soul already knew that this s-Express train took off many years ago. So spending my focus and precious time on something that really mattered seemed to be a much more powerful action step choice as part of my current game plan at hand. Yup. The beloved Universe though stood persistent in its doings and kept leading me back to these many Acting pages. On and on. Stop it! The more that *"little Linda"* got faced with this *"Childhood Dream"* word of hers again, the more my soul began to carry it within my heart. The more that my soul carried it within my heart, the more it became alive again and this reality check really began to bother *"little Linda"* very much. In order to quiet down those "old new" emotions, I then eventually decided to give in and to instead take a closer look on what kept on coming my way by extending those Acting researches across the Swiss borders over to Germany and Austria as well. To my surprise, my eyes quickly came to discover that those schools in Germany happened to be open to any vessels, without any "age" restrictions at all. What?! Are you kiddin' me? Well, this valuable new information flow certainly instantly lit UP my entire inner world like a fireball. WOOSH! Wait a minute. So, did all of this actually mean that it was STiLL possible for Linda Wartenweiler to become an Actress?! Now? What?! The closer I looked, the clearer I saw that my soul, including *"little Linda"* indeed found "themselves" still able to pursuit "our" all time dream with my next-door neighbors, the Germans. OMG. Wow! And this moment truly transformed itself into another very magical and unforgettable reality shift experience. Oh yeah. After some more researches though, I then anew found myself left with one "obstacle" at hand, which put an instant damper onto my soul. Oh no, not again! Yes. The next "problem" that *"little Linda"* found herself facing this time, turned out to be this "audition" requirement for each new student as part of the entry process for any of these available German Acting schools at hand. Ahm. To what? Audition? What on heavens earth does that mean now? As soon as I after some more "digging" found out its meaning, I heard *"little Linda"* repeatedly asking herself of HOW she 1) Possibly could be auditioning for an Acting spot if 2) She had NO clue at all HOW to do so and most importantly, until thus far 3) Gathered no "knowledge" whatsoever yet of even how to BE an Actress. Bummer! The only opportunity that my soul at this point of "her" many *"Living on Earth Game"* adventure creations desired to get, happened to be given a chance by someone, preferably a school, that would teach "her" HOW to become an Actress and that was about it. My logical brain pictured this whole learning process approach about the same way, as I experienced it during my 3 years banking education journey. *"Provide me with all the needed classes and information and I in return will apply everything successfully into my work."* Boom. It's that simple. This approach formula with my then Plan B career choice after all is what led *"little Linda"* all the way to her current managing occupation and the thought of where her path could be taking her to with her ACTUAL *"Childhood Dream"* manifestation opportunity, instantly filled my entire vessel with those tiny "dots" called *Goosebumps*. Ha! Then one night, whilst I found myself busy exploring one of these German webpages, the beloved Universe suddenly responded with its all-time friendly *"Thy Wish is my Command"* gesture by redirecting my clicking's to a difFeRent school's site, which to my surprise said *New York Film Academy (NYFA)*. What? New York Film Academy? Yes, and believe me, my dear *Co-Traveler*, to this very day it actually remains unclear to my soul as of HOW this in New York based page appeared onto my screen, as I certainly did NOT intentionally click on this way too far existing *"The Other Planet"* possibility. Yup. And. Hmmm. Obviously, my fingers somehow must have done so and therefore its appearance instantly ended up surprising my reality with its absolute unexpected approach. BooO! As a first reaction, *"little Linda"* simply kept on starring at this black, white and red colored homepage, while my head voice narrated this entire scene with a *"New York? What? That's insane. I want to stay in the German speaking field. "The Other Planet" is way too FAR away from home. No way, that's not it."* response. Boom. Even though my head voice kept *"little Linda"* quite confused by its resisting and fear-based tactic approach, my heart one on the other hand tried its very best to draw my attention towards its opposite point of view created opinion. *"Head vs. Heart"*. As soon as I decided to direct my awareness towards the pleading latter's narration, I then suddenly witnessed the eFFecTs of a very soothing calmness arising within my vessel, my mouth began to form an intrigued smile, my head to nod softly in agreement and the next thing my soul knew was, that my hand already joyfully took over my mouse's control by enthusiastically scrolling and clicking all over NYFA's entire Acting program pages. Yeeha! Studying my beloved *"Soul Childhood Dream"* in America, on this *"Other Planet"*. Wow, I actually like that thought a LOT. Could this possibly be my "ticket" in order to do the impossible still in this Linda Wartenweiler *"Living on Earth Game"* experience? Is this maybe THE key hobby that I kept on looking for all along, which would unlock and materialize all my many accumulated Dreams, Visions and Desires? Boah. Well that simply would be SO SO cool. Los Angeles. Yes! Los Angeles and Hollywood. Woohoo! And off *"little Linda's"* by then almost 3 decades dated *"Acting as a Leading Lady in a Hollywood Motion Picture"* *"Head Cinema"* trailer right away took. Wow! Alongside with all of this new information flow and perspective-changing outlook at hand, my vessel, including heart simultaneously filled themselves even more so with excitement, whilst my hand got prompted to even faster detect NYFA's application requirements, which ended up stating the exact from *"little Linda"* earlier on asked for *"Pay the yearly tuition fee, know some English and you are in"* solution. Boom. And. Boah. Ah, Universe? Is that what you want me to experience next? But that's crazy and scary in one shot. How could I possibly leave my family, friends, belongings and my beloved Gina behind? We are not talking about Germany or Switzerland here, to where I easily could be moving all my belongings, including my car to and travel back and forth within a SNAP only. No. We are talking about the United States. Another continent. Uhm.

"Planet". Even though this idea sounded a little bit too crazy at first, I "unwillingly" ended up carrying it safely within my heart wherever my vessel brought me to. *"Acting and living in the United States."* Wow. And that is how my secretly kept *"THE Ultimate Childhood Dream Vision"* found its way back into my awareness again by presenting *"little Linda"* a flashback of her initial *"Being able to live on this "Other Planet" via a bank transfer opportunity"* Plan B creation. Hmmm. Yes. This was exactly what my inner voice asked me to look into earlier into my *"Living on Earth Game"* travels and it certainly looked like it, as if I just found another opportunity in order to make this vision happen in its original desired Plan A form. Ha! How about replacing the original bank idea with my *"Acting Dream"*, which instead would bless my reality with a Three in One win-win situation of 1) Finally finding myself able to explore this *"NeverEnding"* within my soul lingering Acting fascination, by 2) Experiencing this whole *"Other Planet"* adventure out of an official residence's perspective and with 3) Finding myself surrounded by my favorite language EVER with the added opportunity to improve it daily. Wow! Yes. This sounded about right. The more that my *"Head Cinema"* went on with the creation of this thrilling new opportunity at hand, the more my soul and *"little Linda"* started to fall in love with what "they" saw and experienced. And let me tell you, my beloved *Co-Traveler*, and this time the seed finally successfully got planted within my heart after the magical Universe's third trial. Yay! Subconsciously, I from then on daily started to nurture and protect my newly found "baby" very preciously. At first, I decided to keep it all safe and sound to myself, as I wanted to avoid the risk of finding *"little Linda"* discouraged anew, caused by any outside resources during this to me quite BiG reality shift adjustment process. After all I just got presented this new opportunity to step into this *"Childhood Acting Dream"* of mine in THiS *"Living on Earth Game"* ride already, without having to wait for another round to start. Yeeha! This whole unexpected reality shift, I at first certainly experienced as quite a frightening, overwhelming and as a very thrilling one in one breath, which therefore instantly left enough room for my all-time concerned and rational head voice to find its discouraging attempts by having *"little Linda"* question herself if Acting truly happened to be a hobby of hers. Ha! And that statement actually revealed itself as truer than true. How COULD I be certain without having its "proper" experience under my belt, right? Thus far, I after all "only" carried those few school experiences and my fascination for this genre as a pre-taste in my backpack and that was about it. Hmmm. And yes, from the logical point of view, this thought absolutely appeared legit and true. How could I truly know. What I DiD know though was that my heart and soul LOUD and clearly found themselves aligned with this whole new outlook and therefore instinctively knew what needed to be done from here on. Yup. Even though these new plans frightened *"little Linda"* quite a LOT at first, I decided to this time direct all of my attention towards my friendly's heart voice first, by simply trusting whatever it would be sending my way. *"Heart over Head"*. YES! And starting from then on, this new Acting

path choice of mine instantly got perfectly well supported and orchestrated by the from the beloved Universe's delivered signs, which I "really" found myself able to decipher a few years later, with the for it required distance, expansion and with the further *"Life Toolbox"* collection extension. Wink. Yes, so looking back from my today's *"Living on Earth Game"* destination has me clearly see HOW eagerly the magical Universe kept on trying to assure and support the still at times doubtful *"little Linda"* that this path with "No Doubt" happened to be THE ONE for Linda Wartenweiler to walk upon next. Now let's dive right into where this reference finds its "birthing" moment. Splash. Shortly after I embarked this new and from the heart led reality creation of mine, things at work interestingly all over sudden started to get very hectic and chaotic. Ha! For the following few months, I literally found myself being bombarded with work and late hours, which resulted in 1) Less Linda time, 2) Less *"FuN Fact"* activities and with 3) An *"ongRowing"* frustration level. Boom. Even though my soul felt very intrigued by this NYFA opportunity, I kept holding myself back from another quite egotistical "friend" of mine in order to get this Acting adventure ball really rolling, introducing *Miss Fear*. Yes. We all know "her" WAY too well. That's right. Directly from her source, *"little Linda"* simultaneously also got infused with a reality creation guided by thoughts like *Fear* of letting go. *Fear* of entering a BiG mistake. *Fear* of losing everything that I created and built. *Fear* of starting over again. *Fear* to be ridiculed. *Fear* of the unknown. *Fear* to fail. *Fear* of stepping outside of my *"Comfort and Security Zone"*. And so forth. Alongside with my *"ongRowing"* frustration level, I therefore allowed this pessimistic friend's opinions to slowly overpower my hearts voice anew by furthermore let "her" put a frozen state of mind spell over *"little Linda's"* sudden appeared whirlwind creation for a little bit longer. Abracadabra. *"Watch Out. Gotch Ya'. Gotch Ya'!"* Alongside with these newly adapted believes, my by then *"Self-*created" with discontent filled *"Living on Earth Game"* experience simply felt as the "safer" choice than stepping outside of this with time very well manufactured "box" into an unknown with *"Not even the Sky is the Limit"* filled adventures "risk", which therefore right away opened the race for a sizzling *"Swimming ALONG vs. AGAiNST the Stream"* inner competition. Oh boy. Yes, and living out this newly created *"Ultimate Childhood Dream Vision"* of mine in my *"Head Cinema"* instead was what *"little Linda"* had to remain "happy" with for a little while longer. Bummer. And. Bravo *Miss Fear*. Well done. *"Head over Heart."* Here we go again. My courage is what I needed to find next in order to break out of this blocking and destructive mindset of mine, which had the HOW word turn into my new game plan mission at hand. Help?! Anybody? Meanwhile, my soul certainly found "herself" quite overwhelmed by the in Erlen presented workload and by this *"Banking. Security. Stability."* vs. *"Acting. Uncertainty. Complete Life Change."* needed crossroad choice. Which path to take? Which one is the "safe and right" one? My wonderful established Swiss *"Security Outlook"* or my *"Soul Childhood Dream"* located on a difFeRent *"Planet"*? Ufff. This decision definitely turned out to be trickier for *"little Linda"* than ever imagined. Dreaming about "the better" definitely felt so much easier than actually taking its very first step towards it. *Miss Fear* accompanied by *"Self*-doubt" with "No Doubt" performed their jobs seamlessly to their finest throughout these past decades. Wow. That happened to be a true fact by now and made me realize that I somehow successfully must have metamorphosed *"little Linda"* into this always undesired "serious, conservative and responsible" adulthood version. Oh NO! How was this possible? Had it to do with this MUM deodorant?! Of course! See, *"little Linda"* knew EXACTLY back then that this "grownUP" stuff happens to be a dangerous formula to apply. Wink. So yes, this reality check of my then "adulthood" stage certainly revealed itself as quite shocking and also very much so as unwanted. At that time, my vessel found itself in its late 20ies count, I had a nice banking career going, lived with my lovely and fluffy roommate Gina in a cool rental apartment in my dream village Bottighofen, owned a in 2002 brand new purchased silver VW Polo, many wonderful friends and enjoyed an overall wonderful *"Living on Earth Game"* lifestyle. At that time, some of my friends also started to get married and to create their own families, which kept reminding *"little Linda"* of the reality truth that our 20ies count soon would be finding its end and that therefore everyone "needed" to step UP their game shortly, by adapting this from society expected more "serious" and "grownUP" considered lifestyle experience, whatever that meant anyway. Hmmm. Further, this to me included to become even more responsible and to therefore most definitely step away from those "crazy, irresponsible and carefree" choices, which still happened to *"wiLD & Freely"* be running through my *"Head Cinema"*, especially these days. After all our 30y decade found itself lingering around the corner, which brought along new *"Living on Earth Game"* rules for the entire mid 70ies generation at hand. Oh Yeah. Getting Married, having Kids, owning a Property, climbing further UP one's Career Ladder plus getting more Settled and Quite certainly appeared as the top ones on that list. Yay. Ufff. Or simply put *Work mORE, growUP, enjoy less FuN and shed those "wiLD & Free" spirited teen and twen days about NOW. Anything else wouldn't look too good and you know it.* Boom. What?! Ughh. These pressure points definitely evoked a LOT of resistance within my heart, as basically none of the above resonated with what my soul initially was planning to live for or to experience during this current *"Living on Earth Game"* opportunity. Hmmm. Creating a family by giving birth to another soul and to therefore getting tied down to a possible part time home-stay mom reality or that sort of image always appeared as one of my last desired *"FuN Fact"* activities to enjoy on my bucket list. Oh yeah! This I knew all along from deep within and still do to this very day. Amen. Experiencing lives magic and its *"NeverEnding"* range of opportunities, including many challenges as *"wiLD & Free"* as a bird happens to be, is what my soul *"ongRowingly"* kept on resonating with the MOST all along of my many thus far "tryouts", as *to Explore, to Experience, to Achieve and to Be in Action* are STiLL playing a BiG part in *"little Linda's"* daily happy and radiant activity choices. Ha! After all I chose this state of mind "set-up" as my starting out position, which perfectly got provided and created by my selected parents Heidi and Urs, the second that my soul got introduced to them as Linda Wartenweiler on that very early May morning in *Münsterlingen TG*. That's right. Now, along with this adulthood stage awareness check of mine, this current cat and mouse ping pong match of which path to choose continued its course for a little while longer. Stability? Insecurity? Stability? Or maybe iNsecurity? Ugh! LOL. *Miss Fear* with "No Doubt" enjoyed "her" doings very much so by further feeding *"little Linda"* with comments like *"Are you crazy? Why would you give up your entire built empire, your family and all of your friends for something that you DON'T even know you will like and/or be good at? And HOW can you even consider starting anew with something unknown and this on a difFeRent continent? Linda, you are a banker in a great position. You have ALL that you need for your journey ahead. Accept that fact and stay reasonable. Please. Thank you."* and so forth. We all know this *"Head vs. Heart"* blah blah battlefield between reason and desire oh too well, right, my dear *Co-Traveler*? Ha! And therefore this *"NeverEnding"* back and forth blah blah match soon successfully ended up transforming my entire inner world into such a confusing and draining whirlwind, that my soul at some point truly wished to in a Time Machine travel right back to those easy-going days from only 10 years ago, to where my belief system still found itself plugged into the *"Not even the Sky is the Limit"* channel. Bummer. Yes, back then, my soul knew with all of my heart that my vessel would be finding itself on this *"Other Planet"* by the time it counted 21 and its actualization seemed so much easier and carefree than what my soul kept on experiencing with my new expansion intentions. Traveling abroad for a few months and leaving everything behind happened to be the most normal and common activity to perform for everyone in their early 20ies and now that I found myself in a similar situation a few years down the road, this entire "thing" suddenly transformed itself into such a complicated and difficult adult task. Wow! Well and this reality check status led *"little Linda"* to wonder if her newly adapted behaviors and belief system ended up being the result of the works of possible *"Self-manipulation"* choices from her end, which throughout the past few decades wonderfully got fed by the accumulated and *"ongRowing"* available adult *"Fear Factors"* at hand, streaming directly and in incognito from those society domestication approaches and from the media's overall "brainwashing" tactics into my daily reality creation? Hmmm. Maybe. Maybe not. Ha! The convenient *"Swimming ALONG the Current"* rather than *"AGAiNST it"* perception therefore transformed itself throughout time into the from society respected and expected lifestyle choice. Yes. The *"Please Feed your "Comfort Zone". DO NOT change Anything once you are settled in and down. And please, PLEASE make sure to NOT stand out."* attitude seems to be an important "SpeCial" life recipe at hand that is supposed to keep each "grownUP" a happy and radiant camper along their many thrilling *"Living on Earth Game"* creations. Hmmm. Well, at least this is the philosophy of how *"little Linda"* always interpreted these "exciting" existing "guiding rules" as from her Thurgau stand point of view. Yup! And I assume that this fine print my soul surely must have skipped as well before "she" reentered this sphere anew back then. Oops. Linda, really?! Yes. Really! LOL. Now, after finding myself in this quite tiring and confusing cat and mouse ping pong whirlwind for a couple of months, my patient soul at some point finally came to the conclusion that *"Enough was Enough"* and that a change needed to happen NOW. After examining my whole new created reality a little bit closer, I came to realize that 1) My "own and original" believes actually always failed to match those from "society" expected view points and that therefore 2) *"little Linda"* needed to keep on pushing forward as truthful to herself as possible by 3) Breaking down all these meanwhile many built UP limiting adulthood walls, so that I on the other end of the rope 4) Determinedly could be marching forward with the recreation of "our" own *Happiness, Freedom* and *Peace* interpretation mission and this 5) All guided by my heart and from my heart only. Boom. *"Heart over Head"*. Let's Go! Once this plan got set in stone was then, when I found myself asking the beloved Universe for its kind help and assistance in regards of my courage finding desire to break out of this blocking and destructive mindset at work. Well, and as for its this time *"Thy Wish is my Command"* reaction, it revealed to me that this "guiding and inspirational" desired hand happened to have been traveling with me all along. What?! Yup. Do you remember, when and HOW my, this third *"Childhood Dream"* adventure attempt got triggered this time around, my dear *Co-Traveler?* That's right. The day after my Heroess' concert in Lucerne, which leads us straight to the "source". What? NENA? Exactly. Smile. Now let's find out what this connection is all about. Shall we? As the *"99 Red Balloons"* star luckily and thankfully happened to be celebrating her 20th performing anniversary in 2002, her soul therefore decided to 1) Push her career path due to a previously own family rising refocusing slowing down phase forward again, by 2) Releasing her genius *"Nena feat. Nena"* anniversary best of album and to 3) Present her soul and her thus far created work LiVE all over Germany, Austria and Switzerland as part of her strong comeback action game plan. Strike! Of course, *"little Linda"* found herself very thrilled, once the news of this brand-new album release reached her awareness, which on top of it all happened to contain all the many songs from her still safely kept tapes, "only" dressed up in an UPdated 2002 "outfit". Sweet. Unexpectedly, this wonderful album ended up inviting my soul onto a magical joyride, whenever I exposed myself to it. wOOsh. First of all, this reinvented best off album always kept transporting *"little Linda"* right back to those tape and singing along days in the mid 80ies and secondly, I suddenly found my soul completely fascinated and drawn towards this singer's, which therefore ignited my desire to experience NENA "LiVE" during her next Swiss announced appearance at the Culture and Convention Center (KKL) in Lucerne LU, on April 25th 2003. Boom. What? Lucerne again? Yes. How interesting, right? Hmmm. Anyway, as this, my very first real time on stage encountered NENA experience even more so sparked my passion for whatever her soul was "doing" and spreading, my soul therefore right away felt prompted to purchase all the many albums that I missed out on throughout the past years. Yup. And this is how and when this *"99 Luftballons"* singer quickly metamorphosed herself into my Heroess, which led me to promise *"little Linda"* that whenever her vessel would be appearing somewhere on Swiss ground, starting right then, that the two of "us" would be standing on it as well. Boom. Certainly, I dedicatedly followed through with this plan, experienced her always very magical performances 7 times in 3 years and that is how Sandy's and my vessel ended up enjoying a FuN weekend in Lucerne the following year. Ha! Now, as soon as I came to realize that NENA actually happened to be my sent by "helping and assisting" hand, it dawned on me that all the support that *"little Linda"* "needed" in order to move through those current blocks at hand, found themselves perfectly well placed within this Artist's work and own energy. What? Yes. Once I allowed myself to REALLY listen and to connect with all my many until then collected NENA songs, *"little Linda"* suddenly to her amazement came to realize that this Musician's soul actually "talked" about EXACTLY what mine was experiencing right then in "her" *"Self*-created" whirlwind reality and that on top of it all most songs were and still are filled with inspirational wisdom and messages. Boah. How cool! Thank you! My soul therefore even more so began to resonate with everything that "she" received from NENA's end, which eventually ended up launching my rocket ship towards my *"Not even the Sky is the Limit"* adventure by brushing off all these accumulated blocks One-by-One, Little-by-Little, along the road. Yeeha! From that moment on, NENA's inspiring and motivational soul, including "light" simply had to be with and around me as much as possible, which left me with the urge to listen to her shared wisdom as a looping back and forth experience in order to switch *"little Linda's"* overall *"Living on Earth Game"* views and believes successfully back into her by nature *"Swimming AGAiNST the Stream"* embedded reality creation approach desire. Abracadabra. *"Thy Will is my Command"*. Boom! Now, what my soul always REALLY loved about the *"99 Luftballons"* singer's soul and about "her" Art is that NENA questions our society, our way of existing including thinking in a to me very sarcastic, super FuNNy and truthful manner, while she further keeps on encouraging her audience to *"Stay True to Oneself"*, to *"Follow Ones inner Voice ONLY"* and to *"Step Over those Limiting Miss Fear based Barriers"* in order to really exist as *"wiLD & Free"* as a bird can be. Ha! Well and right here it certainly becomes quite clear to *"little Linda"* as of WHY her soul keeps on resonating so harmoniously with Missiz NENA's. Right? Wink. Some of my from her end favorite and most helpful offered *"Childhood Dream"* reality adjustment "tools", which keep on hitting my spot instantly whenever exposed to, revealed themselves as *"Es ist niemals zu spät für einen Neuanfang./It's never too late to start over."*, *"Warte nicht, denn Du bist aufgewacht. Sonnenaufgang, die Nacht ist zu Ende, neues Leben, neuer Anfang./Don't hesitate you just woke up. Dawn, night is over, new life, new beginning."* or *"Lass die Leinen los/Cast Off"* and that almost *"NeverEnding"* list could go on. And on. And ON. Oh yeah! Danke schön. Simultaneously to all those many additional from my heart led taken action steps, the beloved Universe of course made sure that *"little Linda"* consciously and subconsciously would nurture this during her NYFA discovery phase planted seed all along in order for it to grow stronger and BiGger by the day. What?! Yes. And therefore, I very soon suddenly found myself in a transformation and preparation cycle for my next BiG and somewhat intense *"Living on Earth Game"* ride ahead. Oh yeah! As my frustration level by June 2005 still very much so got fed by these *"ongRowing"* and hectic work days, which meanwhile also got accompanied by this inner occurring and somewhat "un-matching" added metamorphosis of mine, *"little Linda"* therefore finally felt prompted to gather and test all her newly collected and retrieved courage supply in order to set this *"Childhood Dream"* catching ball into motion. Let's do it! And in doing so, I decided to order this from the New York Film Academy offered brochure, which included all the many details about their available programs at hand. Ufff. At last. Certainly, this action step might come across as fairly "dramatic" from my end and believe me, it was, as deep down in my heart my soul already knew that once my vessel would be holding this brochure in its palms that there would lead no way back to my then considered "normality" state of mind perception. Yup. And so it was. Abracadabra. Very vividly I do recall that to *"little Linda"* quite precious moment, the second her eyes spotted that yellow envelope, which travelled ALL the way from New York City right into her mailbox in Bottighofen, like those three Katja postcards did back then. Hooray! My *"Childhood Dream"* literally found itself lying within my own hands now and all that was required from my end next happened to be to read its content and to further follow my heart's recommendations while doing so. Wow. And. Ufff. That thought truly felt quite scary and oh so right as well my lovely *Co-Traveler*. It truly did. Led by my curiosity and by my newly adapted *"Don't Dream your Life. Live your Dream."* mindset, I therefore shortly after began to read everything that my eyes could detect about their 1 year Acting program and pretty soon came to realize that the Entertainment world's vocabulary very much differed from any of my former English experiences and interactions and therefore already found myself being stopped by expressions like *Monologue, Agents, Casting Directors, Props*, etc. Ufff. Help! Which this time wonderfully got provided by my dear yellow, blue and always reliable translator friend *Duden*, who meanwhile most likely gets considered as an "old fashioned" choice, as Google Translate, Bing and co. by now took over its "manual" activity. Wink. As soon as my translation journey found its very satisfying end, my soul certainly found "herself" vibrating in its HiGHest available notes, *"little Linda"* somewhere lost in her *"ongRowing"* *"Head Cinema"* masterpiece and had me convinced that the *"Acting. Uncertainty. Complete Life Change."* hobby path was THE ONE that I desired to explore next. ASAP. For sure. *"Let's Rock 'n Roll!"* Thank you. The next question at hand that needed to get answered turned out to be the choice of where to possibly study my beloved *"Acting Dream"* within this *"The Other Planet"*. The City of Angels vs. The Big Apple. Hmmm. Now, as Hollywood always remained as my set final destination location, I therefore decided to use one of my still available vacation weeks, in order to 1) Dive right into a "secretive" City of Angels scouting adventure mission, so that I could ensure hands on that 2) A drastic change like this would really be what my soul desired to experience next, before 3) jUMPing into the "unknown" just like that. Deal. After my out of safety reasons felled decision to keep my "real" LA mission plans to myself for the time being, my vessel soon after happily set foot onto California's ground anew by the end of June 2005 and found itself heading straight to Santa Monica, right to where it left off almost 9 years ago. Yeeha! And yes, the Youth Hostel on 2nd Street therefore easily turned into my *"Home Sweet Home"* choice for the 7 days ahead. Finding myself back though truly felt quite weird at first, as this reality check of experiencing everything through the eyes of *"little Linda's"* further thus far *"Living on Earth Game"* explorations and *"Life Toolbox"* ingredient collections at hand made this whole "home coming" moment shine from a difFeRent light than it did almost 1 decade ago. Everything was "good". Just difFeRent. Welcome. Then, the second that I settled in, *"little Linda"* very much so felt the urge to continue her many adventures by exploring her possible new hometown and its territory further with the car rental at hand and that was when this lovely being at home feeling welcomed my inner world instantly again with a warm smile on "its" face. Smile. Now, even though I really enjoyed my time back in my sweet *"Cali Dreamin'"* state of mind reality creation, my oh so stubborn and party pooper friend *Mister Loneliness* for some reason decided on my third day to jUMP aboard as well with its set intention to support my further travels with its "lovely" presence. Oh no. You again. Bummer. Why? Well, my plans of connecting with some interesting and international souls via the Youth Hostel for the time being took on a difFeRent route than desired, which unexpectedly left *"little Linda"* with a LOT more "alone" time and with therefore rather *"NeverEnding"* appearing minutes, hours and days at hand. Oh my. Here we go again. Me, myself and I. Abroad. Help! And this reality check for that reason midway through found itself triggering my urge to fly right back home to where I by now realized Linda Wartenweiler actually belonged to. Ufff. Sadly, *"little Linda"* right then anew came to face the acceptance of another defeat and decided to at least try to make the best possible out of the remaining few days at hand within her dream destination and *"Planet"* by pulling her all time magical *"Positivity Card"*. The wonderful Universe though seemed to have disagreed with my reaction and therefore immediately sent me a friendly and cool Californian girl my way during a grocery shopping adventure of mine, on the following evening. Ha! How our encounter happened slipped my memory for now, though somehow the two of our souls ended up conversing inside the store and the next thing that mine knew was that "hers" invited my vessel to join "hers" and some of "her" friends' for a FuN night out in 24 hours' time. Sweet. Let's! Let's have some FuN with some "real" Angelinos for once so that *Mister Loneliness* gets "his" well-deserved alone time break for the time being. Oh yeah. And as *"Everything ALWAYS happens for a*

Reason", I soon came to learn what this "spontaneous" encounter revealed itself to have been all about. Abracadabra. Once my vessel found itself mingling amongst those newly met American ones a few hours later, my soul furthermore got rewarded with a friendly connection of one of this cool Californian girl's friends, which keeps me ever since convinced that the wonderful Universe planned all of "this" in order to lead *"little Linda"* right back on track again. True fact. Ha! During our getting to know each other chit chatting warming up phase, this friendly young man at some point began to share that his brother happened to be studying Film directing in *Santa Barbara* CA, that he for that reason just returned from a FuN visit a few days prior and that I most certainly should pay this beautiful city a visit now or someday. Excited and a little bit disappointed in one, I then decided to let his soul in on my "real" LA mission plans and into why as *"little Linda"* found herself anew defeated on her chosen *"Acting. Uncertainty. Complete Life Change."* hobby path at hand. Sniff. With a saddened heart, I then revealed to "his" my newly gained awareness state of mind shift that 1) The making friends task seemed to be quite difficult to achieve here in the City of Angels with all these many mainly indoors and in their cars existing vessels at hand. That 2) A relocation from my Swiss safe zone reality into this FAR away existing 9.8 million populated city would surely enhance the chances for *Mister Loneliness* to be present too often and that therefore 3) *"little Linda"* lost her complete interest in proceeding any further on this current path. Been there. Done that. Had my share. Oh yes. And lastly, 4) Meanwhile I even failed on following through on my Acting school researching task, as my soul by now felt way too intimidated and scared to check those opportunities out to begin with. Boom. Yup and anew I allowed myself to slowly accept these head driven motivational speeches over those from my heart delivered ones, as they simply felt very comforting and soothing to *"little Linda"* right then. Bravo *Miss Fear*. You are a true master. Wink. Then, as soon as I ended my mini monologue, this friendly young man understandingly accepted my point of view and continued to share his train of thought by warmly recommending New York City as my other possible dream realization location at hand. What? New York again? Yes. Hello. And as "his" soul seemed to have been quite driven for mine to keep on pushing forward on "her" *"Ultimate Childhood Dream Vision"* path, "he" enthusiastically brought to my attention, that 1) Even though the Big Apple populates about 8 Million souls that the there existing commute system with everyone's own two feet including its many available subways and bus choices actually unites everyone along their travels. That 2) My making friends task should therefore develop itself as easier than in LA and that 3) *"little Linda"* could always continue her *"Cali Dreamin'"* adventure as a respected New York City trained Actress, whenever that *"Living on Earth Game"* ride would be cruising towards its end. Wow. How genius and true this reality check suggestion simply felt. Then, after a little pause, my soul found "herself" Ready to exit the following with a BiG smile on my face *"Do you know what? You are so right. I actually do own a brochure of the New York*

Film Academy in my apartment, as I was considering this option as well. But since Hollywood always remained as my actual ultimate dream location and not New York City, I felt that I should be sticking to my original plans." Boom. And as his words very well resonated with my heart and with my soul, I therefore instantly knew alongside with my reappeared courage that his version needed to be explored next. Yay! *"little Linda"* just returned back into "the game" again. *"Acting Dream"* here I come! After the successful completion of this friendly young man's "mission" and after the introduction of Jeff Buckley's fantastic *"Last Goodbye"* recorded track, we then parted ways, which left me with the wonderful eFFecT of finding myself able to enjoy those remaining *"Cali Dreamin'"* days, now guided by my newly delivered outlook. *"Goodbye"* friendly young man. *"Goodbye"*. Thank you for your powerful help and for your "re-tracking" guidance! It worked. Shortly after my vessel return onto Swiss ground again, *"little Linda"* came to realize that on that particular "spontaneous" City of Angels encounter event, an even further switch within herself must have been put into motion and that whatever spell this friendly young man's soul put on mine, certainly continued its daily *"ongRowing"* magic. Abracadabra. Within the first two weeks, I to my surprise suddenly came to face the urge to slowly start letting my *"Acting Dream"* cat out of its bag, as the planted seed meanwhile found itself being nurtured and strong enough to get presented to some hand-picked souls. What? Are you sure? Alrighty then. My very first choice therefore instantly fell for my always supportive and optimistic "Baer" friend, who reacted absolutely joyous and encouraging about what his auricles perceived. Yay. And. Strike. Well, and with this from my heart led taken action step, the beloved Universe anew already had its interesting plans Ready for *"little Linda's"* further *"Swimming AGAiNST the Current"* journey ahead. As this particular friend happened to be the owner of my, by then considered new "Home Gym", he on his end found himself simultaneously busy with preparing his then girlfriend for her UPcoming Fitness Figure competition, organized by the Swiss Natural Bodybuilding and Fitness Federation (SNBF). Now, as one rule of this yearly held event happens to be that each winner of every category automatically finds itself getting eligible to attend the in usually 1 week after in New York City held World Natural Bodybuilding Federation (WNBF) competition, it suddenly dawned on *"little Linda"* during our *"ongRowing"* conversation, that our wonderful matching Big Apple "coincidence" adventure in progress happened to actually be in tune with my already forged new game plan, of allowing myself to 1) Dive into a further "secretive" *"The Other Planet"* scouting ride in order to ensure hands on that 2) A drastic change like this would really be what my soul desired to experience next, before 3) jUMPing into the "unknown" just like that. Ha! At least last time this formula revealed itself to have been quite useful, right? Wink. With all this information in mind, my soul therefore instantly felt triggered to propose a Milli Vanilli like *"All or Nothing"* pact to the magical Universe in order for it to lead and orchestrate my soul through this entire Acting chapter process the way it was supposed to unfold for *"little Linda"* from here on. Boom. And this is what my soul proposed to the lovely Universe right then. As this SNBF/NYC occasion happened to be only 4 more months away, I therefore informed the trustworthy Universe that I right in that second was going to hand iT over ALL the power in regards of this *"NeverEnding" "Ultimate Childhood Dream Vision"* of mine, so that iT would be finding itself enabled to fully take over my *"Destiny's Path"* and that I would trust it full on with the outcome. Boom. If my friend would end up as the lucky winner in her category, I therefore for that reason would be taking this "wink" from the magical Universe, accompany her vessel to the Big Apple and take a closer look at this NYFA option at hand. And if she would end up with a lower rank, I then in that case would go ahead, drop this *"The Other Planet"* vision immediately and would be putting Germany on top of my checking out list instead. Ok. Deal. *"All or Nothing - Push"*. Let's do it! Once November hit, my vessel as intended found itself amongst the many SNBF visitors in *Horgen* ZH in order to 1) Support the "girlfriend" on stage and to also 2) Find out more about the lovely Universe's plans at hand in regards of the course of my own further *"Living on Earth Game"* ride. Uiii! This event definitely transformed itself into quite an intense and nervous journey, my lovely *Co-Traveler*. This much I can tell you. Ha! Thank God that my soul already found "herself" very familiar with this spectacle's entire process, as *"little Linda"* during its November 2002 happening suddenly felt an impulse to take on this VERY expanding, challenging and with disciplined filled adventure herself in the same category, which occasion therefore enabled for my *"Life Toolbox"* to get extended with many more valuable ingredients throughout the entire year of 2003. Yay. And. Thanks. Now, as soon as those sizzling seconds of the almost 2nd and 1st placed participant announcement arrived, my heart suddenly began its own beating contest against my tenser and tenser transforming vessel, whilst my soul truly realized that "she" really, REALLY wanted to continue "her" *"Living on Earth Game"* adventures in New York City and that therefore my friend simply HAD to win. Help! Like in Trance, *"little Linda"* then immediately closed her eyes and nervously started an inner *"She has to win. She has to win. She simply has to win. PLEASE!"* monologue, while her hands folded themselves into one unit. Then, a few seconds later, THE moment finally arrived during which the winner's name got announced LOUD and clear through all the many speakers placed throughout the hall. And the winner was *My friend*. Woohoo! Yay! WooHOO! Hearing her name evoked this instant feeling within my vessel, as if *"little Linda"* just won the lottery. New York City and you, my *"NeverEnding" "Ultimate Childhood Dream Vision"* here I come. Strike! Thank you. You wonderful Universe. Thank you. Then, 6 days later, my vessel as intended set foot on *Newark* NJ Airport's ground and accompanied as promised my winner friend's and one of a girlfriend's of hers for some FuN Big Apple adventures, which they mainly filled with her WNBF preparation task and I with "mine", whenever possible. Yup. And certainly, *"little Linda"* did as planned hold on to her "secretive" *"The Other Planet"* scouting quest information, as this choice simply felt as THE ONE for my still stronger growing *"Acting Dream"* seed, at least for now. Step-by-Step. One-by-One. Easy. Breezy. Exactly. My first secret mission of course ended up being the planned visit at the New York Film Academy. Once my vessel exited one of the many subway existing entrances at Union Square, I remember how my head instinctively turned itself to its left-hand side once UP and how the "wanted" red flag with its white New York Film Academy spelling letters immediately appeared in the distance. What? *"Red and White"* again? Ha! That just reminds me of my beloved *"Saving Sock"* and of Switzerland's national colors. Hmmm. How interesting, right? Well, and this NYFA LiVE connecting moment anew triggered *"little Linda's"* heart to jUMP UP and down out of excitement with the further added SpeCial eFFecT of her breath stopping for two or three counts. LOL. And off my vessel then headed towards my targeted spot. Once I found myself placed in front of the desired building, this reality check certainly made my soul feel as if "she" somehow just fell into an unexpected dream like state of mind "truth". Wow. Was my vessel truly standing right there in front of this particular Acting school that my eyes "somehow" stumbled upon during my original started Zurich Film Sound School researching task over one year ago? Boah. This all very much simply felt surreal and also oh so goOD. Ha! After my awareness shifted back into the *"Now Moment"*, I then equipped with a dEEEEp breath decided to continue my mission by 1) Diving right into my next BiG life-changing moment at hand and therefore 2) Stepped inside of the building, 3) Walked towards the front desk of this New York Film Academy, 4) Introduced myself to an Albert, 5) Quickly shared my intentions and therefore 6) Immediately got asked by his soul to follow his vessel UPstairs to the first floor to where all the office spaces were located at and to where I finally felt prompted to 7) Exhaaaaaaale. Phew. Done. Yay! Once our both vessels sat across from one another in two red lounge leather seats, *"little Linda"* then as a next step was given the opportunity to address all her open questions and concerns in regards of her *"NeverEnding"* *"Acting Dream"* topic and as for it so often to be happening with those male "souls", Albert's as well went ahead by adding his own magical touch into the mix and smoothly succeeded to dismantle one doubt after another, until *"little Linda"* ran out of any further excuses and "exit door" options. Abracadabra. Which left me with the reality check that I just found myself stripped down to the "truth" that my soul literally found "herself" only ONE MORE action step away from embarking onto my just reappeared personal *"Acting Dream"* s-Express train at its station. Wow. The whole world right then "literally" stood still for a few seconds, whilst *"little Linda"* found herself busy trying to grasp all that magic that was taking place within and around her vessel. Boah. Was that it? Did just burst that SpeCial door wide open, which I perceived as safely locked throughout basically all *"little Linda's"* adventurous *"Living on Earth Game"* travels? Wow. And right then, I suddenly noticed my inner voice's wonderful supporting words *"Yes Linda, that's it. "Thy Wish is my Command". Your "Ultimate Childhood Acting Dream" is yours. Take it if you still want it. This is your desired doorway "in". Now it's up to you* what you make out of it. "All or Nothing", right?" Yes. And that indeed was correct. Filled with excitement and LOTS of respect towards this newly transforming and still in progress existing reality check, my soul then went ahead, UPdated Albert's that "his" just successfully dismantled all my many fears and doubts on that matter and that I therefore found myself with ONLY one option left at hand, *"My application for an UPcoming 1 year Acting program with them."* Boah! What? Did my soul truly just spill out these magical words, which I believed to safe for another *"Living on Earth Game"* ride in a difFeRent vessel? WooHOO! Yes, "she" did. How amazing this whole NYFA excursion exercise simply made *"little Linda"* feel. Strike. After thanking Albert for his kind help, my vessel then happily ever after stepped back outside into the cold and into Manhattans vivacious and pulsating vibes, to where *"little Linda"* instantly felt the urge to reveal to its many avenues and streets that this was "it" and that her vessel would be returning next year in order to FiNALLy pursue her *"NeverEnding"* *"Soul Childhood Dream"* right here at the New York Film Academy. Yeeha! Filled with many powerful "heaven on earth" emotions, I then headed towards the right across the avenue held Union Square farmers market, began my inspirational journey of what I could be purchasing in my very near future, before my vessel happily kept floating UP north on could number 9 towards the Garment District and Time Square, while *"little Linda's"* *"Head Cinema"* already found itself busy running its UPdated *"Not even the Sky is the Limit"* trailer. Wink. Then, soon after a joyful and puRRing reunion with my beloved roommate Gina, my soul as a next step decided to begin with the creation of a newly needed game plan for my further required *"Stepping-Stone"* steps to walk upon on my, this chosen *"Acting. Uncertainty. Complete Life Change."* crossroad path. Uiii. And this task certainly caused *"little Linda"* some more respect, as she knew that this newly opened doorway would be changing EVERYTHiNG that she "knew". For good. Oh boy. A *"So let's then"* turned out to be my *"Positivity Card"* attitude pick by furthermore deciding to simply courageously keep on moving forward, as the beloved Universe after all led my soul to this point and path, which therefore required my trust as an "Actress" to Act upon its given "directions". Ok. Action. After the successful map creation of WHAT needed to get materialized next, I found myself left with seven essential needed transitioning tasks at hand, which included the 1) Filing my NYFA application, the 2) Waiting for my acceptance letter, the 3) Quitting my job and apartment with the each agreed 3 months' notice period, the 4) Applying for a student visa, the 5) Finding a new *"Home Sweet Home"* base in Manhattan for the time being, the 6) Putting all my belongings, including my car into storage, plus the 7) Finding a new "family" for my beloved fluffy "Sniffy" action steps. Sniff. Well and the latter definitely revealed itself as my toughest chore at hand, as *"little Linda"* 1) Became roommate with Gina ever since her vessel moved into her new home in Oberaach right after her return from Charlotte in 1996, which therefore made her 2) Feel very sad to leave her "baby" and travel companion of almost 10 years behind and this even more so, as she 3)

Found herself unsure of if her Swiss-German and cat language explanation skills where enough for "him" to really understand WHY her vessel soon would be disappearing out of his reality into a *"NeverEnding"* new *"Living on Earth Game"* adventure held on an *"Other Planet"*. Oh boy. Sniff. Speaking of "boy", my Gina's soul in fact used to be living in a male recognized vessel, which I ended up adopting from my Oberaach roommate right after we decided to end our rental agreement as part of my then UPcoming Swissair chapter optimizing *"Stepping-Stone"* action step. Yup. Well and this "sex accident" actually occurred during the night of which another former roommate brought this cute fluffy red and white kitty cat home to Oberaach. What?! *"Red and White"* again? What's up with that combination? For real. Hmmm. This reappearing "coincidence" certainly is starting to trigger *"little Linda's"* curiosity. Hmmm! Anyway, as this other roommate apparently was told by Gina's previous farmer "dad", that this few months young kitty kitty happened to be a thus far nameless female creation, he therefore instantly named his new "lady" Gina and found himself quite baffled once the vet told him differently a few days later. LOL. Cute. Well and as "Gina" fitted this sensitive, gentle and adorable "fella" just fine, he ended up keeping his name and got nicknamed *Schnüfeli* and *Sniffy* by *"little Linda"*, as soon as he moved in with her into their new Bottighofen home a few years later, as sniffing on everything happened to be one of his favorite *"FuN Fact"* activities. Well, besides sleeping, eating, puRRing, watching the birds outdoors via the window or to cuddle with his new mommy of course. Wink. My Sniffy with "No Doubt" used to be an amazing companion, my baby, and remains as another heart missed *"Extended Family Member"* of mine, who meanwhile is accompanying *"little Linda's"* many *"Living on Earth Game"* adventures alongside with my father. LOVE. And therefore, the finding a good home for my precious baby boy task revealed itself as the most important one for my soul, which prompted the wonderful Universe to send "us" THE perfectly ideal solution our way. Yeeha! As soon as the word of my newly forged plans started to cruise around in my then neighborhood, one of my lovely neighbors therefore soon happily approached me with the information that a mutual friend, who happened to get along with my Sniffy very well, showed his strong interests in 1) Moving into my apartment, 2) In keeping Gina as his roommate and in further 3) Buying my curtains. Boom. And. Boah! How cool was that, right? Yay! Of course, this "changing of the guards" proposal turned into the most perfect solution for everyone involved, which ensured a very smooth transition for my baby boy and the certainty for *"little Linda"* that her Sniffy would be blessed with a new, loving and carrying roomy, whom he knew and loved very much as well. Ahhh. Thank you! Before I started to put all of these many collected wheels into motion though, I as a next step first needed to fully take care of this reappeared *"Heart vs. Head"* tango contest, which certainly infused *"little Linda"* with some undesired uncomfortable and confusing emotions. Again. Oh boy. Yes, and as *Miss Fear* as usual decided to get things done "her" way, she therefore came to the conclusion to throw an oh so "helpful" *"Am I really and truly doing the "right" thing?"* question into my way by further underlining that these many mapped out action steps after all would be changing EVERYTHiNG with NO return ticket in sale ever, once this entire shifting process got set into motion. Ufff. So true. Even though my heart and soul remained strong in their knowledge that this "universal" felled choice was "it", I at times still ended up paying a little bit too much attention to this sneaky head voice of mine that determinedly kept on trying to stop *"little Linda"* from her "courageous" and "dangerous" plans at hand, which as a result led her to secretly wish for some on the horizon appearing CONS. Help! Anyone? Fact was, that I found myself about to pop this wonderfully over the past decade created *"Comfort and Safety Zone"* bubble and that reality check felt truly scary and amazing in one breath. UiiiAhhh! Well, and the probably most caused "difficulty" at hand, turned out to be the "truth" that my vessel this time around would be taking off for a *"NeverEnding"* declared period, as my soul already knew that the United States would be turning into my new chosen home country. Indefinitely. Yup. And for that reason, this new outlook of mine kept on running its therefore created *"Head Cinema"* clip in its replay modus that showcased Linda Wartenweiler's vessel jUMPing right over the edge into an unknown *"wiLD & Free"* state of falling experience. Ahhh! Help, *"little Linda"* truly needed a helping hand in order to shift that somewhat stuck switch back into her smoothly flowing *"Heart over Head"* desired state of mind channel, for which achievement therefore only left room for ONE success formula at pick. YES, amazing NENA. Ha! My mission this time around therefore ended up being the scanning exercise of all her many shared songs for those to my soul very eFFecTive resonating valuable clues and encouraging words as of HOW to *Start Anew*. HOW to *Step Over One's Fears*. HOW to *Stay Positive*. And most importantly, HOW to *Do Me*. Boom. My final kick and shift in this whole preparation process at hand, I found myself experiencing right after watching the newly purchased *"Nena feat. Nena"* concert DVD, which got recorded back in 2002. Yes. Spending almost 2 ½ magical hours straight "LiVE" with my newly adapted Heroess in my living room, truly filled my cup UP with LOTS of *Love, Joy, Confidence, Inspiration, Courage, Determination, Certainty* and with the result of experiencing my within slumbering and well-hidden *"inner Artist"* longing to burst out of its shell already. Yay! It worked. Thank you! Once I found *"little Linda"* equipped with all the to her "right" reasons and emotions to finally set these many collected wheels into motion, she then eagerly went ahead with her first marked To Do task, picked June 2006 as her starting date and therefore as a next step found herself filling out the in that brochure placed application form for her desired 1 year Acting program held at the New York Film Academy in New York City. Boah! Was this truly true? Yes! Then, on the following evening, December 18th 2005 it marked, I remember very vividly, how my hand found itself secretly slipping this very precious envelope into a local yellow post office mailbox on my way home from work. Done. Off it went. First task completed. Yay! The ball officially found itself rolling a little bit faster by then and with it the *"NeverEnding"* waiting period for

its approval began its course as well. Daily, *"little Linda"* therefore quickly would be checking her mailbox first thing after work in the hopes for another yellow envelope to appear right in front of her eyes, which would have travelled ALL the way from New York City to Bottighofen. Well, and this exercise I kept on practicing diligently Day in, Day out, Week in, Week out without the desired result. Hmmm. After another few weeks of this patience enhancing skill workout, I decided by mid-January 2006 that the arrival of this desired letter took way too long and therefore instantly reached out to NYFA via an e-mail in order to find out more about the whereabouts. Now guess what happened? Yup. My application apparently never made it onto their desk, which ended up being the news that my soul expected to read from their end. Ufff. And. Yay. Very relieved and happy, I therefore found *"little Linda"*, once she got filled with the knowledge that this desired *"Ultimate Childhood Acting Dream"* door presented itself still wide open for her to enter. Anytime. Perfect. Quickly, I therefore as a next step went ahead, decided to this time make use of the to me still kind of new existing online application option and sent it out with even more convincement that this door WAS the one that my soul desired to walk through next. Woohoo! Thank you for this powerful organized "delay". Wink. Then, on the following day, the desired confirmation notice for *"little Linda's"* acceptance into their, in June 2006 held 1 year Acting program already found itself sitting in my online placed mailbox, which filled my vessel with a mix of possibly every positive available emotion. LOL. With a LOUD and startled *"WOAH! What just happened? Did I, Linda Wartenweiler just get accepted to an 8 month Acting study adventure on the other side of the world, on this "Other Planet"? OMG! Is this REALLY happening right now or is this all simply a wiLD dream? Somebody poke me please! Gina?"* narration on this right in front of her eyes occurring life-changing reality shift, it suddenly hit my soul what was happening to "her" at that very *"Now Moment"*. Wow. Somehow, I truly just managed to 1) Metamorphose myself into one of those "lucky ones" from this *"Other Planet"*, 2) *"little Linda's"* almost 3 decades dated *"Acting Dream"* just manifested itself into Linda Wartenweiler's *"Living on Earth Game"* ride experience, which UPdate therefore proofs to me that 3) *"Dreams DO come True"*, guaranteed. Holy cow! And right then the encouraging *"Don't Dream your Life. Live your Dream."* quote my soul quickly adapted as "her" new "companion" by further releasing some *"Yeeha! New York, here I come!"* shouting sounds.

"STOP! In the name of LOVE"
Alongside with the reality check, that all of my many *"Acting. Uncertainty. Complete Life Change."* path created plans and visions gradually started to manifest themselves into the material world, my soul therefore soon developed the required urge to finally UPdate my beloved mom's and the ones of some of my dear friends about what was going to happen to all of us very soon. Uiii. My mom as usual reacted amazingly supportive as soon as she learned about *"little Linda's"* plans and even though she felt quite saddened to know that her only child would be "leaving" her soon

for a far, FAR away and *"NeverEnding"* planned adventure, her loving soul quickly put my needs in front of "hers" and sent me all "her" blessings my way. To this day, I am finding myself enjoying and appreciating her always very supportive, encouraging and loving soul to the fullest and "Heidi" definitely revealed herself as the PERFECT mom for mine, this *"Living on Earth Game"* ride as Linda Wartenweiler. Yup. Danke Mami. Love. My Danny as expected reacted quite saddened about my soon to be disappearance announcement himself and assured for it to be the perfect path to walk upon if it was led by my heart. And yes, a true *"Heart over Head"* decision, guided by my own inner guidance and by the magical Universe only, this decades ago envisioned *"Swimming AGAiNST the Stream"* choice certainly ended up being. At last. Yay! Then, my dear BFF added that his vessel of course soon would be stopping by for his usual visits, which Danny as already hinted earlier also did during my delightful Housekeeping School Adventure. LOL. Yes, and that weekend back then in the early 90ies, during which 1) My Möne and *"little Linda"* took this all the way from the Parkweg traveled "besty" to a by now legendary "Jacque-Files" excursion and the moment of 2) His introduction of my Geneva host families "wonderfully" kept kitchen and carpet situation, certainly remain as our then most favorite collected *"FuN Facts"*. Guaranteed. Wink. Therefore, once again, HOW can one NOT love Danny's kind soul, right? With what an amazing BFF and "brother" I simply got blessed with so early on into my Linda travels. Love. And. Peace. For you. My Danny. Always. As soon as all my further close friends and *"Extended Family Members"* supported my newly forged adventures with their blessing as well, my soul then finally found "herself" ready to release "her" last and most challenging safety attached string. My TKB job. Yup. By now one might probably think that *"little Linda"* meanwhile turned into an opportunity quitting pro, right? Well, that actually happened to be what I assumed for myself up unto the morning of. Oops. How nervous my soul suddenly felt, as soon as my vessel found itself approaching my big boss's office door in order to hand in my 3 months' notice announcement. Oh boy. Part of WHY these feelings arose, surely led back to my knowledge of 1) My boss' appearance of feeling quite happy with my overall delivered work and TKB representation skills throughout the past 5 years, 2) That my soul's vessel this time got hired with more responsibilities and "importance" at hand, 3) The ending of Lucia's and *"little Linda's"* journey as a TKB dream team unit, 4) The arrival of my lasting closing moment of this adventurous, educational, diverse and FuN *"Swimming ALONG WiTH the Current"* TKB ride over a total duration of 10 years and lastly, the from *Miss Fear* underlined awareness "truth" that 5) Those many mapped out action steps of mine after all would be changing EVERYTHiNG with NO return ticket in sale ever, once this entire shifting process got set into motion. Uiii. And instantly, I therefore decided to take on my heart's following advice and found myself courageously jUMPing right over that appeared *"wiLD & Free"* screaming edge by accomplishing what needed to be done next. Boom. Thankfully, my wonderful boss himself ended up reacting very understanding and made my transition from a banker into a soon NYC student to be very easy. Thank you, OBR. Hugs. As far as of my "real" plans, I furthermore stuck to my decision of keeping them safe and sound from the general public ear, as *"little Linda"* still felt the need to protect her *"ongRowing"* Acting seed from any possible *"What? How could you possibly trade your amazing banking career for an unknown Artistic trial and this even abroad? Being an Artist is very hard and almost NO ONE will succeed. Linda, I don't think that this is a smart move for you."* reaction risks. Yup. These sorts of lines, my soul eagerly found "herself" avoiding for as long as possible. After all I happened to grow quite familiar with the typical Swiss mind pattern by then, especially when it gets confronted with an "unrealistic" seemingly *"Swimming AGAiNST the STREAM"* information flow. Ha! And this reality check therefore made *"little Linda"* out of safety reasons choose a more broad *"To study English in New York City for at least 8 months and to thereafter enjoy her life abroad for as long as her soul desired to"* approach for the majority of her interactions, which happened to be the absolute spot on "truth" as well. Ha! That's right. Then of course only 3 days after I mailed in my written notice to the HR Department as well, the magical Universe must have felt quite eager to find out as of HOW *Determined, Committed* and *Ready* *"little Linda"* really happened to be with her current *"Childhood Dream"* realization mission at hand by sending her a wonderful new soul along. What?! Yes. In the late 90ies, I believe it dates, we had this one guy from our Thurgau region, who suddenly kept on feeling an urge to revive the magical 80ies decade by organizing its theme-based genius and wonderful parties on Friday nights called *Wunderbar/Wonderbar* aka *WUBA*, which actually are still flying HiGH to this day. Yeeha! And. Bravo. As these parties ever since merely take place during the cold winter months, *"little Linda"* therefore only got granted a limited amount of "time traveling" opportunities per season, which fact of course had my vessel turn into one of their true and sparkling *"Girls just wanna have FuN"* regulars. Oh yeah! BiGSMiLE. WUBA simply offered everything for my soul to keep "her" a happy camper. 80ies Music All Night long. A 7 minutes' Drive away from my fluffy Sniffy. The Presence of many dear Old and Newly gained Friends, which also included Madeleine, Danny, Andrea, Marco, Sandy and my lovely neighbor for example, alongside with many other Familiar Faces and with the perfect "Family Style" based Atmosphere in a small environment in order for *"little Linda"* to *Let Go*, to *Celebrate*, to *Dance*, to *Perform*, to *Sing*, to *Create FuN*, to *Entertain*, to *Mingle*, to *DO* and *Be Me* during her travels right back to those Parkweg moments, with this as thrilling vibrating Time Machine offer at hand. zoOM. Magical every spectacle always ended up being. Oh yeah. Indeed. Now, on this particular Friday night, which as a reminder marks the 3rd day after my official notice announcement, as I found myself in the middle of celebrating my courageous letting go exercise amongst some of my girlfriends with a *"Rebel Yell"*, was when "it" happened. Ha! Filled with happy *"High on Emotion"* vibrations, *"little Linda"* therefore as usual kept on cruising as *"wiLD & Free"* as she loves to be singing and *"Dancing"* like a *"Maniac"* alongside to some of her favorite tracks on the dance floor and at times *"On The Ceiling"*, as suddenly one of her customers caught her attention in the crowd placed a little further away from her. As his head happened to be turning right at that very *"Now Moment"*, our both eyes therefore ended up meeting at the exact same second, which prompted my vessel to as *"Smooth as a Criminal"* walk towards his in order to for ONE say *"Hello? Is it me you're looking for?"* and to TWO also find out as of how he had been. Then, the closer that I approached, my eyes suddenly started to notice a quite handsome vessel standing right next to my "target", which on top of it also happened to contain a very charismatic soul. Boah. After a short small talk warm up, my friend then right away introduced my soul to his cousin's, or was he his nephew? Hmmm. My apologies. This minor detail completely slipped out of my memory collection right now. Oops. And. Blush. Wink. Well, I guess that gives to show how nervous this soul already found "himself" capable of making *"little Linda's"* feel, during that particular first encountered moment. BiGSMiLE. Very vividly I recall, how my heart instantly continued its beating concert with some even HiGHER chosen emotions, the second our both eyes connected. Yup. There was this bond. This familiarity. This "SpEciAl" connection that my soul only once prior came across during this, "her" current *"Living on Earth Game"* experience at run. Instinctively I felt that his soul resonated in to me rather SpEciAl recognized tunes and that mine wanted to get to know "his" better. Yes, I know, right?! 3 days after my final jUMP into this free-falling state of reality creation, I truly got confronted with this wonderful LOVE element. Really? Right now?! OMG. Timing is everything is all I can say. UFFF. Anyway, after paying my attention to this newly met "stranger" as well, it then turned out that he grew up in Erlen and that I of course happened to know most of his family members. Of course, right? LOL! The magical Universe and its famous synchronicity tricks. Wink. As this immediate attraction got felt on both ends, the two of us agreed, as soon as the party ended, to skip the exchange of our information for now and to instead simply meet again right there at a specific set spot in 7 days. Boom. Of course, this following week passed by a LOT slower than usual, which therefore had me access *"little Linda's"* well *"Head Cinema"* produced short film of last Friday's blessing in an *"ongRowing"* looping mode during this *"NeverEnding"* reconnection period ahead. Wink. Then, EXACTLY at 11pm on the following Friday, I nervously found myself waiting on the agreed spot for about 5 to 10 minutes and even though this lovely soul seemed to be missed, *"little Linda"* decided to pull out her *"Positivity Card"* in order to overpower her *"ongRowing"* disappointment, which pay off right after ended up appearing in front of her. WooHOO! Yes, all over sudden his vessel indeed disclosed itself out of a loosening up crowd just a little bit further away from my right-hand side, which thrilling discovery within a SNAP succeeded to cause for my heart to beat in its happy notes. Yay! He came! And immediately it took another jUMP and as soon as our eyes connected anew, our souls did too. Yup. This moment was all that it needed for my heart and emotions to truly get sparked and for my soul to even more so feel very drawn towards this charismatic "stranger's". Oh boy. Wink. And yes, before our vessels parted this time, we did so by exchanging our cell phone numbers, which led us to an immediate exploration journey on our many discovered mutual *"FuN Fact"* interests outside of this Friday nightspot as well. Smile. Yes, thankfully the wonderful rEvolution of this very convenient device called *Cell Phone* by then already occurred about 6 years ago in Switzerland, which therefore allowed almost everyone to own one. Well, and if someone happened to have missed this "train" at that particular time, then this soul definitely would have been considered as "weird" already. For sure. LOL. What *"little Linda"* instantly loved and appreciated about this new communication opportunity, turned out to be its voiceless feature called *Text Messaging* aka *SMS*. Boah! How cool and convenient this additional modern way of information exchange revealed itself as, which actually quickly reminded me of its "cousin", the e-mail. Yup. With this BiG cell phone shift, everyone suddenly even more so found themselves able to stay in touch with whomever via this incredible offered feature, which ever since allows one to either communicate in "real time" and/or in a "time elapsed" reality. 24/7. Genius this invention simply was, is and therefore it made it so much more convenient and "safer" in order to especially connect with one's new "flame". Wink. Yes. Finally, there showed up a new option that conveniently replaced this nerve wracking and brave Picking the phone receiver UP in real time as a first connecting Attempt exercise by instead simply composing a whatever desired message at any chosen moment of the day or night. Boom. Send. Beep. Beep. Delivered. This electronically fast speeding "paper and pen" technique certainly revealed itself as a very smooth and interesting way for me to get to know someone new better and to furthermore sense WHO this other soul "is" and where this connection possibly could be heading towards to. If at all. Yup. Personally, *"little Linda"* meanwhile very much so fell in love with this feature, especially with the later on born *Emoji's "FuN Fact"* option, which I am VERY certain of, my lovely *Co-Traveler*, you by now most likely kind of have picked up upon. Oops. Wink. LOL. Of course, this SpEciAl "stranger" and I instantaneously started to make use of this wonderful staying in touch opportunity as well and therefore always found my mouth instantly jUMPing into a BiG SMiLE creation, whenever his name appeared on my Nokia display. BiGSMiLE. Amongst the many mutual shared interests, of which to my surprise also belonged the from my "Twin Peaks" director Hero David Lynch's further genius, mysterious and thrilling "Mulholland Drive" motion picture creation, *"little Linda"* soon also came to realize, that the two of them also shared the same humor and that his *"little stranger boy"* kept delivering the exact "right" words at the perfect moment. Oh boy. What a blessing and "bad" timing in one. Of course, I early on let his soul in into my New York City forged plans and certainly right away acknowledged "his" disappointment arising behind "his" eyes. Ufff. Even though our both souls felt very drawn to each other, we agreed that for it to be the best to remain friends regarding our circumstances. "Facts" after all were, that he had his career and family plans set in Switzerland and my further *"Living on Earth Game"* adventures already got dedicated towards *"little Linda's"* reappeared *"Acting Dream"* s-Express train, that soon would be taking her ALL the way to this *"Other Planet"*, for which I found myself in a cat and mouse preparation contest for the past 1½ years by then already. Boom. So giving up this from the beloved Universe chosen *"Acting. Uncertainty. Complete Life Change."* crossroad path opportunity for someone *"SpEciAl"*, who I *"just"* met simply remained as an out of question option for my soul, as "her" love for this *"The Other Planet Dream"* vision counted many more decades at hand. Well, and the added thought of possibly creating a family with him or anyone else, by instead walking down the path of parenthood and wife as my full-time occupation whatsoever, still very much SO reliably happened to evoke quite some resistance within my vessel as well and to furthermore cause for *"little Linda"* to silently scream for *"HELP!"*, whenever confronted with. To this very day. YUP. Wink. Now, even though the two of our souls found themselves aware of all these many "facts", we still decided to spend as much time together as possible, as this SpEciAl existing soul chemistry happened to be alive No Matter what, which agreement therefore allowed for us to enjoy some many more FuN moments with one another. *"Heart over Head"*, here we go. Smile. Then, 1 month down the road, this lovely "stranger" came to confess that he just found himself having a conversation with his cousin/uncle about the two of us and that he right then came to realize that his soul would love to give "us" a shot. Maybe there would be a chance for us, somehow, to make it work and that *"One can Only Know the Outcome of Anything by Giving it its Fair Shot"*. After all, there still remained another 3 months, which seemed a good amount of time to explore what "we" were all about. Boom. His words went straight to my heart, as secretly I already started to really fall for him myself. Blush. Starting then, the two of our *"little Selves"* enjoyed a to me even more so magical adventure together before he then eventually started to pull back. Yup. Ouch. 3 weeks into our blossoming relationship, the beloved Universe already made sure to have his yearly 3 weeks military service course lined up and therefore sent his vessel away, which "only" allowed for us to be in unison over the way too short granted weekends. Bummer. Within every reunion moment, my soul then also started to notice an *"ongRowing"* distance shining from his end, which caused for my heart to beat in its sadder and sadder tunes by the days to come. Sniff. Then, alongside with his vessels last military service day, The End of our, to *"little Linda"* as very magical and FuN experienced unison, unfortunately and understandingly arrived as well. Oh, how my heart felt glOOmy about this newly from the outside world caused reality shift in my, this *"Living on Earth Game"* ride, my dear *Co-Traveler*. We all have Been there. Done that. At least once. Right? After my saddened soul confronted "his" with the "why's" of our sudden and contradictory ending, "his" kind heart then began to UPdate my awareness with a *"Linda, I really love being with you and I believe that you could be THE one. Honestly, I was secretly hoping that you would stay here with me.*

But I also know by now that you MUST DO what you decided to do. I fully support you in that. But I also know that I can't do a long-distance relationship with you. We don't even know for how long you will be gone for. Having you so far away definitely would be very hard for me. I just think that it's for the best to end "us" here before we even get more attached to one another and therefore cause more pain to our hearts." confession. Boom. Hearing his heartfelt and truthful words wounded mine even more so, though it also knew that "his" happened to be completely spot on. From a down to earth perspective, our both' pre-set *"Living on Earth Game"* dream visions simply differed quite a LOT from one another and it all along was crystal clear that his place remained in Switzerland and mine out there in the *"BiG Wide World"* and this as *"wiLD & Free"* as Linda Wartenweiler longs to be. Yup. And this is HOW our short and very crisp *"Love is a Battlefield"* story ended and HOW both of our vessels thereafter continued to follow each's separate adventures anew on their desired and destined OWN picked paths. Bye-Bye. Though know that *"I've had the Time of My Life and I Owe it All to You."* Thank you. With that new reality check at hand, I then, besides the Getting Ready for my Leaving mission, also found myself busy with the additional *"Self*-created" added Taking care of *"little Linda's"* aching Heart task. Oh boy. Even though we both decided to part, the lovely Universe still made sure to have us bump into one another here and there on the weekends and these "accidental" encounters always succeeded to hit my heart and soul with many bittersweet OuchYay vibrations. About 2 weeks prior to my departure, our two souls then mutually, during one of these "bump in" occasions, came to decide, that we should allow ourselves one last getting together in order to leave "us" in a proper and peaceful "goodbye" state of mind behind, which outlook of course instantly left my inner world with the eFFecT of finding myself awfully nervous and excited about this one more granted evening, with this to me very SpEciAl soul. Thank you. As meeting point for our *"Last Goodbye"* evening together, our both souls decided to pick one of my favorite outdoor restaurants that is located right at the Lake Constance in *Uttwil* TG, where we as planned, ended up enjoying a few more wonderful hours talking, sharing and well wishing. Then, after our vessels separated themselves with a final warm and loving hug, *"little Linda"* continued her *"Living on Earth Game"* travels towards Zurich, to where she planned on meeting some of her dear friends in order to celebrate life one more time as a unit in the midst of some smooth and exhilarating Techno and House tunes. Yeeha! *"Let's Rock 'n Roll!"* Interestingly, during this ride to Zurich, it suddenly came to my attention that my soul shifted "herself" into this very much-needed and intended peace of mind reality state and that my heart meanwhile found itself able to accept things for what they were. Wow. And. Yay! And right then, the magical Universe decided to finally reveal its "true" intentions with this entire bittersweet *"Love is a Battlefield"* story at hand, by sending *"little Linda"* some very interesting thoughts, including an "eye-opening" birds view perspective vision her way. Hooray! With meeting this wonderful man, I actually had been granted the opportunity to receive a glimpse of what my current *"Living on Earth Game"* ride could look and feel like on the "other side" of my already chosen new pathway. Meaning, that the loving Universe for that reason made sure to send my soul LOVE "her" way, a SpEciAl someone with whom I maybe could have created a family with and worked part-time as the office help in his already own envisioned future business plans at hand. Then, on my already chosen *"Swimming AGAiNST the Stream"* path, I found *"little Linda"* eyeing on her oh so long desired opportunity to finally get united with her Acting and living in the United States *"Soul Childhood Dream"* vision. Well and this scenario then instantly triggered the very famous "The Matrix" scene into my *"Head Cinema"*, in which handsome Neo aka Keanu Reaves was given a choice of 2 difFeRent pills to swallow *Blue* or *Red*. Depending on his choice, he then would either be continuing his existence with either his "Old, *Blue* and Ordinary" version of life, that also included the erasure gesture of Neo's just discovered very important Life Purpose and Soul Mission at hand and with Neo's *Red* pick, he would be granted to further stay and experience his adventures in "The Matrix" with a Lifetime Commitment with NO return ticket on sale ever, starting right then. Guess which path Neo picked, if you happened to have missed this mind-bending Movie thus far, my lovely *Co-Traveler*? Correct. Neo picked the latter. His Life Purpose and Soul Mission at hand. The unknown, *Red* and "risky" path. And so did I. Boom. Once this very important scenario was brought to my attention, my soul and heart therefore instantly found themselves able to grasp the actual and dEEper meaning of my own two created crossroad options, which allowed *"little Linda"* to know from deep within that her already swallowed *Red* pill revealed itself as THE One and Only. And this with "No Doubt". Ha! And right in that very *"Now Moment"*, I came to witness how my *"The Other Planet" "Living on Earth Game"* mission shifted itself from a I WANT to into a I HAVE to state of reality "truth", which suddenly let the past few months shine in a complete difFeRent light. Wow. Yes, everything truly unfolded itself exactly the way it was supposed to and within the following few seconds, it got clear to me that my soul needed to carry out PRECiSELY, what my lovely SpEciAl soul teacher happened to be trying to teach mine as a last lesson at hand. YUP. And this action step revealed itself as the essential *"Letting go of Something that No Longer Serves One's Growth and Expansion."* equation. Ufff. Ok. Sniff! Abracadabra. And therefore, it officially was time to Move On, to Let Go and to Refocus on what REALLY mattered the most, my *Self*. Thank you! Thank you for this wonderful, electrifying, magical, short, crisp and *"NeverEnding" "Head Cinema"* love adventure file creation opportunity, which *"little Linda"* certainly will always cherish safely within her heart and in her SpeCial treasure box. LOVE. Even though my soul found "herself" cruising in this loving *"Living on Earth Game"* experience throughout these past few months, my focus at the same time of course diligently remained on my earlier preset Seven essential needed Transitioning map and the closer June approached, the busier my days therefore transformed themselves into. Thankfully. Wink. As the time frame for my travels remained as a

"NeverEnding" and uncertain amount of days experience, I decided to further hold on to "little Linda's" belongings. At least for now. Luckily, one of my dearest girlfriends, who definitely counts as another "Extended Family Member" and WUBA companion of mine, at that time used to be the owner of a house with an almost empty attic in "little Linda's" 2nd home base village Romanshorn. Bingo. After checking in with Rebi about the option of having my boxes and furniture stored UP there for the time being, she thankfully instantly agreed by adding that her soul would feel more than happy to at least have part of "mine" close by her vessel, once mine would be taking off in a few weeks. Love. Strike. Merci. Ticked off. VW Polo next. Now, as Rebi happened to know of someone with an empty and unused garage, I therefore as a next step went ahead, reached out to our mutual friend and Boom. Done. Too. Fantastic. Left there were 1) "little Linda's" new NYC "Home Sweet Home" base and 2) The passing of her UPcoming scheduled student visa interview at the US Embassy in Bern BE. As my soul very much so found "herself" being drawn to the East Village at that time, I therefore decided to set my starting out position right in that as Artsy interpreted neighborhood by further making use of this super convenient Internet researching helping tool. Wow. Within a short amount of time, "little Linda" already found exactly what she was looking for and ended up signing a rent agreement of a "hip" and furnished 1-bedroom apartment with brick walls for 8 months that was located in the East Village on 13th Street, between 1st Avenue and Avenue A. Boom. As how easy this apartment hunting on another continent simply revealed itself as. Praise the Internet. And left there was my interview in Bern, which as everything else successfully got completed too within a few heartbeats. Beat. Beat. Beat. Wink. Once my vessel found itself standing in front of an immigration officer and as his eyes spotted my M1 student visa request for the Acting program at the New York Film Academy, his soul then right away happily released a *"Oh you are going to be an Actress? Please remember me, whenever you will be winning the Oscar!"* comment, whilst his hands simultaneously approved my *"Ultimate Childhood Dream Vision"* boarding ticket with its needed stamp and signature. WooHOO! That's it! I made it! And right in that very *"Now Moment"*, "little Linda" finally found herself taking her designated seat in the reappeared *"Acting Dream"* s-Express train wagon, thanked this kind soul with a BiG SMiLE on her face for his priceless and life-changing gesture by furthermore assuring that she certainly would do so and will. Woot! Woot! *"Let's Rock 'n Roll!"* Then, April 30th 2006 brought along my very last day of this further *"Swimming ALONG WiTH the Stream"* trial of another 5 ½ years and an additional important key moment for my many *"Living on Earth Game"* adventures ahead in this Linda Wartenweiler experience. Yup. As soon as my vessel successfully found itself locking the front door for the very last time as a bank manager in Erlen, my replacement, who interestingly happened to carry my father's name, HA, already awaited "little Linda" outdoors as arranged in order for us to exchange our two positions, symbolized by dropping all "my" TKB keys into one of his palms. BOAH. What glorious and powerful emotions this handing over gesture simply ended up triggering within my vessel, the second that I, narrated by a joyful *"Please take good care of "my" little bank"*, found myself enabled to let THE key chain fall into his open hand, which prompted this now new and responsible bank manager's soul to happily assure that "he" would. Boom. Chapter closed. Or as NENA sings it *"Der Anfang vom Ende/The Beginning of the End"*. Yay! Then, as soon as we gave one another our blessings and well wishes, *"little Linda"* right away got welcomed by a new *"Time to say Goodbye"* moment and off her HiGH vibrating vessel with a LOUD *"BYE-BYE"* headed towards her in 2002 UPgraded silver VW Polo. Once I found myself safe and sound placed in it, my awareness senses then all over sudden hit me with a *"OH MY GOD. I did it. I just officially closed my banking chapter for GOOD. That's it. I am Free. WooHOO!"* Yes, this realization truly felt very powerful and led my soul to further notice that an iNCREDiBLE rush of tremendous Freedom and Excitement sped throughout my entire vessel. As those sensations quickly developed themselves into a quite overwhelming level, I therefore decided to release some of them by screaming out LOUD and with some jUMPing UP and down movements on my car seat. Ahhh! AAAHHH!!! Ahhhh. How good and liberating this Letting Go exercise simply felt, my beloved *Co-Traveler*. Smile. Then, once most of these intense energies successfully got removed out of my system, *"little Linda"* happily decided to start the engine of her travel companion, chose an amazing Trance track from her 12-disc CD changer and off these two vessels "flew" right back home, within my already *"Ultimate Childhood Dream"* entered chapter. Yeeha!

* * *

The to me very cool awareness check with this above ignited key moment transition, to my surprise rather quickly revealed itself with the wonderful "truths", that I actually ever since am finding myself cruising within a as Permanent Vacation interpreted state of mind reality creation and that this lifestyle choice on top of it all even within a SNAP succeeded in resonating in its MOST perfect harmonious available tunes with my cheering heart and *"wiLD & Free"* soaring soul. Ha! Way to go. Right?! Now, WHAT exactly am I referring to here. Well, with those to me as quite powerful interpreted discovered decisions of ONE Stepping Outside of my *"Comfort Zone"* by TWO Disregarding my many from my OH so protective and concerned head voice delivered *Miss Fear* based statements and to instead THREE Bravely start *"Swimming AGAiNST this undesired Stream"* at pick, I successfully found myself diving right into my soul's most wanted Own Freedom and Rhythm flow creation, by furthermore floating straight out of the to "her" as rather limiting resonating, though quite enriching appearing "logical system" reality. Bye-Bye. With these many from my heart led *"Soul Childhood Dream"* based action steps at hand, I therefore unknowingly ended up becoming my Own Boss "again", just about the way as my soul used to experience it during those *"NeverEnding"* magical Parkweg days. Woohoo! That's right. And this *"Self*-created" personal "truth" choice meanwhile revealed itself as an absolute priceless gift to my soul and to *"little Linda"*, which furthermore keeps my heart beating in its *"ongRowing"* grateful melodies. *"Moment-to-Moment"*. Day in. Day out. Except for some "minor", soon appearing starting out interruptions. pOops! Wink. Now, have I ever experienced any regrets towards my choices? Nope. Would I pick this *Red "Acting. Uncertainty. Complete Life Change."* crossroad path again? Yup. Within the next heartbeat and this with "No Doubt". Even though my soul got faced with quite some tricky and almost *"NeverEnding"* seemingly *"Living on Earth Game"* challenges on this *"Other Planet"*, I meanwhile thankfully came to realize, that all of it HAD to happen the way it unfolded in order for *"little Linda"* to be able to lastly metamorphose into this Linda Wartenweiler version that my soul from the get-go decided to explore in this current *"Living on Earth Game"* ride of "hers". Yup. A 100%. Now, as for my thus far MOST valuable collected *"Life Toolbox"* ingredient treasure, my soul warmly desires to inspire yours, my fellow *Co-Traveler*, with the once from Oprah's wise *"Follow your Hearts Desires. It will Lead you Towards your Destiny."* shared "truths" upon your many own further Upcoming *"Now Moments"* ahead, by *"ongRowingly"* reminding your *"Self"* that *"Your Time is Limited. Don't Waste it Living Someone Else's Life. Don't be Trapped by Dogma, which is Living the Result of Other people's Thinking. Don't let the Noise of Other Opinions Drown your Own inner Voice. And Most Importantly, have the Courage to Follow YOUR Heart and Intuition, they somehow already Know What You TRULY Want to Become. Everything else is Secondary."* Boom. And so it is, Mister Steve Jobs. Gratitude. LOVE.

* * *

My next adventure in this game called *"Living on Earth"* started on Friday, June 2nd 2006 at around 10am, right one day after my mom's birthday. HAPPY BIRTHDAY. This date also marks another important shift on my, this journey, as my soul found "herself" about to enter a new sphere existing on a difFeRent *"Planet"*, which in other words also could get expressed as *"The Next Level of "little Linda's" thrilling "Living on Earth Game" adventure at run."* Boom. After 3 decades of existing in my beautiful, "safe" and peaceful home country Switzerland, the time for my next BiG and UPgrading challenge finally found its way into my reality, which colorful spectacle alongside with time started to unravel itself as *An Artistic and "Self*-developing*" Boot Camp* exercise. Oh yeah. Now, in order for it to have its BiGGEST and most eFFecTiVE impact possible on Linda Wartenweiler's *"Growth and Expansion"* exploration curiosity, the intense, reckless and *FAST* pulsating Concrete Jungle simply seemed to have been THE most perfect spot for all the many prior to my soul's arrival set curriculum goals to get achieved in, and this as power*FULLY* as possible. *"All or Nothing"* right? Yeeha! That's right. On this particular June morning, my vessel therefore found itself "unknowingly" about to embark onto an 8½ year NYC "joyride", to where *"little Linda"* got presented with the opportunity to peek inside of *Pandora's* famous "magical" *box*, which ingredients revealed themselves as a wonderful *"Ying and Yang"* rounding UP match for her already quite preciously "Swiss" grown *"Life Toolbox"* collection at hand. Yay! FuN, educational, iNtenSe, transformational, wiLD, expanding and super interesting this to me thus far very EXCEPTiONAL Linda Wartenweiler chapter turned out to be. And this with "No Doubt". Welcome Aboard, my fellow *Co-Traveler*. Welcome Aboard. Please Fasten your Seatbelt and enjoy OUR ride. Let's GO!

* * *

NEW YORK CITY or *"Don't Dream your Life. Live your Dream."*

"Let's Get really ROCKED. Yeah. Let's go ALL the way."

After spending the whole month of May in my newly gained freedom with my dear roommate Gina, with all my beloved friends and in my soon "old" to be reality creation, I finally found myself Ready and well equipped with 1) My very loyal ex-Swissair travel buddy, a dark blue Samsonite suitcase, 2) A dark green in 1996 purchased NYC GAP tote bag, 3) A TKB backpack, 4) A from some of my wonderful TKB lady friends gifted "Madagascar" handbag that featured Melman, the hypochondriac giraffe, 5) With my *"Red and White"* Swiss passport, 6) Two one way British Airways tickets, which included a London transfer, 7) With many thrilling vibrations and lastly and most importantly, 8) With my well-produced *"THE Ultimate Childhood Dream" "Head Cinema"* clip, standing amongst my mom's, Danny's and two other dear friends' vessels at Zurich's airport. Wow. Soon. Very soon, my transitioning from the small apple into the Big Apple would be completed and *"little Linda"* therefore truly would be finding herself existing within her for decades projected *"Head Cinema"* creation. Boah! Ha, you probably might be asking yourself "still", what this "small apple Big Apple" comparison is all about, right? Well, as the most apple growth in Switzerland happens to occur within my beloved root canton, it therefore alongside our history path at some point got nicknamed *"Mostindien/Cider India"* by my oh so charming Swiss Confederates, which spot from a "planetary" point of perspective certainly has it appear to me as New York's small "uncle". LOL. That's right. Now, as my lovely support system and I nervously found ourselves in front of the check-in area enjoying the remaining precious minutes as a unit, my eyes suddenly came to spot two surprising "guests", which happened to be the vessel of 1) Another longtime and dear *"Extended Family Member"* of mine, accompanied by 2) Her first born baby boy's. Wow. What an exciting eFFecT their out of the blue appearance simply caused on *"little Linda's"* heart, especially as Andi's and my soul lastly connected the night before over the phone. Ha! Surprise! Very grateful, I therefore instantly felt about this just granted LiVE opportunity to one more time see and embrace my ex-volleyball team member, travel and dance companion Andi-Schätzeli, including cutie boy Lars. Merci. Danke. Yay! Alongside with my dear friend's arrival, my UPcoming next *"Time to say Goodbye"* moment of course kept on approaching with every inhaling breath as well and this reality check definitely left everyone in a quite visible heightened emotional state of mind, especially as this time around my vessel's disappearance counted an "unknown" and *"NeverEnding"* amount of days. Beat. Beat. Heartbeat. Then, as soon as the moment of "truth" finally arrived for *"little Linda"* to start walking on her "own" again, I quickly found myself hugging each one of my beloved ones for a last time, for now, wished them well and got myself Ready to dive right into my newly found MUST DO project at hand. Let's Go! Filled with LOTS of curiosity and excitement about this *"ongRowing" "Acting Dream"* chapter, my vessel therefore shortly after found itself embarking its old workspace of nearly 2 years, which reality check instantly triggered for my vessel to fill itself with those lovely *"Home Sweet Home"* emotions. AHHH. Once my transition in London was completed, I then got granted the opportunity to sit next to a German uncle and his nephew, who gave me some nice company, whilst we all kept shooting through the heavens at the speed of light. zoOM. The flight therefore passed by very quickly and about 7 ½ hours later, our pilot successfully found himself landing the aircraft safe and sound on Newark's tarmac. USA. Yay! Welcomed we all got by a heavy rainstorm and with LOTS of wind. Ha. What a "warm" greeting and start this gesture simply turned out to be. *"Well, well. Hello New York"*. Wink. As the Germans found themselves about to head to Manhattan as well, we therefore decided to share a cab, which provided my soul with some further "home" company feelings, for a little bit longer. Once the two male vessels stepped outside of their seats, the cab driver then dropped mine off at my new home address on East 13th Street in the East Village, whilst the water still kept on smashing these "cats and dogs" down to the ground. Quickly, I therefore carried my few belongings and myself to the dry area in front of the apartment building, that carried the number that my eyes were looking for. From there, I then reached out to my landlord so that he could let me into the dry hallway and hand me over my own set of keys. Once this exchange successfully got completed, his vessel then vanished as quickly as it appeared and left I found myself with my last task at hand. Moving into my new apartment. Yay. Very soon though, my soul came to understand, as of WHY my new and "gentlemanlike" landlord's happened to be so eager to take off as quickly as "his" did. The schlepping procedure of my "few" belongings all the way UP to the 5th floor actually turned itself into a rather heavy-duty experienced workout, which activity instantly reminded my soul of its "then" undertaken Grabbing, Squeezing and Willpower exercise that ended up transporting my vessel from that "small bubble into this BiG earthy one" via its only available exit door at hand. Ha! That's right. Here we go again. Wink. Thankfully, the beloved Universe sent my vessel about half way into my Schlepping everything UP the super steep Staircase task, one of my friendly new male neighbors my way, who ended up happily offering his strength to *"little Linda's"* rescue. Ufff. Gratitude. As soon as everything and myself successfully got placed safe and sound in front of my new *"Home Sweet Home"* floor, the *"Open Sesame"* moment welcomed my reality as the next action step at hand and somewhat exhausted, my vessel then finally found itself entering into its new home space, located in this newly entered "sphere". Hooray! Done. The "apple" exchanging journey lastly got successfully completed. That's it. Boah. Once inside, my eyes then came across a rather tiny Artsy space, alongside with the discovery that its advertised living room area "somehow" vanished. Bummer. After the completion of taking my vessel's newly picked home area of 8 months carefully in, my soul then at some point came to the conclusion that 1) This 1 bedroom apartment definitely appeared a LOT more spacious online then it did in "person", that 2) It's monthly rent therefore suddenly seemed rather HiGH for what I actually was "purchasing" and this awareness check as a result instantly left me with the feeling of 3) Having come across a "Less for More" bargain. Ufff. Yes, and right in that moment, *"little Linda"* warmly got introduced to the Big Apple's charming *"Welcome to New York City, Miss Fresh Off the Boat"* existing reality, which led her to the impulse to end this rather long 2nd of June day with a refreshing shower, followed by some much-needed rest. Splash. Good night. A few hours later, right after the lovely sun began its soothing kissing session on my face, my inner voice then suddenly threw my vessel with a LOUD *"Rise and Shine! Rise and Shine!"* wake UP call out of my bed. Even thought my Nokia screen informed my brain of its early 7am hour, *"little Linda"* certainly felt very excited to for once begin a new day with the "birds", as usually she would feel prompted to simply turn sideways again in order to continue her many adventures in dreamy land for at least another 3 hours. Ha! This morning unraveled itself to be difFeRent and my curiosity instead overpowered my still existing melatonin, which led my, with LOTS of happiness filled vessel to jUMP right out of my quite comfortable bed. New York? Is this really you? Wow. Yes, it really seemed like as if my soul just opened her eyes in my new East Village apartment in Manhattan and this in "real life" and "real time". Boah. What?! Or was I maybe still dreaming? Well, and the only way of solving this puzzle at hand, turned out to be to 1) Get Ready and to then 2) Step onto 13th Street. ASAP. Yay! Once I found myself exiting through the front door of my building a few minutes later, my vessel unmistakably found itself standing in the middle of New York City's pulsating vibrations. How incredible this early morning reality check simply felt. Wow. Yes, everything was still vibrating, LOUD and wiLD exactly the way as *"little Linda"* remembered for it to be, which "truth" still had her questioning here and there, whether this all was "true" or simply part of one of her oh so glorious *"Head Cinema"* productions. Ha! Soon though, I came to believe that I successfully sneaked my way into my *"Childhood Dream"*, as all the many yellow cabs, the sirens, the honking, the various diverse looking vessels, the architecture, the car shapes and sizes, the language and the stores smelled, felt and sounded so foreign, familiar and surreal all in one powerful magical package. Yes, I made it. This by now slowly started to sink in. Yeeha! Then, once I fed myself with a yummy in peanut butter covered and toasted everything bagel from the around the corner located David's Bagel bakery, my soul finally felt Ready to dive into "her" *"ongRowing"* with challenges and opportunities filled *"Living on Earth Game"* expansion ride ahead. *"Concrete Jungle here I am. And yes, NOW I am Ready to get All the way ROCKED. The question is, are YOU?!"* Ha! Now, since the calendar counted 2 more days until my New York Film Academy chapter would be starting its "mysterious" course, *"little Linda"* therefore reacted very thrilled to as a next step jUMP right into her "famous" settling in and adjusting process mission at hand and to afterwards continue her explorations in her newly chosen hometown and this for the first time out of the perspective of a NYC Resident. WooHOO! As soon as my refrigerator found itself equipped with all the desired essentials and right after my new *"Home Sweet Home"* space got decorated and set up to my "cozyfication", my *"inner Adventuress"* was the one, whom I granted my focus next. Oh yeah! Finally, the moment arose for me to further explore Manhattans vibrating streets and avenues and this even accompanied with *"little Linda's"* entire "Swiss" Music collection. Boah. What?! Yes, just a few months prior to my take off, the beloved Universe kindly brought to my attention, that the in the Silicon Valley located Apple company released a very genius Music mp3 devise called *iPod* a few years prior. Well, and this information flow instantly sparked my entire fascination for it, as this cigarette package sized mini-computer found itself able to carry thousands of songs, if needed. Wow. And YES, that WAS needed. Ha! And therefore, I right away went ahead, purchased my, by now "classic" considered black iPod at Media Markt in *Winterthur ZH* and fed it with every single song that I could find in my Sony Vaio iTunes collection, which count ended somewhere within the "early" four thousand's. Oops. Wink. Genius this The Three "AppleTeers" combination truly revealed itself as for mine, in the small apple reproduced vessel during its with *"little Linda's"* Music enhanced new Big Apple *"Living on Earth Game"* adventure creations at hand. Oh yeah. Immediately, I therefore discovered that my two feet, accompanied with my own shuffle "picked" soundtrack blasting through my auricles, turned out to be THE perfect New York City exploration match in order to experience its pulsating vibrations and rhythm hands on. Yes, and these moments even more so transformed themselves into quite Movie and Music clip like experiences, especially whenever certain songs perfectly melted into alignment with my inner and outer awareness reality check. Boah! And right then, my soul began to fly HiGHER than a kite, fueled by many released adrenaline kicks, whilst *"little Linda"* instantly found herself transforming into the leading Actress of her right in front of her eyes appearing own *"Head Cinema"* screen. Into what a very happy camper my soul always ended up turning into right then. Yup. As true *"Don't Dream your Life. Live your Dream."* reality confirmations these moments always revealed themselves as. Woot. Woot. Thank you, Mister Steve Jobs. Thank you for having boosted those Walkman day experiences UP into the heavens, to where *"Not even the Sky is the Limit".* LOVE. Now, one of my first discoveries that I found myself quite baffled and astounded about during those two Manhattan excursion days, revealed themselves with the "facts" that 1) Almost every New Yorker appeared to own one of these

magical iPods or another sort of mp3 player inventions already, that 2) Practically everyone therefore chose to hide behind their earbuds, including sunglasses from the outer world as an *"ongRowing"* indoors and outdoors retreat habit and that 3) Technology literally seemed to slowly overtake every pedestrian as a next targeted game step. Boah! And yes, the latter definitely struck my soul the most, as from where my vessel just zoOMed in from, I actually happened to only be used to experience this kind of scenario associated with a workout routine and that was about it. Here, this new to me phenomena appeared to play an essential part of NYC's culture and lifestyle habit, with which my soul of course instantly resonated with and as a next step adapted as "her" new way of *"Getting into the* exploration *Groove"*. Oh yeah. Being surrounded by Music after all is part of *"little Linda's"* normality, ever since that to her very SpeCial mid 1970ies May Day and therefore reliably throws her right into this lovely *"Super Happy Comfort Zone"* reality, whenever exposed to. Ha! That's right. Then, after the completion of my quite impressive first 2 days settling in quest, June 5th 2006 finally brought along my oh so long-awaited New York Film Academy orientation opening moment, which attracted another about two hundred registered and curious Acting and Filmmaking students from all over the world to its, at the Union Square located headquarter. WooHOO. Action. Let's Go! As soon as all the needed information flow got exchanged and the registration process was completed, every 1-year student then kindly got asked to relocate themselves to their then in SOHO existing location, as all their classes took place "down there". With the arrival of everyone's vessel in their assigned classrooms, the moment then finally arose as well, during which I got introduced to all my fellow Acting classmates. Well and I must admit, that this happening unraveled itself as another quite astonishing reality check, as the entire class count for this first time ever in June starting NYFA Acting program contained a total of 12 souls "only". What?! Wow. Did my vessel somehow just get transported back to Zurich? LOL. And alongside with these news, *"little Linda"* then right away also was given one of her very first *Boot Camp* tasks from its itinerary at hand, which as already in Charlotte experienced turned out to be the all-time lovely age difFeRence "challenge". Yup. Here we go again. Welcome back to *"The Other Planet"*. Smile. Soon, I therefore came to learn that 10 out of my newly introduced "friends'" vessels entered into this earthy sphere within the time span of 18 to 24 years ago, which reality check thankfully left *"little Linda"* with student number 11, who's days count actually ended up matching the EXACT same amount as hers. What?! Yes! And with "exact", I do mean EXACT. Literally. Same day. Same year. Starting out point India. Boom. How crazy is that, right? This storyline actually gets even a little bit crazier. Ready? Sweet. Our both souls already happened to become aware of this super interesting "coincidence" spectacle during our NYFA orientation occasion. Yup. Right after I completed my registration process, I then as directed instantly went ahead UP to the 3rd floor in order to grab a seat in the already quite packed auditorium. Once my eyes detected a great empty bench seat right next to the wall to my left, I decided to occupy it immediately and found myself sitting next to another girl's vessel. Well, and as it so happens, once many strangers are amongst one another, the two of our souls certainly began to chit chat as well during this waiting period at hand and you probably already might be guessing, who this "neighbor" of mine turned out to be, my dear *Co-Traveler*. Exactly. My birthday "Twin". A fellow Kylie Minogue Gemini. Ha! This reality check certainly revealed itself as quite a mind-blowing experience to the both of our souls. Boah! Imagine a room filled with SO many other vessels and our both' happened to be placed right next to one another's. WOW. Two girls. Same birthday. Same year. Same *"Acting Dream"*. Same starting date. Including class. Boom. Impressed, I indeed found *"little Linda"* by then and even more so about the knowledge of having been granted this specific Gemini soul along of my *"Acting Dream"* travels. Well, at least for right now. Yup. Since the ticking of my *"Living on Earth Game"* Boot Camp adventure already began its countdown course, the beloved Universe therefore certainly needed to make sure to present *"little Linda"* with its pre-set and *"ongRowing"* challenging curriculum and continued its magical mission by getting my birthday twin pregnant with her second baby aboard. Boom. Boom. "Baby Boom". And gone her vessel out of the blue was after an Acting period of about 8 weeks. Bye-Bye. Bummer. With my "Twin's" disappearance, I as a result instantly found myself anew in this rather unused and uncomfortable situation of either being surrounded by the teachers quite older and by my remaining classmates younger vessels during each class. *"Oh no. Not again."* is what *"little Linda"* certainly kept on remarking and further found herself wondering WHY this phenomenon seemed to chase her *"ongRowingly"* within this *"Living on Earth Game"* ride of hers. Hmmm. Well, it surely seems to me by now that my soul must have chosen this kind of experiencing pattern for some kind of to me interesting *"Growth and Expansion"* reasons or that sort of "thang". Hmmm. One day, I am certain of *"little Linda"* will be presented with the answers at its perfect *"Now Moment"*. Until then, I shall simply remain *Exploring, Observing, Learning, Expanding, Growing* and *Connecting* all these many appearing dots for my own Life Puzzle at hand, I guess. Yup. And so *"little Linda"* will. One of the next challenges that my soul came to face, turned out to be the reality check, that 1) Basically all my remaining classmates just got granted their very first opportunity EVER to 2) Explore their own existence as freshly graduated High School and College students from every desired angle as *"wiLD & Free"* as they dared for it to be and this 3) Far away from their usual *"Home Sweet Home"* parenting base, just about the same way as *"little Linda"* found herself experiencing it during her delightful Geneva Housekeeping School Adventure. One and a half decades ago. Boom. What?! That long already? Boah. Wink. Well and this newly discovered "freedom" certainly kept on reflecting in their overall attendance and work ethic during the months to come, which on the other hand I find my soul understanding theirs very much so. How could one after all blame them, after being placed in this perfectly created playground, which allows SO much room for ANY heart desired explorations and thrilling *"Living on Earth Game"* adventure creations to choose from. And this 24/7. That's right. *"The City with its many Wonderful and Tempting Distraction Choices"* is how I perceive the Big Apple as of today. Oh yeah. Another few reality checks that our each thus far *"Life Toolbox"* ingredient collection comparison brought along with unraveled themselves with the "facts", that 1) The outside of our classroom-based exploration interests, discussion topics and the overall FuN creation interpretation varied a tiny tad from *"little Linda's"* usual "loves", that 2) She therefore often times caught herself thinking *"Been there. Done that. bzZZ."*, whenever her vessel got placed amongst theirs, that 3) All doors to any available bars and dance club exploration occasions remained regarding of almost everyone's under aged status as closed for a little while longer and lastly that 4) Money in general quickly introduced itself as THE reliable *"FuN Fact"* party pOoper to the crowd. BooO. There you go. And all these many added UP "truths" therefore had me realize quite soon, that once more the time had arrived for *"little Linda"* to bravely continue her many *"NeverEnding"* adventure creations on her own, as she already practiced it right after her Yoshi and Hitoshi road trip "trial" one exact decade ago, by further making use of her all-time helpful and magical *"Positivity Card"*. Abracadabra. During my newly created finding a "like-minded" soul quest, I therefore even more so intensified my already prior initiated scanning attempts of all the other available SOHO NYFA students at hand for a possible deeper connection opportunity, which option quickly started to fade away as well. Bummer. Very soon, my soul came to realize that 1) Every Filmmaking vessel already got bombarded with a Monday through Sunday filled classes and shooting schedule and that 2) All the other prior started few fellow same aged Acting student candidates already found themselves very well equipped with either a bestie and/or with an over the past 3 to 6 months formed strong class cohesion. Ufff. This whole *"Connecting and Belonging"* mission truly started to reveal itself as quite a bit more complicated than initially assumed in the City of Angels one year ago. Its "avoidance" after all showed UP as the number one reason, as of WHY *"little Linda"* considered the Big Apple as her possible *"Home Sweet Home" "Acting Dream"* study location after almost being defeated again. Hmmm. Well, there clearly must exist a very good reason for this reoccurring "bumper", as the magical Universe after all guided my vessel into this *"The Other Planet"* adventure. That's right. It really seems to me by now, that 1) This *"Connecting and Belonging"* task did play a very important role in my further own *"Growth and Expansion"* process at hand and that 2) The location of my studies actually ended up being secondary. What?! And yes. This reality awareness check would have been quite helpful to have come across earlier, as *"little Linda's"* magical *"Acting Dream"* s-Express train therefore could have dropped her vessel off in her original LA-LA-Hollywood-Land *"Cali Dreamin'"* envisioned destination instead. Oh men. Now, as I after all believe that *"Everything always happens for a GOOD Reason"*, my *"inner Adventures"* as a next step as usual went ahead, accepted things for what they were and decided to simply keep on pushing forward with all the newly attracted elements at hand. Alrighty. Let's Go then. Even though that I always tried my best to ensure to keep *"little Linda"* as much of a happy camper as possible by spoiling her with many of her favorite *"FuN Fact"* choices, her urge and desire to finally get to meet a "like-minded" soul in crime, with whom she could be sharing all the many inner and outer experienced Big Apple *"Living on Earth Game"* adventure creations with, by further being enabled to even happily giggle at the world as a unit, certainly kept *"ongRowing"* with every passing week. Yup. A few times, I actually found myself getting quite close for this desired bonding procedure to occur. However, these opportunities usually ended up missing the for its actual CLiCKing needed last two or three magical elements and therefore the search had to go on. Bye-Bye. Besides my own initiated Entertainment creation choices outside of the classroom environment, I therefore at some point decided to slowly begin to accept these incoming NYFA hanging out invitations anew, as being surrounded by their familiar vessels meanwhile started to invoke those soothing "home" feelings within my own. Even though that these *"Connecting and Belonging"* opportunity choices failed in the sense of hitting *"little Linda's"* spot the way that she REALLY loved it, I forced her to at least give the selected situations a fair trial and to make it work. Somehow. One never knows after all, right? Right. *"Head over Heart"* here we go, I guess. Smile. Staying *Positive* and *As Open As Possible* remained as my usual game plan choices at hand, which results mostly welcomed my reality anew with the *"NeverEnding"* "truths", of finding myself 1) Being uncomfortably bzZZ bored with where my vessel got placed in and that 2) *"little Linda"* seemed to *"ongRowingly"* apply the "wrong" keys in order to shift those opportunities back towards her happy state of heart desire. Hmmm. And that is how my very dear and loyal travel companion *Mister Loneliness* welcomed "himself" with a this time very LOUD and joyous *"SURPRiSE, I AM HOME"* announcement back into my newly created reality again. Oh nO. Here "he" was again and this even though, I prior eagerly tried my BEST to get rid of "his" existence once and for all, as *"little Linda"* TRULY disliked this very uncomfortable and all time low vibrating eFFecT that his presence caused to her soul. Ouch. Go AWAY! The stronger his appearance grew, the more I therefore kept on pulling my beloved *"Positivity Card"*, which to my surprise at some point slowly started to lose all of its magical and helpful powers. Abracadabra. Abracadabra! ABRACADABRA!! Help!!! Anybody?! Please?! Well, and the most useful help in that particular *"Now Moment"* probably would have been the UPdate for *"little Linda"* on the "truth" that her core *"The Other Planet"* *"Life Toolbox"* ingredient lesson simultaneously to *Mister Loneliness'* appearance already began to run its *"ongRowing"* course in this colorful Concrete Jungle *Boot Camp* adventure chapter of hers. What?! What are you talking about?! Well, let's just dive right into it, my beloved *Co-Traveler*. Shall we? Splash. This core *"The Other Planet" "Life Toolbox"* ingredient lesson, out of my one decade later *Dot Connection* opportunity exercise delivered conclusion, revealed itself into my awareness as *"The Management of a to my soul preciously granted infinite "Abundance of Time" gift, which "she" EXCLUSiVELY gets to share with Linda Wartenweiler on a difFeRent "Planet", FAR away from "her" usual accessible "Comfort Zone" reality exit door opportunity."* Boom. That's right. What a genius game plan, this move on the chessboard simply turned out to be in retro perspective. Ha! Indeed. Wait! Though, WHAT exactly was *"little Linda"* supposed to GAiN out of this from the magical Universe delivered generous "Abundance of Time" gift with my own *"Self"*? Well, let's find out then. Wink. This quite unexpected, exquisite and powerful gift, I came to realize only recently, actually ended up being part of my entire and own personal accustomed NYFA *"Living on Earth Game"* adventure experience. What? That's right. By the end of my first week within my oh so desired *"Acting Dream"* reality, *"little Linda"* soon came to realize that those 3 full school days, including the assigned homework for the remaining 4, provided her with a LOT more free time than assumed. To study my *"Soul Childhood Dream"* as a full-time student from my end got interpreted and expected as to find myself about as busy and pre-occupied throughout these following 8 months to come, as my Filmmaker friends happened to experience it. My soul after all desired to grow as much as possible as an Actress, by learning "everything" of its to me very valuable craft, so that *"little Linda"* right after her graduation in January 2007, could be heading out there and "play" and this as *"wiLD & Free"* as she loves her *"Childhood Dream"* to be. Boom. Well, and right around that time, I came to realize that my soul's ambitious *"Growth and Expansion"* outlook differed quiet a tad from the world of Art, or at least from the one that the New York Film Academy provided. Bummer. At first, it actually happened to be really easy for me to make the most use out of this unexpected extra provided time at hand. *"Fun Fact"* activities like *Attending* my all day filled *Classes* on Mondays, Wednesdays and Fridays, one hour Meisner Technique *Rehearsals* with my assigned classmate, completing my other assigned *Homework*, *Reading* "The Da Vinci Code" in English at a Starbucks, *Watching Movies* on the "actual" cinema screen or on TV, with difFeRent *Excursions* and *Explorations*, occasional *Meet Up's* with other souls, *Working Out* at New York Sports Club, *Improving* my English, NYFA student *Short Film Shoots* here and there over the weekends, *Listening* to *Music* at the back then still at Union Square existing Virgin Megastore or on this genius iPod "classic" invention, with my first *Swiss Accent Reduction Mission* approach, *Adjusting* and *Finding* "little Linda's" *New Flow* and with *Getting to Know New York City's "Soul"*, including its other approximately 1.5 Million inhabited ones better, therefore ended up receiving most of my attention, which actually kept my soul a quite happy camper. For some time. With "No Doubt". Oh yeah. At some point though, *"little Linda's"* magical MUST DO To Do list found itself running towards its end, "normality" in exchange began to welcome her newly created reality, which eFFecTs as a response left her with 1) An *"ongRowing"* "Abundance of Time" gift at hand and with 2) A by then quite strongly developed "like-minded" soul in crime company awareness desire. Ufff. During these small apple Big Apple transitioning and adjusting days, my soul then further came to notice that "her" overall being back in Manhattan reality check on one hand truly felt *"Dream come True"* like and on the other also a tiny tad more intense then all "her" previously experienced "culture shock's" in count. That's right. Well, after all my vessel "just" relocated from the with 1'900 populated Bottighofen into this city's quite crowded developed mish mash creation. Ha! Go figure, right? small apple. Big Apple. Crunch. Yum. And yes, certainly *"little Linda"* had existed in this quite "wiLD" pulsating environment a few times prior, though always out of the eyes of a visitor and this for maximum of a few days in a row, which reality check left my count UP onto this Big Apple reunion with 4 Days in 1996, 3 Nights in 2005 and a few layovers of 1 or 2 nighters per rotation during my adventurous Swissair chapter. Oh yeah. With these past-created experiences at hand, I therefore of course found *"little Linda"* still floating quite FAR off from being a Big Apple pro or from being a "real" New Yorker per se. Ha! Well and in order for anybody to properly and successfully metamorphose into this quite interesting "New Yorker" *"Empire State of Mind"* phenomena, it takes one according to a saying approximately 7 years, which UP unto this shifting point leaves all those many "New Arrivals" travel in its from the native New Yorker's considered *"Fresh Off the Boat"* awareness experience. Yup. And so it is. Been there. Done that. Confirm it. Wink. Now, even though I suddenly found myself standing in front of all these quickly accumulated inner and outer presented Concrete Jungle challenges, my *"inner Adventuress"* thankfully ended up reacting the least impressed and therefore even more so decided to eagerly keep on pushing forward on this, her chosen *"Acting. Uncertainty. Complete Life Change."* reality creation path and this equipped with LOTS of *Passion, Determination* and through the this time *"Eye of the Tiger"* chosen perspective. Growl. One happy factor that *"little Linda's"* heart always instantly prompted to vibrate in its higHER available tunes, happened to be the thrilling outlook of all the many already confirmed, including the further *"ongRowing"* inflowing *"Extended Family Member"* visit announcements, starting September until February 2007. Yay! About 20 dear soul friends, mine therefore soon would be able to welcome Two-by-Two in "her" quite narrow 1-bedroom Big Apple apartment, which actual materialization result transformed itself each time into its own very SpeCial, absolute FuN and memorable *"Living on Earth Game"* adventure. LOL. Oh yeah! And right here follows my BiG THANK YOU to all of those many supporting souls, who found their ways to my cozy brick wall East Village apartment during these to me quite challenging transitioning days, by filling UP my well magically well. Precious all the many air mattress and bed sharing moments truly remain within my heart, as they reliably trigger *"little Linda"* to GiGGLE about as hard, as she experienced it back then with beloved Heidi and Urs. Giggle. Giggle. Giggle. Wink. Love. Now guess, who showed up as my VERY first visitor? Yes? Yes! My beloved BFF of course. Woohoo! As promised, his and his partner Harry's soul immediately went ahead and purchased their flight tickets to JFK, the second everything in terms of my schedule and housing situation got revealed. Ahhh. Now, even though The Third Musketeer this time around already got provided by Danny, the beloved Universe on top of it all decided to spoil *"little Linda"* a bit further by adding our Geneva buddy Möne with a few days overlapping "coincidence" as a perfectly forth vessel match into this *"Extended Family Member"* reunion mix. Yay! And yes, it officially was family time and those many soothing and FuN reconnecting hours throughout the granted 10 days in a row, certainly unraveled themselves as the perfect "opening" Act for my further travels ahead. Gratitude. Both of my loyal Musketeer members actually ended up stopping by in a total of 4 times during this colorful New York City *"Living on Earth Game"* Boot Camp ride of mine. That's right. Every other year. True love. The first three occasions actually turned out to be ordinary planned trips and number 4 arose as a wonderful and well appreciated universal "accident", which incidence sides *"little Linda"* instantly got interpreted as a *"Magical and Unexpected Gift from the Heavens."* LOVE. Now, as both of my beloved friends in 2014 decided to spend their vacation in sunny Cali for once, the magical Universe therefore had them book an appealing flight from Zurich to Las Vegas, which included a short transfer stop at *JFK* NY. Then, since the Three of our Musketeer vessels for some soon to be revealed reasons found themselves being kept apart for a quite *"NeverEnding"* period of time already, the supporting Universe therefore swiftly went ahead and used this opportunity to have them "accidentally" miss their connection flight to Las Vegas. Yeeha! And. Strike. Well, and *"little Linda"* with "No Doubt" very much so found herself delighted about this unexpected UPdate via her meanwhile UPgraded silver black iPhone 5s device, that both of their vessels got stranded in "her" city, until the following morning. Ha! Absolutely thrilled about this wonderful incidence, I therefore instantly confirmed my BFF's request of allowing them to spend the night in my then *Williamsburg*, Brooklyn *"Home Sweet Home"* base, where the Three of our souls out of the blue ended up enjoying those precious granted few hours to the fullest, reunited as The Musketeers, before a green cab returned my beloved friends back to the airport, early in the am. Bye-Bye. For now. The Universe simply rocks so much at times, right, my beloved *Co-Traveler*? Oh yeah! Though before all these many pre-announced reunions found themselves being able to occur, my *"inner Adventuress"* first of all needed to make sure to keep herself, during this *"NeverEnding"* seemingly September 2006 arrival waiting period and throughout my overall Big Apple adjusting phase, as happy, connected and productive as good as possible. In regards of my then available "home" communication and connecting options, I definitely found myself quite excited about what the magical world of technology by then had to offer. Wow. Besides those by now probably "ancient" considered past two availabilities of 1) Pen and paper and of 2) Landline phone calls with a cheaper pre-paid card version, if desired, *"little Linda"* as of then found herself able to extend her choices from an additional added palette of 3) Those oh so convenient and with its 40 cents per use still quite costly text massages, of 4) Writing personal or mass e-mail messages and of this 5) Generous free and new online communication application tool called *Skype*. Ha! And this UPgraded selection at hand absolutely revealed itself as quite an improvement throughout this past decade, especially in regards of staying in touch with ones already pre-created *"Connecting and Belonging"* loved ones from aFAR. Thank you. My then favorite pick instantly fell towards the forth invention, as many of my lovely small apple friends expressed their wish to stay UPdated about my many Big Apple *"Living on Earth Game"* adventure creations. *"Thy Wish is my Command"* and therefore I would be placing my vessel, equipped with my then quite slow and hardwired Sony Vaio laptop and with my diary, on my East Village apartment desk, whilst *"little Linda"* happily found herself typing away all the numerous to her interesting impressions and experiences as part of the absolute perfect "outlet" option remedy at hand. Send. Well, and this monthly to by-monthly developed tradition, I eagerly kept up throughout my entire 1 year Acting NYFA spectacle, before my soul then alongside with "her" successfully completed graduation decided that its *"Time to say Goodbye"* moment simultaneously arose as well. Bye-Bye. And yes, these reports certainly still remain safe and sound in my, for them eSpeCially NYC created online folder. Oh yeah. Speaking of online, 2006 also turned out to be the year, in which my auricles and eyes, besides Skype, started to come across terms like *Myspace, YouTube* and *Facebook* via my many in their early to mid 20ies traveling fellow NYFA students at hand. Ha! That's right. As for its Music advertised genre, *"little Linda's"* first curiosity therefore instantly fell for this Myspace option. Though as quickly as this attraction hit her interest, it also found itself fading away again shortly. Yes, and right during those small apple Big Apple transitioning days, I suddenly found my soul anew getting exposed to this reality shift, during which the magical world of technology even more so arose and this time in its most eXPLOSiVE and mind-blowing form. Ever. Boah! 2006 to me therefore with "No Doubt" marks the tipping point of this eNOURMOUS and still *"ongRowing"* technological metamorphosis, which with the help of numerous inventions like *Social Medias, MP3 Players, Apps* and *Smart Phones* for example out of nowhere enabled for this entire "Universe" of ours, to 1) Connect and communicate as a unit 24/7, to 2) Sp*EED* everyone's instant experience and information flow UP within a fingertip and this with the main intentions, I assume, to 3) Create an "easier", more accessible, FuN and very convenient *"Living on Earth Game"* experience ride for each and every interested soul. Boom. And. WOW! What an incredible rEvolution the world of communication simply has undergone ever since, or better put, ever since my vessel's magical transition from that small bubble into this BiG earthy one. Ha! And therefore *"little Linda's"* Gemini instincts find themselves VERY curious as to find out, alongside of her own *"ongRowing"* and expansion journey, of WHAT further interesting surprises the wonderful and swift Universe carries within its delightful *"Living on Earth Game"* toolbox from here on. "West World", here we come?! You bet. *"Winter certainly is here."* Wink.

Besides those many UPgraded happy factor communication options, including this *"NeverEnding"* September outlook at hand, my soul thankfully found herself all along equipped with the MOST reliable and powerful element, that instantly dissolved all the many at times quite unpleasant *Mister Loneliness* "interactions". And the winner is The Magical World of Acting. That's right! Very soon, *"little Linda"* luckily came to discover, that this early on recommended *"Childhood Dream" "FuN Fact"* activity revealed itself to as well contain this wonderful dust, which reliably succeeds to swing open that from her so beloved *"Super Happy Comfort Zone"* door within a SNAP, the second that my soul gets exposed to it. AbracadabraaaAAH! One of my very first realizations, throughout this *"ongRowing"* Acting passion journey of mine, turned out to be the fact that the topic communication actually plays a BiG part in it and on top of it all even counts as its MAiN ingredient at hand, which the Artist synchronically is supposed to express in a smooth and *"NeverEnding"* dance between its Vessel, Intuition, Mind and with its Mouth. Ha! *"Your vessel is your instrument and therefore use it as colorful as Mozart used to play his."* appeared as one of my teachers first from my end as "secret" interpreted MUST DO ingredient for my magical *"Life Toolbox"* collection at hand, which I soon came to understand, that its implementation certainly sounded much easier in theory than in its actual practical form. Oh yeah. For one, I rapidly came to notice, that *"little Linda"* in addition right away realized that this ambitious chosen *"THE Ultimate Childhood Dream Vision"* of mine, required the quickest development possible of 1) My current Artistic "mindset", including skills at hand and 2) Of especially the for it needed words. And this ASAP. That's right. Oh boy. How limiting my entire English vocabulary selection simply revealed itself as throughout those first few creative NYFA starting out months. Uiuiui. On top of all the many useful given Acting tips and tricks, *"little Linda"* first needed to ensure that 1) She understood the given English words properly in order to then find herself being enabled to 2) Discover the meaning of the jUST heard of with her dear yellow, blue and always reliable translator friend Duden, which activity therefore transformed this wonderful helping tool into my newly found "dude" at hand. Wink. My Shakespeare class definitely by FAR turned out to be the most "FuN and thrilling" one, let me tell you, my beloved *Co-Traveler*. Oh boy. Most of the times, I truly found myself completely left in the dark with what was going on throughout these classes, as my regular and contemporary English knowledge already happened to be on a quite limiting level, which reality check therefore kept my mind very busy trying to hold up with my other "normal" classes for starters. "Monologue, Agents, Casting Directors, Props, etc." over and over anew. Oh yeah. So HOW on heavens earth was I supposed to 1) Understand, what my "Lady Macbeth" was trying to express with this horse raven that she heard outdoors in my assigned soliloquy and to on top of it all 2) Memorize the whole "monologue" in order to present "her" as natural and authentic as possible?! AaaAH. Exactly. One probably can only imagine the outcome of this quite frustrating *"FuN Fact"* given task.

LOL. Well, and whenever my dear American born classmates found themselves being called to present their own assigned and wonderful sounding soliloquy, *"little Linda"* always immediately caught herself trying to figure out the meaning of these very gibberish sounding stories and furthermore wondering if they even truly "understood" what on mother earth their soul was reciting from A-Z. Good old Shakespeare days. R.i.P. Wink. Now, one very significant SpeCial eFFecT that this overall quite alarming gap detection reality check within this, my "newly" found passion, combined with some of my teachers remarks that the MORE foreign that I sounded, the less my vessel would be getting hired evoked, turned out to be the iMMEDiATE necessity of a *FAST* speeding "fixing" game plan creation. Oh yeah! As a matter of fact, the thought of finding *"little Linda"* restricted and limited within her OWN created *"THE Ultimate Childhood Dream Vision"* truly made the least sense to my soul, which therefore instantly triggered my *"inner Warrioress"* to awaken as well by finding her VERY determined to proof them all wrong. That's right. And therefore the *"I, Linda Wartenweiler will get restricted because of my beloved Swiss roots? What?! NO WAY! That's impossible."* reaction turned out to be my immediate full on adapted first New York attitude chosen approach in order to take on this newly given *Boot Camp* challenge at hand. Ha! After all this awareness "truth" once very elegantly got clarified by Audrey Hepburn with a *"Nothing is impossible. The word itself says it I'M POSSiBLE."* statement. How genius. Well and in addition to this very determined warrior instinct wake-UP call, my soul certainly must have thrown my childhood friend Marco's very wise and inspirational teachings, to *"Always follow your Hearts Desires as Radiant as possible by ensuring to Keep On Pushing Any presented Boundaries with a Living Life to its Fullest possible Approach and to therefore absolutely NEVER take NO for an answer, No Matter what, as Not even the Sky is the Limit."*, into the mix as well. And so it is. Amen. As far as of my *FAST* speeding "fixing" game plan creation answer, I then as a next step came up with the resolution to *"Instantly Eliminate ANY "little Linda" Behaviors and Traits that would reveal her Swiss-German Roots to ANY American born and English-speaking soul in general."* Boom. And in order to achieve this desired outcome, my soul therefore needed to metamorphose itself into an in *"The Other Planet"* born vessel as authentic and *FAST* as possible. That's right. Now, with eliminating I literally meant ANYTHiNG that this "Swiss Linda Wartenweiler" version was and did. Exactly. *"Let's go All the way. Let's Give Yourself Away. Yeah."* Which in other words meant, the *Disappearance* of my entire *Swiss-German Accent* by adapting the so called *Standard American English* door opener "requirement" instead, to *Acquire* a "well-rounded" *English Vocabulary* selection, including proper *Grammar*, *Speaking Habits* and *New York's* quite "exquisite" *Behavior* and *Expression* choices, by also *Switching* my entire *Thought* and *Head Counting* pattern into *"The Other Planet's"* invented one. Boom. Well and this *"All or Nothing"* set *"Head over Heart"* approach certainly revealed itself with time as THE PERFECT formula for the successful abandonment of *"little Linda"* out of my entire "existence", by eventually finding my soul completely striped down to a "Lost in Translation" identity. Strike. And. Hooray! pOops. WHAT?! Now, with all these many newly set goals in my pocket, I then happily went ahead and instantly applied everything One-by-One into the daily practice of my further *"Living on Earth Game"* adventure creations to come. Boom. Whenever my vessel crossed path' with another Germanic originated one for instance, I then instantaneously would make it a habit to either try to avoid "it" completely or to at least converse in English as much as possible and as soon as *"little Linda"* would come across of a fellow Swiss-Germanic reproduction, then I very consciously chose to dismiss any of those presented networking and "like-minded" friendship opportunities at hand, unless this soul turned out to be a NYFA Filmmaking student. Yup. And therefore, my Swiss Linda Wartenweiler version only got allowed to appear during either these Germanic based NYFA interactions or during any soul visits resulting from her "previous" existence. For any other opportunities, I as a solution quickly adapted the from my supportive head voice wonderfully and legit provided justification slogan that *"If I wanted to be surrounded by my Swiss-German Confederates, that I as a matter of fact very much so could have stayed in my "old" "Comfort Zone" reality creation with my beloved souls. After all I got guided to study my precious "Acting Dream" right here within the USA and therefore this has to be done as authentic and eFFecTive as possible."* Boom. And that was how simple this explanation ended up being. Of course, I found my soul very aware of the "truth" that this newly created *"Dream Catchin'"* believe pattern right away dropped the bars a couple of levels on "her" oh so desired "like-minded" soul connecting quest, which reality check I based of the city's million more opportunity offer with "No Doubt" more than willingly decided to "risk" with all of my heart. A *"Walking the Extra Mile"* truth, this entire *"Acting. Uncertainty. Complete Life Change."* picked pathway at the end of the day included anyway. So, might as well simply just go *"All the way"* from A-Z. Right? That's right. Well and this action step choice to my surprise actually ended up developing itself into a from my perspective quite interesting and satisfying direction. At first, I found my soul attracting and connecting with many other *"Fresh Off the Boat"* cruising ones, who happened to have started their own *"Living on Earth Game"* spectacles spread out all over mother earth' availabilities, which within this Swissair style like experienced reality check even ended up allowing some room for a few lovely German-English speaking exceptions. Ha! Then, with every passing year, I came to notice that my vessel more and more found itself surrounded and connected with many of those on *"The Other Planet"* entered ones and that my adaption and metamorphosis creations certainly wonderfully worked their eFFecTive magic along with the reliable *"Thoughts become Things"* reality "truth" formula. Ha! And so it is. Love. As far as of my further communication gap detecting journey, within this entire *"THE Ultimate Childhood Dream Vision"* materialization chapter at the New York Film Academy, I "of course" from the get-go found myself facing quite a few misunderstandings as well. What?! For real? For real. LOL. In our Meisner Technique class for instance, my classmate's and my soul found ourselves being taught all the wonderful Mister Meisner discovered approach suggestions from one teacher, whilst our Acting Technique teacher simultaneously enthusiastically passed us along all his own over the decades gained believes, "knowledge" and secrets, which on the other end caused *"little Linda"* to "logically" exactly apply all the newly discovered *"Acting Toolbox"* ingredients into her work in the other class. And vice versa. Then, all over sudden the other teacher as a reaction would be starting to criticize my choices, including approach by furthermore pointing out that this was NOT the way of doing "it". Hmmm. Alright then. Confused over his comments, *"little Linda"* as a next step of course instantly obeyed to his criticism with a *"Thy Will is My Command"* attitude and "corrected" her actions into his desired direction. Happily, about another success at hand, she then quickly went ahead and passionately applied those newly gained inputs into her work in the UPcoming other teachers class, who to her surprise right away ended up reacting with LOTS of disagreement towards her just for "right" declared choices from the previous teacher by kindly asking *"little Linda"* to please apply his teachings only into her work. What?! OMG. You probably can only imagine how my frustration level got built up. Day in. Day out. Oh yeah. That's right. And this newly created cat and mouse tennis match at hand lasted for about 2 or 3 weeks, before my soul decided to step in with its *"Enough was Enough"* boundary setting command, which immediately let me to express my *"ongRowing"* frustration and irritation level to one of these teachers. Ha! Well and his soul as an instant clarification explanation approach brought to my attention, that 1) We were dealing here with Art, that 2) Therefore "rules" officially would be out of existence and by further adding that 3) *"All ways lead to Rome Linda. Use whatever works best for you, as we here at NYFA only provide you with as many difFeRent Acting tools as possible for your OWN creation and interpretation journey ahead. But for now, please stick to each taught technique within every class only, so that you can get the fullest experience out of them all separately."* Boom. What?! Hmmm. Somewhat dazzled, I took this newly arrived information flow in, which soon left *"little Linda"* with this remarkable epiphany "truth" that in Art, the from her "logical" brain half commanded 1 + 1 equation NEVER equals 2 and that it therefore out of the right half viewed perspective all over sudden was allowed to equal 103, 9'328, 47 or any other soul's desired number. Boah! How cool, eye opening and refreshing this reality check experience simply revealed itself as. Wow. All over sudden ANY "results" floating around the for quite boring and mundane considered *"Safe Zone"* number 2 option appeared to be the preferred and "interesting" à la Mozart creative state of mind outcome. Ha! Now, as this freeing awareness shift absolutely resonated with my soul, I therefore quickly found myself very intrigued and curious to enter onto my own creative exploration journey within this sudden *"Not even the Sky is the Limit"* appeared palette at hand. Instantly, *"little Linda"* therefore happily went ahead by trying to figure out what exactly this creative "truth" implementation "meant" translated into action. Hmmm. And yes, this for it required *"Head TO Heart"* transition formula certainly caused for my soul to remain confused and frustrated for a little while longer, as my *"inner Artist"* still eagerly kept on trying to please each teacher with their own provided teaching technique with a "logical" Step-by-Step implementation approach. Until one day, the moment finally arose, during which I with all of my heart decided that I have had it with this tiring trying so hard procedure at hand and that a "to surrender" strategy therefore needed to get tested next. Abracadabra. Ha! And this instinctive choice of silencing my mind, by trusting my own inner wisdom and guidance instead, to my surprise truly found itself unlocking the for it required magic in its many available sparkling colors and shapes. Yay! Anew my *"Heart over Head"* formula revealed itself as THE satisfying winning choice at hand, which then thankfully started to dissolve my overpowering "logical" Artistic mindset more and moRE by granting *"little Linda"* access to an Abundant and UPlifting *"wiLD & Free"* creative experience. WooHOO! And. Thank you. Of course, right after this task got ticked off from my *Boot Camp* itinerary list, the beloved Universe swiftly went ahead and presented me my following Acting challenge within the next heartbeat in order to provide my soul with its *"Growth and Expansion"* curiosity desire, which as a matter of fact roots all the way back to "her" *"NeverEnding"* floating in the womb experience. Ha! As soon as our needed Acting foundation steps firmly got established throughout all of the assigned classes, the memorizing a "real" scene task finally got unlocked on our skill developing schedule as well and this *"FuN Fact"* activity ended up disclosing itself as THE toughest one throughout *"little Linda's"* entire NYFA *"Acting Dream"* materialization journey. Oh boy! Let me tell you, my dearest *Co-Traveler*. Oh boy. What a messy whirlwind experience this newly presented challenge brought along with it. Uiii. As for my very first scene, I found myself very happily accepting the from my Meisner technique teacher handed few pages out of Clifford Odets "Waiting for Lefty" Theater play. Excited, *"little Linda"* therefore quickly went ahead and began to read her very first casted part as "Edna", which activity more and moRE ended up filling her vessel with confusion and disappointment, as she anew had NO clue of what really was going on within this given storyline. Oh NO. Not again please! Ufff. Now, as Clifford Odets set this in 1939 published play in 1935, it therefore right away confronted my soul once more with a quite difFeRent vocabulary and scene structure choice then I used to experience it from today's way of communication. Help! How was I going to solve this challenging task at hand successfully in order to be able to eventually present this entire about 4 pages long scene with my assigned American partner without letting him down? AaaH! "Facts" were, that at this point I already found myself quite challenged with those lovely Shakespeare classes, the memorization of any assigned contemporary short exercise lines introduced themselves meanwhile with their own added difficulty level into my reality as well and now suddenly finding myself being faced with this kind of early 1900s way of speaking, including lifestyle, simply was it for my soul. HELP! My frustration level therefore instantly arose to its top level, which left *"little Linda"* at times entirely out of hope and ideas as of HOW to complete this memorization task in time or even at all. Sniff. help. My first few read through experiences presented themselves with the reality check that my brain continuously tried its very best to understand its content and to pronounce all the newly found words correctly, somehow, based on my own interpretation skills and with the then followed attempt of remembering each presented line in its very time consuming correct order. Word-by-Word. Until at some point, I felt Ready enough to as a next step add the trying to figure out the true meaning of each memorized line into my entire preparation approach. Yup. Well, and the then further required Connecting with the Text task by getting the entire scene into my "muscles", therefore needed to stay patient for quite some time longer, as this required magic enhancing skill with "No Doubt" presented itself with an almost "impossible" outlook at hand and with some even further added *"To connect with the text, the words and to then get them all into my muscles? What?? Hey, I am already quite busy with getting everything "out" in the EXACT correct order and with its proper pronunciation. So can we please, PLEASE wait with this connecting and into the muscle exercise? Whatever this is supposed to mean anyway. Please?!"* confusion. OMG. Help!! YUP. All of this is what one eventually is getting by choosing to study something completely difFeRent and new on another *"Planet"*, in a foreign language, including culture. Ha! Even though I found my soul struggling quite a LOT during these beginning few memorizing moments, I thankfully always found my *"inner Warrioress"* more than determined to solve this obstacle with the use of her all-time precious *"Where there is a Will there ALWAYS is a Way"* *"Life Toolbox"* attitude ingredient, as dEEp down in my heart my soul knew, that with *Hard Work, Practice, Patience* and with *Time* all those seemingly BiG hurdles eventually would dissolve themselves into many magical, playful and fulfilling moments. And so it was. Yay. The more that I practiced these memorizing and creative muscles, just as I knew it from my many beloved gym adventures, the more breakthroughs my soul therefore ended up earning, experiencing and enjoying as a rewarding gesture from the supportive Universe, throughout this rather tidies *"Growth and Expansion"* process, and those many released energies and inspirations as a next step then wonderfully infused and encouraged my *"inner Artist"* to approach the many *"NeverEnding"* thereafter presented tasks, "hurdles" and level UP jUMPing's One-by-One. And so forth. That's right. Well and looking back, I must admit that this *"Walking the Extra Mile"* strategy, guided by LOTS of Determination and Endurance, actually revealed itself as quite a powerful recipe in regards for any soul, who desires to undergo rapid *"Self-development"* results. *FAST* speeding breakthroughs are definitely guaranteed. HA. Oh yeah!

"Put your hands UP in the Air. Put your hands UP in the Air."
Alongside with *"little Linda's"* long-awaited NYFA 1 year Acting graduation approach, the wonderful question of *"What's next"* certainly welcomed her reality creation anew, which led this task right away transform itself

into the next important puzzle solving piece at hand. Even though I still found myself accompanied by *Mister Loneliness* quite often within this *"ongRowing" Boot Camp* experienced adventure of mine, I all along also very much knew with all of my heart, that 1) This MUST DO *"Acting. Uncertainty. Complete Life Change."* entered path remained EXACTLY as THE One on which my soul desired to continue traveling upon, that 2) *"All Beginnings* after all *are Hard"* and that 3) The attraction of a new perfect visa match therefore appeared as my desired next *"Stepping-Stone"* to focus upon. In a helpful meeting with NYFA's friendly international student advisory, I quickly came to learn that from my graduation period on *"little Linda"* was given a selection of two new paths to choose from, which resulted in either applying for a 2 months Work Permit or to continue my *"Acting Dream"* adventures with a 2 months Optional Practical Training (OPT) visa. Then, as soon as this friendly advisory completed her UPdate with all the additional revealed details, my soul instantly knew that the first choice was THE winning option and therefore found "herself" absolutely thrilled, the second its approval notice reached my reality 2 weeks later. Yeeha! Certainly, this extra provided *"Childhood Acting Dream Catchin'"* opportunity provided my further career path creation desires with only a tip of the iceberg required amount of time, especially with my still heavy existing Swiss-German *"little Linda"* accent aboard, with my very present *"Fresh Off the Boat"* awareness point of view within this *"The Other Planet"* environment, accompanied with the "truth", that my vessel would get considered as a "very young" Actress, for probably another year or two longer. The wonderful chance that this newly granted "in between" visa solution for my further *"Don't Dream your Life. Live your Dream."* reality exploration provided though, ended up being the perfect sneak peek opportunity for *"little Linda"* to get a sense of the "real" Big Apple and Acting world existing outside of any safe classroom walls and this guided by her own instincts and thus far gathered *"Life Toolbox"* ingredients only. Ha! Then, parallel to my graduation date, the termination of my Artsy East Village *"Home Sweet Home"* base lease found its way into my reality as well, which therefore instantly prompted my soul to look out for a cheaper and fairer deal via a webpage called *Craigslist*. Oh yeah! How we all love that one, correct? LOL. As far as of the approach of this newly adapted task, I came to decide to settle for another 6 weeks for now, in order to match the date with *"little Linda's"* first Switzerland visiting boarding ticket and to therefore peacefully take care of my further whereabouts sometime before my return to the city, which facts as a result ended up leaving my soul with a quite flexible and open attitude, as to where "her" vessel would be vacating at during this very educational NYFA wrapping up chapter at hand. Within a short amount of time, this lovely Craigslist page choice already proved itself to be of success by leading my soul to its ideal and desired next matching sublet option, that this time turned out to be a furnished room in one of those typical three-story buildings located in *Bedford Stuyvesant*, Brooklyn. Ha! Well and this granted mini Brooklyn *"Living on Earth Game"* excursion, certainly provided my *"Fresh Off the Boat"* floating Swiss country style soul with a further quite remarkable and interesting view point expansion opportunity and with the soon understanding as of WHY all expenses in that neighborhood are set WAY cheaper than in Manhattan. Oh yeah. Two Bed Stuy "facts", that I happened to be unaware of at that particular moment in 2007 turned out to be that 1) This neighborhood mainly got inhabited by African Americans and that 2) Its reputation over the past decades molded itself into a *"Bed Stuy. Do or Die"* attitude reality check. Oops. What?! Oh boy. AAHH, dear Universe? What happened to be your educational intent for *"little Linda"* with this quite abstract delivered *"Growth and Expansion"* opportunity at hand?! Getting rid of *Miss Fear* maybe? LOL. Yes, maybe. Well, the one further very useful *"Life Toolbox"* ingredient that this Big Apple adventure certainly did end up helping me with, turned out to be the development of the in this Concrete Jungle rather useful *"Better leave "little Linda" Alone"* attitude protecting "veil" that my soul according to outside resources, with the help of her in this athletic appearing, ¾ Swiss-German and ¼ German background wrapped vehicle, non-verbally sends out, whenever "worn". Ha! That's right. *"Watch Out. Watch Out."* And. Abracadabra. Very vividly I actually do recall the beginning moments of this newly discovered *"Life Toolbox"* ingredient, which origin most likely travels all the way back to one of *"little Linda's"* first subway rides "home" to the on the C train located *Kingston-Throop* stop. As I found my vessel gathered amongst many other from station to station changing ones, it at some point came to my attention that the closer the train approached my desired stop that the more my fair skin suddenly began to stand out even more so and this UP to the moment, of finding my female considered vessel as the ONLY white one left in the entire full cart. Oops. Hmmm. Yes, and this quit unusual awareness check certainly left my Thurgau originated soul with many skeptical and unsure *"What to Do. What to Do."* vibrations by immediately leading me to wonder, whether this presented scenery should be interpreted as endangering or as still safe. Hmmm. Help? Which as a next reaction step had me decide to follow through with my inner voice's suggestion of simply staying alerted and aware. Just in case. And that this action step was all that it needed in order for my vessel to remain safe and sound. In and out. Boom. Great. With a *"Thy Will is My Command"* attitude *"little Linda"*, therefore quickly went ahead, gave this easy flowing directed task its fair trial and ended up finding herself with "No Doubt" very pleased with its outcome. Sweet. Well, and the more that she actually kept on playing around with this newly discovered "outfit", the more *"little Linda"* suddenly began to discover its quite helpful and unexpected contained magical powers. BooO! Boah! Yay! Then, once my vessel as predicted returned safe and sound to its temp home again, I decided to share my "just" experienced with my female roommate, who ended up confirming, as of my immediate standing out color, to simply remain aware and alerted and to preferably choose well-lit streets during any nighttime walks from or to the subway station. Sweet. Quickly, I therefore went ahead, added those newly and valuable granted insider

Bed Stuy neighborhood tips into my *"ongRowing"* own Big Apple adjusting and transformational repertoire and pretty much ended up enjoying this very crisp and impressive complete standing out experience of 6 weeks "As Good as it Gets". Oh yeah. Then, with the arrival of March 12th, a new *"Time to say Goodbye"* moment welcomed my reality as well, which meant *"little Linda's"* first break from her *"ongRowing" "Acting. Uncertainty. Complete Life Change." "Dream Catchin'" "Living on Earth Game" Boot Camp* path experience. Ha! Switzerland here I come and this time as a freshly backed NYFA Actress graduate. WooHOO! What?! And this *"Childhood Dream"* realization fact still found my awareness as quite unbelievable. Boah. My set plans for those UPcoming few weeks back in my souls comforting root environment, amongst "her" many beloved blood and *"Extended Family Members"*, resulted in 1) To simply enjoy everyone and everything to the fullest and to 2) Parallel also begin "her" mission with the attraction and creation of "her" next desired *"THE Ultimate Childhood Dream Vision" "Stepping-Stones"*, so that *"little Linda"* happily ever after would be able to continue her many *"Living on Earth Game"* adventures in her desired *"Don't Dream your Life. Live your Dream."* reality. Oh yeah! After the allowance to store my still little belongings at the house in Bed Stuy, my vessel shortly after found itself filled with many gathered new impressions and with a wonderful emotional mixture in its "old" office space shooting through the heavens towards its beloved *"Red and White"* flagged other *"Home Sweet Home" "Planet"*. Yay! Setting foot onto Zurich's ground again, after being exposed for 9 months straight to probably THE MOST active and dynamic melting spot availability on mother earth, certainly revealed itself as another rather unexpected interesting experience. Wow. Suddenly, everything and everyone appeared SO much slower, cleaner, cuter, quieter, smaller, politer, super organized. Well, simply picture perfect. Ha! Welcome to Switzerland. Jodeliuuuhuuu! And right then, my soul to my surprise instantly got thrown into "her" next culture shock at hand and this even in "her" birth origin and *"Home Planet"*. LOL. Yes, my vessel has been absented for quite some time prior, though this occasion brought along my very first extreme *"Yin and Yang"* duality experience of finding my soul *"ongRowingly"* floating within a reality check of its opposite "Apple growth" and therefore outside of the as so conveniently perceived *"Comfort Zone"*. Yup. Switzerland these days after all populates a total of 8 million vessels and this spread out over 26 difFeRent cantons, which head count alone equals the city of New York. What?! Boah! And the One fact that *"little Linda"* therefore continuously finds herself fascinated with in regards of this newly explored metropolis at hand, is the "truth" that somehow, someHOW with "No Doubt" it truly seems possible for all the many on mother earth invented *Cultures, Religions, Believe Systems, Sexual Orientations* and *Skin Shades* to exist and interact peacefully united with one another, and this on a *"Self-*created" own *"Planet"*, on which ANYTHiNG is possible. 24/7. Boom. That's right. Well, and this entire mother earth formation melted down onto one magical and HiGH vibrating Concrete Jungle "truth", I actually came to witness works miraculously well, which ever since convinces my Thurgauer soul entirely, that in the end *"WE ARE ALL EXACTLY THE SAME"*, No Matter one's appearance, "position" or preferences. HA. That's right! Every soul after all finds itself vacating a from itself chosen pre-programmed vehicle, which throughout everyone's Own and Personal further accepted outer and inner resources very much defines as of HOW each souls' *"Self-*created" *"Living on Earth Game"* experience unfolds itself and this guided by a wonderful mixture of one's Free Will and of one's *"Head over Heart over Head over Heart"* action step decisions. *"Moment-to-Moment"*. Day in. Day out. And so it is. Love. Now, the reality check of finding my vessel amongst all my beloved and "like-minded" Swiss souls and Confederates again, I must admit, my dear *Co-Traveler*, transformed itself into a much-needed MUST DO excursion. How good it simply felt to express myself again as *"wiLD & Free"* as *"little Linda"* loves to be, by finding myself being understood a 100%. Ahhh! Those cup filling and adventurous 5 Swiss chosen traveling weeks, my soul happily ended up enjoying with many of "her" beloved *"FuN Fact"* activities like *Reconnecting, Being, Reflecting, Snowboarding, Hugging, Laughing, Sharing, Celebrating, Indulging, Planning* and all of this very much to its fullest possible, as on the other end of things the "truth" also existed, that 1) Most of my meanwhile within the Big Apple created networking souls found themselves in the midst of spreading their vessels out all over mother earth again, that *"little Linda"* therefore 2) More or less would be facing a renewed starting over spectacle once back, which reality check this time around got placed 3) Outside of any pre-set *"Safe Zone"* environment at hand. Boom. Oh well. Let's then. As far as of my further planned next perfect visa match attraction *"Stepping-Stone"* approach, I very soon found myself connecting with the solution of taking advantage of the since 9/11 for every European non-visa holder reduced granted 3 months visiting in a row opportunity as part of my UPdated master plan, by further deciding to 1) Give this back and forth cat and mouse dance a maximum of the magical Three's A Charm trial and to therefore 2) Anew hand all my *Trust*, the *How's* and the *What's* right over to the all-time helpful Universe. That's right! After all iT was the one that led my soul into this *"THE Ultimate Childhood Dream Vision"* reality in the first place and along of my many travels as Linda Wartenweiler I further came to witness that iT thus far always reliably just in time ended up providing *"little Linda"* with whatever she "needed" next for her many in the past created *"Living on Earth Game"* adventures. Yup. And this awareness "truth" therefore had me stay VERY confident for this quite magical teamwork dynamic to remain in its *"ongRowing"* creation mode. Ha! With this chosen outlook in my pocket, I then quickly went ahead, accepted one of my Filmmaker friend's offer to vacate in his apartment for a week or two as a starting out *"Home Sweet Home"* base solution by then completing my getting Ready quest with the purchase of a one-way ticket to JFK, dating my mom's dad's birthday *April 16th 2007*. Bye-Bye. After a nice and quiet short felt flight, my vessel finally found itself equipped with LOTS of *Hope, Inspiration, Respect, Eagerness* and *Curiosity* for this meanwhile already second Big Apple *"Childhood Acting Dream"* started chapter, safely back on American ground again. Yay! Now guess, my wonderful *Co-Traveler*, what awaited *"little Linda"* right there at the airport? Ha! Charming New York truly anew decided to welcome my appearance with the EXACT same "joyous" SpeCial eFFecT, as it already did on June 2nd 2006. LOL. Exactly. With a heavy rainstorm that this time even lasted for a couple of days. *"Hello and welcome back "Miss Fresh Off the Boat". We surly missed ya' that many teardrops much. Oh yeah!"* Wink. Well and this repeated cats and dogs falling down from the skies scenario "coincidence", certainly struck my soul as quite odd, as these two occasions happened to be the ONLY ones at count, throughout my since June entered Concrete Jungle *Boot Camp* adventure. Hmmm. Maybe the beloved Universe intended to bring a point across? Hmmm. Maybe. Maybe, we shall be able to detect an answer along of our mutual *Dot Connecting* journey. Let's see. Ha! Now, as soon as my vessel arrived at my friend's studio apartment at Union Square, I as a next step quickly made my way to Bed Stuy, collected all my few belongings and Ready my soul thereafter felt for "her" further *"Don't Dream your Life. Live your Dream." "Dream Catchin'"* reality creation mission. My first focus I thereafter immediately directed towards the attraction of my new own *"Home Sweet Home"* base starting May 1st, the latest, which time frame parallel certainly also would provide *"little Linda"* with enough hours to adjust and settle back into this now faSTER and wiLDer vibrating "Apple" at hand. BuzzZZZZZ. Craigslist, I therefore anew chose as my solution technique, which opportunity this time to my surprise failed to match any of my requested and interesting sounding options. Weird. Then, whilst my vessel found itself equipped with *"little Linda's" "Positivity Card"* eagerly solving its *"Home Sweet Home"* attraction quest on one of NYFA's provided computers the night before its planned moving out date, the magical Universe reliably as usual swiftly went ahead and sent me as its *"Thy Wish is my Command"* gesture another dear just graduated Filmmaking friend my way. Ha! Well, and as it so happened, right after my soul finished expressing "her" *"ongRowing"* frustration experience at hand, "his" happily ended up sharing that the second furnished bedroom in "his" current *Astoria*, Queens rental home base actually would become available, starting the following noon, which rent even equaled the EXACT amount of my "order". Boah! What?! What an amazing "coincidence". Thank you, my beloved Universe. Thank you. Of course, my soul immediately jUMPed aboard on this out of the blue appeared offer and this even more so, as his very kind, respectful and loving soul seemed to be THE perfect next "in-between" solution at hand in order to grant *"little Linda"* with a further familiar vessel for another 3 1/2 weeks, before my friend's would be moving itself back to India. For good. Boom. This, in New York City's Greek influenced neighborhood located apartment, revealed itself as a wonderful 1 month settling back in opportunity, which led my soul, along with my pleasant friend's disappearance and as of our quite noisy and time-consuming landlord lady, consult this Craigslist page anew, with a this time quick and satisfying "Mission *I'mPOSSiBLE*" outcome. Yay! This newly attracted *"Home Sweet Home"* base of mine presented itself as a furnished room in a three-bedroom apartment, which conveniently found itself being located only a few blocks further UP from my then current address. Sweet. And. Strike! This space my vessel ended up sharing with an American office worker and with a Dutch drummer for a duration of 15 months, before a new appearing opportunity led *"little Linda"* to the Upper East Side in Manhattan and then to her final Big Apple Italian neighborhood based destination in Williamsburg, Brooklyn in 2010. Ahhh. *"Home Sweet Home"*. Now you are all done. Grazie.

"Step-by-Step. Oh yeah. I really know it's just a Matter of Time."
Now, before all of these mentioned moves took place, I of course first needed to finish my NYC settling back in task during my May Astoria temp-home base ride, which at its completion quickly led the beloved Universe to direct all of my attention back to its already pre-delivered and from *"little Linda"* quite undesired "Abundance of Time" gift at hand. *"Oh no! Please stay away from me. You are not welcomed here. Leave. NOW!"* Boom. And back it was right before my eyes, which reality check instantly prompted for my soul to occupy "herself" a LOT more ASAP, in order for this uncomfortable TOO much *"little Linda"* bzZZ time setup to disappear. During the following few days, I therefore right away steered all of my focus back towards my beloved *"Childhood Acting Dream"*, the main reason why my vessel found itself back on this *"The Other Planet"* after all, by the instant creation of Linda Wartenweiler's Acting profiles on all the recommended few young Actor starting out websites, so that *"little Linda's"* audition adventure finally could begin its course as well out there in the "real" world, followed by my first attempt of getting this for decades longed Acting career started. WooHOO! Let's Go. Soon though, this Entertainment business approach revealed itself as a much more overwhelming experience than expected and questions like *"Where to start? What to do exactly? How to proceed? How do I write a great introduction letter and this in English in order to find 1) An agent and 2) Free work for now? What is important?"* therefore already found themselves able to successfully stop all of my many enthusiastically started doings, including further forged game plan creations within a snap. SNAP. And this moment then right away introduced itself to my very passionate and eager vibrating soul with the reality check "truth", that this time around "she" got required to march even more than *"The Extra Mile"* in order for this "baby" to get anything close to started. *"Oh boy. And now I am even on my own with all of this. Help. Help!"* Yes, my classmates and I did receive some suggested Do's and Don'ts along our FuN NYFA education ride from some of our teachers. Though, whilst my attempts of putting those theoretically shared tips into practice, I quickly came to realize, that 1) This helpful faculty somewhat seemed to have only scratched the tip of the iceberg of this to *"little Linda"* rather delicate subject at hand and that 2) There happened to be so much more to this whole entered Acting cat and mouse business game than what was shared

or she picked up on. Ufff. And therefore, it anew officially was time to pull *"little Linda's"* magical *"Positivity Card"* by simultaneously deciding to simply take it all *"Step-by-Step"*, Day-by-Day and to therefore for now, shift my focus back to the audition process, which *"FuN Fact"* activity at least provided my *"inner Artist"* already with some successes here and there. Yay. As this Acting career start up mission of mine unraveled itself with a LOT slower progression pace than desired, I therefore inevitably found myself once more being faced with a little bit too much of this "Abundance of Time" gift at hand, which reality check instantly prompted my soul to activate "her" already in Switzerland prepared "emergency" Plan B. Ha! Abracadabra. Yes, and this especially for this situation created Plan B this time involved the attraction of a waitressing job in one of the few existing Big Apple Swiss restaurants for starters. Boom. My thoughts and goals with this newly invented action step resulted in providing *"little Linda"* with the opportunity to 1) Gain some regular income in order to grant her *"Red and White Saving Sock"* account a little breather, to 2) Find her vessel being exposed to a "like-minded" public community on a Steady basis, which hopefully would assist to quiet down her *"ongRowing"* *"Connecting and Belonging"* desire, with the further chance to 4) Maybe meet one or two nice souls with whom "hers" could be sharing some quality time outside of the working environment and lastly, with 5) An activity that preferably would occupy my *"little Linda"* with a LOT of FuNNy giggly moments and with many new *"Living on Earth Game"* adventures for her collection. Yeeha. For this waitressing quest at hand, I therefore found myself Ready and equipped with my valuable Swissair resume, as this global *"Swimming AGAiNST the Stream"* traveling choice thus far happened to be my closest experience to the world of gastronomy. That's right! The Swizz restaurant in Manhattan therefore appeared as my first planned *"Comfort Zone"* target and as with my *"ongRowing"* audition and visa process journeys at hand, I decided to approach this *"Connecting and Belonging"* task exactly in the same *"Moment-to-Moment"*. *"Step-by-Step. Oh baby."* manner. Ha! On the following morning, I then found my vessel entering the NYFA building in SOHO and this equipped with LOTS of determination and excitement about this new project at hand and with the intent to print out a few copies of my Swissair resume, which my friend Sandy offered to scan and email to my account during our last gathering at her house, as she thought for it to be a great idea to also have my precious paper accessible in its digital form as a second option at hand. After all this new and convenient online job application trend found its way into our earthy reality as well and being UP to speed on that matter, certainly seemed to be a mighty good idea. Perfect. Now guess what "miracle" welcomed my reality this time during my NYFA computer session, my dear *Co-Traveler*? Any idea? Wink. And. Ha! The magical Universe truly must have full on agreed with my just launched new *"Stepping-Stone"* at hand, as its wonderful *"Thy Wish is my Command"* gesture practically found my way over night. Boah! Yes. As soon as I sent out my order of 20 copies to the selected printer, one of my Film Academy staff friends suddenly called my vessel over to the front desk, as his soul felt a strong intuitive impulse to introduce mine to a just in the room appeared Swiss-German Filmmaking student. Sure. Let's. Within the following few breaths, *"little Linda"* then got informed that her in the 1970ies entered vessel started her *"Living on Earth Game"* ride in Zurich and that her inner child currently happened to be studying "her" Filmmaking passion right here at the Film Academy. Ha! Then, right after our brief and crisp introduction, she then from my end desired to find out what my further plans from here on were, now as a just from the small apple returned graduated NYFA Actress, which instantly caused *"little Linda"* to happily reply *"Oh, I literally am printing out my Swissair resume right now, as I am planning on heading to the Swizz restaurant in Midtown later this afternoon in order to find out if they might be in need of my waitressing services."* Boom. And this newly provided key moment was all that it needed for what's to come next. Yeeha! And. Thank you. Quickly, her kind soul then informed mine, that 1) "Her" manager at "her" current Italian restaurant part-time occupation happened to be in urgent need of a food runner, preferably a guy though, that 2) I definitely should be stopping by there at 5pm today and give it a shot, as one never knows after all, if I liked to of course and that 3) I should be asking for the manager Nini, by then informing her that "her" soul sent mine Nini's way. Ha! What?! Sweet. Of course, I shall. Yay! With that our two vessels then parted and with it also my already made plans for this day ahead. *"Thy Will is My Command"*. Smile. At exactly 5pm on this particular Thursday in early May 2007, my vessel then as directed curiously found itself walking into this restaurant called *Grotto*, which used to be located on Forsyth Street, between Broom and Grand Street, right at the borderline of the *Lower East Side* and *Chinatown*. The second that I entered through the already open doorway, my eyes immediately came to notice a very busy and in a hurry seemingly girl with dark glasses behind the bar, who kept herself busy with getting all the candles Ready for the night ahead. Shyly, *"little Linda"* then went ahead, asked as instructed for this Nini manager and right away came to learn that she already found herself in the midst of talking to her. Bingo! Perfect. Quickly, my soul therefore went ahead, let "hers" in on my story and intention, which caused "hers" to respond rather relieved and with a slight French sounding accent *"We Really, REALLY need someone Right NOW. Could you be back in 1 ½ hours with a black t-shirt and start with your first training tonight?"* What?! Tonight already? Wow! Super astounded about this TURBO SPEEDing *"Thy Wish is my Command"* delivered result at hand, my vessel then exited this Grotto with a happy *"Yes, absolutely. Sounds great. See you in 1 ½ hours."* responds. Boah! That really turned out to be another perfect *"Timing par Excellence"* experience. WooHOO! Excited about this whole twist of my just entered job hunting adventure, I then took off, purchased the required t-shirt somewhere on Broadway and returned just in time again, Ready to *"Rock 'n Roll!"* Yeeha. A lovely French waitress then took *"little Linda"* under her wings for the night and showed her all the ropes needed for this available runner position at hand. This "down on earth" gastronomy spectacle certainly right away introduced my soul into a complete difFeRent experienced *"Living on Earth Game"* reality check by further providing "her" with many more unknown expressions, with new approaches and with the introduction into New York's famous fast paced *"Are you Ready to get ROCKED?"* restaurant/working rhythm. Oh yeah. Then, at the end of my mutually successful perceived completed first training session, my quite pleased manager ended up happily inviting my vessel back for the following evening, as her Swiss-French originated soul very much resonated with our "like-minded" work dynamic and interpretation. Wink. Well, and as my soul very much so felt drawn to this newly attracted *"Growth and Expansion"* challenge at hand, I instantly found myself accepting my fellow Swiss Confederates *"Connecting and Belonging"* opportunity invitation and kept on returning for many more throughout the following 4 ½ years. That's right. Ha! Who would have thought that this Plan B mission completion would reveal itself into such a smooth and easy flowing ride by providing *"little Linda"* after some unexpected magical twists and turns with exactly the desired "Swizz" gastronomy outcome. *"Coo-coo-cool. Yeah, yeah. This is so cool."* Wink. The result of a *"Heart over Head"* chosen strategy, this storyline certainly ended up carrying. This I remain certain of. Oh yeah. Well, and as this wonderful perfectly timed *"Connecting and Belonging"* opportunity seemed to need a little bit more of a magical touch in order to assure my soul that "she" found "herself" absolutely on track, I within my first 2 Grotto months came to face two to my soul quite mind-blowing *"Synchronicity par Excellence"* experiences. Ready? Let's Go. My very first "coincidence" took place with my friendly new manager, who, as already mentioned, started her *"Living on Earth Game"* ride on the opposite side of my beloved Lake Constance area, which happens to be in a small village right at the Lake Geneva. Ha! That's right. Now, early on into our getting to know one another journey, Nini at some point shared that her in the late 1970ies appeared vessel grew UP in this with 14'000 populated village located right next to Lausanne called *Morges*. What?! Did she just say Morges? Morges, VD? NO way! YES way. Her Swiss *"Home Sweet Home"* base of over 2 decades truly turned out to be the EXACT same spot, during which my Möne and I each Friday experienced the honor of getting taught all the many magical tips and tricks of HOW to become a "perfect" housewife and housekeeper for 10 months straight. LOL. Yup. Nini even ended up reminding *"little Linda"* of our delightful Housekeeping School's name, which at this point of her travels "mysteriously" seemed to have slipped her mind. pOops. Wink. *Marcelin* it was and this word to this day actually reliably finds itself *"ongRowingly"* filling my entire vessel with many giggling vibrations as soon as it somehow pops UP. Giggle. Giggle! Giggle!! Yes, this synchronicity certainly threw a quite impressive eFFecT onto my soul, as the chances of 1) Encountering someone from that exact rather tinny Swiss spot in this very crowded Concrete Jungle experience, I perceive as very, VERY slim and to then 2) End up working for this particular soul for quite some years and this 3) Even in the field of my, in her hometown undergone education in 1991. Boah! That must even more so explain as of why she felt very satisfied with *"little Linda's"* work ethic. LOL. Hey, and who knows, maybe the two of our vessels even happened to have first crossed paths back then already. *"One way or the Other."* Ha! Who knows, right?! Well and right within this interesting ice breaking Marcelin discovery spectacle, our nicknames found its birthing moment as well, which ever since left Nini as *"La Maman"* and *"little Linda"* once more as *"La jeune Fille"*, which terminology indicates a Teenaged girl's Housekeeping Apprentice Function at hand, within any French speaking mentioned environment. Wink. Love. Then, my second interesting incidence followed a few weeks after, on a June evening at around 6pm, whilst I found myself in the midst of my backyard station getting Ready mission. Very vividly I do recall, how my vessel therefore quite quickly slid behind the indoors located wooden bar in order to grab some clean water glasses from the shelve, as suddenly one of the just entered vessels released the unthought-of *"Hey, did you by any chance ever work as the branch manager at the TKB in Erlen?"* line. Holy Moly! WHAT?! What did this girl just ask me right now?!?! Somebody poke me please! Gina?! And this question instantly managed to stop my entire existence for about 3 seconds, whilst my soul came to realize that my Swiss past just caught UP with my, on this *"The Other Planet"* newly created *"Now Moment"* reality. Boah! Absolutely dazzled and somewhat shocked I then slowly turned my face towards an unfamiliar appearing face by further instantly confronting her with a *"Who on heavens earth are you?!"*, by then wanting to know HOW she possibly would own the knowledge of my previous function set within a reality existence located far, FAR away from Grottos ground. Yeah! Please tell me. Quite excited, her soul then went ahead and began to explain in her right in that very *"Now Moment"* into the familiar Thurgau switched dialect *"Oh, we actually met at your work a few years back. Do you remember? I used to weekly stop by during my apprentice years for my boss XY in order to exchange some important data tapes in his safety deposit box before I then moved to Paris for 4 years and then to Manhattan. Oh, and my hair used to be very, VERY short at that time."* CLiCK. And right during her clarification speech, *"little Linda"* straightaway found herself able to successfully detect its matching tape within her well-kept *"Head Cinema"* archive by furthermore remembering EXACTLY, who this from then teenaged Sinéad O'Conner "look alike" into that a now shoulder length with bangs styled twens metamorphosed Thurgauer vessel was. Boah! What another quite crazy "coincidence" this interaction truly turned out to be. Out of the blue, this former indirect TKB client, who also happened to know my dear *"Extended Family Member"* Lucia, suddenly appeared incognito in my next attracted *"Connecting and Belonging"* work environment and this in this tinny and rather unnoticeable Big Apple Grotto location. Wow. WoW. WOW. The magical Universe. The magical and all time surprising Universe. Ha! Now let's jUMP back to my overall experienced Grotto journey, which *"Living on Earth Game"* chapter soon happened to reveal itself as a true jackpot on all levels and this for many various reasons. Oh yeah. During my first 2 years for example, I weekly found my vessel being called in for my speedy, friendly and reliable runner services, whenever an extra set of hands and feet were needed, which usually occurred during their busiest hours on Friday and Saturday evenings, and occasionally on Thursdays. So whenever *"little Linda"* found herself surrounded within her desired *"Connecting and Belonging"* environment, she then therefore always ended up feeling quite excited about the opportunity, to 1) Dedicate a few hours of her granted "Abundance of Time" fortune towards some useful service to others activities and to 2) Exist amongst some "like-minded" souls during its execution. Well, and her excitement, including love for this quite diverse FuN food runner occupation and for all the many there encountered souls must have ended up sparking so much passion within her vessel, that at some point, the from *Munich* originated Germanic owner, including La Maman decided to increase her hourly rate with another 5 bucks. Boom. Boah! What? How amazing. Thank you! Yes, and as this from their end quite motivating first and Only Ever granted runner salary raise infused my entire work ethic and overall enthusiasm even more so, my vessel then eventually ended up getting fired from my food runner services a few months later. What? What?! True fact. And all for the wonderful one reason, of finding myself getting promoted to a newly opened waitressing position instead. Ha! That's right. Well, and Nini's reasoning for this adjustment, alongside with the completion of my further Acting studies, turned out to be that the moment finally had arrived, in which my soul's quite advanced social and selling skills needed to get implemented more in the front side of things and that this tweaking action step certainly would reflect a positive light onto both ends income numbers. Ha! And spot on her soul certainly was with this fortune prediction. Wink. Now, even though I found myself quite excited about this UPgraded position at hand, I on the other end also ended up detecting some lower occurring vibrations mixing up my overall emotional awareness state of mind, as this job after all very much so grew on my soul throughout this really FuN food runner *"Living on Earth Game"* excursion of 2 years. Yup. Quite saddened about this unexpected appeared *"Letting go of Something that* "apparently" *No Longer Serves One's Growth and Expansion"* experience at hand, *"little Linda"* therefore instantly found herself approaching La Maman after this getting "fired" reality check UPdate, with the request to at least being granted to keep one of her weekend runner shifts for now, in order to please her attachment for this then super FuN given Grotto door opening opportunity at hand. Hesitantly her soul after some pondering understandingly ended up supporting *"little Linda's"* desire for about 2 weeks, before she then kindly got asked to execute her letting go exercise ASAP in order to make room for a replacement of my choice. Boom. Alrighty then. Deal. After some reflecting over a possible "perfect" fitting soul match, my inner voice suddenly brought a dear ex-NYFA *Paris,* France originated classmate as The One to my attention, who truly ended up being THE pleasing solution for this transition at hand. Yay! Shortly after, I therefore found myself in the position of passing along all the needed ropes to "Ma Chouchette" for her newly attracted runner position by taking her under my wings for the time being. Voilà. Ça y est. Boom. Then, once I allowed myself to fully let go of "The Past" by embracing the *"Now Moment"* with this UPgraded waitressing position at hand, my soul actually at some point ended up realizing that somehow "she" managed to 1) Find "herself" floating within a *"Work equals FuN"* environment, that 2) Even included "her" favorite state of *"Being able to Work Freely in My Own Style and Rhythm"* by *"Being Fully Trusted with No Direct Boss in my back"* reality creation. Boah! *"Coo-coo-cool. Yeah, yeah. This is so cool."* Yay! And merci La Maman. Bisous. Looking back, I also happily find myself sharing with you, my beloved *Co-Traveler*, that this from the swift Universe delivered Grotto *"Connecting and Belonging"* chapter indeed revealed itself as the from my soul perfect and literal life-changing requested *"Game"* and *"FuN Fact"* enhancer solution. That's right. And as life-changing this Plan B Swissair resume printing out resolution I certainly do find myself perceiving this opportunity as, as most of my newly created network and "like-minded" friendship bonds, within this second *"little Linda"* Big Apple *"Childhood Acting Dream"* ride, my soul successfully ended up tying throughout my vessels travels at this German owned Italian restaurant. Ha! Who would have thought that this magically delivered package would include truly everything that my soul very much felt attuned with, right at that exact moment of "her" travels? Abracadabra. This *"Thoughts become Things"* theory certainly proved itself to be of "truth", as it blessed my *"ongRowing"* Boot Camp ride with *Delicious* and *"real" Food, Great* and *FuN Co-Workers*, many provided *Challenges* and *Lessons* to support my soul's *FAST* speeding and *"ongRowing" "Growth and Expansion"* development desire, new "like-minded" *Friends* and *Acquaintances, "little Linda's"* in NYC based *"Extended Family Member"* community, which partly even rooted back to Switzerland and Germany, LOT's of *FuN* and *Freedom*, a Steady *Income, Deep Conversations, "ongRowing" Responsibilities*, the taking care of feeding my *Entertaining, Socializing* and strongly emerging *Helping Syndrome* urges in a *"wiLD & Free"* environment, quite crazy *Parties*, many *Incredible* and *Unbelievable Anything Goes* Big Apple *Experiences* and all of those countless memorable adventures even got topped off with *"little Linda's"* meanwhile further developed favorite own Music taste, in the form of a in the background as spotlessly orchestrated soundtrack delivery and this *"All night long. All night. OOH YEAH."* Boom. Boom. And. Hooray! Thank you. Speaking of "quite crazy parties". Ha! Well, the countless *"Dancing and Celebrating this "Living on Earth Game" adventure of mine as often as possible"* granted opportunities, certainly keep on presenting themselves as probably one of my MOST favorite embarked Grotto spectacles at hand, which announcement usually found itself taking place in a monthly set rhythm and this in the form of its original *Who is Sexy?* named experience, which identity along with time found itself transmuting into a *Deep and Juicy* excursion, followed by its in January 2014 ending and meanwhile legendary *Sweet' N Low* known formation celebration. That's right. Legend says, that this ritual found its birthing night all the way back to a surprise 40th vessel celebration spectacle of a in *Nice,* France originated former Grotto coworker, which La Maman's soul happily organized for this dear grown friend's of "hers", as soon as all the stoves got turned off at around midnight, and this *"All night long. All night. OOH YEAH."* Ha! Well and this celebration spectacle must have unfolded itself with so much FuN, that many attendees instantly requested MORE of this "wiLD wiLD East" experienced adventure in an *"ongRowing"* avalanche appearing SpeCial eFFecT approach. Boom. As Nini's Swiss originated soul thankfully as well very much so finds "herself" attuned with the *"FuN Facts"* to 1) Celebrate "her" own *"Living on Earth Game"* ride with as much FuN as possible and this 2) Accompanied with preferably Deep House, Electro and other Funky chosen beats, "she" therefore right away found herself more than open to officially continue this then born monthly Who is Sexy? ritual after the from the owner granted green light. Yeeha! Of course, *"little Linda"* reacted more than thrilled about this out of the blue appeared, every last Saturday of the month *"I Can't Stop Raving. I Can't Stop Raving."* After-Hour extra treat at hand and those time traveling opportunities most definitely served as a true enhancement towards her overall undergone *"Connecting and Belonging"* Grotto journey by simultaneously also successfully evoking many of these *"Home Sweet Home"* desired vibrations with each passing month. Yup. And this is how it all worked. As the floor plan of this restaurant found itself divided into two separate long and narrow dark wooden dining room areas, they based on their overall appearances therefore started to carry the names of *The Dark Room* and *The Red Room*, of which the latter description most certainly last appeared into my awareness during "Twin Peaks'" final episode in season 2. Ha! *"The Owls are NOT what they Seem."* That's right. LOL. Then, parallel to midnight's approach, the overall staff's goal of converting The Red Room into a dimmed and cozy dance floor area and to equip it with its temporary created DJ booth, including its quite experience enhancing sound system, slowly started to arise as well. Boom. My vessel's responsibilities from the get-go always remained in the 1) Stacking of all the dining tables and chairs into the outdoors Area exercise, in 2) Ensuring that every possible previous dinner indications vanished, in the 3) Care taking of the desired hominess SpeCial eFFecT Spreading vibrations by adding many candles into its dimmed space and in 4) To lastly switch the inviting and quite bright OrangeRed Grotto neon sign into its OFF-mode state of appearance. Switch. Once these tasks successfully got accomplished, my following mission then resulted in altering The Dark Room into its matching loungy theme-based space. The German owner "Schauzi", who gained this nickname via La Maman, based on a from his end quite FuNNy picked Deep and Juicy Halloween black mustache costume detail on a particular year, and the main DJ of the night would always simultaneously to *"little Linda's"* doings take care of the setting the BiG LOUDspeakers, including the DJ booth with a few tables Up task and of any further required technical installments, in order to provide every arriving *"wiLD & Free"* wired soul an amazing vibrational excursion. *"Music is the Answer to your Problems."* Yup. That is where it all happened. Ha! Then, in order to provide every Grotto attendee an as smooth and professional as possible Dinner into an Underground "Club" transition ride, the on duty staff's goal and focus during those particular evenings therefore always resulted in the coordination of letting The Red Room getting filled UP first by ensuring that after a certain set time any newly arriving dining guests would be welcomed into The Dark Room area, in order to secure for their many available senses to enjoy their just entered indulging journey to the fullest and this in an "undisturbed" manner. That's right. As soon as I found myself in my UPgraded work of state reality position, my vessel therefore instantly got declared as THE set waitress in The Red, my favorite Room, on these SpeCial Saturdays, so that I closely would be finding myself being enabled to as *"Smooth* as an *Operator"* overview, orchestrate and guide the entire *"ongRowing"* ceremony into its *"Let's get Ready to Rock 'n Roll"* converting flow. And. Let's Go. Another reality check happening, that my soul truly loved about these quite adventurous nights, unraveled itself with the "fact" that some of our *"wiLD & Free"* spirited regulars decided to embark onto their Sweet' N Low journey with some yummy Grotto food first, by then further celebrating each's granted *"Living on Earth Game"* opportunity as a unit throughout the following few hours, UP onto this point, during which either their souls or ours found themselves Ready to travel back *"Home Sweet Home"* for some well-deserved bzZZ moments. Ha! And now you might be finding yourself wondering, my curious *Co-Traveler*, as of how LATE our doors would remain open for then. Right? Well and that answer is EXACTLY why this entire "anything goes" spectacle quite soon got well known in New York's After-Hour underground scene and this mainly by its convenient and *FAST* speeding Word-to-Mouth delivered advertising tool, as *"little Linda"* already experienced it throughout her small apple travels. Wink. Now, the last on set spinning DJ usually would be starting to slowly tune down those many fine vibrating tracks as soon as the warm sun welcomed mother earth anew somewhere between 6am and 7am, or whenever the spirit of this mini Burning Man organized celebration on a rare occasion began to fade away earlier. Yup. That long. Our busiest and craziest hours though, as for its After-Hour theme, therefore typically unfolded themselves any time after 4am, alongside with the arrival of all the many *"wiLD & Free"* spirited Concrete Jungle night owls, who instantly kept enhancing Grotto's already quite *"Maniac"* existing magic with the contribution of their own *"Let's Go Crazy" "Self"*. Ha! Certainly, those late-night celebrations at times even ended up attracting the attention of any by passing cops, which possible party pOoper endangerment Nini's soul thankfully always intuitively knew how to dismantle within a SNAP with her "innocent" Swiss charm, once being alarmed from our hired bouncer, whilst the entire gathered Grotto community supported her doings as "Silently as Lambs" indoors. Snap. Then, as soon as the green light was back, the Music got turned on anew and all the remaining vessels continued their celebrations even more so with a now newly added *"Let's Go Crazy"* reason. Oh yeah! Fortunately, our many close by Forsyth Street neighbors all along reacted very understandingly throughout those many Who is Sexy?, Deep and Juicy and Sweet' N Low rides at count and some of them even ended up joining our festivities on a regular basis, which incidences always succeeded in adding an even more SpeCial touch onto this family style happening at hand. Oh, and yes, these last Saturdays of the month shifts might somewhat appear as rather LONG ones. So they truly were indeed. Though super FuN ones and the time during these quite interesting unfolding time traveling hours always sped by within a SNAP and sometimes even way TOO fast for *"little Linda's"* taste. Ha! That's right. Well, since my soul got provided with so many *"Super Happy Comfort Zone"* boosting *"FuN Fact"* criteria's, with Freedom, with Belonging, with "HER" style of celebrating this quite precious granted *"Living on Earth Game"* ride as Linda Wartenweiler, "her" collecting all the empty glasses and bottles, including the stacking the bar with whatever was needed tasks, therefore always made those many on duty hours appear as being out and about, rather than being at "work". Oh yeah. And of course, I at times even put on my dancing shoes in order to test the DJ's work. Ha! That's right. What a great combo these shifts simply turned out to be and on top of it all, my soul even got paid for enjoying a difFeRent style of an *"I've had the Time of My Life"* experience. Thank you. With this unexpected *"What Other Hobby, besides watching Movies and TV shows, enjoying Music, Dancing and Celebrating this "Living on Earth Game" adventure of mine as often as possible, could I possibly turn into a FuN paying profession"* opportunity, the magical Universe definitely succeeded in introducing *"little Linda"* to a further quite appealing income resource style, which presented itself as a *"Help. Dance. Play."* formula. OOOh! As "sweet' n juicy" this discovery truly keeps on resonating with my soul ever since. Love. Then, as with everything on mother earth's plane, change is an inevitable *"NeverEnding"* occurring reality "truth" and therefore things at my beloved *"Connecting and Belonging"* Grotto opportunity slowly started to take their own twists and turns as well by instead reliably creating the required room for every then involved soul to embark onto their own further individual designated *"Expansion and Growth"* adventures. Beloved coworkers therefore started to move on and new ones appeared instead. Regulars turned into strangers and new strangers into regulars. Along with these *"ongRowing"* vibrational shifts, new ones arose as well in which a sudden appeared Taking advantage of Generosity mind set called in restrictions on all ends and that chain reaction eventually caused for this with magic filled Grotto bubble to in one smack EXPLODE right in front of *"little Linda's"* eyes. POOF. Bye-Bye. And these shifting moments therefore then left my *"Connecting and Belonging"* opportunity of 4 years melt into a serious, mundane and quite chaotic cat and mouse whirlwind dance, which as for its exchange rate successfully assisted my *"ongRowing" Boot Camp* journey to take off to its finest, by providing it a LOT of wood to ignite *"little Linda's"* second and third NYC experienced break downs within one month time, accompanied with a rapid loss of appetite, including pounds for starters. Yeeha! *"One way or Another, I'm gonna Get Ya'. Warned Ya'."* Ufff. Then, 5 months into this new *"Self-created"* unhealthy and somewhat low vibrating Grotto experience of mine, my soul finally came to accept this from my heart quite a while ago announced new *"Letting go of Something that No Longer Serves One's Growth and Expansion"* reality check and the therefore required, procrastinated, uncomfortable appearing and more than overdue *"Time to say Goodbye"* action step prosecution. Oh NO! Sniff. Yes, that's when it also dawned on me that the kind Universe seemed to have provided me all along with the required letting go indicating signs and this in the same manner, as it already did during *"little Linda's"* frustrating last few months in Erlen. What?! Hmmm. Yes, this entire new whirlwind spectacle at some point suddenly triggered the back then recorded tape onto *"little Linda's" "Head Cinema"* screen, which re-run with "No Doubt" seemed to match the *"ongRowing"* scenario at hand. Boah! As how interesting this awareness "truth" simply kept on striking my soul. Certainly, I instantly found myself asking as of WHAT further precious *"Life Toolbox"* ingredient *"little Linda"* was supposed to gain out of these two matching "coincidental" insights at hand, by then wondering if it maybe resulted in the *"Whenever the easy flow of One's "Living on Earth Game" ride is starting to get bumpy, accompanied with some inner "ongRowing" resistance, that a change of some sort would be of help in order to then successfully being enabled to step back into this magical "Easy Rider" state of experience again, if desired?"* awareness interpretation. Ha! Well, my soul meanwhile very much finds "herself" resonating with this "truth", after having come across a few more of those "Déjà Vu" SpeCial eFFecT revelations within "her" further undertaken travels and adventures through time and space. That's right. In mid-December 2011, *"little Linda"* therefore finally found herself Ready to switch her awareness state back into the helpful *"Heart over Head"* mode by sadly handing in the overdue 2 weeks' notice to her very understanding Schnauzi boss, after an unforgettable, wiLD, amazing, quite crazy, challenging, expanding and enriching 4 ½ year *"Connecting and Belonging"* Grotto opportunity ride as a unit. Sniff. And that is how my wonderful Plan B solution chapter found its bittersweet end and how the *Caterpillar* with the help of the all-time supporting Universe decided to slowly call in "her" metamorphosis journey into a so-called colorful *Butterfly* by stepping right back into the from my mom's early on provided valuable *"Spread your Wings my Child and Fly HiGH" "Life Toolbox"* ingredient attitude. Bye-Bye. Looking back to my entire New York City *"Don't Dream your Life. Live your Dream." Boot Camp* collected souvenir list, from where my soul is speaking to you today, my wonderful Co-Traveler, I must admit that *"little Linda's"* most dear and favorite *"Living on Earth Game"* memory creations actually occurred during her magical *"Work equals FuN"* Grotto ride, between 2008 until the end of 2010, which got enhanced by her NYC Dream Team and so-called *"The Other Planet" "Extended Family Member"* formation of *PutshkiPatshki, DoggyDoggy, SchneidySchnupp, La Maman, Ma Chouchette, Miss Colombia, il Bastardo, Leo, Jorge, Schnauzi* and by all the many souls, who enabled for our many mutual adventures to take place with their lovely presence, support and indulging desires. That's right. And therefore, I am shouting out a BiG THANK YOU to y'all, as each one of you furthermore assisted *"little Linda"* to lastly *Belong*, to *Connect* and to also evoke those wonderful *"Home Sweet Home"* vibrations within this entire *"THE Ultimate Childhood Dream"* Concrete Jungle *Boot Camp* chapter. Well and certainly, I always find *"little Linda"* jUMPing right back into this Grotto *"Super Happy Comfort Zone"* groove, whenever she chooses to time travel, by either playing some of those various from La Maman and PutshkiPatshki provided DJ set recordings, that often times added a SpeCial background sound eFFecT to our dinner adventures, which originally got created by *Moos Juh, Gusto, Sid Vaga, Wiseacre, Sabo, Nickodemus, Gilles Wasserman* or *Zile Maravic* or whenever she chooses to recreate that atmosphere by picking some specific tunes from her overall Grotto experience of 4 ½ years *"Self-*created" playlists from her iTunes or iPod "classic" treasure box collection, which lets "Thievery Corporation" and "Bonobo" with "No Doubt" rank as the leading throwback Artists at hand. That's right. *"Because we are your friends, you'll never be alone again. Oh, come ooon"* LOVE. Always. Then, as every closing door based on its *"Cause and eFFecT"* truth always instantly evokes to for minimum one new one to swing open, the kind Universe therefore swiftly went ahead and provided *"little Linda"* with her next income opportunity and this "only" a few days after her notice given taken action step. Ha! On the following Wednesday, at around 6pm, I remember how my white iPhone 3 device suddenly got my attention, as soon as its incoming call signal reached my auricles, which at that time resulted in some of *"little Linda's"* favorite Sweet' N Low tunes of either the Lovebird's *"Want you in my Soul"*, *"Turn me On"* by Black Coffee or Hendrik Schwarz's version of *"Feeling you"* by Omar *"Boom. BOOm. BOOM."* sneak peek track. Now, even though this call resulted from a to my contact list unrecognized number, my curious inner Gemini once more overpowered my suspicious mind by answering it immediately with a *"Hello? Is it me you're looking for?"* first reaction. To my surprise, I instantly came to recognize the voice of a to me known soul, whom *"little Linda"* often times came across during the "early" hours of our monthly SpeCial Saturday spectacles or whenever my vessel attempted to enter the from Grotto close by *Nublu* venue for some LiVE Music or DJ hosted *"FuN Fact"* excursions. As soon as my friend found himself happy about my, to his opening question provided bartending skills description, his soul then further shared, that 1) He recently took on a manager function of a fairly new opened bar in the East Village, that 2) His usual Wednesdays hired bartender just dropped his shift and that 3) He therefore would love for my vessel to fill in this emergency gap at hand, and this at 8pm. Ha! Excited about this swift and out of the blue appeared new opportunity, I right away approved his request, as the time frame happened to be fitting my schedule just wonderfully. 2 hours later, my vessel therefore found itself being placed in a quite interesting bar called *Bamboo*, which used to be located on 1st Avenue between 1st and 2nd

Street, right underneath the old residence of the legendary Drag Queen Chinese restaurant Lucky Cheng's, mixing regular drinks, Long Island Iced Teas and Caipirinhas and the latter two for the very first time. Oh yeah! *"Where there is a Will there ALWAYS is a Way"* and with the wonderful guidance of today's quite convenient smart phone Google access possibility, I therefore within a snap found myself happily and successfully able to add those quite easy pouring cocktail creations into my overall liquid mixing repertoire as well. Sweet. After a FuN and busy Brazilian night, my friend must have found himself quite pleased with my performance, as his soul alongside with my almost departure ended up offering all the following Wednesday night shifts, including the opportunity for some possible Saturday fill-ins to my vessel. SNAP. Well, and as his kind proposal appeared to be the perfect next match for 1) My soon lose to be transforming schedule at hand, so that I lastly 2) Would be able to grant my, over these past 6, as quiet intense experienced Grotto months' tired fallen vessel its desired Resting, Resting, Resting and Recovering time-out period and as it 3) Also seemed to accommodate *"little Linda's"* further urge to move her *"ongRowing"* in the background pounding initial *"Acting Dream"* chosen path back to its number one focused priority, my soul therefore happily found "herself" accepting my friend's trusting offer on the spot. Boom. At first, this newly delivered "team for two" TKB Erlen style dynamic opportunity provided my soul with a LOT of FuN, whilst my friendly manager's kept "himself" busy with "his" very skilled doorman abilities and mine with "her" expanding bartender ones, and all of this set in a MUCH slower and more relaxing overall environment than from where my vessel just came from. Ufff. Then, as most of these Wednesday night shifts ended up unfolding themselves as rather slow and as my vessel after a relaxing duration of 5 months, collected enough of those for new challenges and *"BiG Wide World"* adventure creations required Duracell molecules, I therefore came to the conclusion that my time anew happened to be worth more than the 30 bucks' tips that I on most nights ended up schlepping *"Home Sweet Home"* after many bzZZ experienced spectacles. 30 Bucks?! What? Yup. That's right. Wink. The ONE most valuable, priceless and newly gained *"Life Toolbox"* ingredient that *"little Linda"* found herself able to gain out of this entire out of the blue provided Bamboo opportunity though, to her surprise actually ended up being the genius transformation from the early on discovered *"Being able to Work Freely in My Own Style and Rhythm"* and *"Being Fully Trusted with No Direct Boss in my back"* lifestyle desire into its UPgraded and very head to toe soul resonating *"Working by mySelf and on my Own"* version, which newly discovered *"Swimming AGAiNST the Stream"* career style path ever since decided, to present itself from its own *"ongRowing"* and multifaceted unraveling side. Boom! Very grateful I therefore feel towards this quit expansion enhancing attracted next transitioning key *"Stepping-Stone"* in this, my *"Living on Earth Game"* journey as Linda Wartenweiler. Thank you, Malik and dear Universe. Thank you. Then, as soon as I found myself, parallel to my meanwhile successfully refocused *"Acting Dream"* path with still quite a LOT of my available "Abundance of Time" gift at hand, my inner voice therefore right away guided my vessel back to my lovely Big Apple "dad" Schnauzi in order to find out if his soul possibly might be having any here and there FuN involved available income resources at hand. After all my vessel happened to be living in the money-oriented business capital New York City, in which opportunities lie on every corner, if one stays open and flexible to ride this already discovered *"Cause and eFFecT"* wave. Ha! And. Oh yeah. A further Grotto adventure though, certainly remained as an out of question option and my interest with this suggestion therefore gravitated more towards Schnauzi's in 2002 launched "Mother-Ship" and *"Self"* operated catering company creation, known as *Monterone*. Once reached out to my friendly ex-boss's iPhone, our two vessels as a result found themselves on the following AM as desired in a meeting and guess what, my wonderful *Co-Traveler?* Ha! Exactly. Anew, I found myself quite surprised about this further, from the all-time supporting Universe sent *"Thy Wish is my Command" "Synchronicity par Excellence"* solution package. Boah! After a warm and crisp catching up phase, within the walls of Schnauzi's office space located above The Red Room, his soul happily began to UPdate *"little Linda"* about Monterone's just newly taken on expansion journey and that therefore he happened to be in the need of hiring new staff. Right NOW. Bingo. Furthermore, I came to learn that 1) His "Mother-Ship" would be taking over the in-house existing coffee bar in one of NYC's top leading, from industry innovators chosen photo studio's, which finds its home base in the *Meetpacking District*, in 2 weeks' time, that 2) Monterone's catering services in addition to its already "coffee" set presence would be advertised as part of any occurring project bookings, spread out to the entire then 7 available creative spaces at hand, that his following step on this newly entered venture of his literally occurred in 3) Hiring the for it required barista staff and that 4) Our reconnection therefore revealed itself as THE perfect *"Synchronicity par Excellence"* jackpot solution. Yay! That's right. And. Thank you, my beloved inner voice. Thank you. Then, at the end of our short and crisp meeting, I happily found myself replaying *"Yes"* to this newly appeared and creative sounding *"Living on Earth Game"* adventure opportunity at hand, as my soul very much so resonated with everything that "she" came to hear. Certainly, my Grotto "dad" would have loved to hire *"little Linda's"* presence as a full-time barista resolution, though his soul already found itself during "his" proposal very aware of the fact that her priorities meanwhile shifted themselves back to her beloved and somewhat neglected *"THE Ultimate Childhood Dream Vision"*, which also included some deeper scouting excursions of Big Apple's opportunity availabilities within her *"Swimming AGAiNST the Stream"* desired awareness "truth". Boom. That's right. After all, my vessel already spent quite a BiG amount of my all-time available "Abundance of Time" gift within Grotto's "save" walls and therefore the *Caterpillar* found itself MORE than eager to as *"wiLD & Freely"* as possible keep on extending its explorations of what further valuable ingredients this *"All or Nothing"* Concrete Jungle had to offer for *"little Linda's"* valuable *Boot Camp* "Life

Toolbox" collection. Ha! Very understanding, my dear Schnauzi boss then went ahead and gave me the liberty to choose the to my soul preferred days, on which "she" desired to be in charge of his, our new "baby", as my vessel happened to be the first hired barista on board. *"Coo-coo-cool. Yeah, yeah. This is so cool."* Tuesdays and Fridays therefore suited my taste just well for starters and for the remaining three days, he kindly asked me to please go ahead and check within my meanwhile quite wide ranged grown NYC network, if one soul would appear as the additional and available perfect match. *"Thy Will is My Command"* and within a day or two, another out of my NYFA chapter gained friend happily found herself jUMPing aboard too. Boom. Done. With the successful completion of our "team for two" barista formation, our two souls then found ourselves "lucky" to obtain a full-on barista training at our newly attracted workspace located within Industria Superstudio's walls on the second floor, which got hosted by a professional instructor. Those 3 with coffee filled hours, to my surprise very much unraveled themselves as a very educational awareness check and *"little Linda"* certainly found herself more than astounded about the newly discovered "truth" of HOW MUCH of a complex passion choice, this from especially those "Manhattatian's" acquired strong java love, revealed itself to be. Wow! Well and this passionate and knowledgeable connoisseur most definitely left a very impressive mark on my soul, as *"little Linda's"* own coffee journey ever since transformed itself into a quite "awakening" and respectful experience. Cheers. By mid-June 2012, the with Industria Superstudio teamed up first Monterone Coffee Bar ever then found itself finally Ready to get launched into its own unique adventure, which newly attracted *"Connecting and Belonging" "Stepping-Stone"* opportunity right away led my soul to be spoiled with a wonderful mix of "her" *"Work* equals *FuN"* desired lifestyle, *Freedom, Peace*, plenty of *Caffeine, Responsibility, Creativity,* a full-on breather for my *"Red and White Saving Sock"* account, *Networking* opportunities, with the continuity of this just newly UPgraded *"Working by mySelf and on my Own"* reality check and with just enough time at hand for myself, for my beloved *"Acting Dream"* and for *"little Linda's"* further NYC *Boot Camp "Growth and Expansion"* exploration quest. Perfect! The only "real" challenge that I as a meanwhile perfectly adapted New York City Night Owl ended up facing, turned out to be these spontaneous transitioning attempts into an Early Bird, twice and towards the end even more per week. Uiii. b*zZZ*. Yes, those from the get-go into my *"Don't Dream your Life. Live your Dream."* discovered 6:48am intervaled *"Rise and Shine! Rise and Shine!"* wake-UP calls by then definitely found themselves anew as quite "disturbing", as usually *"little Linda"* would feel prompted to at this hour simply turn sideways again with the goal, to continue her many adventures in dreamy land, for at least another 3 hours. That's right! Thank God that on each one of these Early Bird occurring mornings, my vessel always found itself able to leave its Williamsburg *"Home Sweet Home"* base assured of the fact that its rewarding salvation kept on welcoming it right at the destined arrival destination, in the form of a delicious *Red Eye* at 8:00am, which contains a cup filled with freshly brewed drip coffee, topped off with one or two strong espresso shots. Oo-WAH! Yes, and this magical *"Alive and Kickin'"* morning ritual always reliably took care of its satisfying awakening transformation into a promising new day ahead, and this for 2 years straight. Love. Aside from my *"ongRowing"* expansion journey into a coffee making expert, this *"Working by mySelf and on my Own"* part-time barista opportunity certainly provided *"little Linda"* with many more valuable ingredients, experiences and insights for her further *"Life Toolbox"* repertoire collection. Yay. And this is why. As Industria mainly gets booked for a variety of advertisement projects, my Artistic and Thurgau originated soul therefore ALWAYS felt quite honored, whenever the kind Universe presented "her" with the further Early Bird treat of being able to either interAct or to even spoil the at times as celebrity declared appearing vessels, of for instance *Heidi Klum, Katie Holmes, 50 Cent, Susan Sarandon, Debbie Harry, Eva Mendes, Forest Whitaker, Demi Lovato, Willem Dafoe, The Olson Twins, Kelly Osbourne* and *Helena Christensen*, with their pick of *Coffee, Tea, Smoothie's*, freshly squeezed *Veggie Juices* and/or available *Snacks* at hand. Ahhh. And. Snap. *"little Linda"* certainly *"ongRowingly"* ended up enjoying these spontaneous, in front of the TV or Movie screen presented Abracadabra SpeCial eFFecT moments of those many "like-minded" creative souls to the fullest, especially in this quite unique and in a way private set environment. One of the Olson Twins' vessel btw already welcomed my reality during my very first Grotto summer and this out of the eyes of a still *"Miss Fresh Off the Boat"* awareness cruising food runner perspective. Ha! So "running" into them "again" in the form of a Happy Hour package about 6 years later, by "still" being hired by the same boss, presented itself as another quite *"Coo-coo-cool. Yeah, yeah. This is so cool."* experience. Ha! Another additional three hiGHlights that find themselves standing out to *"little Linda"* in this entire Monterone-Industria "marriage" chapter, for ONE is the extra treat of having been granted a very interesting sneak peek opportunity into the world of the model and fashion industry via the at times for fashion shows and other kinds of events booked venues, with TWO the for any Gemini born soul's required diversity, surprises and creativity filled *"Work* equals *FuN"* experience, which let these days at times truly *SPEED* by in one breath only and on other ones they appeared in a *"NeverEnding"* counting contest against my *"ongRowing"* b*z*ZZ state of awareness and with THiRD of all, the creation of a wonderful *"Extended Family"* style work relationship with many *Recurring Creative Souls*, with the *Entire Industria Crew*, which also included the so generous and all time VERY friendly Italian co-owner couple *Fabrizio* and *Geraldina*. Grazie. Yes, and even though my vessel always happened to be the only Monterone representative on duty, *"little Linda"* with this newly presented set-up quite soon found a new way of how to boost her *"Connecting and Belonging"* desire to its extended next level. Abracadabra. Yup. This entire Monterone-Industria adventure actually ended up developing itself UP onto the point, during which Industria started to here and there require my Swiss service skills for their own end of things on my off-days as well, which back and forth switch of employers always revealed itself as a FuN, flexible and perspective changing exercise. The most honored my soul certainly felt about the co-owners' request of hiring my vessel as a trusted staff member for their UPcoming wedding ceremony, which actually took place a few weeks AFTER my last Monterone-Industria shift. Yay! With "No Doubt", I therefore immediately accepted their very sweet "invitation" and found myself able to close this overall coffee-making chapter within the walls of Industria Superstudio in the form of an absolute fabulous, magical and loving last celebrational gig. Grazie mille. Now, as by Spring 2014 my dear Schnauzi "dad" came to decide that his soul desired to practice a to "him" overdue *"Letting go of Something that No Longer Serves One's Growth and Expansion"* action step with his, our 2 years ago launched Monterone-Industria "baby", I found mine as quite a happy camper as well, as *"little Linda"* meanwhile pretty much grew out of her barista shoes, which caused for her further *"Growth and Expansion"* cravings to secretly *"Knock, Knock, Knockin' on her "I Want to Break Free" door"*, a little while ago already. Perfect. Well, and alongside with this shifting point within my overall *"Living on Earth Game"* ride experience, another quite spectacular key moment ended up welcoming itself into my awareness as well, which to *"little Linda's"* surprise called in the reality "truth" of suddenly finding herself being thrown into this opportunity puddle of being able to sell her many with time adapted service *"Life Toolbox"* skill ingredients in the form of a diversity of income resources to her throughout the past 8 years *"Connecting and Belonging"* created Big Apple community. Wow! What?! Yes, finally my, what some souls consider "hard work", started to pay itself off by further metamorphosing this from 2 ½ years ago detected *"Working by mySelf and on my Own"* existence into its ever since adapted and truly embraced *"Working by mySelf as my Own Boss"* freelancing choice, which income form *"little Linda"* already very well found herself being familiar with from her beloved *"Acting Dream"* reality. Ha! That's right. And this is how this to me precious rocket ship "unknowingly" got launched. As soon as my soul spread the word about "her" immediate service skills availability over the meanwhile incredibly transformed social media *"Planet"* platform, my vessel *"ongRowingly"* got requested for a wide range of opportunities, which let this entire *"Work equals FuN"* flow appear as a quite colorful rainbow made out of On call Hostessing and Food Running at my ex-Grotto coworker's then newly in my neighborhood opened Barcelona-style restaurant *El Born*, Babysitting, Catering and Bartending Assistance at Monterone's hired events, a couple of fix recurring *Airbnb Cleaning* gigs, *Coat Checking* at La Maman's and Schnauzi's in 2013 newly opened smooth and classy Restaurant/Lounge/Club creation *Louie And Chan/303* plus *Bartending* on privately hosted events, which allowed *"little Linda"* on one occasion to even serve some yummy cocktails to David Schwimmer as a surprise SpeCial eFFecT appeared "Friends-ly" guest. Ahhh. *"Life is Good."* Interestingly, except for one from the beloved Universe delivered proposals, I to my surprise found myself being able to backtrace all the way to *"little Linda's"* adventurous and most favorite NYC chapter, which is *TatAAA!* Yes, to Grotto. Boah. This May 2007 Plan B Swissair resume printing out mission truly revealed itself once more as quite a powerful *"Cause and eFFecT"* taken *"Stepping-Stone"* at hand. Who would have thought, right?! Wow. WoW. WOW. Well and during those transitioning days, it really started to dawn on *"little Linda"* as of HOW BiG of a network she actually found herself able to create throughout these entire 8 with opportunity filled *"Don't Dream your Life. Live your Dream."* Boot Camp chapter years on this *"The Other Planet"* sphere. That's right. This reality check very much so presented itself as quite a satisfying, proud and powerful awareness moment. Well done! Yup, my oh so dutiful Swiss originated soul worked "her" way UP and most importantly *Through it ALL.* Yeeha! Thank you. Thank you. THANK YOU. To each single soul out there that supported this part of *"little Linda's"* *"Living on Earth Game"* ride with your kind work contribution, with your trust and with our at some point formed connection. Hugs. And. Blessings.

"I got the Poison and the Remedy. I got the Pulsating Rhythmical remedy."
Now, as "Every Mirror always has Two Faces", we therefore of course do come across this phenomenon along of my many *"Living on Earth Game"* travels as well. Ha! We better, right? Wink. Well and by now, my lovely *Co-Traveler*, you might be finding yourself wondering about the further unfolding of *"little Linda's"* beloved *"THE Ultimate Childhood Dream Vision"* and as of why my focus thus far mainly kept on being directed towards those many "safe" *"Connecting and Belonging"* income adventures, when in fact my soul's *"Don't Dream your Life. Live your Dream." "Acting. Uncertainty. Complete Life Change."* chosen path desire appeared as the actual reason for my vessels small to the Big Apple transformation in 2006. Hmmm. Well, and this is exactly one of the many, MANY questions that I at some point down the road found myself asking as well in the form of *"What just happened to me throughout all these many past years? What am I doing. To my "Self"? OMG. I COMPLETELY am "OFF track". Oh NO! Help!!"* Yup, and this divinely delivered epiphany wake-UP call lets us right away dive into *"little Linda's"* earlier on mentioned *Artistic and "Self*-developing" *Boot Camp* experience, which my soul at this very *"Now Moment"* does feel the urge to take yours on a little detour in order to equip it with my NOW eagle eye gained perception of WHAT I believe happened within my vessel, during this VERY spectacular chapter at hand. Further, I also would love, as part of my *"One Thing ALWAYS leads to Another in its magical "Cause and eFFecT" unfolding truth."* believe, direct our focus on the latter first. Ready? Yeeha! Me too. As already revealed, this in 2006 undertaken small apple Big Apple transformation naturally brought along many new challenges and lessons for my Linda Wartenweiler repertoire at hand, which very much so left me with countless impressions, resources and perspectives in return. Living in this *FAST* passed, energetic, charming, sneaky and fascinating metropolis *"ongRowingly"* for 8 ⅛ years, surely thus far metamorphosed itself into my MOST valuable and demanding

journey of them all, this my soul knows with all of "her" heart. Well and the giving birth process to this *"Self*-interpreted and created" US-Swiss Linda Wartenweiler version, this time surely required quite a few more grabbing, squeezing and willpower efforts from my end than back in the 1970ies. Ha! That's for sure. Thankfully, after almost a decade of a tireless, determined and with a rewarding countless colorful filled trials and tricks collection at hand, my soul eventually discovered its releasing combination out of that *"PandoraWombBox"* entered experience as well and here I am today with another exciting victory in my pocket. Hooray! Which in a longer breath means, that this in 2006 undertaken relocation action step very much so introduced my soul to an absolute contrasting reality check and this in every sense of the word. Duality of its finest. That's right. Within these mutually first three explored decades of my many *"Living on Earth Game"* adventures, I mainly found myself being exposed to nature, animals, kind and helpful souls and by a much slower paced lifestyle. Alongside with my arrival in this Concrete Jungle's madness, my soul as a matter of fact very much so found "herself" suddenly consistently floating within its contrasting opponent, which situation indeed requited quite some advanced adjusting skills. Now, as duality happens to be another *"NeverEnding"* existing law that this *"Living on Earth Game"* experience keeps on offering on every single end and moment, I therefore meanwhile came to the understanding that it incredibly much so gets intensified within those *FAST* pulsating and vibrating New York City occurring energies. Meaning, that if one disregards this law or simply remains unaware of its existence by instead trying to ride these newly appeared opportunity waves based on all the from any other existing realities imported rules and believe systems, that then as a result some very interesting SpeCial eFFecTs will be arising into ones *"Now Moment"* creations. Sooner or later. Guaranteed. In my case, distractions and any sorts of health issues kept on insisting in becoming my new BFF's by promising and securing my soul an unforgettable ride throughout this magical Candyland par excellence. True fact. Now, as I on top of everything decided to raise the stakes for this *"Soul Childhood Dream"* realization quest of mine even hiGHer by throwing my vessel into a *"NeverEnding"* puddle filled with unknown souls for starters, I therefore at first only found myself having access to my own inner guiding system, including my many thus far collected past occasion experiences in order to be led through this entire new given game plan at hand. Then, alongside with the *"ongRowing"* inner and outer appearing resistances, which arose whilst my soul kept on applying all those wonderfully adapted Swiss rooting choices, I therefore as a reaction instinctively found myself reviewing and adjusting whatever I thought would be necessary in order to secure a smooth traveling solution based on my many past experiences. Yes, and that was then, when my entire pre-set *Believe System, Behaviors, Actions, Approaches, Looks, Humor,* including *My Way* of *Being, Thinking* and *Speaking*, simply ANYTHiNG, that out of MY interpretation seemed to be standing in my way in regards of the fulfillment of my beloved *"American Dream"* needed to get adjusted as good and as *FAST* as possible.

Oh yeah. And this success formula then furthermore brought along this, from my end for a couple of years overlooked probably quite important side SpeCial eFFecT of *The Abandonment of my OWN identity and of my OWN True "Self"*. Oops. An additional to me quite important reality check that I found myself experiencing throughout my small apple Big Apple adjusting phase, resulted out of my *"ongRowing" Being Nice*, my *Pleasing* and out of my *Helping Syndrome* developing symptoms. Yup. Prior to my NYC existence, kindness and being of help used to be the most normal and common traits to practice amongst my Swiss Confederates. Certainly, my soul kept this wonderful habit up, as my experience with it mostly resulted in excellent outcomes towards my own well-being and happiness. Now, once I found myself overwhelmed with this generous "Abundance of Time" gift at hand, my desire to share it with others very much so got enhanced alongside with time and with it the practice of those three "symptoms". Even though my adventurous soul by nature already happens to be a passionate YES-sayer, my desire for using this FuN habit even more so grew stronger by the day in order to ensure that I was being *Liked, Recognized, Busy* and/or *With Company*. jUMPing onto every being busy opportunity that arose in front of my eyes therefore turned into another new behavior choice of mine and responses like *"Yes, I can, No Matter what"* and *"No, I don't need help"* into a deconstructive, from my head voice led developed attitude spiral instead. At some point, I even found myself adding a little extra SpeCial touch onto all my "doings", then from those many past experiences I already learned that this formula always worked its satisfying magic. And guess what? It also reliably did on this new quest of mine and to my surprise, this delightful added touch actually ended up working even better in this *FAST* pulsating city than anywhere else before. Hooray! The end results out of this genius developed tactic of mine this time around turned out to be, that 1) My batteries got used up much faster and quicker by the year and that therefore 2) Enough room for these many existing low vibrational side SpeCial eFFecTs got created as its rewarding gesture. Strike. Which suddenly led words like *Burnouts, Breakdowns, Anxieties, Being Drained and Sad* infuse my vocabulary selection in regards of my overall well-being and state of mind description to others. What?! Yes. At first, my "almost" recovery phases passed by fairly quickly. Then with time, my vessel, including immune system decided to slow things down for me for a little while, as they most certainly must have gotten VERY annoyed by my *"ongRowing"* recovery requests. Both though indeed eagerly tried hard to bring their point of having me *STOP Doing* what I *Kept on Practicing* across. Even though I at times did hear their callings, I still ended up being too busy being busy and disregarded any further warnings in disbelieve with a *"Ahhh. I can do this. I am fine. Everything will be wonderful again very soon. No worries."* reaction. Along with that process, this beloved *"Positivity Card"* trick of mine therefore more and moRE found itself getting replaced by its opponent and the city's kind spirit probably supported my successful transformation with a cheerful *"Welcome to New York Linda. Soon, VERY soon you will be one of us. Keep*

on doing what you are practicing. You are doing GREAT. Woot WOOT."
attitude. Yup. Surely, my further habits of *Constantly being on The Run, Carrying for Others More than for mySelf, Looking for Love and to Be Loved, the Need to Belong*, my *24/7 Availability rate*, my *Priority Settings*, the many *Distractions*, my *Being a "Good" and Responsible Employee/Co-Worker/Friend Desire* and the adaption of an *Unhealthy NYC Lifestyle*, helped rounding this turning point of my adventurous *Artistic and "Self-developing" Boot Camp* journey UP, in which I allowed my soul to enter into a from my end as darker perceived *"Living on Earth Game"* exploration ride. Now, as my soul never experienced such a LONG, intense and *"ongRowing"* Linda Wartenweiler darkness period prior, it therefore took me quite some time to realize what actually was happening to and with me. Somehow, my usual inner magic suddenly started to vanish and everything that I touched seemed to be of momentary happiness, success and "gold" only. Something very much was "off". This I knew and felt all along. What the cause of this "hasty" appearing whirlwind resulted in though, stayed blurry to my soul for another few more years. pOops. *Caterpillar Butterfly* metamorphosis eFFecT? Hmmm. Maybe. Then, as a further reward for my many undertaken efforts, a difFeRent kind of domino eFFecT soon started to introduce itself into my newly created reality as well. The more drained that I felt, the unhappier I decided that I turned. The more helpless that I Acted, the darker situations, thoughts and souls I allowed to enter into my awareness and alongside with this shift, those 20 pounds/10 kilograms and my hopes started to successfully melt away as well. *"Moment-to-Moment"*. Day-by-Day. Boom. And. Ouch. The darker my awareness grew, the more my soul as a result started to rebel against my *"ongRowing"* life choices with anything that "she" was able to find. Resistance of its finest. Once I allowed myself to become more *Aware, Attentive* and *Concerned* about my overall well-being, it suddenly dawned on me that I somehow ended up giving WAY too much of myself away to others. What?! Yes. The side eFFecT that this generous distribution of my many existing goods attitude in this Apple version brought along with, turned out to be that my soul with time began to trade LOTS of "her" *Inner Light, Sparkle* and *Positivity* with an on my end very unbalanced and lowering vibrational experienced outcome. And. Another. Ouch. "OUCH." In Switzerland exists this great and matching German proverb *"If you give someone your Small Finger then sHe will be taking your Entire Hand."* Well and this exact attitude happened to be the kind of "taking" that my soul found "herself" being used and accustomed to, up until then. In New York City, my soul then got granted the priceless opportunity of getting introduced to an even MORE extreme existing interpretation of this saying, which I came to experience as a *"If you give someone your Small Finger then sHe might as well be taking your Entire Hand, your Arm, your Body, your Energy, your Light, your Aura, your Dreams and Anything Else that You Allow your opposite to get from you."* reality check. OUCH! And yes, this metropolis' sneaky approach obviously varies just a tad from my known Thurgau version. LOL. That's right. And that is part of WHY and HOW my *Being Nice*, my *Pleasing* and my *Helping*

Syndrome symptoms started to play against my own *"Self"* and against my initial Big Apple dreams. Now, while my batteries discharged themselves more and moRE without me "noticing", I parallel with it also decided to switch my priorities from my beloved *"Soul Childhood Dream"* to those many available *"Comfort Zone" "FuN Facts"*, for a little while at least, as they simply felt more soothing, "rewarding" and "easier" than this *"ongRowing"* tiring, confusing and frustrating *"Acting. Uncertainty. Complete Life Change."* path choice at hand. Yup. And as this kind of behavior seemed to be getting practiced by almost every "Manhattatian" anyway, Linda Wartenweiler on top of it all finally found herself fitting in perfectly well in this new kind of comfortable *"Swimming ALONG WiTH the Current"* attitude choice. Ha! Here we go again. *"One way or Another, I'm gonna Find Ya' and Get Ya'. Watch Out."* Of course, this UPdated action plan once more right away put my entire *"THE Ultimate Childhood Dream Vision"* continuously on a daily hold, as I already "unknowingly" used to practice it in my dear Switzerland *"Living on Earth Game"* chapter, until the concerned and all time supportive Universe in 2013 decided, to literally put it on hold, and this until further notice. Boom. Yup. Sniff! And while all these instant available *"FuN Facts"* slowly transformed themselves into my first new chosen passion, my beloved *"little Linda"* as its *"Cause and eFFecT"* result therefore gradually began to turn smaller and quieter by the day as well. Bye-Bye. Floating in all those many Candyland distractions at first really felt amazing, as they momentarily succeeded in keeping my unpleasant and unwanted *Mister Loneliness* companion away by furthermore assisting to nurture all these newly accumulated soul wounds on an *"ongRowing"* basis, for a short amount of time, at least. Then, during those few hours that my vessel actually spent *"Home Sweet Home"* alone, I as a result came to face a *"NeverEnding"* inner cat and mouse resistance battle in regards of using my whatever time and energy resources I had left towards any of those from *"little Linda"* desired Acting proActivity opportunity creations, be it with auditions, Acting researches and/or with any type of networking approaches, within this then as still rather confusing and frustrating perceived foreign Entertainment industry at hand, which reality check therefore easily let for my *"Self*-confidence" to call in the assistance of *The Thief of Time* master, who probably better is known to you as *Madam ProCrastination*. Hello. Oftentimes, I already found myself quite lost and overwhelmed by trying to get the ball rolling only a tiny tad further, as my soul very much felt unsure, still, as of Where to start and How to find legit representation and better auditions. So instead of creating my own opportunities by being proActive, I therefore decided to be guided by this soothing and comforting new adapted *"Too much work. Maybe tomorrow."* mantra of mine. With that, my *"ongRowing"* disorientation and frustration level led me to choose the "easy" way out option by welcoming *Madam ProCrastination*, including the magical *"Self*-sabotage" ingredient into my game plan. Yay. The next action step, that my newly created US-Swiss Linda version alongside on this abandonment adventure of my True *"Self"* started practicing, turned out to be the habit to disregard my *Own Wants, Needs, Desires* and *Dreams*, as at some point I felt too numb and deaf towards that inner and outer created reality at hand. Boom. And successfully, I found myself being trapped again within a by *Miss Fear* orchestrated *"Head over Heart"* lifestyle. Bravo. Hey, this is part of New York's game after all and I definitely played it very well. *"All or Nothing - Push"*. Right? Ha! Then, after an enduring and stubborn fight with my Own *"Self"*, my *"ongRowing" Boot Camp* program in Summer 2013 lastly had me there, where it needed me to be, so that my BiG inner transformation finally could get triggered. Destination *Rock Bottom*. Abracadabra. Once I fully became to understand with all of my heart that I ended up running into a *Complete Undesired and to me "Wrong" Direction* and that my soul very much so got intoxicated by this city's spirit and by its sneaky methods, I as a result instinctively knew what needed to be done next *Survival Mode Button ON*, while putting the many on all levels ASAP required changes and adjustments into action. Boom. By doing so, I furthermore came to the understanding that if I wanted to create *Instant Powerful Shifts*, that I for ONE slowly and surely needed to let go of my still always *Nice, Kind, Understanding* and *Friendly* existing Swiss Linda habits and that I therefore inevitably had to prepare myself to possibly get TWO confronted with some uncomfortable outer provoked resistances and to THREE here and there for once being "disliked" reactions. Ufff. Additionally, to this awareness set strategy, I also decided to start applying "their" methods in order to protect my *Self* from all these incredible destructive existing behavior patterns and energies that my soul allowed to experience inside out. *"Tit for Tat"*, boundary settings, starting to say *"NO"* and to gradually standing UP for my *Self*, whilst choosing *"little Linda"* first, again, therefore more and moRE returned into my new habit choices on my moving forward path. Those action steps as a result then ended up creating a harder and bitchier version of my *Self*, as we say it in New York, and exactly after these predicted 7 years, Linda Wartenweiler's metamorphosis into a "real" considered "New Yorker" finally came to its almost *"NeverEnding"* seemingly completion. HOORAY. That's right. The side eFFecT that my soul out of this defensive mechanism came to experience though, introduced itself this time in the form of the usage of a LOT more available energy resources out of my system than expected. Wow. All those many new created choices simply felt like SO much unnecessary hard work on top of all the other challenges that this wiLD city already kept on offering to me. As already mentioned, prior to my Big Apple chapter, my "Linda soul" never really got forced to apply any of these harsh protecting tools and therefore, I certainly needed to first figure out as of HOW to use them properly and efficiently. The word in itself actually already sounds quite incredible and mind-blowing to my soul. "Protecting Tools". What?! That very much so is complete crazy non-sense and on the other hand it also is a 100% truly justified. After all we are talking about the Concrete "Jungle" here, which with time created its own human dance version between its predators and their targeted preys. Growl. Prior to this *"Living on Earth Game"* adventure chapter, I found myself being used to be functioning within a community mind-set, in which every soul almost always shared the needed respect and well-meant interest for one another. It seemed like a standard way of living, an unspoken agreement. A soul looks out for the other with its BEST interest for everyone involved by automatically having each other's backs, with probably only minor to no *"Self*-centered" and profitable conditions knotted to those chosen action steps. That's right. What other wonderful duality example this kind of human behavior those difFeRent two Apple *"PlanEts"* truly bring along indeed. Ha! Even though I found myself trying hard to adapt and to stick to my newly found New York City attitude mission, my by nature Positive, Kind and Optimistic mindset mostly started to take over again as soon as I felt more *Safe, Comfortable* and closer to *mySelf* and that comforting into *"little Linda"* shift as a result then naturally tempted me to break my many opposite set life choices right away. Over and Over and Over. Anew. Boom. What a frustrating stepping back into the light process this cat and mouse dance now turned out to be. *"The ONLY Person standing in Your Way is YOU"* attitude therefore with guarantee is what strongly applied towards my own *"Growth and Expansion"* process during this new invented phase of mine. Ha! One quite important key ingredient that I began to "decode" during this colorful *Boot Camp* adventure, turned out to be the "fact" that whenever I chose to put my*Self* on 2nd, 3rd and/or even 4th position, that I right in that very *"Now Moment"* actually always successfully worked AGAiNST my *Own Happiness, Dreams, Health* and *"Self"*. What?! Yes. Then, the braver and more courageous that I turned in regards of allowing my 1st priority to shift back towards deserving *"little Linda"*, the more my soul as a reaction *"ongRowingly"* found "herself" delighted about its eFFecTs. Wow. The more that I then began to *"Push"* this newly discovered *"Self*-loving" remedy forward, the more I then as a further result suddenly became to experience that whenever I dared to put myself even on 2nd, 3rd AND 4th position, that my entire awareness creation gradually started to shift into an even MORE magical and delightful mixture than ever expected. Abracadabra. What a powerful reality transformation, filled with a LOT more *Love, Peace, Well-Being* and *Harmony* this seemingly small shift simply turned out to evoke. Boah! The more that I then found myself able to allow my*Self* to follow really through with this newly discovered *"Self*-love" remedy choice by further permitting my*Self* to surrender to my true *"Self"*, the more it dawned on me that I very early on during my *"Miss Fresh off the Boat"* state of mindset somehow got caught up in a by *Miss Fear* lead *"Head over Heart"* choice spiral, which SpeCial eFFecT triggered me to throw the love for my*Self*, including for my soul over board. Bye-Bye. Splash. After my own conditioning of this *Miss Fear* based state of mind reality creation throughout a couple of years, my soul and vessel then at some point urgently tried to wake-UP my heart by shaking my mental and physical well-being with signals like *Destructive Thoughts and Behaviors, Anxieties, "ongRowing" Sadness and Sickness* symptoms, *Loss of Appetite* and with it those 20 pounds/10 kilograms down to 117lbs/54kg, *Nervous Breakdowns, Tears, Disorientation, Panic* and

Hyperventilation Attacks, by rounding this *Boot Camp* exercise UP with the eye-opening awareness check that those newly adapted choices simultaneously also triggered my apparently somewhere within *"little Linda"* hidden *CoDependency* tendencies. What?! Oh my. Furthermore, it then suddenly dawned on me that whenever I allowed myself to enter into a hurtful state of mind reality perception, that my soul actually only happened to be re-experiencing a reflection of an unfinished past occurred situation that mostly was/is rooted somewhere in *"little Linda's"* early on collected "growingUP" travels, which situations at the end only kept on asking for my Attention, Forgiveness and for my Love all along. Hmmm. Meanwhile, I thankfully allowed my soul to embark onto this from "her" end desired recovery journey and with the remarkable help of this *"the DOiNG ME PROjECT"* project, I as a result simultaneously even ended up unexpectedly succeeding to shine a LOT of LOVE and LiGHT onto many of these discovered past occurred "wounds" of "hers", which adventure even more so had me convince that *"Everything happens for a Reason and this Always at its Perfect time."* That's right. Hooray! And. Thank you. And yes. This all might sound like quite a whirlwind to exist in, which it truly was. Especially when a soul "unknowingly" throws "herself" into a this kind of an extreme duality organized reality for the very first time. Smile. Fortunately, the to my soul quite powerful *"Where there is a Way iN, there Always is a Way OUT"* collected *"Life Toolbox"* ingredient, is what my inner voice kept on reminding and fueling "her" with. Day in. Day out. *"Moment-to-Moment"*. And this quite eFFecTively. Strike. Today, I happily can state that this quite precious *Boot Camp* ride of mine revealed itself after all as a necessity for so many reasons and it also turned out to be an absolute success on every level, which my soul finds "herself" VERY grateful for. At last. Gratitude. Now, in order for me to successfully find my way out of this rather intense and messy experienced low vibrational *"PandoraWombBox"* maze back into my with time as "uncomfortable" and "weird" perceived positive *"Super Happy Comfort Zone"* again, I instinctively ended up deciding to trust the help of my inner and outer all time available *"Heart over Head"* guiding system every *"Step-by-Step"* on the way. As much as possible. Until I MADE iT. Through. Congratulations. Yes, and as we both just came to experience as a unit, I myself sooner or later became, what I used to call *"A Victim of the Beast"* and thankfully with the assistance of a LOT of *Focus, Determination, Trust, Perseverance, Awareness* and with many *"Self*-love" based developed taken action steps, I eFFecTively found myself able to *"ongRowingly"* shift this, to my soul as rather blocking perceived "vicTiM" state of mind awareness set, back into its *"wiLD & Free"* glowing "vicTORY" mode. Abracadabra. Yay! And therefore, I today proudly consider my precious *"little Linda"* *"A brave Survivor of her Own inner accumulated Dragons."* Yup. That's right. Well done. *"You* after all *Always Are what you Thinkest."* Ha! Three additional, from the wonderful Universe sent powerful and to me very significant elements that tremendously ended up assisting my entire *"Finding back Home again"* rebirthing journey, introduced themselves in the form of 1) *"sHe, who looks OUTside DREAMS. sHe, who looks iNside AWAKENS"* and as 2) *"Change the way you Look At Things and the Things you Look At Change"* awareness shift suggestions, by then leading my soul into this quite mind-blowing adventure of 3) Writing all these many stories and thoughts of *"little Linda"* down right here alongside with you and for US, my dear, dear *Co-Traveler*, accompanied by a variety of other undertaken action steps resulting from my entire *"Growth and Expansionary" Artistic* and *"Self*-developing" *Boot Camp* repertoire, which I happily will be sharing with you as well at its perfect arising time. Yup. *"When the Student is Ready, the Teacher will Appear."* Wink. And right at this very precious *"Now Moment"*, I am feeling an EXTREME soul urge to Thank YOU, my wonderful new/old soul friend for your kind attention, curiosity and for your generous mental support thus far. It is my pleasure to have you aboard. Muahs. What I in retro perspective truly came to love and realize about this *"All or Nothing - Push"* NYC *Boot Camp* chapter of mine, is that this quite catalyzing exercise actually ended up offering an excellent opportunity for my many, with time created *Walls, Lies, Masks, False "Self", illusions, Believe System, iNsecurities* etc. to get stripped down, which therefore allowed me to rebuild everything anew from "scratch" and this guided from a complete difFeRent perspective, angle, approach and awareness mindset. In return, my soul this time around found "herself" being sent into a wonderful awakening *"Living on Earth Game"* journey, which rewarded my newly adapted lifestyle choices *"ongRowingly"* with a LOT more *Love, inner Peace, Harmony, Happiness, Magic, Balance, Awareness, Positivity, "Self*-love", *"Self*-respect", *"Self*-worth", *"Self*-confidents", *Willpower, Trust*, with my personal *BiGGER Picture interpretation Discovery, Playfulness, interDependency, Knowing, Truthfulness, Curiosity, UPlifting Thoughts*, with the *Stability* of my *Mental* and *Physical Well-Being*, with the reconnection success of my a LOT *Truer "Self"* and with the at last, extreme *reBonding* outcome with my magical *"little Linda"* as my first, second, third AND fourth priority and responsibility at hand. Yay! That's right. Then, whilst I found myself being busy and committed to my new being busy FuN task at hand, I at some point suddenly started to notice that the more that I allowed for my *Self* to embrace *"little Linda"* as my actual very first "met" BFF, that my dear *Mister Loneliness* buddy as part of "his" *"Cause and eFFecT"* reaction step decided to slowly call in "his" vanishing transmutation process. Sweet. Proudly I must admit that this "little one" out of this friend trading exercise very much so happened to have enlivened and enriched my entire *"Living on Earth Game"* spectacle enORMOUSly, ever since our reunion in Spring 2016. How much I truly missed her sparkly, FuN and giggling presence throughout those many years. Welcome back my *Love*. *"sHe, who looks OUTside DREAMS. sHe, who looks iNside AWAKENS."* A further powerful shift that this entire whirlwind spectacle offered to my soul, turned out to be the jUMP-start of the from "her" end to me by now quite obvious desired spiritual journey adventure, by therefore having "her" undergo an extreme personal *"Growth and Expansionary"* exercise, so that I lastly found myself able to acknowledge the importance of the bond healing necessity between my neglected *"True little Linda Self"* and I, which also included the ones of dear and amazing Heidi's and Urs'. Finally. And therefore, I am sending out my BiGGEST gratitude ever to you, my beloved Universe for your tireless patience during this stubborn Linda waking-UP call quest of yours. We made it. Yay. Love. On top of this wonderful faced and embraced opportunity, I meanwhile also came to the conclusion of WHAT this granted *"Living on Earth Game"* ride of mine actually seems to be all about, and yours most likely as well. Ha! Ready? It is as simple and wordy as *"The Overcoming of One Challenge After the Other in its "NeverEnding" loop "truth" and this instant "Growth and Expansion" created "Cause and eFFecT" dynamic as a result allows the soul to propel itself synchronically to the Sun's and the entire Universe's own "ongRowing" rhythm forward, orchestrated by its specific vacated vessel's own magical Free Will existing pace and manner choices."* And in super short put *"The Overcoming of One Challenge After the Other in its "NeverEnding" loop "truth", in order to provide the soul with its evolutionary desired "Expansion and Growth" experience."* Boom. That's right. Wink. Now, the rather enticing "fact" about this discovered reality law presents itself to me in the approach of the WHEN's and HOW's of each presented challenge, as each opportunity after all leaves as much room for EXACTLY as many difFeRent interpretation and option choices as we find any kind of soul vessels in count, and this within nature's wide ranged psychological behavior miracle, meanwhile truly triggered my souls fascination tremendously as its side eFFecT "EffECt" along of this "newly" taken on *"the DOiNG ME PROjECT"* challenge. Yup. It basically presented itself as a new hobby of mine. Ha! *"Found Ya'."* Wink. Yes, and this newly gained awareness check therefore eventually led me to realize, what kind of an unexpected incredible Acting research opportunity my soul after all has been given to "enjoy" with this granted *Boot Camp* experience at hand. Boah! In addition to my many, during the in total three NYFA embarked adventures provided Acting *"Life Toolbox"* ingredients, the kind Universe blessed my Linda Wartenweiler soul with this rather incredible chance, to furthermore explore a very difFeRent inner and outer world existing reality possibility than the one from my usual as *"Comfort Zone"* perceived awareness perspective and this even as the leading Actress in my own created and LiVE produced *"NeverEnding"* Story Feature Film. Yeeha! And this just shared *"Living on Earth Game"* conclusion of mine in other words finds itself very much so reflecting and translating within my soul's current most challenging, powerful, *"ongRowing"* and *"NeverEnding"* seemingly *"Where there is a Will there ALWAYS is a Way"* puzzle "peace" experience at hand. Which is *TatAAA!* My Visa. Abracadabra. OUCH. That's right. Before we continue our travels with this specific topic though, I would love to wrap up this NOW eagle eye gained perception chapter with one more needed ingredient, so that our two souls thereafter more or less will be cruising along on the "same page". Wink. Ready? Steady? Go. One of the to my soul rather most interesting phenomenon that this Concrete Jungle formation brings along with, is its incredible hunger for its green paper currency, including the therefore on it based created lifestyle. Hmmm. Out of my perspective, the being busy and staying active tasks probably are the number one executed action steps of most "Manhattatian's", which includes its during or afterwards following soothing numbing oneself remedy process that this tempting Candyland keeps on offering to everyone with its *"NeverEnding"* 24/7 availability selection choices. Ha! And this classical *"Yin and Yang"* reality eFFecT tactic then mostly seems from the chosen vessels to get tied to the goal, to hopefully receive its desired assistance to help it keep their inner and outer energies as balanced as possible, whilst their fragile souls slightly might be undergoing some here and there appearing challenges, caused by this ruthless NYC paced energy flow. Finding THE "right" mixture, I believe contains the magical required formula to absolutely being able to get the MOST out of this lovely city's experience, if one sticks around longer than less, however this might be easier said than done. *"One Only Knows the Outcome of Anything by Giving it its Fair Shot"* and therefore I am certain of, that it is possible, once one is AWARE and Ready for this sort of adventure. Ha! *"I'M POSSiBLE"* after all. And so it is. So, what exactly am I trying to bring across here. As we all know, the Big Apple itself already is an absolute hectic city and therefore finding oneself physically alone is an almost impossible occurrence to experience, especially during daytime. 8 million vessels somehow co-exist in one spot and this piled UP in subways, cars, buses, skyscrapers, buildings, parks and in the many available streets and avenues. Wherever one goes, one continuously is exposed to other souls, to concrete and to all kinds of difFeRent energies and vibrations. The reality of things is that most of these energies happen to vibrate on a lower end of the scale, as there simply exists rather little room for someone to ACTUALLY rest and/or to recharge those used up batteries properly, as time after all is money. Yup. That's right. Now, if you are adding all these many tall buildings into your own *"Head Cinema"* creation, which simultaneously happen to eat up most of those soothing and for the human vessel essential vitamin D carrying sunray resources on their ways down, then remove most trees, animals, insects and plants, give everything an expensive price tag, overall little and narrow available private spaces, set the hourly work wage to a minimum of a in 2009 eFFecTive $7.25 per hour for example and then round this wonderful fusion UP by throwing ALL the many HiGH figure income existing souls, including their luxurious availabilities into this duality puddle and voilà, here is your Own and Personal provided Operation Concrete Jungle sneak peek experience. Enjoy. Ha! Well, and with this concept at hand, many souls therefore certainly get forced to either choose to work in the conventional Getting hired in several jobs Agreement solution in order to keep up with their monthly expanses or to possibly come up with their own creative income resources as an alternative. Yes, and this part of NYC's hectic existing domino eFFecT also explains as of WHY it is an absolute normality and necessity for especially low-income employee's and young aspiring Artists to spend most of their precious time in a whirlwind of a minimum two jobs situation agreement. In the Artistic world, we call the first few *The Survival Jobs* and the very last one on that list would end up appearing as *The Pursuit of One's Creative Dreams* or *The Actual Reason as of WHY One's soul currently is tolerating this Jungles' Madness*. That's right. Now, for those entrepreneurs that choose to create their own income resources, I came to learn that ANYTHiNG goes in this to me rather fascinating and somewhat shocking *"Head over Heart"* dictated *"Be as Creative, Smart, "Self-centered", Ruthless and Persistent as you can be, whilst you chase after YOUR desires and you shall get rewarded with them ALL, eventually"* approach. Hmmm. And Boah. What?! Yes, and that is when the Art of Taking, Using, Abusing, Lying, Cheating, Scamming, Calculating, Manipulating and so forth, orchestrated by Snoop Dogg's *"With my Mind on my Money and my Money on my Mind"* mindset is able to take its fairly interesting twists and turns, whilst the predators find themselves determined of getting their hunger met. *"You HAVE it. I WANT it. I'll GET it. No Matter what it TAKES. Promised."* That's right. Welcome to the "Jungle". Money exists and flows everywhere, as it is New York's main soul purpose and therefore basically everyone and everything is ruled by it. Alongside to this income spectacle, I believe that any soul existing in New York City preferably should be considering adjusting its mindset to their *"What is in there for ME? What can I get out of it?"*, including the *"Don't trust anyone, as almost every vessel wants something from you"* attitude ASAP, whilst being exposed to those many multidimensional strangers and behaviors in order to be able to stay on top of this metropolis' game plan at hand. Yup. And I guess that this is HOW and WHEN my Little Finger story slowly starts to make sense. At least a "little" bit more. Right? Ha! Then, besides all the many difFeRent physical occurring exchanging methods, there of course simultaneously also exists its opposite form, which therefore *"ongRowingly"* takes place in the unseen and subconscious sphere, introducing *One's Own personal and precious "Time and Energy" resources*. That's right. Meanwhile, I actually came to the conclusion that those two elements very much so appear to be the probably MOST valuable, unaware and MOST globally traded daily merchandise in any soul's *"Living on Earth Game"* experience. Yup. And the "truth" of this matter is that the more a vessel actually "owns" of each in a itself balanced and foundational unit, the more thrilling, magical and sparkly a soul's journey as its wonderful *"Cause and eFFecT"* response therefore will unfold itself as, which results with "No Doubt" will always remain more powerful, lasting and blissful than the impact that ANY of these "temporary" physical and outer soul provided interactions ever are capable of providing. This, my soul finds "herself" quite convinced of. And so it is. To me the actual function of any of those countless wonderful existing and created physical availabilities, which includes any fellow soul traveler, meanwhile revealed itself into my awareness as mainly being enhancement tools for our by nature already *"NeverEnding"* provided and all time accessible HiGH vibrating inner occurring reality experience in order to assist each soul, during its Own just discovered inner and outer *"Experiencing, Growing* and *Expansion"* process, throughout their entire individual *"Living on Earth Game"* quests as a pleasant reward. Well, and whenever that magical eFFecT at some point stays afar, then this temporary reality "truth" might seem like a mighty wonderful opportunity for anyone, to possibly call in a *"Heart over Head"* time-out session in order to check in with one's *"little Self"* of what outer and/or inner created resources possibly would require some sort of immediate improving tweaking. If desired of course. Wink. Today, I thankfully am finding my *Self* aware of the fact that Linda Wartenweiler has been given this wonderful "Abundance of Time" gift from the beloved Universe for a specific reason and therefore my soul at some point down this *"THE Ultimate Childhood Swimming AGAiNST the Stream Dream"* road found "herself" embracing and surrendering "herself" to it *"Moment-to-Moment"*. Day in. Day out. With the attempt of making the BEST possible use of it for my *"True little Linda Self"* experience, plus for my soul's mission at hand. Ha! And this awareness collected *"Life Toolbox"* ingredient treasure therefore finds itself wonderfully reflecting in Mark Twain's once magical shared *"The TWO Most important Days in your Life are THE Day when You were Born and THE Day when you Figure Out Why"* discovery "truth". Thank you. And so it is. It actually took me until very recently to kind of fully understand its tremendous value and to be able to grasp the "fact", that I ended up trading *"little Linda's"* many dear *"Life Toolbox"* treasures, including *"FuN Fact"* passions with many to my soul lower vibrating responding "objects" and choices, which awareness check as a result instantly left me once again with the feeling of having come across a "Less for More" bargain situation. Uiuiui. Here we go again. Wink. In regards of this *One's Own personal and precious "Time and Energy" resource* discovery, I very much so came to believe that its value actually tremendously gets heightened in this just talked about metropolis. Yup. This spectacular Candyland after all offers an amazing and intensified opportunity for all those many souls out there, who consistently are on the run from their Own *"True little Self"* in the hopes to be able to numb and cover their *"ongRowing"* shadows UP with any outer Cry for Help available resources in the form of an unbalanced and deconstructive distraction mix of *Money, Love, Physical items, Activities, Conversations, Social Media, Work, Substances* and/or with *Any Other* available *Preferences* on the market. Hmmm. Looking for one's *"ongRowing"* and *"NeverEnding"* desired lasting happiness from outside resources therefore is how MOST of the, especially in The Western World populated souls seem to perceive this magical all time appearing SpeCial eFFecT to occur, when in "True Snapple Fact" everything required for it already exists safely locked within each owns vessel from the very get-go. Always. *"sHe, who looks OUTside DREAMS. sHe, who looks iNside AWAKENS."* Ha! And this train of thought just now leads me into this chapter's closing message, which expresses itself with an *"Always keep on Treating, Carrying and Using those two Magical Power Resources of YOURS with its Needed Respect, if they happened to be dear to you, my friendly Co-Traveler. And this Wherever you Go. By "ongRowingly" remembering to "Watch Out. Watch*

Out."" Wink. Well and if you happen to be up for a daring *"Let's Rock 'n Roll!"* adventure right NOW, or in any other arriving *"Now Moment"* ahead, then give the following exercise a shot or two or three, which with GUARANTEE eventually will lead your soul towards a VERY precious and powerful treasure, which is *Your "True little Self"*. WooHOO! *"The Key to your Own inner Happiness lies in your attempt to Bravely Embrace and Look those possibly within YourSelf existing Dragons with LOTS of LOVE and COMPASSiON into the eyes by simultaneously Surrendering Yourself with all of your Heart and Trust into the whirlwind appearing Chaos, knowing that this is HOW Your beautiful Caterpillar successfully metamorphoses itself into the so-called magical Butterfly. Abracadabra."* Yup. Been there. Done that. You can do it TOO. With "No Doubt". LOVE. Always. Alrighty, and with all this additional for your own *"Head Cinema"* creation soon *"Hmmm, this actually kind of makes sense"* to be gathered information flow, I now would love for the two of us to finally find out WHAT exactly happened within *"little Linda's" "Don't Dream your Life. Live your Dream." "Acting. Uncertainty. Complete Life Change."* entered *"PandoraWombBox"* path. Welcome back.

"Here we Go again with total Dedication."
Acting Visa. Yes, this is the topic that we will be directing our two focuses' on throughout the following few pages, which has us jUMP right back to my grandfather's April 16th 2007 birthday date and to where my vessel finally found itself equipped with LOTS of *Hope, inspiration, Respect, Eagerness* and *Curiosity* for this then already second Big Apple *"Childhood Acting Dream"* started chapter safely back on American ground again. Yay. Which occasion furthermore brought along my soul's intents, to approach this then non-visa holder experienced reality check with the UPdated *"Moment-to-Moment". "Step-by-Step. Oh baby"* master plan exercise of 1) Giving this back and forth cat and mouse dance a maximum of the magical Three's A Charm trial, which decision therefore caused for me to 2) Hand all my *Trust*, the *How's* and the *What's* anew right over to the all-time helpful Universe, as iT after all was The One that led my soul into this *"THE Ultimate Childhood Dream Vision"* reality in the first place. Ha! Remember? That's right. After an, in the following August moment occurred interaction with this, during my NYFA *"Connecting and Belonging"* printing out Plan B session introduced 1 year Filmmaker student and meanwhile into a Grotto coworker transformed Zurich friend of mine, my soul interestingly suddenly came to learn that the kind Universe happened to have delivered its *"Thy Wish is my Command"* next *"Stepping-Stone"* solution on that matter as well in the form of another Happy Hour surprise. Wow. For real? For real. And thank you. One very important information flow, that struck my instant attention during our then experienced conversation, revealed itself with the "fact" that her vessel found itself in the possession of an approved and more valuable F1 student visa. What? How come!? Hmmm. With that UPdate in my pocket, I then immediately went ahead and consulted the same already earlier met friendly international student advisory at the Film Academy in order

to find out, what this difFeRence to my meanwhile expired M1 visa was all about. From her end, I then came to learn that the Film Academy finally experienced their desired school status UPgrade in January 2007, which ever since allowed them to accept any international F1 student visa holders to their available programs as well. Hmmm. And this "minor" seemingly change therefore also brought along the UPdated "detail" that all those from any NYFA 1 year program graduating students with that got granted the wonderful opportunity to apply for an UPgraded 12 months OPT visa next solution, if desired. Boah. 12 months? Wow. What luxury to have. Oh my. Now, as my by then back and forth traveling choice slowly started to get under my skin, I then out of my Gemini's curiosity happened to wonder about my own current OPT attracting options at hand, which *"Cause and eFFecT"* action step she to my surprise ended up answering with the following *"Ask and You shall Receive"* offer *"Well, you could be taking our newly created 2nd year Acting program in January 2008, graduate in 8 months and then apply for your desired 1 year OPT visa."* Ha! This really sounded like a wonderful plan up unto that moment, during which "her" soul mentioned the number of their increased tuition fee. Immediately, my vessel as a reaction therefore quickly found itself filling with LOTS of resistance towards this rather expensive "Less for More" proposal at hand, which as a next step right away let me to express my unwillingness to pay so much money towards a "just" new student visa solution. Boom. That's right. Well, and I guess that my soul's reaction must have been one of my very first *"With my Mind on my Money and my Money on my Mind"* adapted and instinctively applied New Yorker tricks at hand, whilst defending my own green paper resources, as this friendly advisory right away understandingly proposed to talk my situation through with one of her big bosses, in order to find out what my overall options with them were. Fantastic. Sounds great. About 1 hour later, she then reached out to my then "old school" owned Nokia cell phone device and shared the wonderful news that NYFA found themselves happy and willing to support my additional *"Childhood Acting Dream"* journey in the form of a 50% discount rate. WooHOO! What?! Strike! Yes, these words absolutely sounded like Music to my ears and therefore made me accept their kind offer with "No Doubt" within a snap. SNAP. *"I've got the Power."* Yeah! Now, as I at that time still happened to be the proud owner of my silver 2002 VW Polo, I therefore decided to call in a *"Letting go of Something that No Longer Serves One's Growth and Expansion"* moment, by instead using this lovely Swiss based "companion" as the perfect "fair" trading solution, as its selling amount matched about exactly those newly appeared expanses. Sweet. Let's. My next created To Do's from here on then resulted in 1) Returning back to the small apple in November in order to sell my beloved Polo friend and to 2) Simultaneously also apply for this precious F1 student visa for my hopefully in January starting 2nd year NYFA Acting program venture. Yes, and "hopefully" for that reason, as up onto my departure date "only" another fellow soul found itself being interested in embarking this newly created advanced Acting study journey at hand, which for its actual "happening" therefore very much so required for a few more vessels to sign up. Hmmm. Well, thankfully there remained still a few more weeks within this then soon "old" to be considered 2007 year and this extra time at hand as a result certainly could change its 2 students count on any appearing day. Yup. Fingers crossed. Nevertheless, I decided to stay hopeful, as *"Wunder Gescheh'n/ Miracles happen"* on and on after all. Ha! As soon as my vessel found itself back on Swiss ground again, I therefore fairly quickly put my lovely silver car with its amazing equipped sound system enhancement up for sale on Switzerland's Craigslist version called *Fundgrube* and immediately ended up finding a nice couple, who in return to its keys handed me the almost exact needed tuition amount in a white envelope in exchange, which gesture certainly must have symbolized and called in another "important" key moment within *"little Linda's" "Living on Earth Game"* ride. Ha! Thank you. And. Bye-Bye, my loyal friend. Farewell. Sniff. Then, once my desired F1 visa also found itself safe and sound anchored in my *"Red and White"* Swiss passport, my soul happily decided to enjoy those last few weeks ahead with "her" dear blood and *"Extended Family Member"* ones full on, as I very much so knew that this time my vessel would be remaining absent for quite some time longer. Bye-Bye. As soon as I, after a for once sunny and warm JFK welcoming gesture, found myself in the middle of December filled with many additional *"Head Cinema"* added creations in my Astoria *"Home Sweet Home"* base again, I on the following AM, therefore quickly made my way towards Union Square in order to UPdate the friendly advisory on my behalf. Well, and that was then, when my soul came to learn, that 1) "Her" desired January 2008 2nd year Acting program, as for its unchanged registered souls just got cancelled and that my vessel as an alternative 2) Could be entering its desired OPT quest by joining all the many sufficient, for the in September 2008 signed up 2nd year students instead. Cool! Wait. What?! September? With BiG EYES I instantly kept on gazing into hers, whilst my unsatisfied soul made it quite clear, that 1) I just landed with the from her end suggested F1 visa solution in my pocket, which mutually got knotted to my 2) Ultimate set goal of attracting this magical 1 year OPT door *"Stepping-Stone"* opener, that alongside with its approval right away would be unlocking *"little Linda's"* legal and official opportunity status, to finally get hired for a still rather quite limited range of paying Acting gigs and that therefore 3) The suggested waiting around period of another 9 *"NeverEnding"* months, happened to be out of my interest at this point of my travels. Boom. That's right. Anew this friendly advisory went ahead and comforted my soul with a *"I understand. Let me check in with one of the big bosses so that I can find out what we can do for you this time."* chosen response. Great. About another hour later, my soul then got confronted with about the same *"Ask and you shall Receive"* Nokia scenario as last time, which in that emerged *"Now Moment"* presented itself somewhat like this *"Ok, I just talked to one of the big bosses and this is what we can offer as a solution. Why don't you repeat the 2nd semester of the 1 year Acting program that will be starting at the end of January*

2008, for free, which would have you graduate in May. And then, as you would be allowed to get hired by us with your current F1 visa, you could apply for a Residential Advisory (RA) position for our, in July starting 8 weeks summer Acting programs for High School students, which would provide you with housing and food as compensation. And then in September, you finally could enter into your desired 2nd year Acting program for the same tuition fee as discussed and celebrate your 3rd NYFA graduation in May 2009." Wow. Excited about what my auricles just came to hear, I as a next step instantly felt prompted to double check its "for real" factor with a *"Did you just say that I can repeat the 2nd semester for FREE?"* follow up responds, which the voice on the other side of the line instantly confirmed with a happy *"YES"*. Boah! Splash. And on board I therefore right away jUMPed onto this free Acting semester cruising by boat, by further expressing my interest in the rest of the just offered game plan as well. Sweet. Yes, and right then my soul very much so felt appreciative towards the all-time lovely Universe's gesture, including about its attached delivered message, which left me assured that everything found itself moving along just fine on my precious *"Childhood Acting Dream"* chosen path, by furthermore ensuring once more that for every presented hurdle or route change eventually always exists its yet still unknown, though perfectly well fitting *"Everything happens for a Reason"* puzzle piece. Especially, when approached with one's heart and in peace. Yay. Now, whilst my soul found "herself" enjoying this out of the blue granted 2nd semester 1 year Acting free ride with new classmates, including with some newly added teachers, I actually very soon came to realize, as of how valuable this with many AHA eFFecTs filled study gift revealed itself as. Wow. Suddenly all those many exercises, techniques, words and teachings finally started to truly make "sense" and therefore all these many over time English and Acting undertaken *"Walking the Extra Mile"* skills transformation action steps, therefore right away assisted my soul from then on to continue "her" Artistic *"Growth and Expansion"* quest with a valuable and fueling breakthrough collection for my *"ongRowing"* repertory. WooHOO. And. Thank you NYFA. With my second graduation diploma in my pocket, I then as offered found my vessel being hired as one of NYFA's summer camp RA's during daytime, whilst I decided to parallel also keep my beloved Grotto running shifts on the evenings. Well, and this with duality filled adventure, certainly unraveled itself into another quite interesting NYC ride. Yup. And this so, as with my choice of keeping myself busy with both tasks during these 2 months, I as a result for the first time succeeded to *"Push"* myself towards some quite uncomfortable mental and physical appearing challenges. That's right. *"Let's go ALL the way."* Soon into my summer camp adventure, I as a matter of fact came to learn that this taken on opportunity mainly required the presence of Linda Wartenweiler's vessel and this with many to my soul rather unusual waiting and bzZZ sitting around filled hours reality check, therefore *"ongRowingly"* kept on provoking my brain, including vessel to AAAH rEvolutionize. Yes, the from my souls desired workout and being busy routine, I with "No Doubt" always promptly got provided during my three weekly Grotto runner shifts. Oh yeah. Though 6 weeks of this with sleep deprived developing back and forth *"Buffalo Stance"* dance seemed to have been enough time for my "reliable" Swiss batteries to empty themselves out and to as a result successfully throw my first NYC burnout symptoms into my newly created *"Living on Earth Game"* adventures at hand. Strike. And this "truth" factor therefore once more triggered my soul, to exactly 2 years later, long for another September arrival moment to occur and to furthermore add "her" desire for this *"NeverEnding"* seemingly 2nd year Acting OPT quest to be completed already, as its overall game plan after all still ended up providing my journey with an "undesired" waiting and sitting around situation of 3 months. Ufff. And. Ha! *"Thoughts become Things"* and this spectacle certainly happens to just now be triggering the earlier on *"What's up with that, right? Well, as my knowledge of "how" the magical Universe interprets a soul's order happened to be at a zero at that time, I therefore found myself unaware of the fact that it actually only focuses on the during the order produced "Head Cinema" created clip and that any additional No's and Not's added SpeCial eFFecT "specifications" remain as an insignificant detail" Law of Attraction* order discovery into my awareness. What? And so it is. Always. Also here. Wink. Then, shortly after the completion of my 3rd NYFA graduation ceremony in May 2009, my long awaited 1 year OPT next door opener resolution got approved within a heartbeat as well and this to my soul rather important and powerful key moment finally allowed for my vessel to apply for this, within this *"The Other Planet"* for paying work required own magical social security number. Abracadabra. Yeeha! This shifting *"Dream come True"* materialization achievement at hand, truly marked a thrilling new milestone along of my current *"Don't Dream your Life. Live your Dream." "Acting. Uncertainty. Complete Life Change."* chosen path and furthermore immediately ended up filling my entire vessel with an endless stream of proud vibrations. Horray. With this new vicTORY in my pocket, I of course already kept my eyes and auricles open for my following *"Dream Catchin'"* options, as my soul after all "only" got granted with an opportunity window of an exactly still rather short 12 months. Once I started to put the word of my intents out on my by then actively operated Facebook social media account, one of my foreign Acting friends right away ended up recommending her lawyer to my soul, as theirs just successfully happened to have attracted "her" first O1 Artist visa into my friends reality. Yay! Congrats. Now, as this friend of mine spoke rather highly of this lawyer's work, including persona, my intuition therefore led my vessel in January 2010 to reach out to him as well, in order to receive my first heads up in regards of what needed to be accomplished from my Artistic end, within those 5 remaining OPT months at run. After all I learned out of my former banking experiences, that 1) Any called in paperwork collection exercise usually easily takes up quite some time and that 2) A rushing into things approach out of my *"Life Toolbox"* ingredient selection always appears to leave too much room for "mistakes" and/or for any possible undesired outcomes to occur. At the end of our first meeting, my soul then, equipped with all the desired information flow, right away decided to hire "his" as well for this quite important journey ahead and thereafter continued this newly picked up O1 Artist visa quest of mine, by setting the directed gathering of all the for it required Linda Wartenweiler material, including recommendation letters into motion. Let's Go! One of my, within this process from the magical Universe provided golden tickets, for sure led my memories travel back to this precious and "private" granted Kristen Johnston Acting teaching opportunity, who's vessel very much so got known via the 90ies TV show hit "3rd Rock from the Sun", which in it performed character even ended up providing her with the honor to win two Primetime Emmy Awards for a wonderfully and convincing completed job. Boah! BRAVO. How amazing. So yes, as you can see, my lovely fellow *Co-Traveler*, the wonderful Universe further kept on aiming for my *"Childhood Acting Dream"* education and networking skills *"To Grow and to Prosper"* and this is how the to my soul as rewarding interpreted graduation gift found its igniting way into my awareness within once again, the magical NYFA SOHO front desk walls. Ha! What?! Yup. Whilst my alumni vessel paid this schools location a quick visit in June 2009, I happened to be crossing one of my former Acting teachers', who's soul found "herself" curious about How things were moving along out there in the "real" world now and How my further Acting plans would look like from there on. After the delivered *"little Linda"* UPdate, this friendly teacher then continued her train of thought, by recommending for my vessel to join her friends' UPcoming 10 days private Acting class group, which Kristen intended to be hosting at her house and that therefore she happily would be emailing me all the for it needed details later on. What?! Kristen Johnston happened to be her friend? Wow! What a small planet our mother earth once more simply appeared to be and alongside with this delivered awareness check UPdate, my soul also got shown spot on, that one truly never knows with whom another soul finds itself connected with. Therefore, always *"Watch Out. Watch Out."* Wink. Of course, I right away expressed my HiGH interest in her wonderful and valuable proposal and after a FuN and nonchalant interview within Kristen's living room walls, our two souls right away agreed to add my vessel into the already almost filled up group puddle of another 9 students. WooHOO! This 10 days Acting adventure as assumed developed itself into one of my MOST favorite and inspirational craft experiences, which even got topped off by getting the opportunity to observe a real and seasoned Acting pro demonstrating as of HOW to dive into the magical world of our mutually "hobby" chosen passion PROFESSiON. Love. Very grateful my soul therefore always will be feeling towards this thrilling *"Growth and Expansionary"* provided chance, including for having been put in touch with Kirsten's very easy going, FuN, humorous, kind, straight forward and down to earth soul. Thank you. Now, as my O1 Artist visa application quest required as many "powerful" recommendation letters as possible, I after an instinctive first Gwen Stefani autograph replicated Swiss style *"Heart over Head over Heart over Head over Heart"* *"Buffalo Stance"* dance, finally hesitantly dared to also reach out to Kristen in order to ask for her possible help as well. *"One Only Knows the Outcome of Anything by Giving it its Fair Shot,"* right?! Right. And let me share with you, my dear *Co-Traveler*, how flattered my soul felt, the second that my eyes found out about "her" instant willingness to be part of *"little Linda's"* thus far gained *"The Other Planet" "Acting Dream"* support troop and this even more so, once I in the actual letter came across the quite encouraging statement that America needed an Actress like my kind. Yay. And. Gratitude. Once I by April found myself in the possession of all the required material, my vessel thereafter instantly met up with my lawyer's in order to proudly share my entire collected treasures with his soul. Pleased with my presented Artistic gathered evidence, he then as a next step felt confident for us to officially let the ball for this O1 Artist visa application quest of ours rolling and this with the from my soul's end of May 2010 chosen starting out date. Yay. Let's Go! Shortly after our submission got handed in, we promptly heard back sides the immigration office with a request, to hand in some additional Linda Wartenweiler desired skills evidence, in order to assist the assigned immigration officer in his or her further evaluation process. Sure. Whatever you need. Then, a few weeks after the newly sent in paperwork requirement, the visa puzzle pieces finally seemed to have found themselves to be strong enough to as well convince our assigned immigration officer, that *"little Linda"* should be allowed to continue her desired *"Soul Acting Dream Catchin'"* mission within this *"The Other Planet"* realm. *"Hip Hop Horray! Ho. Hey. Ho."* We did it. My UPgraded yellow US *"Acting Dream"* key door opener got approved until the end of May 2013. OMG. And yes, certainly my both eyes instantly filled themselves with many salty relieving and happy teardrops, once this wonderful and significant milestone achievement found itself getting presented to my soul via a from my lawyer's colleague's received phone call in the beginning of August. Ufff. And. Thank you. Very excited about those news, I then right away went ahead, purchased a flight ticket to Zurich and off my vessel took a few days later, in order to get my trophy anchored in my precious *"Red and White"* Swiss passport as well. After a lovely and always recharging Swiss adventure of 2 weeks, I then, eagerly and driven by my desire to continue *"little Linda's"* dear *"THE Ultimate Childhood Dream Vision"* as a then proud owner of the magical O1 Artist visa, headed back to the Big Apple right into the newly created reality check, that granted her with an immediate UPgraded "better" audition access rate of about 40% to all the, within this *"The Other Planet"* existing Acting opportunity market. Yeeha! *"Let's Rock 'n Roll!"* Oh, how liberated my soul truly felt from here on about the fact that this time around my vessel finally got granted a gap of about 2 ½ years, before the following visa hunting season would be opening itself up again. Ufff. With this knowledge in my pocket, I then decided to allow my soul, after a continuous and with pressure experienced visa quest of 4 years straight, to call in a much-needed mental resting and breathing period in order to celebrate this granted *"Living on Earth Game"* ride of mine a little bit more from an overdue *"wiLD & Free"* side of things and Grotto therefore right away revealed itself as THE perfect All-in-One solution. Ha! And. AHHH. Alongside to this newly "temp" set lifestyle choice at hand, I furthermore added the from my lawyer pre-discussed Artistic path development vision into my overall game plan, which included 1) The importance to *"ongRowingly"* and powerfully establish Linda Wartenweiler's vessel as an Actress within this *"The Other Planet"* sphere, so that I then 2) Would be finding myself being enabled to provide my lawyer with all the for our in 2013 planned second O1 Artist visa journey required skills evidence paperwork, which additional, until 2016 approved *"Stepping-Stone"* desired goal, then furthermore lastly would allow for us to 3) Quite promisingly apply for *"little Linda's"* last *"THE Ultimate Childhood Dream Vision"* required puzzle piece. Yup. The ultimate all door *"Open Sesame"* key formula *The Green Card*. That's right. And with this crucial MUST DO game changer milestone achievement, upon my souls *"Don't Dream your Life. Live your Dream." "Acting. Uncertainty. Complete Life Change."* chosen path, *"little Linda's"* precious *"Soul Acting Dream"* destiny then lastly would be finding itself equipped with everything needed in order to call in its true unfolding journey, within this *"The Other Planet"* sphere and this as *"wiLD and Free"* as the kind Universe all along planned for it to be. Namaste. Now, as soon as the year 2013 found itself sneaking around the corner, I as of its from three years ago revealed success formula came to decide, to approach this UPcoming second O1 Artist visa quest of mine the same way as my soul already did back then. Yes. Let's! By the end of December 2012, I therefore anew reached out to the exact same lawyer with my exact same requests to 1) Schedule a heads-UP meeting in January 2013, so that 2) Our two souls once more peacefully and early enough could be establishing WHAT possible action steps would be required from my Artistic end in order to grant us with a as smooth as possible second journey experience. Instantly, my lawyer anew found himself responding within a snap and January 10th 2013 therefore ended up being set as our new ball rolling date. Yay! Once my vessel found itself being placed across of his within his meanwhile own established law firm office space in Midtown, everything seemed to move along EXACTLY the same way as 3 years prior, EXCEPT for one quite significant ingredient, *My UPdated inner World Creation*. Hmmm. Very clearly I do recall, how MUCH of a struggling contest I found myself being exposed to against my own soul during my desired joyful and other positive vibration recreation efforts and how my inner world instead kept on insisting in entering into this after all quite important meeting, with an emotional mix of *Anxiety, Fear, Desperation* and *Disorientation*, which quite uncomfortable reality check UPdate furthermore led my awareness to witness how disconnected and absent I actually felt from my own *"Self"*, including vessel. Hmmm. HMMM. Thankfully, the overall course of this meeting seemed to pass by fairly well and my soul certainly found "herself" quite relieved and pleased after my lawyer's very promising *"Linda, you will be fine. This will be a Piece of Cake case. There is nothing for you to worry about. On top of it all know that I won't charge you with any of my own UPcoming expenses, as one-third out of my, within the past 3 years experienced successes lead right back to your many sent referrals, which gesture even helped me to extend my services to the West Coast. Therefore, you to me are "Saint Linda" and as for my Thank You to you, I will release any of my fees."* material reviewing end statement conclusion. Boom. And. WOW! This all definitely sounded like a new BiG strike on my horizon and flattered I accepted his soul's very kind offer. Thank you. Once my lawyer found himself in the possession of all the needed documents, his soul then by the end of April confidently decided, to officially let the ball for this, our second O1 Artist visa application quest rolling, with a this time seamless end of May replacement intent. Sound great. Yes. Let's. About 4 weeks after our submission got handed in, we promptly heard back sides the immigration office, with the Déjà Vu request for us to hand in some additional Linda Wartenweiler desired skills evidence in order to assist the assigned immigration officer in his or her further evaluation process. LOL. Sure. Whatever you need. Been there. Done that. No problem. And again, I as quick as a bunny right away went ahead and organized all the further requested "exposure" evidence material, which this time also included the from my end almost forgotten first-ever Music video performance of mine from 2007, with its then 1.2 Mio YouTube counted hits. Boah! What?! Yeah. Circa Survive's *"The Difference between Medicine and Poison is the Dose"* it is and shows my vessel being wrapped in a red dress and my forearms hooked to two tubes. Ha! Who would have thought that one of *"little Linda's"* first in the "real" world granted *"Acting Dream"* opportunities and this in a Music video for a to her until then unheard of apparently "famous" band, would end up being clicked at over 2 Mio times at this very *"Now Moment"*?! Love. And. Gratitude. Then, after another passing month without any further UPdates sides my lawyer, my impatient growing soul therefore decided, just as I found myself about to switch off the lights on that June 20th 2013 Thursday PM, to send his vessel an e-mail in order to find out more about the whereabouts. After all this new waiting around scenario also brought along the to my soul rather disturbing "facts", that ONE Linda Wartenweiler's *"The Other Planet"* visa status meanwhile transformed itself into a "pending" on hold situation, which *"Cause and eFFecT"* truth instantly threw my vessel from its TWO By the end of May for the first time going to be on TV presented Acting opportunity, which happened to be "The Slayer of Seven" episode, in which I portray Frank Lloyd Wright's mistress *Mamah Wright*, for the on the Travel Channel aired Monumental Mysteries reality TV series creation, accompanied with an until then finally well-rounded gained freelancing agents, managers, including network portfolio at hand, THREE At exactly the very first occurring second of May 25th 2013, with one BiG SLAM back into a *"NeverEnding" "All or Nothing"* re-appearing very minimized employable sitting around situation, alongside with my newly sent precious "Abundance of Time" gift at hand, that this time would be lasting until this Piece of Cake case would be finding itself getting answered and closed. Boom. Poof. Ufff. In addition to these *Boot Camp* added ingredients, I also came to deal with the "truths", that with every passing "on hold" day, *"little Linda's"* Acting and creative talents found themselves simultaneously missing out on *"ongRowingly"* being able to 1) Collect any additional powerful *"Dream Projects"* for those in 2016 planned Green Card evidence requirements and to 2) Establish Linda Wartenweiler as an Artist within this *"The Other Planet"* sphere. What in detail meant, that whenever the "MUST" approval of this second "yellow" key desired *"Stepping-Stone"* would be finding its way into my awareness, that No Matter its arrival date, it instantly would be beginning its seamless replacement journey, starting May 25th 2013. Ouch. And. Yes. Therefore, those many *"NeverEnding"* and with rather pressure filled career stopping *"Dream Catchin'"* seconds, in return found themselves VERY much so enhancing the course of my overall, by then as rather "destructive" experienced state of mind adapted well-being choices. *"Moment-to Moment"*. Day in. Day out. And this UPdated *"Living on Earth Game"* reality creation therefore *"ongRowingly"* allowed for my soul to get in touch with the REAL meaning and understanding of this from mankind quite valuable created measurement called *Time*. That's right. AAAH!!! *"I Want to Break Free."* On the following Industria Friday morning, I therefore, during my many coffee and tea preparation tasks, anxiously caught myself *"ongRowingly"* checking my iPhone Mail App, in the hopes to finally receive a to my soul quite overdue news UPdate sides my lawyer. AAAHbracadabrAAAH! And at exactly 8:35am, my desired *"Thy Wish is my Command"* e-mail request flew successfully into my mailbox and this with the powerful and magical opening line, that 1) Yes, he actually would have some NO good news for *"little Linda"*, that 2) The immigration office just happened to have sent him a new letter the day before, in which "his" soul came to learn that 3) We basically would NOT meet the required criteria, though that we 4) Luckily got granted with a second chance to hand in some further Linda Wartenweiler evidence material by then deciding to exit this conversation with an apology that "things" weren't moving smoothly. SLAP. OUCH. Well, and this unexpected and with SpeCial eFFecTs packed content with "No Doubt" revealed itself to successfully have added the last few needed drops to cause my already unsteady and low vibrating mental well-being glass to instantly spill over. CRASH. BOOM. SPLASH. There you go. *"Ah. Push it. P-Push it REAL GOOD."* Yes, my lovely *Co-Traveler*. *"Enough was Enough."* Once again. And this time FOR REAL. Those rather painful resonating vocabulary choices, including the additional announced 90 Linda Wartenweiler skills proof sitting and waiting around opportunity days, then for some reason right away led my soul, on this very unique June 21st 2013 solstice day to believe, that my desired request got denied, which shocking "UPdate" therefore meant that I just successfully called in my first and most important BiG time failure EVER, plus The End of all *"little Linda's"* many unlived *"Head Cinema"* dream creations at hand. POOF! And once again, my entire *"THE Ultimate Childhood Dream Vision"* bubble found itself popping in its LOUDEST notes possible right in front of my eyes and this time its "loss" felt MORE than real. Goodbye. Farewell. OH. MY. GOD. Yes, and dEEp down in my heart, my soul instantly knew that the concerned Universe with this gesture urgently aimed for my stubborn *"Self"* to stop practicing what I kept on insisting in and therefore I finally allowed my*Self* to acknowledge, that I 1) eFFecTively jeopardized *"little Linda's"* entire precious *"Soul Acting Dream"* career with my choices of 2) Carrying for other souls *Wants, Needs, Desires* and *Dreams* more than for my OWN, which *"Cause and eFFecT"* truth nevertheless ended up resulting from this meanwhile 3) Unfitting US-Swiss Linda version transformation source at hand. *"All or Nothing - Push"* and therefore I finally succeeded to nudge my own *"Self"* over the unthought-of edge, which newly called in key reality shift as its rewarding gesture allowed for my own *"Caterpillar"* to witness how my entire inner world collapsed within one LOUD SLAM and how this inner occurring earthquake experience simultaneously blew away all my many within these almost four *"little Linda"* decades created *Hopes* and *Dreams*, including all my whatever *Energy* and *Willpower* resources there were left. SWiSH. Game Over. Congratulations. Then, as soon as I found myself able to switch my focus back to my vessel's outer placed surrounding, I furthermore came to witness how my soul as a next step found "herself" entering into a completely changed *"Living on Earth Game"* awareness experience, which unexpected transmutation suddenly let every appearing minute melt into a heavy, *"NeverEnding"* and with salty teardrops filled journey. Oh my. How on mother heaven's earth was I supposed to survive this LONG work day ahead as professional and put together as possible?! Oh boy. Well, somehow, alongside with my many developed Acting skills and with this into a thankfully slow mutated bzZZ shift at hand, my soul made it work and therefore tremendously felt relieved, once this with challenges filled Industria task found its bitter-sweet end. Then, as soon as my quite exhausted vessel, including suffering soul found themselves equipped with my sunglasses able to exit its Graham station on the L-train, my all-time reliable feet finally found themselves able to drag "us" towards our *"Home Sweet Home"* base on Monitor Street, where my soul furthermore suddenly felt the urge to spend some much-needed alone time in the nearby located McGolrick Park. Oh yes. Nature. Please make me feel better. As soon as my auto-pilot had me stop at a peaceful and with many trees surrounded wooden bench area, set close by the there in 1923 placed Angel of Peace statue, I finally found my*Self* enabled to let go and to fully surrender to whatever was boiling itself together within and that was when I came to realize, that at this point of my many *"Living on Earth Game"* created adventures truly Nothing mattered anymore. That was it. *"Great job Linda. Well done."* Boom! And out of nowhere suddenly everything turned pitch black, whilst my lovely head voice kept on narrating this most vulnerable experience ever of mine, by *"ongRowingly"* reminding me about my thus far BiGGEST produced failure and that I just officially wasted 7 years out of my precious granted *"Living on Earth Game"* journey, including all the for it invested *Time, Money, Health, Energy* and *Effort* resources towards *"little Linda's"* priceless and never returning *"Soul Childhood Acting"* dream. *"Truly well-done Champ!"* And this reality UPdate therefore right away let everything, that I very hard and diligently kept on working for, disappear within another BiG BANG by replacing my further *"Head Cinema"* creation with a vision of experiencing my own vessel embarking into an airplane, which transported it straight back "home" to Switzerland as part of its, for this bravely in 2006 entered *"Don't Dream your Life. Live your Dream." "Acting. Uncertainty. Complete Life Change."* chosen *"PandoraWombBox"* path wrapping UP gesture. Bye-Bye. And. Yup. Linda Wartenweiler will be returning as THE predicted failure, which "truth" factor therefore will proof that all those existing *NAY*sayers, including my lovely *Miss Fear* friend ended up being spot on all along. Who would have thought, right? Ufff. Shame on me. How embarrassing. How embarrassing this "truth" simply made my soul feel. Ouch. Oh well. What can you do? Over is Over. That's it then. Bye-Bye, America. Bye-Bye, my *"Childhood Dream"*. It was a pleasure meeting y'all. You will be missed. See you hopefully in another *"Living on Earth Game"* ride again. Take care for now. Sniff. And right in this particular appearing instant, my soul for the very first time came in touch with the true understanding as of WHY my father decided to put an end to his own *"Living on Earth Game"* experience and this based on the reason, as "his" soul as well ended up losing everything that "he" cared for in one BiG SLAP. Yup. The older that my *"little Linda"* vessel grew, the more my soul therefore simultaneously also came to learn about my father's many, over his three *"Living on Earth Game"* decades accumulated inner existing dragon "friends", which important "facts" therefore *"ongRowingly"* granted my own *Dot Connecting* journey with the awareness understanding, that his own *"True little Self"* from quite early on, as part of his experiences decided, to "befriend" a lower vibrating reality perception as his *"Comfort Zone"* choice. Oh no! Yup. And those darker vibrating energy choices certainly very much so found themselves getting enhanced on this particular day, during which his shattered soul under a mixture of a couple of beers and "his" prescribed depression medication decided to set an end to all of our three, including to our cat's journeys. Ufff. And. HELP. Thankfully, my strong and "Karate Kid" skilled mother instantly succeeded to free herself under his first choking attempt and to furthermore storm with *"little Linda's"* vessel under her arms right out of our Amriswil *"Home Sweet Home"* base, whilst my soul apparently very clearly, after "his" voiced curiosity if we would return, assured that "he" would NEVER EVER see us again. EVER. Well, and sadly those words manifested themselves into an instant *"Thy Wish is my Command"* reality "truth", as "his" soul very likely found itself at its wit's end with "his" *"ongRowing"* unhealthy choices in count. Sigh. On the following day, my brave mother, whom I meanwhile also perceive as my savior and as another Heroess of mine, found my beloved father's vessel, during her mission of getting some clothes for the both of ours out of our home, gassed in our garage. UFFF. Yes, and this quite shocking discovery second, my childhood friend Marco actually recalls having witnessed, during one of his outdoors created *"wiLD & Free"* adventures and this in the form of a scream from afar. Oh boy. What life changing and dEEp soul marking shift this probably rather disturbing awareness check must have left on my mom's further inner and outer reality perception. Sniff. And therefore, ALL my LOVE and BLESSiNGS to them both even more so. Always. Yes, and as tragic as this story might be sounding, this is what happened, and everything simply remains perfect the way things are, as *"Everything keeps on happening for a Reason or Two or Three or even More."* That's right. And this rather powerful *"the DOiNG ME PROjECT"* project, that you happen to be holding within your own palms right now, my lovely *Co-Traveler*, certainly assisted my entire "understanding" of it all even more so. Yup. And. Thank you. Now, as I found my own *"Self"* in the midst of this quite unexpected and brief granted Standing within my father's Shoes experience at hand, my soul very much so developed a LOT of sympathy for his own over all inner created universe and this *"Cause and eFFecT"* entered exercise then furthermore led *"little Linda"* to remind my own *"Self"*, that "his" loving soul all along kept on tirelessly traveling alongside of my many countless *"Living on Earth Game"* created adventures. *"Moment-to-Moment"*. *"Step-by-Step."* And that "he" actually happened to be floating right there next to my left-hand side. NOW. WOW. That's right. And this awareness "truth" therefore straightaway propelled my *"True little Self"* to share with "our" father that I absolutely found myself understanding WHAT he went through and that I forgave him with all of my HEART and SOUL. Well, and this unexpected and rather magical occurred re-connection with my beloved unseen parent indeed turned out to be a VERY soothing experience for my soul, including for *"little Linda"*. LOVE. Then, another few breaths later, I suddenly came to notice a different, much lighter, warmer, briGHter and VERY encouraging sounding voice within myself, which appearance right away triggered my Gemini's curiosity to shift its attention towards its eye-opening *"Dear Linda, please listen to me. Yes, it might seem that you messed up, but know that your dreams and time are NOT vanished or wasted at all. Remember? Your immigration officer ONLY asked for more evidence and that's it. There still is a 50% chance for your visa to get approved. BUT here is the deal: You MUST start making up your mind about where to you would like to head from here on. Do you really want to keep on neglecting yourSelf or would you finally consider a drastic change for your OWN HiGHer good? Is your concern about others and all those many distractions truly worth the cost of your own unlived Wants, Needs, Desires and Dreams? Or would you rather like to jUMP back on track again on your OWN personal interpreted Well-Being journey? You have just been given an opportunity in order to start taking many healthy action steps towards your OWN fading inner TRUTH and Happiness. Think about it. The Choice is Yours."* delivered message. Boom. And. Wow. This rather powerful parenting delivered Abracadabra dialogue definitely succeeded in igniting a tinny flame within my overall experienced emptiness, just as I remembered it happening at the almost very end of "The *NeverEnding Story*", which reality check therefore instantly triggered my own slumbering *"inner ARTreyu Warrioress"* to jUMP right aboard onto this newly appeared briGHt liGHt on the horizon by knowing EXACTLY what needed to be done. Starting the following morning. Danke Papi. Equipped with this additional collected *"Living on Earth Game" "Life Toolbox"* ingredient experience within my backpack, I then eagerly made my way back into my Monitor Street based bedroom, where I as a next action step fully allowed for my soul to grieve and to release many of these throughout this rather intense *Boot Camp* chapter years accumulated energies, so that I would be finding myself Ready to enter into this just accepted *Adjusting, Healing* and *Rebuilding* journey as cleansed, free and refreshed as possible. Oh yeah. *"Let's get Ready to Rock 'n Roll again! Oo-WAH!"*

"Get UP my Darling and Get Your Dreamin' before your Chance is over."
As soon as the lovely sun a couple of hours later, welcomed my soul with one of its soothing kissing sessions back into a fresh new day, my strong willed and with LOTS of hope filled vessel thankfully found itself immediately Ready Steady to jUMP out of bed as well, eager to get this recommended "fixing" chapter journey rolling. ASAP. Which newly taken on *"Stepping-Stone"* attitude approach with "No Doubt" from the get-go very much so *"ongRowingly"* got approved by the magical Universe. Yay! The to me probably most significant and encouraging supporting gesture actually "already" ended up occurring within the time span of the first 2 hours, during my next Monterone-Industria shift, 4 days later. Boah. That swift? Yup. That swift. Smile. As I found myself well equipped with my new mind-set and with my beloved Red Eye "savor" setting up the coffee bar with all the needed supplies, including snacks, a very friendly producer woman from two rented out studios on my floor, all over sudden interrupted my flow by requesting for me to please have all the many snacks removed from the counter for the day, as Heidi happens to try to keep her kids away from them as much as possible. Sure. *"Thy Will is My Command."* Now, whilst I put that soul's request into action, my inner voice simultaneously for some reason kept on repeating this "Heidi" word over and over, which as a first reaction thought of course immediately triggered my beloved mother's face onto my *"Head Cinema"* screen, before iT hit me. W-w-w-wait a minute. Heidi?! Did she mean *Heidi Klum*?! What?! Holly Molly. No Freakin' Way! Almost blown away from this quite interesting reality discovery, my soul therefore right away felt the EXTREME urge to get this assumption cleared by this friendly producer woman and truly found myself thereafter completely baffled about her conformation, including the timing of this universal exactly NOW delivered "coincidence" attraction "truth". Boah! Up until this very *"Now Moment"*, I actually completely forgot that Heidi herself ended up inspiring and encouraging *"little Linda"* with her own *"The Other Planet" "Dream Catchin'"* created story, the second that she handed in her notice in January 2006. Ha! That's right. And this is how Heidi's helping hand found its way into my awareness. Parallel to the wonderful inspiration of my NENA's many through her lyrics and through her magical soul's spread wisdom, I in addition of course *"ongRowingly"* also kept on listening to my own inner supportive heart voice guidance, which action choices therefore one day led me to bump into Heidi's then

still quite new captivating briGHt green covered modeling career book with the enticing German title *"Natürlich Erfolgreich/Naturally Successful or Heidi Klum's Body of Knowledge, in its English edition"* in a bookstore in Constance. Now, as Heidi and the top German cable TV channel PRO7 during that time frame decided, to launch the first episode of "Germany's Next Topmodel" on January 25th 2006, she for that reason even more so awoke *"little Linda's"* interest, as her vessel after all happens to contain a fellow Gemini started out soul with a similar birth origin, including year, who as a matter of fact truly made it in a related Entertainment genre on this *"The Other Planet"* formation. Boah. Congrats! Well, and as those timely well delivered facts of her "vessel's" showing up seemed to have been enough reason for my own soul, to also start taking a closer look onto Heidi's *"Living on Earth Game"* path creations during *"little Linda's"* Big Apple preparation journey, I therefore quickly decided on that day in Constance/Konstanz, to add this auspicious book into my overall preparation repertoire. Perfect. Let's Go. Within a short amount of time, I then successfully ended up indulging this entire newly discovered *"Life Toolbox"* ingredient treasure and as a result found my soul for ONE Even more so aligned with *"little Linda's"* chosen *"Acting. Uncertainty. Complete Life Change."* path and ADDiTiONALLY quite inspired by 1) Heidi's shared modeling success stories, by 2) Her soul's UPlifting, FuN and positive appearing energy and lastly, 3) By all her interesting sounding advises. My favorite definitely remains the one, in which the top model uses a stone filled bracelet as a reference tool for one's *Success Road* to walk upon. Meaning, that Heidi happily shared how she perceives each piece as a one step at the time *"Stepping-Stone"* approach reminder upon every soul's set *"Dream Catchin'"* and desire fulfillment quests, for which she furthermore underlined the importance of a diligent One-by-One, *"Step-by-Step"* following-through strategy, excluding any cheating or skipping attempts. Boom. Way to Go. And as this advice immediately found itself resonating with my own soul within a snap, I therefore right away took it to my heart and still remind myself of its "truth", whenever needed. Yup. Thank you, Heidi. Well and this gratitude expression has us right away jUMP onto a to me in 2006 meanwhile as rather mind-blowing interpreted *"Thy Wish is my Command"* uttered "coincidence" desire. Ha! As Heidi's book unexpectedly turned out to be another important inspirational tool choice for my own *"Don't Dream your Life. Live your Dream."* adventure creations, I for that reason caught *"little Linda"* at some point strongly stating, as she already prior did about NENA's kind support, that one day, ONE DAY in the future my Linda Wartenweiler vessel would be granted with the opportunity to thank both Germanic considered souls in person for their unconscious kind help, guidance and inspiration. Boom. And so this almost forgotten first request and opportunity found itself arising right in front of my eyes EXACTLY 4 days after my BiG inner shift or 7 1/2 years after its sent-out order. Boah! What?! Dear Universe?! *"Ask and You shall Receive at its PERFCT Time."* WOW. And Thank YOU. So, the second that my *"Head Cinema"* successfully projected this entire Heidi storyline back into my awareness, it furthermore dawned on me that our two vessels actually even found themselves about to spend all day quite close to one another's. LOL. And yes, this realization check, therefore instantly caused myself to laugh out LOUD, which further led me to thank the amazing Universe for this incredibly well timed *"Dream come True"* materialization opportunity, including for its soothing *"All is good. All is well. You are doing wonderfully Linda. Woot. Woot."* attached approval message delivery upon this newly entered *Adjusting, Healing* and *Rebuilding* journey of mine. LOVE. Then, about 2 hours later, while I still found myself quite busy trying to grasp everything that was happening within and around me, since this quite SpeCial past Friday triggered Monterone-Industria experience, my in 2006 "foreseen" moment decided to begin its opening Act by having Heidi's vessel suddenly appear out of one studio and to as a next step have it directly aim towards my coffee bar. Oh no! Help! Anybody?! Her stepping closer moves definitely through me right into quite a nervous state of mind awareness check and quickly, I therefore caught myself trying to figure out a game plan as of HOW to make the best use of this unexpected chance, if even. Hmmm. Oh boy. And here she already was, by also bringing along a newly created *"Truth or Dare"* exercise, which situation with "No Doubt" immediately reminded *"little Linda"* once again of her back then Gwen Stefani entered spectacle. Boom. As soon as this super model's vessel found itself placed right in front of mine, her soul then quickly expressed "her" Latte desire, which caused mine to react with a *"Mit welcher Milch denn?/With what kind of milk?"* icebreaking response. Somewhat surprised about my Germanic sounding origin, Heidi then as a next step UPdated me with a smile about her preference and off my vessel therefore quickly "escaped" with my just given task at hand, including with my still *"ongRowing"* inner battle of WHAT TO DO. Ufff. Then, once the end product found itself all hot and fresh sitting within my palms, my soul knew that THE *"Now or Never"* moment just arose in front of my eyes as well and that I HAD to do iT. Ok then. HELP. After the intake of a dEEp breath and whilst I simultaneously also kept myself busy gathering all my available courage, *"little Linda"* then bravely went ahead and nervously began to express everything that she back then intended to share, including her gratitude towards Heidi's wonderful bracelet advise. SPLASH. And out it was. Hooray! "Mission *I'mPossible*" completed. Ufff. Heidi's soul then happily thanked mine for everything, before her vessel quickly disappeared to where it just came from a few minutes earlier, by leaving my awareness with the quite unthought-of ticking this *"Living on Earth Game"* goal task off from *"little Linda's"* MUST DO To Do list gesture and with an enhanced inspirational confirmation flow in continuing my chosen approaches *"ongRowingly"* upon this just entered Taking very good care of my*Self* mission at hand. Danke schön. *"Thy Will is My Command."* In regards of my current visa situation, I meanwhile heavy hearted came to decide to follow through with my lawyer's advice of fully taking advantage of those additional 90 granted Stronger Linda Wartenweiler skills Evidence collection days at offer, which reality check as far as of my overall until

2016 set *"Childhood Acting Dream"* goals meant, to mercilessly melt away for another at least 4 to 5 months. Best-case scenario. OMG. AAAAH! After I gave this quite catastrophic waiting and sitting around presented outlook some deeper thought, I decided to give my *"Positivity Card"* its magical trial and to therefore use this from the kind Universe just anew and in a way forced delivered "Abundance of Time" gift at hand full on towards 1) The *Healing* and *Rebuilding* necessity of my neglected *"Self"* and towards 2) The *Adjusting* action steps of my somewhat messy created lifestyle choices. Ufff. Ok then. Might as well use this time wisely for once, right? Yup. And that was then, when my inner voice strongly suggested for me to jUMP-start this entire *"Finding back Home again"* journey from my very inner core, the heart center area on outward by further letting me in, that 1) If my soul succeeded in getting to the source of what REALLY kept on holding me back from my true unlived *"Don't Dream your Life. Live your Dream."* reality experiences, that I therefore as part of the next essential *"Stepping-Stone"* at hand, graciously would be given the chance to 2) Allow my*Self* to start making peace with whatever as uncomfortable perceived outcomes would be entering into my awareness and that I then would be granted with the further opportunity, to replace iT all with a new and loving seed instead, if desired, which then additional into motion set *"Cause and eFFecT"* shifts eventually would 4) Provide my soul with another refreshing round of many new UPlifting and exciting *"Living on Earth Game"* adventure experiences in the form as Linda Wartenweiler. Abracadabra. Then, this loving voice continued explaining that if I decided to follow through with this quite powerful and *Patience* required *"The ONLY Person standing in Your Way is YOU"* liberating game changer at hand, that the next vital step therefore would appear of UTMOST importance, which revealed itself as the TOP ONE responsibility for me to *Nurture* and *Protect* this newly planted treasure *"ongRowingly"* with LOTS of *LOVE, CARE* and *RESPECT* in order for it to be able to grow and *"grOW and Expand"* and GROW stronger by the day, just about as *"little Linda"* used to practice it with her *"Acting. Uncertainty. Complete Life Change."* hobby desired dream seed and replenish my entire vessel this time around with *"little Linda's"* beloved *"NeverEnding"* love and light stream *"Comfort Zone"* experience, so that I eventually would be finding my*Self* swimming within an Abundance puddle of LOVE and LiGHT, which remains I THEN happily could be sharing with other soul travelers, if desired. Boom. Then, I suddenly came to witness how my *"Head Cinema"* production began its demonstrating run of HOW this within my heart rooted seed developed itself *"ongRowingly"* into every available direction, all the way outside of my *"little Linda"* vehicle by eventually presenting itself as a GiGANTiC, firm and dEEp-rooted oak tree made out of many strong branches and filled with numerous dark green leaves. Wow! And as my soul by then found "herself" more than sold by this just exposed game changer proposal at hand, I therefore happily and inspired decided to follow through with this lovely given advise, which keeps me to this very day a 111% grateful that I eventually did, my dear fellow *Co-Traveler*. Oh yeah. Indeed. VERYBiGSMiLE. Once my *"inner*

ARTreyu Warrioress" found herself Ready Steady for this magically sounding *"Finding back Home again"* challenge at hand, I as a next step right away jUMPed onto this newly presented *"Living on Earth Game"* exercise with LOTS of persistence and willpower. Yeeha. *"Let's Rock 'n Roll!"* After many eager countless effort attempts though, of putting all these in theory SO much easier sounding *"Growth and Expansion" "Stepping-Stone"* recommendations into action, my soul soon came to face the newly arising "truth" that any lasting desired performances presented themselves to be of much trickier nature than expected. Hmmm?! Yes, and those many stopping moments then eventually guided my*Self* to the quite disturbing cognition, that this within these past 7 1/2 years created US-Swiss Linda version ended up being quite difFeRent from whom I remembered *"little Linda"* to have started out as, on that to me precious May Day early morning. Oh boy! Yup. And this reality "truth" therefore required the immediate pre-action step from my end, to FiRST figure out into WHOM on heavens earth I actually transmuted this once so *"wiLD & Free"* spirited little one into, before my actual solid foundation recreation quest could be beginning its proper and eFFecTive course. Oh my. What a mess. Sniff. Thankfully the all-time magical Universe once again reliably and swiftly showed up as the wonderful guiding hand, by making right away sure to have my eyeballs stumble over the to my soul quite striking and eye-opening quote *"He, who looks OUTside DREAMS. He, who looks iNside AWAKENS"* on my Facebook wall first and once more about 18 hours later, within one of my neighborhood stores called Awakening. Ha! *"Gotch Ya'."* Now, as this rather controversial line within its second "coincidence" strike very much so succeeded in captivating my Gemini's curiosity, I therefore instantly felt prompted to start a researching quest on it with this brilliant all-knowing Google webpage tool and therefore quickly found myself slightly surprised about its Thurgau origin. Boah! Hold on. What?! Did I just read Thurgau?! YES. And suddenly, the magical Universe started to reveal to my soul that this amazing statement happened to have been expressed a LOOONG time ago by one of my fellow Swiss Confederates, the famous psychiatrist and psychoanalyst *Carl Gustav Jung*. WoW! For real? For real. And this newly created *"Now Moment"* then right away decided to continue its teachings with the Updates, that 1) "His" soul PRECiSELY a 100 years prior to my re-appearance ended up deciding to start out "his" next *"Living on Earth Game"* ride in a tiny, at the beautiful Lake Constance boarding village called *Kesswil* TG, that 3) Happens to be situated "only" a 10 minutes car ride away from *"little Linda's"* Parkweg rooted *"Home Sweet Home"* base, which she and two of her Herr Keller classmates on top of it all back in the thrilling 1980ies for some secret remaining reasons at some point 4) Started to nickname *"Stingi/Stinky"*. Ha! Oops. Now it's out. Oh no! Sorry Sonja and Alexandra. Though I shall keep the rest of it safe and sound within. Wink. So yeah, since this additional *"Coo-coo-cool. Yeah, yeah. This is so cool."* added Cider India reconnection immediately ended up striking my soul as another significant mind-blowing "coincidence", I as a next step right away decided to direct this rather dEEp diving sounding *"He, who looks OUTside DREAMS. He, who looks iNside AWAKENS"* quote some further attention and found myself rather surprised about my inner voice's suggestion, of having my soul picking UP a daily meditation practice. Meditation? Are you asking for my soul to start meditating, so that I will be able to better complete my WHO did I Become discovery quest upon this newly entered *"Finding back Home again"* path? Hmmm. Well, even though this proposed task sounded rather b*zZZ* to my auricles, I as part of this tremendous "Abundance of Time" gift at hand decided to give this *"One after all Only Knows the Outcome of Anything by Giving it its Fair Shot"* statement its *"Fair Shot"*. Boom. Now, as my experience with this topic happened to be limited to the a few months prior via this Google search engine attracted many free downloadable Orin samples, of which same pronounced Auryn expression *"little Linda"* recently interestingly furthermore took notice of in a beginning scene of a during a newly entered "The *NeverEnding* Story" movie adventure, and this in the form of a to Atreyu for guiding and protecting purposes handed mystical necklace, I after some more researching attempts came to decide to give those many on YouTube available guided mediations their fair trials, on where my soul at first connected the most with an acquaintance's brilliant Kelly Howell recommendation. Thank you. Then, a few weeks into this newly gathered, twice a day, *"sHe, who looks OUTside DREAMS. sHe, who looks iNside AWAKENS"* tested *"Life Toolbox"* ingredient, already proofed itself of tremendous help upon my overall mental and physical well-being stabilization quest. Yay! And all these many UPlifting released *"sHe, who looks iNside AWAKENS"* created *"Cause and eFFecT"* vibrations, actually found themselves already rewarding my awareness within the very first few trials and this in the form of experiencing my soul to be more *Relaxed, Calm, Balanced* and more *Aware* again of my own inner *"Self"*, of my surroundings and of this friendly love driven inner existing *"Heart over Head"* voice. Strike! Way to Go. One of my further significant awareness checks, that this newly experienced *"Living on Earth Game"* lifestyle shift brought along with, turned out to be the fact that I suddenly *"ongRowingly"* started to catch my soul being pre-occupied with figuring out the question as of WHY "her" vessel still found itself placed within this rather unsatisfactory and as outdated resonating *"The Other Planet" "Home Sweet Home"* base choice, resulting from 7 years ago. That's right. Obviously, this once as SO magical and thrilling perceived Big Apple *"Dream come True"* experience, meanwhile somewhere down the road truly seemed to have lost all its many powerful sparkles in order to keep my soul anything close to the so-called *Happy Camper* preferred state of mind *"Comfort Zone"* creation, which "truth" furthermore let me to lastly accept the "facts", that 1) This Concrete Jungle's soul mainly gets ruled by the world of the from *"little Linda"* in 2006 escaped *"Swimming ALONG WiTH the Current"* based business "aquarium" reality check and by 2) An Abundance of stage based *"Swimming AGAiNST the Stream"* opportunities within the magical world of Acting. Hmmm. Yes, and therefore those newly from my end approved conclusions finally led my soul to accept the already "known" reality check, that my vessel actually found itself meanwhile kind of cruising within a rather misplaced and "off" the original desired *"Don't Dream your Life. Live your Dream. Catchin'"* track formation, and this No Matter the then current b*zZZ* visa status spectacle at hand. What?! Oh boy. Yes, the "truths" of the matter after all remained, that my soul for ONE *"ongRowingly"* caught "herself" feeling the most drawn, passionate and MOST loving towards any presented on-camera creation opportunities and that *"little Linda's"* original and still very valid *"THE Ultimate Childhood Dream Vision"* SECOND of all results in the very thrilling desire to *"Act as a Leading Lady in a Hollywood Motion Picture"*. Yeeha! That's right. Wait a minute. What?! OhhOops! EXACTLY. And as one thing always leads to another, my wonderful *"Head Cinema"* production therefore immediately went ahead and guided my awareness right back to the in 2005 in Santa Monica created memory file, on which this friendly sent young man as his third *"Childhood Acting Dream Stepping-Stone"* master plan proposed, *that 3) "little Linda" could always continue her "Cali Dreamin'" adventure as a respected New York City trained Actress, whenever that "Living on Earth Game" ride cruises towards its end.* BOOM. OMG. This I almost forgot! Was this maybe the point that the magical Universe all along eagerly tried to bring across? Oh no! Yup. That is HOW my slumbering *"Cali Dreamin'"* desire finally successfully got awoken again within one SLAP and HOW my soul then came to decide, that this from *Madam ProCrastination* terribly well-guarded *"Living on Earth Game"* adventure as a matter of fact soon called for its proper attention, accompanied with the further execution of a just appeared long overdue *"Letting go of Something that No Longer Serves One's Growth and Expansion"* action exercise choice. Ok. Got it. *"Thy Will is My Command."* The more that I from that *"Now Moment"* on began to carry this rediscovered *"Childhood Cali Dreamin'"* option within my heart, the more it dawned on me, that my soul within those sunny *"wiLD wiLD West"* Coast offered lighter and loving vibrations, most likely would be finding "herself" a LOT moRE in tune with the from her end, almost 4 decades ago, original Linda Wartenweiler experienced *"Comfort Zone"* notes. Oh yeah! A further "True Snapple Fact" that let this City filled with Angels light UP as a more fitting territory for my *"inner Artist"*, meanwhile also resulted in my discovery that mother nature decided to equip *"little Linda"* with all the necessary tools in order for her to effortlessly and apparently convincingly portray any female villain character. Ha! Oo-WAH! *"Watch Out. Watch Out."* Wink. Yes, throughout time, I *"ongRowingly"* have been told that my soul happens to come across as rather creepy and scary as soon as my transformation into one of these darker appearing characters found itself being put into action. Abracadabra. And this without me even trying. LOL. Oops! Well, I very much so assume that all these many Horror Movies, including Danny's and my souls "kind bully" episodes from back in the day, certainly must have taken their sweet tiny toll on *"little Linda"*. Wink. Which developed skill on top of it all with guarantee perfectly well ended up getting expressed by whatever battlefield my *"inner Warrioress"* right then happened to be floating in. Ha! GROWL. Now, as this female villain genre revealed itself with time as one of my "SpeCialTies", a dear Filmmaker friend of mine, who actually ever since our first Artistic encounter in 2011 came to decide to use *"little Linda's"* many acquired talents as his set muse for all his own *"ongRowing"* Horror and Thriller story creations, happened to synchronically to my own inner *"Cali Dreamin'"* occurring realization journey, pointing out whilst on set for his in mid-July 2013 own written, produced and directed Short Film called *"Imprisoned Souls"*, that 1) My soul's skills in his opinion would do rather well in the magical Movie Mecca based in Los Angeles, that 2) Most Horror Movies within this *"The Other Planet"* sphere actually happen to be produced over "there" and that 3) My vessel therefore possibly should be considering to relocate itself to the more suitable *"wiLD wiLD West"* Coast formation. Boah! What?! Dear Universe?! LOL. Certainly, his words found themselves straight traveling to my heart area, which reality check immediately caused the beloved Universe to take advantage of this just ignited *"Cause and eFFecT"* momentum by sending *"little Linda"* a wonderful *Boot Camp* ending indicating next fitting *"Stepping-Stone"* gesture her way. Yay. About 1 week later, while my soul found "herself" busy with an occasional Instagram interaction with a dear like-minded Swiss-German LA based Actress friend of "hers", whom *"little Linda"* with LOTS of joy briefly happened to get connected with throughout her thus far unmentioned NYC MCTC Theater Company member journey of 4 years, this particular friend rather "randomly" suddenly found herself for the first time wondering, when my vessel would be paying hers a visit. Boom. What?! WOW. Very thrilled about this newly appeared *"Synchronicity par Excellence"* opportunity at hand, I therefore quickly UPdated this kind friend on the "truths", that 1) I, as part of another LA scouting adventure exercise, literally just found myself in the middle of eyeing into traveling towards her direction in September and that 2) My soul very much so would love to reconnect with "hers" in "her" current *"Home Sweet Home"* base chosen city. Then, as soon as this line found itself posted on our Instagram thread, lovely Marem instantly went ahead and kindly offered her cozy couch for my vessel to rest upon during my planned stay. Hooray! How sweet. Merci. Yes, and as this next Swiss Confederate based "coincidental" delivered supporting gesture revealed itself as enough of a *"Comfort Zone"* reason for my soul to feel Ready Steady *"Cali Dreamin' Catchin'"* Go, I within a short amount of days, with "No Doubt" quickly went ahead and purchased my next precious LAX airfare ticket. Yay! Los Angeles, here I finally come. Again. Yeeha. Then, alongside with the arrival of a third *"NeverEnding"* September waiting period at hand, our additional 90 days granted Stronger Linda Wartenweiler skills visa Evidence collection period thankfully found its dragging end a few days prior to my departure as well, which reality check therefore caused for my lawyer to send out everything required as promised. Wonderful. Fingers crossed. With this UPdated taken action step under my belt, my vessel then happily embarked the aircraft on the chosen mid-September date towards a newly entered *"wiLD wiLD West"* Coast adventure and this for the first time as a New York City trained and with its "famous" attitude equipped Actress. Ha! After a lovely and relaxing flight, my vessel then finally found itself anxiously and with *"How will this Movie metropolis feel like, now out of the eyes of a well transmuted Actress/ New Yorker/Ex-Banker perspective? Would my soul finally fit in and feel Ready for this original and by now probably so much easier felt challenge at hand? A small LA "Connecting and Belonging" community I meanwhile after all found myself able to create, with all the from the Big Apple's madness already escaped Acting and Filmmaking friends in count"* filled thoughts, reconnecting with the City of Angels' ground, after a this time break of a little over 8 years. Woaw. 8 years? That long already?! Yup. That long. And this being back reality check, my dear *Co-Traveler*, as usual felt SO "right" to my soul. Let me tell you. Yes, and therefore this city's and my sweet Swiss friend's warm and joyful welcoming gestures, as part of its *"Cause and eFFecT"* reaction, instantly succeeded in triggering these from *"little Linda"* much-appreciated soothing *"Home Sweet Home"* vibrations back into my awareness. Ahhh! Hello again. Woot. Woot. And. Thank you. This rather thrilling and well-replenishing scouting week, I happily ended up filling with several "old" NYC soul *Reconnections* and with *Networking* in general, with two spontaneous attracted private *Photo Shoots*, with *Revisiting* many of *"little Linda's"*, in especially 1996 created memory places, whilst the magical soul of Santa Monica anew decided to put another loving spell onto mine and with simply *Enjoying* my *Self* within this warm, sunny, soothing, relaxing, with nature filled and easy going offered energy flow of this SO MUCH quieter city filled with many angels experience. LOVE. Then, one day prior to my departure, the beloved Universe decided to further encourage my *"ongRowing" "Cali Dreamin' Catchin'"* mission by spontaneously granting my *"inner Artist"* with the opportunity to meet up with a there based manager, with whom a friendly casting director friend of mine put my soul in touch with, a few days prior. Yeeha! As this meeting from A to Z went by truly well and as our two souls immediately ended up CLiCKiNG in a rather FuNNy "Tag Team" way, we therefore both with "No Doubt" decided to jUMP onto a bicoastal freelancing based collaboration for starters and this as soon as the green light of my rather draining visa spectacle would appear within the hopefully very soon arriving *"Now Moment"* horizon. Strike. With all of these many thrilling impressions and inspirations at hand, it therefore truly felt rather easy for my soul to say *"YES"* to this original *"THE Ultimate Childhood Dream Vision"* experienced *"Head Cinema"* creation, whilst back UP in the air again, which reality check instantly led my attention travel back to my, in Santa Monica once *"The Key to your Success is to keep your Dream in Focus and to have the Courage to do things Other's WON'T do"* received attitude formula. Sweet. Ok. Let's. Once my vessel found itself in the late dark PM safe and sound placed on JFK's ground again, I right away experienced myself almost cracking UP about HOW welcoming, charming and friendly this rather ruthless and sarcastic city simply decides to present itself at times. LOL. After my discovery of the airport staff's decision, to get some apparently required construction work done on the for all passengers to the subway stations and terminals in between connecting solution required AirTrains tracks, and this *"All night long. All night. OOH YEAH."*, I therefore right away found myself for quite some time patiently waiting for its replacement bus. Then, as soon as this Plan B vehicle about 45 minutes later dropped my vessel off at its desired L-train station stop, my soul as a next adventure step instantly came to face the almost exact same Déjà Vu experience from earlier. What?! Yup. That's right. The presented changes this time around though appeared in the form of learning, that 1) One part of my *"Home Sweet Home"* transporting L-train line found itself experiencing some UPdating repairing work as well, which reality check furthermore meant, that I in that very *"Now Moment"* needed to 2) Wait for another replacement bus, somewhere in a rather sketchy appearing Brooklyn neighborhood area, so that it then 3) Would be able to release my vessel onto its from then on properly operating L-train stop experience. Boom! OMG. GROWL. After an almost *"NeverEnding"* 2 ½ hours, instead of its usual 1 hour duration experienced ride back to my lovely Williamsburg *"Home Sweet Home"* base, my frustration level synchronically very much so happily ended up throwing itself back on track again, which in its awareness "truth" for my soul meant that "her" Concrete Jungle re-adaption process found itself in its successful completed status mode as well. *TatAAA!* Well done. Yes, and therefore, this city's message hit my reality with a clearer than clear *"We are delighted to have you back lovely Linda. We truly missed you here. Though NEVER do this LA thingy EVER again! Alright? You better Watch Out. Watch Out."* welcoming home gesture. Ha! LOL. As far as of my newly set *"Cali Dreamin' Catchin'"* game plan at hand, I based on my *"ongRowing"* visa waiting and sitting around spectacle of another UP to 90 possible days decision making process time frame normality, right after my resettling in phase came to decide, that mid-January 2014 therefore seemed to be the ideal *"wiLD wiLD West"* Coast transition period to aim for. Yeeha! In the middle of October though, I to my surprise out of the blue came to learn that my *"Living on Earth Game" Boot Camp* journey for ONE Still seemed to be walking in its *"ongRowing"* shoes, whilst my soul TWO Suddenly got presented with the iNCREDiBLE news, that the entire immigration office a couple of days ago decided to call in a *SURPRiSE!!! Strike Period.* Excuse me?! *"Seriously?!?"* They are on strike. NOW?! OMG. What the heck! Filled with MANY more of these as frustrating described collected vibrations, I therefore iNSTANTLY found myself dialing my lawyer's iPhone number in order to find out WHAT on heavens earth this newly appeared delaying mystery at the horizon was all about. From his soul mine then came to learn that 1) Unfortunately everyone involved needed to remain in their waiting shoes, until this very unpleasant situation would be finding its hopeful end soon, which "truth" therefore 2) Called in the further *"Patience is a Virtue"* method as its *"ongRowing"* game plan at hand. Bummer. Absolutely unpleased about this rather nerve-wracking introduced spectacle, my soul then decided to finish the conversation with the further discovery that my entire world found itself all shaken UP again. AAAH! As soon as I succeeded in letting most of my built-UP emotion flow out of my system, my *"inner ARTreyu Warrioress"* then immediately came to decide to give those newly discovered *Positive Affirmation "Life Toolbox"* ingredient tricks their fair trial by furthermore pulling *"little Linda's"* oh so magical *"Positivity Card"* for help with the intent to hopefully succeed in raising my overall as rather heavy perceived existing state of mind vibrations towards a desired final visa approval end result. Then, after a strike duration of a total of 2 weeks, the immigration office staff FiNALLY decided to jUMP back on their regular work schedule again, which reality check therefore right away prompted my soul to even more so plead the kind Universe to PLEASE guide my responsible immigration officer towards the approval of my longed for O1 visa *"Childhood Dream Catchin'"* ticket. ASAP. PLEASE! Well, and as by mid-November this *"Patience is a Virtue"* method very much so got *"Pushed"* with an *"ongRowing"* and *"NeverEnding"* *"Enjoy the Silence"* reality check, I anxiously and with "No Doubt" instantly picked UP my iPhone anew and dialed my lawyer's number with the intent to receive ANY kind of UPdate on the whereabouts. 6 VERY precious and valuable months after all slowly have been snailingly melting by my awareness at this very *"Now Moment"*, which "truth" of experiencing my desperate evolving *"inner Artist"* being on hold for THAT long, simply caused for my *Patience* practicing soul to gradually freak out. Understanding as usual, my lawyer's soul then right away expressed "his" sympathy for my *"ongRowing"* concerns at hand, by quickly continuing his cheering up attempts with the information flow that 1) "He" happily would love to call up the immigration office in order to hopefully receive any news on my behalf, thought that 2) This task, as part of the experienced strike *"Cause and eFFecT"* reaction result, would rather appear as an unwise choice, as every immigration officers desk after all must be finding itself being staked UP with 2 weeks of additional produced work, which "truth" factor therefore very much so happened to be slowing down the entire visa process journey for every soul involved. Boom. And then, in order to round this entire evolving debacle the most elegantly way possible UP, my lawyer decided to exit our conversation with the wonderful further appreciated cherry on top added Piece of Cake awareness check ingredient, that 3) As for the cheerful around the corner slumbering Christmas Holiday season at hand, the pace at the entire visa department usually would experience some slower productivity as well and that my soul therefore 4) Needed to remain *Patient* until most likely January 2014. The very earliest. If my *"inner Artist"* gets lucky. SLAP! WHAT?! January 2014, THE earliest? Are you FREAKiN' KiDDiN' me?! OMG! Beloved Universe?! Hellou?! What are you doing?!! SNiFF. Yes, and these very words, accompanied with the knowledge that my ENTiRE, until 2016 powerful career establishing Green Key evidence hourglass, kept on running lower by the day as well, therefore instantly found themselves, as you possibly can imagine, my dear, dear supporting *Co-Traveler,* *"Hitting"* my heart and soul *FASTER* than the speed of light *"With its Best Shot"* possible.

OUCH!!! HOW on heavens earth was this from my end by then as ABSOLUTELY unacceptable and disastrous *"Don't Dream your Life. Live your THE Ultimate Childhood Dream Vision"* perceived reality check possibly possible. Was this outcome truly the result of my, throughout the past few years inner and outer US-Swiss Linda undertaken thought and behavior pattern adjustment choices, which UPdated results therefore within this very *Boot Camp "Now Moment"* "truthfully" started to reflect their *"You Are what you Thinkest, as Thoughts become Things and Energy Flows where one's Attention Goes"* results in its materialized mirror eFFecT? OMG. What a mess. Help. HeLP! HELP! And right in that further arriving *"Now Moment"*, I then as for the usual reaction approach and as of *"little Linda's"* trusted *"Everything happens for a Reason"* collected *"Life Toolbox"* ingredient, forced my*Self* to stay stronger for longer. PLEASE. Now, as a relocation to the City filled with Angels with this VERY limiting visa pending status at hand seemed like a nonsense choice to my logical evolved mindset at that particular time of my many created *"Living on Earth Game"* adventures, my soul therefore heavy hearted came to decide to synchronically *"Push"* this desired *"Stepping-Stone"* action choice forward, to my hopefully soon arriving yellow key visa approval moment. Deal. What I with this re-mastered game plan found myself unaware of though, revealed itself with time with the awareness discovery, that I on the other rope of things subconsciously also ended up putting my own *"Self"*, including *"little Linda's"* entire *"Acting Childhood Dream"* quest on hold. Yup. And therefore, I later on came to realize, that sneaky *Miss Fear* anew succeeded in convincing my still rather whirlwind inflicted inner *"Self"* to believe, that a stepping outside of my newly adapted NYC *"Comfort Zone"* reality seemed to be a too risky of a choice, accompanied with WAY too much involving work and that for that reason another from *Madam ProCrastination* demanded *"Wait-a-While"* attitude adaption needed to get called in. Until further notice. ASAP. Yes, and certainly this *"Head over Heart"* suggested game plan at hand, instantly found itself resonating with myself for the very two reasons, that for ONE, despite of the slow and sure improvement steps of my overall experienced well-being, I on the other hand still kept on witnessing my mental and physical impulses to promptly gear themselves into resistance mode, as soon as any images of whatever brave and mysterious proposed new *"Living on Earth Game"* adventures appeared on my *"Head Cinema"* screen, which *"Cause and eFFecT"* truth therefore easily convinced my positive wired *"True little Linda Self"* to accept this TWO suggested *"Wait-a-While"* choice at hand with "No Doubt", as its translation on top of it all also happens to reflect my last names meaning. Ha! That's right. Which discovered equation therefore equals a Linda *"Wait-a-While"* existence "truth". LOL. Alrighty. Let's then. Ufff. Yes, and this *"FuN Fact"*, ever since its awareness realization moment, as a matter of fact keeps on successfully prompting *"little Linda"* to proudly and properly honor its "truth" whenever required. Oh yeah. From then on, this newly entered *"NeverEnding"* *"Wait-a-While"* procedure at hand, which my soul probably last came to experience within "her" inguinal hernia hospital adventure almost 4 decades ago, I with LOTS of effort kept on *"Push*ing" my*Self* to take as much advantage as possible out of this daily disastrous and uncomfortably expanding "Abundance of Time" gift at hand, which reality check as for its result *"ongRowingly"* ended up developing itself into a rather spectacular undertaken rollercoaster joyride. WooHOO! Welcome aboard. As this *"NeverEnding"* seemingly *"Enjoy the Silence" "Wait-a-While"* period in regards of ANY reaction sides my lawyer and therefore from the immigration office as well, happened to be cruising along in its unbroken mode by March 2014, still, I as a result for the first time, within this Linda Wartenweiler created *"Living on Earth Game"* ride, came to experience HOW my mental state of mind slowly started to lose iT. Uiii. Yes, my beloved *Co-Traveler*. At this point, within my many accepted *Boot Camp* adventure tasks, my driven and tireless *"inner ARTreyu Warrioress"* found herself confronted by MANY various inner and outer accumulated pressure creations, which as a reaction cause further triggered this tremendous *"ongRowing"* longing within, to find my vessel surrounded by all *"little Linda's"* dear, beloved and missed blood and *"Extended Family Member's"*, including all her many other close and "like-minded" collected Swiss Confederate ones, within my oh so dearly known soothing Swiss roots *"Safety Realty"* zone. SNiFF. AAAH! And therefore, my bleeding soul found "herself" on this mid-March Monterone-Industria workday morning anew *"Push*ed" to the point, during which "she" came to decide that *"Enough was Enough"* and that this as absolutely unnecessary, dragging and as painful perceived nonsense needed to STOP. ASAP! Impatiently, I then as usual, as part of this apparently by now into a cat and mouse Piece of Cake business relationship established tango, immediately reached out to my unknowing lawyer as of WHAT the causes of this delaying *"Enjoy the Silence"* immigration attitude were and demanded a One-on-One get together, the fastest and earliest time possible. Thankfully, the kind Universe granted for our two souls to meet up again for the first time after a 9 months break, right after this snail-like paced ending coffee making work shift at hand, during which occasion I actually for the VERY first time ever, within this *"Living on Earth Game"* opportunity of mine, got *"Push*ed" very close to the point, of allowing this within my vessel slumbering and raging discovered "Black Panther" force to take control over my entire behavior and action choices. Oh boy. GRRRROOOWWWL! Yes, and this UPcoming and unplanned "performance", my wonderful *Co-Traveler*, with "No Doubt" would have granted my *"inner ARTreyu Warrioress"* with the outstanding achievement of carrying home one of those golden miniature statues called *Oscar*, if this female villain portrayed scene would have been recorded for one of those on the BiG screen projected *"THE Ultimate Childhood Dream"* creations. This, I know from the bottom of my heart. And so it is. Now, whilst my soul found "herself" OUTrageously busy spilling EVERY single accumulated emotion, including thoughts volcano-like out of my system, I on the other end of things all over sudden started to realize as of HOW MUCH Linda Wartenweiler actually found herself walking on EXTREME mental thin ice and that I therefore from that very second on, needed to pay ENORMOUS close attention to ANY of my further by *Miss Fear* driven executed reaction choices. Yes, this rather eye-opening slapping wake-UP call of experiencing my *Self* almost pushing my sanity over the from society considered "unhealthy" edge, upon this a few months ago joyfully *"Finding back Home again"* entered healing path, certainly right away succeeded in evoking every, within my vessel UPlifting and loving existing vibration, to pull my *Self* with LOTS of inner control back into the *"Now Awareness Moment"*, which undertaken procedure, as part of its *"Cause and eFFecT"* reaction step, quickly ended up triggering for my breathing-in mechanism to interrupt itself from working properly for about a 30 *"NeverEnding"* felt seconds. Boom. Now you REALLY have to *"Watch Out. Watch Out."* Linda. Oh boy. Yes, and that was when and how my soul, including *"little Linda"* for the first time came in touch with a so-called *Panic Attack* experience and how my superhero friend *Miss Fear* furthermore felt prompted, to even more so appear to my rescue. HELP. Witnessing my own self *"ongRowingly"* trying very hard to catch any of the in Abundance right in front of my lips and nostrils available floating oxygen supply with an only very little success rate at hand, certainly felt enough of a reason for my soul to ignite some more of these panic vibrations and to therefore plead my somewhat very confused and helpless appearing lawyer for help, as by then I with "No Doubt" felt enormously overwhelmed by whatever was happening within and outside of me. And certainly, so felt he. After I eFFecTively found a way to calm this outraged and erratic escaped "Black Panther" of mine down, my rather perplexed lawyer then, as part of our just earlier UPdated game plan creation at hand, right away felt prompted to very much so confirm and assure, that he 1) Would be submitting the Additional discussed O1 visa to be Created case material within the UPcoming few days, alongside with his strong attached hopes for 2) The newly to be involved officer to grant us with a LONG overdue and unexplainable reaction gesture soon. Yes. PLEASE. And that is HOW this somewhat very irritating Piece of Cake *"Wait-a-While"* period continued its *"ongRowing"* course of silence for actually quite some time longer. And lonGER. And LONGER. My beloved *Co-Traveler.* Which reality check therefore eFFecTively succeeded, to weekly throw more and moRE wood into this open blazing fire desire of finding my vessel, especially during this rather as challenging, helpless and as being left alone perceived mental *"Growth and Expansion"* exercise, placed amongst all my beloved ones within this other *"Home Sweet Home"* planet of mine, from whom *"little Linda"* always truly felt understood, supported and loved. Oh my. Ufff. Some further obstacles that I within this *"NeverEnding"* seemingly *"Enjoy the Silence"* *"Wait-a-While"* rollercoaster period came to face, certainly resulted in my knowledge that for 1) August 2011 marks, yes markS the last time, that I found myself happily and as for granted taken floating amongst EVERYONE missed, that 2) Those almost by then 3 years in a row experienced Switzerland separation break in count, revealed themselves as a new record for my vessel to have been "vanished", that 3) The latter inevitably would be continuing its adding course and this UP unto this very instant, during which 4) Any decision making gesture, sides either of these by then open O1 visa case numbers would be finding its way into our reality. Sometime in the hopefully near appearing future. PLEASE. Yes, and therefore the idea of finding my *Self* surrounded by my own-kinds within those as rather heavy and darker experienced *"Living on Earth Game"* adventures of mine with "No Doubt" seemed to be THE magical formula for my soul, in order to travel as smooth as possible through this entire *"Childhood Dream"* crashing dilemma at hand. Sniff. Certainly, many of my, in Switzerland located loved and dear ones, simultaneously *"ongRowingly"* found themselves wondering, when *"little Linda"* would be presenting herself next for some LONG overdue celebrating and catching up *"Living on Earth Game"* adventure creations within their mutual rooted planet, while many of them furthermore began to express that her *"wiLD & Free"*, FuN and giggling spirit actually would be missed quite a LOT. Ufff. And so felt I. Yes, my *"little Linda"*. Where are you?! SNiFF! Heavy hearted, I therefore over and over anew found myself explaining to each one of them that currently I choose to stay within this *"The Other Planet"* Boot Camp formation until further notice, as the reentering attempt of Linda Wartenweiler's vessel to her *"Home Sweet Home"* base of over 8 years by then only would be granted with an approved and valid visa status anchored in my *"Red and White"* Swiss passport and that with all the thus far rather bitter experienced Piece of Cake tasting bites at hand, an exiting without this desired UPdated *"Acting Dream"* s-Express train ticket in my pocket, would remain as a WAY too risky move on this current with action packed chess game at play. Yes, and on top off it all, those further accumulated and collected inner pressure points in count, my lovely intuition all along also kept on reminding my soul, that The End of this *"NeverEnding" "Enjoy the Silence"* entered waiting and sitting around period of "hers" would be remaining out of sight for quite some time longer, which reality "truth" unfortunately, or maybe one day this all actually will appear as a VERY wonderful and fortunate *"Everything happens for a better VERY AMAZiNG Reason"* blessing discovery, my inner voice proofed itself to be right. As usual. AAAH! And all those many rather as overwhelming experienced inner whirlwind created vibrations, instantly led for my soul to strongly plead this ruthless Concrete Jungle's to present itself from its gentler and more soothing side for once, by furthermore asking the all-time supporting Universe to PLEASE provide my many *"Living on Earth Game"* adventures with some much desired positive and enlightening shifts, ASAP, whilst this entire *"Childhood Dream"* crashing Boot Camp exercise at hand found itself about to successfully release all the many of my, within this *"Finding back Home again"* journey re-gathered *Hopes, Desires* and *Dreams* right out of *"Pandora's* magical *WombBox"* again. help. Now, as my mental well-being, besides the help of my more or less daily adapted meditation routine, within this one year inner beating up behavior routine by May 2014 with "No Doubt" happened to be successfully tangled within this in the Big Apple established unhealthy *"Head over Heart" "Spiderwebs"* reality check again, the concerned Universe therefore found itself rather determined to catch my *"Patience is a Virtue"* practicing heart's *"Enough is Enough"* attitude attention, by sending my vessel a sarcastic and LOUD *"LiNDA. STOP. LiNDA! LiSTEN TO ME! YOU NEED TO STOP DOiNG WHAT YOU ARE DOiNG TO yourSELF! HELLOU?!"* first ear infection ever my way. HA! That's right. Its message in retro perspective certainly appeared as rather crisp and clear, though my heads interpretation and view of it all at that particular time of course arose in a complete difFeRent light, especially after the from a soon visited doctors 30 ANTibiotic pill prescription remedy solution, over the course of 10 days straight. Boah. Let me tell you my beloved *Co-Traveler*, this medical healing treatment choice with "No Doubt" developed itself into another quite unforgettable joyride, as my immune system right then for the first time ever within those many *"Living on Earth Game"* created adventures, found itself getting exposed to such a long and intense PRObiotic bacteria removal action plan. Uiii. About 5 days into this newly entered *Healing* journey, I alongside with my *"ongRowing"* inner whirlwind producing attitude, to my surprise truly succeeded in evoking my vessel to out of safety reasons shut itself down by sending my soul into a since then thankfully last experienced breaking down and hyperventilation attack excursion. Yes, and as my inner sarcastic and dramatic *"Self"* seemed to have desired to end this rather unhealthy unraveling *"NeverEnding" "Enjoy the Silence" "Wait-a-While"* rattle with a glorious and remarkable exit, I therefore, about 10 hours later, made triple sure to give my VERY best in order to repeat this with SpeCial eFFecTs filled body shutting down scenario full on anew by this time adding a hint of some hyperventilation symptoms and the thrill of almost being run over by a car, into the mix, whilst my vessel found itself escaping from its triggering source. Hooray! GREAT job. Then, with the extra eye-opening added symptoms during day number 9, of witnessing how these magical "healing" pills suddenly enabled an *"ongRowing"* inner uncomfortable appearing itchiness to spread itself all over my entire vessel by furthermore leaving my awareness with some heavier breathing-in results than usual, the beloved Universe's trick finally succeeded in order to get through to me. And this time for REAL. Strike! Yay. Right in that very powerful appearing CLiCKiNG waking-UP *"Now Moment"*, I therefore instantly promised to my*Self* to 444% that *"Enough WAS Enough"* and that things HAD to change. Starting 8 seconds ago. As I within every *"little Linda's"* existing cell came to know that my soul, my sanity, including my vessel just officially reached their limit and that therefore any further created strains with guarantee would be leaving my awareness check, including my oh so beloved *"Soul Childhood Acting Dream Catchin'"* intentions with rather serious undesired consequences. *"The Choice is Yours."* Boom. That's right. Now, as *"Everything always happens for a Reason and this at its Perfect time"*, I would love as part of our *Dot Connecting* exercise point out to you, my wonderful *Co-Traveler*, that all of the just experienced interestingly literally and EXACTLY ended up occurred, whilst my dear Schnauzi "dad" came to the realization, that his soul desired to practice a to "him" overdue *"Letting go of Something* that *No Longer Serves One's Growth and Expansion"* action step with his, our 2 years ago launched Monterone-Industria "baby", which let mine appear as quite a happy camper as well, as *"little Linda"* meanwhile pretty much grew out of her barista shoes, which caused for her further *"Growth and Expansion"* cravings to secretly *"Knock, Knock, Knockin' on her "I Want to Break Free" door"* a little while ago already. Boah! What?! Yes. And the combination of 1) Those many *Knockin'* undertaken attempts, including my *"inner ARTreyu Warrioress'"* determination and commitment of 2) Seriously picking her neglected *Adjusting, Healing* and *Rebuilding* mission UP as its number ONE priority upon this out of sight fallen *"Finding back Home again"* journey, somehow must have been THE success *"Cause and eFFecT"* formula, which allowed for the numerous in front of my eyes locked doors to instantly swing wide open and to furthermore throw surprised *"little Linda"* into this opportunity manifested puddle of being able to sell her many with time adapted service *"Life Toolbox"* skill ingredients, in the form of a diversity of income resources to her throughout the past 8 years created *"Connecting and Belonging"* Big Apple community. Wow! No way! Yes way. And this to me as just rather mind-blowing perceived inner and outer *"Synchronicity par Excellence"* timeline revelation at hand, therefore reveals itself in this very *"Now Moment"* as THE then appeared magical key requirement, which granted my *Self* with the awareness experience, of witnessing HOW my from some souls considered *Hard Work,* unexpectedly started to pay itself off, by furthermore letting this from 2 ½ years ago detected *"Working by mySelf and on my Own"* existence metamorphose into its ever since then adapted, truly embraced and "unknowingly" launched precious *"Working by mySelf as my Own Boss"* freelancing choice. Ha! How crazy, right?! Boah. One gotta love life. Oh yeah! And therefore, my soul will always remain in "her" very grateful happy camper state of mind appreciation "shoes", towards especially the from my Schnauzi "dad's" then powerful indicated stepping outside of my *"Comfort Zone"* action shift, as its opened doorway, alongside with my immediate thought pattern and attitude undertaken adjustment choices, apparently ended up rewarding my CLiNKiNG revelation with the attraction of all those many supporting, FuN and diverse helping opportunities from my by then built *"Connecting and Belonging"* Grotto network and with the further rather satisfying awareness outcome, of experiencing HOW my oh so dutiful Swiss originated soul worked "her" way UP, and most importantly *Through it ALL. "Step-by-Step. Oh baby."* Abracadabra. Horray! *"Eventually all Things Fall into Place. Until then Laugh at the Confusion. Live for the Moments. And Know that Everything happens for a Reason."* There you Go. And so it is, Herr Albert Einstein. LOVE.

"Keep on Movin' my Darling. Ooh ooh-ooh ooh."
Now, with all these many, since my Rock Bottom visit up unto this experienced 444% *"Enough WAS Enough"* CLiCKiNG waking-UP revelation May 2014 *"Now Moment"* mental and physical accumulated undertaken adjustment decisions under my belt, there most certainly

must have something rather important gotten unlocked within this *Boot Camp "PandoraWombBox"* adventure chapter of mine, as things interestingly thereafter soon started to develop themselves towards many of those earlier on ordered refreshing experiences, which also included a secret set heart wish desire, that I, especially after my logical *"Head over Heart"* voice's success of convincing my soul to postpone "her" City filled with Angels relocation action step up unto the point, of the MUST GET approved yellow key occasion came to express. That's right. Very vividly I actually do recall those many occasions, during which my vessel found itself exhausted resting in my comfortable bed early in 2014, whilst my *"Head Cinema"* nevertheless nonchalantly continued its many *"Childhood Dream Catchin'"* adventure creations, whenever either put in touch with some of my Kelly Howell picked meditation sessions or simply on its own, whenever permitted. One to me rather significant through this *"sHe, who looks iNside AWAKENS"* process ignited SpeCial eFFeCT, soon introduced itself into my awareness with my acknowledgment, that 1) My soul actually *"ongRowingly"* kept on developing this strong desire to escape this city's madness, at least for a little while, so that I would be finding my*Self* able to "peacefully" dive into a 2) Much needed re*Booting* and readjusting healing challenge of this entire *Boot Camp* created US-Swiss Linda "mind-set" and to furthermore been enabled to 3) Direct all the required *"Heart over Head"* guided attention towards my rather unattended *"Finding back Home again"* oak tree mission vision at hand again. Well, and as I instantly found my*Self* resonating with this soothing away from everything sounding *"Living on Earth Game"* proposal and as my Switzerland desire *"ongRowingly"* kept on floating within its on hold status for who knows how much longer, I thereafter with "No Doubt" secretly began to add my still unlived and very present Los Angeles *"Cali Dreamin'"* dream location into this enticing emerging retreat fantasy adventure as its Plan B option. AHHH. Now, as my heart, throughout this rather as hectic experienced *"NeverEnding"* seemingly *"Enjoy the Silence" "Wait-a-While"* period, still happened to react with a LOT of resistance towards any actual possible brave and mysterious outside of my by then as *"Comfort Zone"* declared set new *"Living on Earth Game"* adventure proposals, I therefore as its compromising option simply continued to explore these many escaping action steps within my *"Head Cinema"* creations for the time being, which scenario each time ended up triggering my heart to yell *"WooHOO! I would LOVE to!"* One additional wonderful idea that this entire *"sHe, who looks iNside AWAKENS"* process vision found itself evoking though, resulted in this genius fantasy of renting out my Williamsburg *"Home Sweet Home"* room for a couple of months, to preferably a soul resulting from my own thus far created community network, so that mine would be finding "herself" enabled to truly dive into this entire magically vibrating *"wiLD wiLD West"* Coast *"Finding back Home again"* master plan as *"wiLD & Free"* as "she" after all always desires to be. Oh yeah. Now, as those many Los Angeles *"Cali Dreamin'"* undertaken escaping excursions also happened to be taking place alongside of my rather frustrating *"The ONLY Person standing in*

Your Way is YOU" stepping back into the light cat and mouse dance exercise, I interestingly, right after this fairly powerful 444% *"Enough WAS Enough"* CLiCKiNG experience, came to witness, how suddenly the gears of this truly committing to my *Self*, including well-being improving mission at hand, seamlessly started to shift themselves into my hearts and souls VERY first set priority. Finally. Hooray! At last. Yes and the *"Cause and eFFecT"* result out of this newly created *"Self*-care" attitude formula, therefore rather soon introduced my awareness into this earlier mentioned impressive reality SpeCial eFFecT creation observation, that 1) Whenever I chose to put my many OWN *Wants, Needs, Desires* and *Dreams* on 2nd, 3rd and/or even 4th position, that I right in that very by *Miss Fear* orchestrated *"Now Moment"*, actually ALWAYS successfully ended up working AGAiNST my *Own Happiness, Health* and *"Self"* and whenever I 2) Bravely allowed its opposite *"Heart over Head"* duality choice to occur, that my vessel to my surprise ALWAYS instantly started to fill itself with *Strength, Willpower, Sparkles, Determination, Love, Approval, Satisfaction* and with the reconnection outcome of all the many from patient *"little Linda Wait-a-While"* on hold put *"Living on Earth Game"* adventure To Do desire list. Boah. Abracadabra! And with all these many determined and magical undertaken improvement *"Stepping-Stone"* action steps towards my *"True little Linda Self"*, I am assuming that the loving and supporting Universe must have found itself rather pleased with my *"ongRowing"* inner and outer undertaken lifestyle adjustment choices, as alongside with 2014's September arrival, it 8 years later made sure to once more reproduce a in 2006 experienced SpeCial eFFecT event, which was *TatAAA!* Yes? Bingo, my wonderful *Co-Traveler!* The very spontaneous and "accidental" 4th couples of hours visit of my two dear and missed Musketeer souls Danny and Harry during their transit to Las Vegas. WooHOO! THANK YOU. Well, and as my overall progress, upon this once accepted *Boot Camp* challenge at hand, furthermore seemed to successfully have develop itself towards its *"PandoraWombBox"* exit door, my heart and soul therefore found themselves, about 28 hours after our bittersweet goodbye hugs and kisses exchange ceremony, on top of it all in the "possession" of a further magical and unexpected from the heavens sent *"Ask and You shall Receive at its PERFCT Time"* gift. Abracadabra. Introducing THE desired *"Dream come True"* materialization opportunity of their secretly envisioned Los Angeles *"Cali Dreamin'"* escaping fantasy. Boom. OMG. What?! YES. And this is HOW its unlocking key unraveled itself into my reality. On the following early September Monday morning, whilst my still UP HiGH on cloud 88 floating soul found "herself" busy with getting Ready for this newly started day ahead, I happily recall how my attention suddenly got drawn from my brand-new Danny and Harry recorded *"Head Cinema"* tape rerun spectacle, towards an incoming WhatsApp message resulting from a in Zurich based friend of a friend of a friend, whom I 1 year prior briefly came to meet during a Big Apple visit of hers. Now, as she found herself wondering if I happened to be available for a quick NYC Q & A FaceTime meeting any time within this week ahead, the two of our faces, as for the mutual perfectly arisen *"Now Moment"* at hand, therefore spontaneously ended up seeing each other's monitored on our iPhone screens, a few breaths later already. Ha! Jodeliuuuhuuu! Hello. Hello. Switzerland. After a FuN and short few warming up minutes, this friend then as a next step began to share, that she 1) Happened to be in the middle of organizing a much-needed Swiss sphere escaping *"Living on Earth Game"* adventure, in the form of a 6 months English improving excuse within this favorite metropolis of hers and that those 2) From her picked schools offered Manhattan student housing options somewhat seemed to appear as rather HiGH priced, for what she actually would be "buying". Ha! Sounds kind of familiar, my dear *Co-Traveler*, remember? LOL. That's right. *"Miss* soon *Fresh Off the Boat"* to be. So it is. Welcome to New York. Wink. Which train of thought then led her soul to express "her" curiosity if 3) Maybe mine would know of someone, who happened to be in need of a subtenant, starting January 2015 for the time being. Boom. Instantly, my all-time helping and supporting driven *"Self"*, then guided by my usual reflexes, found itself *speed*ing through my entire NYC collected memory library in the search for any possible fitting opportunities, which as for its immediate unmatching results triggered my soul to release a *"I'll happily keep my eyes and ears open for you"* responds and to for my inner voice to suddenly start screaming at me in its LOUDEST available *"LiNDA! LiNDAAA!! LiNDAAAAAA!!! HOLD ON! What are you doing??! This request is sent for YOU! YOU are in need of a subtenant, remember?! LA! Los Angeles! Your all time "Cali Dreamin'" wish!? Hellou?!"* notes. Oops. Oh. YES! That. Was. True. LOL. This unexpected, out of the blue arising unthought-of secret *"Dream come True"* arriving option truly "almost" slipped my brain. Ha! Let's blame this one on my still *"Rock 'n Rollin'"* Danny and Harry flash. Wink. Well, as soon as this rather important information flow successfully found itself hitting all my many brain cells within my own Las Vegas jackpot entered experience, I therefore filled with LOTS of excitement, instantly caught myself interrupting my friend's sentence with a LOUD *"OH MY GOD, WAiT! Do you know what? I actually am in need of someone. I almost forgot. Oops."*, which reality "truth" therefore right away succeeded for my slumbering *"little Linda"*, to absolutely pleased giggle out aLOUD about this somewhat TOO crazy to be true sounding Abracadabra, *"Thy Wish is my Command"* delivery at hand. First this random Danny and Harry *"Extended Family Member"* reunion treat opportunity and only about 1 day later this?! What was going on?! Lovely Universe?! Wow. WoW. WOW. And. AaaaHH. *"Life is Good"*. After all. Happily, I thereafter quickly went ahead and UPdated that Swiss friend's soul about this secretly kept *"Cali Dreamin'"* fantasy creation of mine by then wondering if maybe she might be interested in considering MY BEDROOM as her *"Home Sweet Home"* base for this Big Apple study venture to come, whilst my vessel nonchalantly and as *"wiLD & Free"* as my soul very much missed for it to be, would be finding itself as envisioned able to dive into this just magical appeared *"wiLD wiLD West"* Coast "test ride" opportunity, placed within this City filled with Angels formation at hand, as part of a possible, though much-needed next moving forward *"Stepping-Stone"* to think about strategy at hand. Ufff. And spilled out this idea, including words finally were. OMG. Which *"Cause and eFFecT"* truth then right away succeeded to 1) Instantly fill my vessel with many more of those as UPlifting and thrilling perceived vibrations and to furthermore inform my awareness, that 2) This once with inner resistance infused experience on that matter *"irgendwie/Anyhow"* down this truly committing to my*Self* road, mysteriously seemed to have dissolved itself. *"Irgendwo/Anywhere. Igendwann/Anytime"*. POOF. Boah. What?! Hooray! And that was when my *"inner ARTreyu Warrioress"* determinedly found herself with a LOUD *"Rebel Yell"* jUMPing right out of her hiding corner, Ready Steady and Driven to full hearted enter onto this next spectacular appeared *"Growth and Expansionary" "Living on Earth Game"* opportunity level. *"Let's do this Linda. Let's Rock 'n Roll!"* Yeeha. Ha! Then, as soon as our two souls found "themselves" after a LiVE FaceTime tour of my by then *"Home Sweet Home"* base of 4 years, including the exchange of all the necessary details, absolutely resonating with this spontaneous win-win city swapping miracle at hand, we then came to decide to set this perfectly matching *"All or Nothing"* ball into its *"Push"* position, by setting our two focuses onto the collection of the three further green light requirements, upon this our just mutually re*Booting* entered *"Dream come True"* materialization path at hand, which OK's resulted sides my lovely and always supporting roommate's, including landlord's souls and in getting my friend's student visa application approved. Within a hopefully "normal" speed of light duration. Wink. Boom. Yes. Let's. Things from that very *"Now Moment"* on, then thankfully started to move fairly quickly and these from my end required two *YES*es, I as assumed found myself a couple of days later already able to, within a SNAP and with "No Doubt", switch on. WoohOO. Gratitude. Dear. Emily. And. Lenny. LOVE. And these two ignited reality shifts as a matter of "truth", instantly succeeded in furthermore releasing my soul's knowledge and certainty, that "this" most likely was "iT". For me. Uiii. Yup. And this awareness UPdate therefore in detail meant 4 more months to *Prepare*. 4 more months to *"Enjoy"*. 4 more months to *Go*. Before my "Linda Wartenweiler" soul would be daring, to execute this much and LONG overdue *"Letting go of EVERYTHiNG that No Longer Serves MY Own Growth and Expansion Desire"* pre-cutting exercise, as a soon further "almost" *"Dream Come True"* like, bi-costal ON HOLD set Actress to be experience, upon this from the beloved Universe mysteriously orchestrated *"Don't Dream your Life. Live your THE Ultimate Childhood Dream"* oak tree quest at hand. Wow. Then, with the arrival of the 3rd day in December, the long awaited third green light welcomed itself into my soon temp-room-taking-over-mate's to be and my awareness as well and this final *"Open Sesame" "Stepping-Stone"* collected key therefore right away slammed opened the first page of our mutually entered new *"Living on Earth Game"* re*Booting* chapter at hand, which furthermore meant, that my friend's vessel officially would be moving into my *"Home Sweet Home"* base in about 4 weeks' time and that I therefore "freely" could materialize the from *Madam ProCrastination*, for exactly one year straight, very well guarded task of purchasing *"little Linda's"* MORE than deserving, mid-January 2015 dated one way LAX ticket. Yeeha! SNAP. Finally. Yes, and this newly manifested spectacle at count, soon led my awareness to notice, that 1) The from my soul's and heart's diligent for 12 months straight, revisited *"Cali Dreamin'" "Head Cinema"* Plan B recreation, found itself about to actualize EXACTLY the way as "predicted" and that 2) The *Law of Attraction's "Cause and eFFecT"* delivery "truth" resulted in a 100% ACTUAL "wanting" outcome success, without any of those "NOT wanted" elements. Ha! Remember? *"Thy Wish is my Command"* vs. *"The Power of released Words and images"* Boah! And therefore, once again a heartfelt *"Thank you. Danke schön. Thank you. You magical Universe you."* Now, as far as of my overall back "then" entered *"Acting. Uncertainty. Complete Life Change."* reality creation path at hand, my soul to my surprise actually 2 months prior to my vessel's departure came across an additional, rather impressive from the beloved Universe organized and with SpeCial eFFecTs packed two *"Don't Dream your Life. Live your THE Ultimate Childhood Dream"* encouraging *"Keep on Movin' my Darling. Ooh ooh-ooh ooh."* gestures, within this New York City *"Don't Dream your Life. Live your Dream"* transitioning wrapping up chapter at hand. Ha! Ready? Oh yeah. Let me please share this one with you too, my wonderful dear *Co-Traveler.* Buckle UP! Thank you. Let's GO. This adventure started its course on a particular mid-November Monday morning, whilst I as usual found myself busy checking all the many overnight "in flown" e-mails, from which the *Free LA January 2015 Pilot Season Workshop Information Event hosted by Actors Connection* line succeeded in catching my soul's and saddened *"inner Artist's"* immediate attention. Ha! OMG. This would be SO COOL! Ufff. Driven by my Gemini's curiosity to find out more about this very thrilling and time frame matching appeared subject at hand, I instantly kept on examining its content and found my soul by the time that "she" came to learn, that 1) This 6 days workshop filled with 18 significant pre-announced vessels out of this Movie, TV and Commercial Mecca's industry collection, would begin its magical journey 2) 4 days after Linda Wartenweiler's LAX arrival date and this within the magical Universal City environment formation, which happened to be set in between 3) *"little Linda's"* ultimate Hollywood Hills *"Home Sweet Home"* dream base and the legendary Universal Studios, MORE than lost within *"little Linda's"* all-time *"THE Ultimate Childhood Dream" "Head Cinema"* reproduction screening. Oh MY! Then, the second that my eyes espied this event's attendance confirmation note of an out of sight lost mutual David Lynch fascinated former MCTC Actress friend of mine, the wonderful Universe once again succeeded in sprinkling the perfectly required ingredient mixture onto all my many available senses at hand, in order to spark my soul's instant trusted knowledge, that 1) This with "coincidental" dream like filled occasion with "No Doubt" was calling for my vessel's attendance and that 2) The many from my end meanwhile inner and outer adjusted and executed *"Stepping-Stone"* choices towards the *Wants,*

Desires, Needs and *Dreams* materialization for my OWN precious *"Self"* even more so must have found themselves aligning on an *"ongRowing"* basis towards *"little Linda's"* OWN desired happiness *"FuN Factors"*. Yeeha. *"You Always Are what you Thinkest as Thoughts become Things"* right?! Ha! Certainly, I therefore right away went ahead by confirming my vessel's seat as well and found my *Self* once ticked off, rather thrilled about this absolutely inspiring MUST DO next introduced *"Living on Earth Game" "Stepping-Stone"* experience to come. Oh yeah. With this overall, thus far rather magically developed *"I Want to Break Free"* manifested *"Dream come True"* ticket in my pocket, my impatient vibrating soul then as a next action step first felt triggered to dial my lawyer's number for once in order to receive ANY as usual overdue reaction or some kind of UPdate information exchanges, upon this *"NeverEnding"* and *"ongRowing"* with LOTS of silence filled fading *"Childhood Acting Dream" "Wait-a-While"* experience in progress. GrOwL. Some rather as disturbing considered "facts" at that particular point after all resulted in the "truths", that 1) Meanwhile almost 2 rather precious, unique and with action packed years found themselves, since our two vessels "promising" as Piece of Cake case declared initial meeting, nonchalantly powering by my *"inner Artist's"* dreams realization hindering awareness check, of which 2) 19 months belonged to my *"inner Artist's"* aching moRE or less creative being shut down mode journey and 7 months towards the 3) Immigration office's second O1 case received reception confirmation reaction notice. OUCH. OUch. ouch. Oh yeah. *"Keep on Hitting me with your Best Shot. Fire Away. Common."* Now, as for my *"ongRowing"* impatient *Patience* practicing soul's newly chosen ASAP solving approach, of this by then as iNCREDiBLY annoying, outrageous, blocking and disrespectful experienced FREE Bye-Bye Green Card established Saint Linda cat and mouse Piece of Cake business relationship tango deal at hand, I for once decided to apply the within this *"The Other Planet"* often times "magical" *"With my Mind on my Money and my Money on my Mind"* short cut door opener strategy, which option move though instantly found itself getting dismantled by my lovely and VERY "carrying" lawyer's all-time returning Déjà Vu *"Cause and eFFecT"* reaction choice of 1) The assurances that any green paper exchange remained as an out of question solution from his end, that 2) His soul truly kept on walking in the dark over these mysterious *"NeverEnding"* and silently running visa cases at hand, that 3) The only action step within his power would result in calling the immigration office, once again, in the hopes of getting ANYTHiNG from their end, as SNAP *"They've Got the Power"* and that therefore 4) The only activity from our ends therefore remained in holding our focuses' on the *"Patience is a Virtue"* exercise. For longer. OMG. For real? I MEAN. For real. REAL?! O.M.SUPER.G. What was new, right, my lovely and co-*Patience* practicing *Co-Traveler*? WOW. And that was when my somewhat rather annoyed over this truly by then as rather ridiculous and with LOTS of non-sense filled developed BLa*BlA*BLA b*zZZ* WHATEVER visa lullaby turned soul found "herself" anew successfully *"Pushed"* over this

"Enough was Enough" edge, by furthermore gaining the awareness conclusion, that I truly had it with this absolutely destructive established waiting around procedure at hand and that it therefore was at the time for my "inner ARTreyu Warrioress" to also keep on moving forward upon "little Linda's" fading "Childhood Acting Dream" path. "With or Without You." As on top of it all, my vessel ultimately found itself about to finally test-relocate-ride, this since October 26th 1911 established magical Movie and TV Candyland à la "Mulholland Drive", just as "little Linda" "accidentally" happened to blur it out to Frau Marzoli, exactly two decades ago. HA! That's right. LA-LA-Hollywood-Land. Here I come. Abracadabra. Well, and I assume that these incoming vibrations then furthermore instantly must have aligned my soul with this early on to "her" as wise and philosophical interpreted "Life Toolbox" ingredient attitude treasure, to "Always follow your Hearts Desires as Radiant as possible by ensuring to Keep On Pushing Any presented Boundaries with a Living Life to its Fullest possible Approach and to therefore absolutely NEVER take NO for an answer, No Matter what, as Not even the Sky is the Limit", as my heart thereafter instantly led my vessel as for its next action "Stepping-Stone" choice to reach out to the responsible Actors Connection LA Pilot Season Workshop soul and happily found myself, after an inspiring and convincing meeting, signed up for this with Magic, Goosebumps and Adrenaline filled Acting connecting and networking "Living on Earth Game" exercise opportunity ahead. Boah! And HOW grateful my soul remains over this "Heart over Head" accepted master plan decision, as this "With or Without You" entered "THE Ultimate Childhood Dream" venture revealed itself as one of my MOST powerful Acting experiences thus far. WOOHOO! Yes. This choice of allowing my soul to find "herself" being exposed to "her" beloved "NeverEnding" Acting passion for 6 days straight, within this "Dream come True" like "Knock, Knock, Knockin' on Hollywood's opportunity doors" reality formation truly felt like Heaven. On. Earth. WOWOWOW. And. Thank you "Linda". Smile. The wonderful outcome out of this "The Key to your Success is to KEEP your Dream in Focus and to have the Courage to do things Other's WON'T do" entered "Don't Dream your Life. Live your THE Ultimate Childhood Dream" adventure at hand, resulted in 1) The gathering of many valuable LA-LA-Hollywood-Land based contact information, which therefore furthermore included 2) 18 incredible and precious exposure opportunities for my Artistic Linda Wartenweiler vessel to reach back to and properly make use of at the perfectly destined arising "Ask and You shall Receive" "Now Moment", the 3) Release of all the many accumulated creative energy vibrations amongst the from my "inner Artist" as Real Deal perceived souls by simultaneously gaining 4) Even more so confidence in "little Linda's" "wiLD & Free" creative choices and lastly, 5) A spectacular 18 months Commercial contract representation offer, of a from "little Linda" right after her first NYFA graduation celebrations in 2007 secretly desired bi-costal agency, starting as soon as my vessel officially would be deciding to reside within this City filled with Angels formation. Boom. WOW. How thrilling this "Don't Dream your Life.

Live your THE Ultimate Childhood Dream" adventure offer certainly felt and sounded like. Oh yeah! Though, as my magical *"NeverEnding"* seemingly *"Enjoy the Silence" "Wait-a-While"* spectacle at that very particular appeared mid-February 2015 *"Now Moment"* still happened to *"ongRowingly"* be floating *"Somewhere over the Rainbow"*, my aching *"inner Artist"* for that reason heavy hearted found herself being forced to postpone this additional *"Dream come True"* delivered representation opportunity. Until further notice. Ouch. Bummer. Sniff. Which reality achievement check then thankfully soon led my soul, to after a *"Change the way you Look At Things and the Things you Look At Change"* undertaken *"Positivity Card"* trick exercise, burst out a celebrating *"Yeeha! Congratulation my dear "little Linda". Very well done."* reaction *"SHOUT"*. That's right. And to furthermore translate this from the wonderful Universe delivered message into a clear *"Keep on Movin' my Darling." "Step-by-Step. Ooh ooh-ooh ooh baby." "Just Hangin tough. Oh. Oh. Oh. Oh. Oh."* encouraging *"Boom. BOOm. BOOM."* advise. Now, as one of the last existing TO DO requirements on this 8 1/2 years ago accepted, though towards its end running Artistic and *"Self*-developing" *Boot Camp* itinerary at hand, must have resulted in a spontaneous *"Now Moment"* mirroring reflection inventory exercise of *"little Linda's"* entire inner, throughout this precious *"Acting. Uncertainty. Complete Life Change."* chapter undertaken metamorphosis achievements, I therefore, 6 weeks prior to my *"Don't Dream your Life. Live your Dream."* wrapping up date, which to my surprise turned out to be 5 days after my soon temp-room-taking-over-mate to be's incoming last green light achieved newsflash, found my *Self* getting confronted with another rather magical *"Synchronicity par Excellence"* reality spectacle. WoohOO! Ready?! Ready! Well, this storyline actually interestingly found itself once again getting set into motion, via a for this time for some whatever reasons in my spam mailbox landed e-mail discovery and this right after a LOOOONG and FuN, on this particular second Monday December later PM evening, ended Skype catching up meeting with my lovely mom. Now, as this e-mail, with its quite enticing *Self Tape!!!!* chosen subject line ended up resulting from my, in *Long Island* NY based agent, my soul therefore instantly felt prompted to find out more about this absolutely unexpected, with its following day appeared audition opportunity indicated due date gesture. To my *"ongRowing"* surprise, I therefore soon came to learn that this wonderful agent of mine decided to, despite of her knowledge of my *"NeverEnding"* visa quest at hand, submit my information to the casting directors of the from 2014 until 2015 on Cinemax aired TV show "The Knick", starring Clive Owen, and that they therefore requested for *"little Linda"* to record two difFeRent attached, for their 2nd season wanted character sides, until the following afternoon. BOAH. What?! WHAT!? Certainly, this newly from the always surprising Universe provided *"Dream come True"* like information flow, welcomed itself into my awareness with a LOT of bafflement and with a thrilling Goosebumps SpeCial eFFecT attack and this even more so, as Cinemax happens to be owned by my favorite TV network channel *HBO*, which reality UPdate though furthermore meant, that this company, according to my knowledge "Once Upon a Time" decided to exclusively hire American citizens and Green Card holders for their creative projects and that therefore all the many from HBO offered Acting opportunities find themselves cruising along within this for ANY yellow key holder inaccessible 60 % creative puddle. Hmmm. Now, as my Gemini's curiosity, guided by this always enticing *"Everything happens for a Reason"* collected *"Life Toolbox"* ingredient very much so found itself *"All Fired UP"* a few breaths later, my soul therefore quickly decided to put this appeared questioning mode of mine on hold and to instead simply move forward by testing the waters within this just appeared *"Don't Dream your Life. Live your Dream."* delivered opportunity at hand. *"One after all Only Knows the Outcome of Anything by Giving it its Fair Shot."* Ha! That's right. Quickly, I therefore right away reached out to my as well, during *"little Linda's"* MCTC journey gained roommate friend, in the hopes that she would be available and willing in assisting my newly picked up project as my reader, including camera operator on the following day. Now, even though her Tuesday schedule ended up being quite filled already, my supportive roommate thankfully found herself willing to grant my *"inner Artist"* with the only available time slot, which turned out to be during her lunch cooking session in our kitchen. LOL. What?! Yup. Well, and this creative adventure of watching her vessel move *"Back, Back, Forth and Forth"* like a *"Smooth Criminal"* between her steaming pots and pans mission and recording task of my sizzling performances, certainly with "No Doubt" transformed itself into a rather FuN and priceless spectacle. LOL. Oh yeah. Indeed. And therefore *"Welcome to the Magical World of Filmmaking"*, my curious Co-Traveler. Ha! As soon as the first trial of scene one found itself safe and sound locked within my silver black iPhone 5s device, our two souls, as for Linda Wartenweiler's vessel quite certain unhireable existing "truth", combined with my *"inner Artist's"* satisfying work quality, came to decide that this one was iT already, which criteria also ended up getting applied for the second scene, after its second recording. That's right. And therefore *Send. Bye-Bye. Mission completed.* Well, and to our surprise, my roommate and my astounded *"Self"*, a couple of days later then actually suddenly came to learn that those from our both ends experienced time crunches, including my choice of approaching this granted *"Dream come True"* like *"FuN Fact"* exercise with a for once easy breezy *"Less is More"* attitude approach, seemed to magically have worked in our favor. Ha! Yes, and therefore my soul certainly reacted rather startled about my agent's, on the following Monday AM incoming phone call news delivery, that ONE as the "The Knicks'" casting director found "herself" being pleased about *"little Linda's"* delivered creations, her vessel therefore TWO got called into Cinemax's Greenpoint office space on the following early morning, in order to audition for a newly chosen character pick and to furthermore bring back the one that we recorded once. Boom. AH. What?? WHAT?! Ok?! Hmmm. As soon as those absolutely magical vibrating words, including kindly provided complement sort of slowly found themselves sinking into my awareness, my soul as a next *"Cause* and eFFecT" step felt prompted, to first verify with my lovely agent's if my vessel truly would be able to get hired with this annoying and "NeverEnding" seemingly pending O1 visa spectacle at hand, iF. From her end, I then instantly came to learn that everything looked OK, as any usual visa requirement guidelines happened to be missed in this particular posted casting call, which thrilling information flow then happily led my soul with a cheerful *"Coo-coo-cool. Yeah, yeah. This is so cool."* confirm its vessel's attendance. Oh yeah! Equipped with both directed and within my "muscles" locked characters, I then even more so excited found myself a few hours later, *"Eye-to-Eye"* sitting across a very friendly casting director, who desired to tape my own and two from her end directed interpretations of each character and this SpeCial, from the magical Universe delivered first time ever Real Deal Acting jackpot treat with "No Doubt" succeeded in throwing *"little Linda"* right UP HiGH into her quite out of sight lost *"Super Happy Comfort Zone"* reality sphere. ABRACADABRAHHH. WooHOO! Now guess WHAT, my amazing *Co-Traveler*? Ha! Another couple of days later, my soul truly found "herself" more than amazed about a newly from my agent received e-mail stating that 1) Linda Wartenweiler's vessel found itself being put On Hold, that 2) The "The Knick" producers, as for the last 2014 approaching Holiday celebration season decided, to continue with their final season 2 2015 shooting schedule in the beginning of January and that we therefore 3) Thereafter would be hearing back from them with more news. BOOM. Excuse ME?! WHAT?! My precious *"little Linda"* found herself being put On Hold now?! HOLLY MOLLY. How on heavens earth was this simply possible!!? Now that I tried the LEAST bit to book this job, every door suddenly seems to slam wide open within a SNAP?! Hmmm. Lovely Universe?! Hellou?! WOW. Certainly, this rather satisfying achievement, within this second ever to Linda Wartenweiler granted Real Deal audition opportunity, kept on producing a LOT of those thrilling *"Not even the Sky is the Limit"* vibrations within my vessel and furthermore infused my Gemini's curiosity to wonder about How Much further my *"inner Artist"* would be succeeding in *"Keep on Movin'"* forward, upon this magical *"THE Ultimate Childhood Dream"* guided "The Knick" path. Ha! Well. Now guess WHAT-WHAT, my lovely *Co-Traveler*?? Exactly! The *"I'mPOSSiBLE"* truly happened. Boah! 9 days prior to my vessel's *Artistic and "Self-*developing" *"Don't Dream your Life. Live your Dream." Boot Camp* exiting *"Stepping-Stone"* experience, my mind finally found itself a 188% blown away, the second that my eyeballs came across a from my dear agent forwarded e-mail stating, that "The Knick" team happily would be loving to hire my Linda Wartenweiler vessel as a newly offered character for 1 episode in their UPcoming 2nd Season production. BOOM. OMG! O.M.G! OHHHM.And.Super.G! Yes, and as you most likely can imagine, my friendly dear *Co-Traveler*, my soul right in that very with many *"Dream come True"* SpeCial eFFecTs filled created *"Now Moment"*, found "herself" ECSTATiCALLY and completely lost floating *"Somewhere HiiiGH UP over the Rainbow"*, alongside with NENA's magical and all-time inspiring *"99 Red Balloons"*. For a few seconds. Before my thrilling and also still "UP there" existing *"NeverEnding"* seemingly *"Enjoy the Silence" "Wait-a-While"* party pOoper decided to pop this just appeared and with LOTS of *"HiGH on Emotion"* filled 100th red appeared balloon, by reminding my soul to instantly place my feet down on earth again and to as a next step instead share with my dear agent that 1) My *"inner Artist"* within this very heart beat moment ABSOLUTLY would love to accept this *"Dream come True"* like gesture, iF 2) This vessel of mine TRULY and OFFiCiALLY would be finding itself being allowed to get hired by Cinemax. After some more *"Back, Back, Forth and Forth"* e-mail exchanges, the beloved Universe then decided to finally let the assumed cat out of its bag by having "The Knick" UPdate my dear agent, including my*Self* that a green key happened to be the minimum requirement for this *"FuN Fact"* job at hand and that they therefore unfortunately found themselves being forced to offer this magical opportunity to another talent instead. Bummer. PUFF. Oh well. Hopefully, I will be getting to see you again some time *"At its PERFCTLY arising next Now Moment."* Bye now. Shortly after my*Self* thereafter succeeded in accepting this entire with magic packed "The Knick" spectacle for what it actually from the get-go was, my heart voice then suddenly brought to my attention that I actually would find all the many wonderful reasons to feel proud and confident about this just experienced *"Living on Earth Game" Boot Camp* closing *"Now Moment"* mirroring reflection inventory exercise of *"little Linda's"* entire inner, throughout this precious *"Acting. Uncertainty. Complete Life Change."* chapter undertaken metamorphosis achievements at hand. UFFF. That's right! Wink. "Facts" after all were, that 1) This precious "The Knick" provided experience happened to be my vessel's first, within a LONG period of time practiced audition performance, that 2) My current undergone *"NeverEnding"* yellow key quest to my soul's relieve eFFecTed the final outcome in NO way, that passionate *"little Linda"*, with this to her 3) Second thus far presented Real Deal Acting job opportunity 4) Ended up scoring her BiGGEST achieved *"Childhood Acting Dream"* booking success, including green money offer thus far, that 5) This final casted part appeared as an additional suggested character that my vessel DiD NOT audition for and lastly, the rather interesting awareness insight, that 6) This from my hearts, from decades ago collected *"Empty your Mind and become Water my Friend"* chosen *"Life Toolbox"* ingredient strategy, must have Played a significant Part within this entire *"I'mPOSSiBLE"* success story at hand. Oo-WAH! And therefore *"BRAVO "little Linda". Well done. Now you know that "YOU've Got the Power"* and this with *"No Doubt"."* Ha! That's right. *"Hip Hop Horray. Ho. Hey. Ho."* Yeeha! And. Gratitude. For. That. Awareness. UPdate. LOVE. With all these many spectacular and encouraging last up until January 22nd 2015 collected Big Apple *"Living on Earth Game"* impressions safely zipped within my backpack, I then FiNALLY found my*Self,* precisely 12 months after the from *Madam ProCrastination* original taken over and well-guarded aimed for shifting materialization quest, excited, relieved and as *"wiLD & Free"* as my soul so MUCH missed for it to be, Ready, Stead and Driven to release my vessel and soul out of this LOOOONG overdue *"I Want* to Break Free" Boot Camp "PandoraWombBox" experience, whilst my lovely temp-room-taking-over-mate took over *"little Linda's"* beloved *"Home Sweet Home"* base spot for the time being. Yeeha! Bye-Bye you Concrete Jungle YOU. See you in about 6 months. *"Oops. I did it again."* Now it's time to *"Rock 'n Roll!"* with some Angels for once. Jodeliuuuhuuu!

* * *

LOS ANGELES or *"Finding back Home again"*

"Love and Devotion, my "True little Self". Please come back into my Life."
As soon as the airplane a couple of hours later, safely dropped my vessel off at *Burbank*'s CA airport on that Thursday evening, I remember how instantly many of those thrilling *"Not even the Sky is the Limit"* vibrations in lighting *SPEED* began to fill UP my entire inner space from head down to my 10 toes, by furthermore witnessing how my soul simultaneously decided to quietly shout out a LOUD *"HELLO? "CALiFORNiA LOVE", iS iT ME YOU'RE LOOKiNG FOR?"* line. Ha! And yes, right in that very *"Now Moment"*, I must have felt about exactly the same way, as brilliant and inspiring Naomi Watts magically chose to demonstrate it in "Mulholland Drive's" opening scene, which reality check certainly stimulated *"little Linda"* to therefore embark onto her own dream-like and with duality filled interpretation experience of this genius David Lynch created flick within her *"Head Cinema"* production. Oh yeah. *"Silencio. No hay Banda."* Wink. Filled with these many extra added impressions, I then, equipped with my two luggages found myself thereafter next to a lovely palm tree excitedly waiting for this dear, WAY earlier introduced first Monterone-Industria ex-coworker and NYFA friend of mine, as her kind soul, aside from "her" generous offer for my vessel to rest upon "her" air mattress during my first 2 settling in weeks at hand, furthermore came to express that "she" on top of it all even happily would be loving to welcome my presence at the airport already. Yay! *"Hay esta un Banda."* LOL. Et. Merci. On the following early AM, I then, inspired by these many to my soul unusual from an entirely blue sky traveling warm and soothing famous *"Cali Dreamin'"* late January sun rays, including the few more in front of our door spotted welcoming palm trees, instantly felt prompted to slowly get the ball for the two most important pre-set 14 days game plan at hand rolling, which included 1) The preparation of my *Self* for this thrilling first within *"little Linda's" "THE Ultimate Childhood Dream Vision"* provided LA-LA-Hollywood-Land realization adventure to come, plus 2) The look-out for THE next perfect temp *"Home Sweet Home"* base for the soon remaining 5 ½ months ahead, so that my soul thereafter finally and peacefully would be finding "herself" enabled to 3) *"OngRowingly"* dive into this much-needed re*Booting* and readjusting healing journey of this unfitting detected US-Swiss Linda creation, whilst I parallel also would be dedicating 4) All my available focus towards the proper "completion" desire of this meanwhile picked up *"Heart over Head"* guided *"Finding back Home again"* oak tree

vision mission at hand. Once my first task found itself 1 week later successfully locked within my overall Acting *"Life Toolbox"* ingredient collection, I then as a result thankfully got provided a 100% access rate to any further required *"Time and Energy"* resources in order to get this remaining open second task settled as well, which completion success though to my surprise decided to sail along by an easy breezy appeared mojo flow. Hmmm. Now, even though this important settling in setting up puzzle piece at hand still happened to be swimming in its uncompleted mode 2 days prior to my vessel's moving on date, my soul therefore, based on my inner voice's provided recommendation to in general stay away from any of those by *Miss Fear* orchestrated impulsive rushing into things adapted Big Apple action choices, came to decide to instead simply allow my*Self* to approach this newly entered *"wiLD wiLD West"* Coast test-relocate-ride chapter with a cool head, accompanied with this city's presented speed and to furthermore *"ongRowingly"* keep on putting my trust into this, from *"little Linda"* a few months ago, magically *"You must be my Lucky Star"* created *"Positivity Card"* trick. That's right. *"Patience after all is a Virtue"* and this with rather thrills and chills filled *"Life Toolbox"* ingredient practice nevertheless happened to have proofed itself as a quite valuable success formula thus far. It certainly worked its wonders with *"little Linda's"* Astoria *"Home Sweet Home"* base solution on April 30th 2007 and confident my soul therefore remained, that the beloved Universe, guided by my choice of this once intuitively trusted *"Stepping-Stone"* approach, anew reliably would be delivering its next matching *"Ask and You shall Receive"* gesture just *"at its PERFCT arising Moment"*. Oh yeah. Abracadabra. Yay! It worked. And this with SpeCial eFFecTs filled *"Thy Wish is my Command"* epiphany this time around found its way into my awareness, during my soul's meanwhile diligently and daily performed *"sHe, who looks iNside AWAKENS"* Transcendental Meditation (TM) collected *"Life Toolbox"* power ingredient practice, in the same afternoon. Boom. Now, as my soul within this 3 ½ months TM spectacle at count, *"ongRowingly"* came to realize that this technique, besides its rather quickly detected increasing *Happiness, Energy, Appetite, Peace, Focus, iNspiration* and *Clarity* experienced awareness levels, furthermore seemed to provide my soul's overall undergone *"Living on Earth Game"* ride with some interesting suiting and satisfying insights, including recommendations whenever desired, I therefore instantly and with "No Doubt" once again came to know what needed to be done, as soon as my soul found "herself" in the *"sHe, who looks OUTside DREAMS"* reality state of sphere again, a couple of minutes later. Ha! With my newly picked up *"Thy Will is My Command"* attitude selection, I therefore as directed found myself within a snap reaching out to another friendly, and just a few days ago reunited ex-June 2006 NYFA classmate, in order to find out if 1) My vessel possibly would be able to rent out his and his wife's on Airbnb posted extra bedroom in their LA condo for a couple of nights, so that I 2) Could "buy" myself the required time, until this open mission at hand would be finding itself in its Ticked Off mode. Send. Then, after a short, crisp and satisfying returned phone call from his soul a few hours later, the all-time supportive Universe to my surprise once again made sure to enhance this assigned *"Cause and eFFecT"* undertaken *"Open Sesame"* key exercise, by having us close a from my ex-classmate's fantastic proposed deal, which included the FREE use of their couch for the time being in EXCHANGE of my services in their rather quite booked Airbnb days ahead. How perfect. Absolutely. Yes let's! Strike. 2 days later, my vessel therefore as planned found itself exactly after these 2 first offered starting out weeks, transitioning from one, during *"little Linda's"* many NYFA adventures gained friends, to another, which newly granted *"Connecting and Belonging"* opportunity furthermore let this former classmate of mine once again turn into my friendly "neighbor". Ha! What?! Yes. That's right. As "coincidence" has it, the two of our souls actually, through some from his end occurred interesting twists and turns already ended up residing in the EXACT same East Village building throughout almost our entire June 2006 NYFA created adventures, with the difFeRence that his, in Texas originated vessel happened to be located on the ground floor, alongside with our Mexican considered ex-classmate's, whilst *"little Linda"* happily enjoyed all the many Swiss visitors UP on the legendary 5th floor. Ha! How FuNNy, right my dear *Co-Traveler*? Then, about 1 ½ weeks into this newly embarked Free couch Airbnb exchange *"Living on Earth Game"* adventure, those friendly two temp-roommates of mine one evening came to decide to approach my vessel with the urge of having a talk with my soul and this from my end rather unexpected perceived action choice instantly triggered my brain to jUMP into its very well Concrete Jungle adapted defense mechanism mode, by furthermore expecting to find myself about to get confronted with some lowering and as negative perceived vibrations. Yes. This reality check after all remained as my absolute uncomfortable ingrained *"Comfort Zone"* experience and thankfully, my soul this time around found "herself" getting presented with a further *"You must be my Lucky Star"* SpeCial eFFecT offer, whilst my soul came to learn that my presence, including assistance within their own daily routine for ONE happened to have increased their overall experienced life quality and that therefore both of them TWO happily came to decide that they would love to extend our deal for as long as I desired for it to flow. Abracadabra. What?! Wow. Yes, and as these rather unexpected flattering appeared words very much so succeeded to resonate with every within my vessel existing cell, I therefore relieved and excitedly felt prompted to accept their kind offer with a joyful *"YES, I would love that too."* Boom. Horray! And that is, how I ended up attracting and completing this from the get-go set second desired THE next perfect for the meanwhile remaining 5 months temp *"Home Sweet Home"* base task, which reality shift therefore instantly let my vessel melt into its official roommate relationship status with this friendly couple, their two cute little doggies and with their 3 months in "baby on board" spectacle in growth. That's right! Congratulations. Well and this, for the first time ever from a daily placed front row seat witnessed *"Growth and Expansion"* miracle adventure at hand, with "No Doubt" developed itself *"ongRowingly"* into its own absolutely unexpected mind-blowing *"Living on Earth Game"* journey, including in retrospective discovered much required and with power infused puzzle "peace", alongside of my own undertaken *Adjusting, Healing* and *Rebuilding* travels ahead. WOW. Who would have known. Oh yeah. Soon, soon certainly, my dear *Co-Traveling* friend, you shall be finding out for your*Self* what the magical Universe's intents were, with this additional and incredible provided *"Everything happens for a Reason"* exercise. Ha! With this new easy peasy in-flown granted last settling in accomplishment under my belt, I then FiNALLY found myself peacefully able to fully shift my entire attention and focus back onto this somewhat annoying *"NeverEnding" seemingly "Enjoy the Silence" "Wait-a-While"* whatever to call it by now at hand and towards the cleaning UP of my inner and outer Big Apple produced whirlwind. Uiii. My supportive *Co-Traveler.* Let me share with you, what BiG of a pile filled with LOTS of uncomfortable work ahead my soul right in that very presented *"Now Moment"* came to spot. WOW. Ufff. Oh my. Driven by the powerful *"Where there is a Will there ALWAYS is a Way"* truth, the question of WHERE to Start therefore right away presented itself as one of my very first figuring out tasks, which reality check once again led my soul to trust the guidance of this lovely voice located within, whilst I simply would be floating in the speed of this in sunny Cali offered refreshing bree*zZZ* from One Moment into the Next, by executing the discovered action requirement choices, *"Step-by-Step. Oh baby."*, alongside with the reappeared wonderful "Abundance of Time" gift treasure in its 100% availability and accessibility rate. Ha! Welcome back. YOU. you. Hmmm. Yes, and with this newly created game plan, including lovely set up, placed FAAAR away from everything that I at times still allowed to lower my vibrational level, my determined *"inner ARTreyu Warrioress"* then instantly cheerfully jUMPed back onto the field, Ready to get this life-changing ball rolling and Steady with the further taken *"Stepping-Stone"* decision move, to dedicate all my *"ongRowing"* emerging *Personal and Precious "Time and Energy"* resources towards The One and Only to my soul meaningful detected responsibility at hand. *The Well-Being of my "True little Linda Self"*. OH YEAH! Now let's do this for REAL. *"All or Nothing - Push"*. And. GO. One of the next received insights about this rather HUGE and challenging seemingly *"I'mPOSSiBLE"* quest at hand, introduced itself with my hearts very strong suggestion, to at first direct my main focus towards the regaining of the for this *"Growth and Expansionary"* mission ride required physical, including mental strengths, for which further encouraging priority clue purposes the lovely Universe succeeded in directing my attention towards a newly from it, the night before my vessels into its second *"Home Sweet Home"* base undertaken transfer, provided *"Life Toolbox"* ingredient. TatAAA! A bright P!NK and white "SCREAMiNG" postcard stating *"LOVE YOURSELF Love yourSelf FiRST and Everything else Falls into Place"*, that I "accidentally" came across on a shelf placed in a gym store called *Lorna Jane*, located within a BiG shopping mall. Ha! *"Gotch Ya'."* That's right. Yes, and as this rather soothing, inspiring and emPowering received P!NK message instantly succeeded in 1) Resonating full on with my soul and to further spark my Gemini's curiosity desire, to 2) Find out more about this wonderful *"Self*-love" sounding advice, including its 3) ACTUAL "true" into action put *"Cause and eFFecT"* experience, I therefore with "No Doubt" within a SNAP decided, that this just presented treasure MUST assist my soul as a daily reminder of this rather important seemingly *"The Truth About* self-*Love"* exercise suggestion at hand. Abracadabra. And. ThanXOXO. Interestingly, this newly gained life-enhancing ingredient then right after its appearance, kept on *"ongRowingly"* flowing into my awareness in a loving stream by furthermore awakening my soul's curiosity in this enticing topic called *Life Coaching* and by simultaneously "randomly" finding my*Self* getting put in touch with an in NYC based Grotto Swiss friend's very dear in LA based Swiss originated vessel, as her inner voice shared with her that our two, apparently very similar vibrating souls, should be connecting with each other. Boom. Well, and as soon as my eyes read in this friend's Facebook message, that this suggested Swiss Confederates soul happened to be working as a Life Coach, I certainly right away understood the magical Universe's WiNK and found myself immediately following through with its requested next *"Stepping-Stone"* task to take. After a FuN and successful back and forth connection period with this suggested Swiss Life Coach, her warm, friendly and UPlifting soul then shortly after suggested, that 1) Our two Swiss Made vessels definitely should be uniting any time soon, for which occasion she therefore 2) Happily would like to propose a *"Self*-love" workshop that a Life Coach friend of hers would be hosting in the following week. Ha! What?! WOW. Of course, this occasion came in at THE perfect *"Now Moment"*, and as my calendar in general happened to be filled with LOTS of flexibility, my soul absolutely thrilled jUMPed right on board onto this wonderful appeared and with SpeCial eFFecTs filled Two-in-One "coincidence" opportunity at hand. Yay. After a successful and very inspiring completion of the from this Life Coach provided *"Self*-love" introduction gesture upon my own further *"Finding back Home again"* path, my *"inner ARTreyu Warrioress"* then even more so felt Ready Steady Oh Yeah, to keep on exploring more of this from my end apparently on January 22nd entered *Candyland of Spirituality* reality sphere. WOW. What?! For real? How matching. Ha! Yes, this from that hosting soul's shared information flow about the Southern part of sunny Cali, to my surprise instantly and with "No Doubt" unexpectedly even more so started to light UP every available cell within my vessel with a LOT of passion and craving to experience more and MoRe and MORE of this newly provided Candyland version at hand. WooHOO. Now, in regards of this sudden and *"ongRowing"* sparked interest of my soul in this mentioned Life Coaching topic, my *"Head Cinema"* tape keeps revealing on its screen, that it originally most certainly must have been ignited via this incredible and inspiring Acting book that my eyes somehow "accidentally" stumbled upon online a few months prior, that I ended up indulging twice within a short amount of time, of which the latter inner *"Growth and Expansion"* exercise got chosen to assist *"little Linda"* to prepare herself for her UPcoming LA-LA-Hollywood-Land adventures ahead. *"How to be a HAPPY ACTOR in a Challenging Business. A Guide to Thriving Through it All."* is the title of this to my soul rather magical, emPowering and then spot on fitting *"sHe, who looks iNside AWAKENS" "Life Toolbox"* ingredient opportunity lecture, that happened to be created by an Actress, Life Coach, Author and Hypnotherapist named *Justina Vail Evans*. Ha! What a lovely combination in retrospective, right? LOL. Yes, so therefore, I am assuming that this planted Psychological and Spiritual theme-based hobby seed *"ongRowingly"* must have gotten nurtured by my subconscious all along UP onto the almost same *"Now Moment"*, of the discovery of this precious with PINK filled *"Self-love"* postcard. What?! YUP. True "fact". Hmmm. Hmmm?! Yes, very vividly I actually am able to recall this occurred "coincidence" spectacle on its recorded tape, during which a in the Concrete Jungle placed soul, about one hour later, recommended mine to look closer into this further genius, famous and rather successful Life Coach practicing vessel known as *Tony Robbins*, the second that "she" learned about this newly found interest of mine in a short catching up iPhone session. Sweet. *"Thy Wish is my Command."* Done. As my own soul right after "her" famous Google researching completion achievement, found "herself" vibrating with even moRE excitement about this topic, I therefore instantly felt the desire, to share this new Tony Robbins discovery with my ex-classmate, somewhere within the first 20 minutes of my vessel's completed moving in action step, on the following afternoon. Well and to my absolute surprise, my new roommate then with a BiG smile on his face responded to my shared idea with the gesture, of pointing to his bookshelf by furthermore kindly asking for *"little Linda"* to grab its there placed 10-disc CD collection box called *Get The Edge*. OK?! Certainly, I right away did as told and now ONLY guess ONCE, my dear *Co-Traveler*, what name my eyes came to read on its Black Box? EXACTLY. Yes! Unbelievably Tony Robbins'. OMG. Right?! WOW. Then, as soon as my friend furthermore let me in on the information flow, that his soul actually ever since his vessel's 11th count happened to be following and applying this Tony's teachings, I definitely found my *Self* very much so baffled and convinced that THiS just next, within my own "Mulholland Drive" created experience provided *"EdgyBlackWombBox"* puzzle "peace" at hand, needed to get explored. ASAP. Oh yeah. *"Strike it UP." "Though. Hay una Banda?"* Well let's find out. Wink. Equipped with these two enticing Two-in-One provided foundation expanding suggestions, my *"inner ARTreyu Warrioress"* then right away found herself thrilled, eager and Ready to Get her way all the way to The Edge again, which newly taken on *"Living on Earth Game"* mission this time around though would be taking its loving duality course, guided by every available, of its prior opponent based taken action step choices. As much as possible. Oh yeah! Boom. Let's Go. Now, whilst I found my *Self* rather busy with this as fascinating unraveling regaining of my physical, including mental strengths entered journey, my up onto that years Valentine's Saturday arrival still *Patience* practicing soul already must have arrived at one of those aimed for Edges, as my heart on this for "self-*LOVE*" declared day, out of the blue started to with a *"Rebel Yell"* scream at my soul that *"ENOUGH was ENOUGH"* in regards of this absolutely disserving and annoying magical *"NeverEnding"* seemingly *"Enjoy the Silence" "Wait-a-While"* whatever at hand and that THiS situation therefore required an iMMEDiATE COMPLETE change of strategy. That's right. That's it. As *"I've Got the Power."* YES. An obvious "True Snapple Fact" at this point of *"little Linda's"* many experienced *"Living on Earth Game"* adventures with "No Doubt" appeared with the "truth", that whatever I mentally and physically kept on practicing over the almost past 2 years, on this of my *"inner Artist's"* on hold set *"Don't Dream your Life. Live your THE Ultimate Childhood Dream Vision"* path, resulted in "The Nothing" and that therefore the execution of a further *"Letting go of Something that No Longer Serves One's Growth and Expansion"* action move needed to get called in. NOW. Abracadabra. Inspired by my *"You must be my Lucky Star"* experiences at count, I therefore happily accepted my inner voice's suggestion of considering a change in the front side of things, as for ONE my lawyer truly seemed to be unable to get this FREE *"Acting Dream"* Piece of Cake melting away disaster fixed any time soon, which reality check led for my soul to realize that TWO "her" overall faith and trust in "his", meanwhile found themselves floating somewhere lost WAY beyond any appearing rainbows in outer space. pOops. Go figure. GROWL. Yes, and therefore a new, more trustworthy and powerful representative needed to get recruited by yesterday already, in order to take over control of this sinking ship "aboard", for which *"I'mPOSSiBLE"* mission I decided to start googling a possible new "captain's" name, that happened to be mentioned to my *"inner Artist"* twice, during my soul's prior two *"Help! I need Somebody."* social media call outs, in this *"NeverEnding"* resolving Story*line* in motion. Action. To my surprise, I then quickly found my soul rather impressed about this recommended lawyer's overall career achievements, status, including network community, once my eyes scrolled over this on his persona created Wikipedia page. WOW. Alongside with the intake of all the gained information flow and of seeing pictures of his vessel shaking the hands of the at that very *"Now Moment"* incumbent President of this *"The Other Planet"* formation Barack Obama and the one of Hillary Clinton for starters, I furthermore came to learn, that this lawyer's father on top of it all found himself a few decades ago able, to help "rewrite" the books of the immigration law with a successful outcome of an *"I'mPossible"* considered Green Card case. Boom. Congrats. Well and therefore, my intuition right away happened to share with my soul that if this hiGH end established NYC based law firm would be failing in helping my *"inner Artist"* to fix this entire produced *"Enjoy the Silence"* mess the best way possible, that most likely no one else would be able to do so. That's right. Ha! Fully inspired, I then instantly dialed this in Manhattan located law office's number on the following Monday morning and found myself, after a short conversation with this targeted new "captain's" secretary, in the "possession" of a first Skype meeting time slot at his earliest convenience, which turned out to be in 3 weeks. 3

weeks?! LOL. Oh boy. Alrighty then. *"Good Things* apparently *take Time"*, of which I after all, kind of, had plenty to spare. Wink. Then, as soon as I received my purchased opportunity, to UPdate this new lawyer's soul via my MacBook Pro screen in a short cut version about this magical, throughout the past 2 years experienced *"NeverEnding"* seemingly *"Enjoy the Silence" "Wait-a-While"* spectacle at hand, my *"inner ARTreyu Warrioress"* as a next action step passionately found herself driven to obtain all the existing available paths, that would be leading towards my *"inner Artist's"* heart desired green ultimate all *"Opening Sesame"* key puzzle "peace" treasure. Instantly, I therefore came to learn that according to my current established visa reality check, Linda Wartenweiler would be granted with TWO options to choose from. *Number ONE* resulted in the lawful "truth", that one of these two mysteriously "stuck" open cases needed to get approved first, before my vessel could be proceeding with the application process for this precious last desired s-Express *"Acting Dream"* train ticket, within *"little Linda's"* almost 4 decades dated *"Don't Dream your Life. Live your THE Ultimate Childhood Dream Vision"* creation and *Number TWO* revealed itself with the undesired and with my then anyway *"I'mPOSSiBLE"* single status at hand option, to tie a knot to an American citizen declared vessel. Ufff. Alrighty then. Let's *"Keep on Movin'"* straight forward as had. After some more interesting information exchanges, we then ended our meeting with the mutually forged game plan, for my just newly hired lawyer to take over the in April 2013 first submitted O1 visa case ASAP, for now, by furthermore applying the *FAST speed*ing and extra costly Premium File option to his soul's further *"Stepping-Stone"* procedures ahead. That's right. *"Enough was Enough"* and therefore I, alongside with the *"ongRowing"* change of strategy undertaken adjustment choices, came to decide to finally pull this fancy available and with SpeCial eFFecTs filled *"All or Nothing - Push"* joker card, which would force the responsible immigration officer to provide us with THE decision result, within 15 business days. HA. Yup. At this point of my travels, my soul's main objective truly resulted in SiMPLY getting ANY kind of reaction or UPdate within this tedious *"NeverEnding"* seemingly *"Enjoy the Silence" "Wait-a-While"* GRRR at run and at this very *"Now Second"*, you most certainly might be detecting some similar vibrations within your own vessel, right, my beloved *Co-Traveler*? Ufff. Well, and now guess WHAT?! May 13th 2015 it dates, on which afternoon I happily found myself answering an incoming iPhone call resulting from my new lawyer aboard, who right away informed my soul, that we 1) As desired were given some information sides the immigration office and that 2) The result most likely differed quite from what I might be expecting to hear. Ok?! Whatever. Just shoot it. *"I Want to Break Free!"* Please. What is it? What is it?? What is going on?! AAAH. Right?! Well, and the *"Cause and eFFecT"* result out of this newly taken on visa solving quest at hand, presented itself with the reality "truth" that the immigration department for ONE currently found themselves unable to provide us with their decision, as for TWO my case happened to be under security check. EXCUSE ME?! Under what?! Security check??? WHAT does that

195

even mean!!!? And this, from my end somewhat confused appeared reaction responds about this rather unlawful and "illogical" sounding feedback, therefore right away got clarified with the UPdate, that either my Linda Wartenweiler identity or the one of my precious previous lawyer's, has been put under a Homeland Security Investigation reality check, as most likely something went off the "normal" with my cases. NO KiDDiN'. And that any further details remained unknown to his awareness. For now. At least. Oh my. What a mess. Indeed. Sniff. Yup, and these news, definitely differed quite a LOT from what I assumed to be learning at that very *"Now Moment"*, even though the just heard of after all also, in a way, instantly felt MORE than "logical". Oh boy. Somewhat relived about this final pEek-a-BooO granted clarification UPdate at hand, my soul furthermore felt prompted to find out How Much More of my preciously fading *"Acting Dream" "Wait-a-While"* time resources this unraveled security Easter Egg spectacle would be taking up, which provided information flow this time around included the "facts", that 1) As this mystical revealed investigation quest happened to get solved by a third, outside of the immigration office placed party, that 2) Our responsible officer's hands for that reason found themselves being tied down, up onto the very arising *"Now Moment"*, in which this vessel would be delivered with The End result, that 3) This counting down phase therefore would allow for my soul to *"ongRowingly"* keep "herself" busy with the mastering skill of this from my *Boot Camp* generated *"Patience is a Virtue"* task, for another unknown amount provided days, weeks or months longer, and that I lastly 4) As part of the failed 15 business days final visa decision experienced reality check, would be given the entire invested Premium Filing fee back and that my case however 5) Would be remaining in its Premium filed status. OH BOY. Strike! To the latter. Sure. About the rest. With this double achieved shifting success package in my pocket, I thereafter happily thanked my newly hired "captain" for these very quick and honest delivered "truth" facts and ESPECiALLY for having been able to at least break this *"I'mPOSSiBLE"* enduring *"NeverEnding" "Enjoy the Silence"* spell at hand. Ufff. And. Hooray! Finally, more clarity found its way into my awareness, alongside with the wonderful Universe's rewarding agreement gesture to the many, from my *"inner ARTreyu Warrioress'"* thus far Edgy undertaken transformational choices. Yay! And. Thanks. And these, from *"little Linda"* celebrational chosen accepting steps, then even more so got enforced by my lawyer's impressed impression comment towards this apparently rather unusual, very positive and optimistic appeared reaction outburst regarding the just presented circumstances. Ha! That's right. *"Enough* after all *remained to be* to 444% *Enough"*, No Matter what, as all the many, since this from almost 1 year ago powerful experienced CLiCKiNG awakening *"Now Moment"* undertaken *"Heart over Head"* adjusting choices, with "No Doubt" proofed themselves to cause my soul to vibrate in MUCH hiGHer and a LOT more soothing tunes again, compared to whatever I at some point decided to practice in this other *"Yin and Yang"* existing sphere. Been there. Done that. Had my share. Oh YEAH. Then, once the two of our souls found themselves separated again, my instinct right away led my fingers to share those magical Premium unlocked discoveries with my old lawyer's, via a most likely somewhat sarcastic composed e-mail, in order to keep "himself" in the loop about "HiS" whereabouts. That's right! Well, and as expected these lines remain to this very day in its unanswered state of reality and my *"inner ARTreyu Warrioress"* ever since quite certain, that *Miss Fear* successfully took care of WHATEVER this lawyer's soul had been practicing behind my back at the expense of *"little Linda's"* precious fading *"Don't Dream your Life. Live your THE Ultimate Childhood Dream Vision"* at hand. BOOM. THANK YOU. VEry. much. For this FREE *"With YOUR Mind on YOUR Money and with MY Time and Well-Being on MY invoice"* Saint Linda Piece of Cake deal. LOVE. it. Tremendously. Peace. Yes, and right in that encountered second, it very much so got clear to my soul that nevertheless EVERYTHiNG holds its price tag, *"One way or the Other"* and that the one, for this in Spring 2013 enduring entered joyride, certainly revealed itself as a rather HiGH investment in regards of my *Own Personal and Precious "Time and Energy"* resources. Hmmm. Oh well. With this new *"Wait-a-While"* established period in my pocket, my soul then calmly shifted all "her" focus back to the at this point as top four declared *"Finding back Home again"* oak tree vision mission priority mixture, which included the further *Cleaning UP* of this entirely inner and outer, within my *Boot Camp* produced *Whirlwind* reality, the *Exploration* of this soothing and enticing *"The Truth About self-Love"* sounding adventure, the *Completion* of that mysteriously delivered *"EdgyBlackWombBox"* puzzle "peace" and with the *Familiarization* of this interesting vibrating *Life Coaching* topic. Alrighty, let's Go. Some of the encouraging "side eFFecTs", within this *"ongRowing" "Self-loving"* metamorphosis entered journey, rather soon revealed themselves in the form of enabling my soul to experience how suddenly all those many over the past few months, years appeared hurdles, One-by-One more and moRE smoothly began to clear themselves in front of my eyes, by each time even granting my *"inner ARTreyu Warrioress"* with its own sort of reward, with the additional pleasure of receiving opportunities to release many, over the past 4 decades built UP energies, and with the wonderful reality check of witnessing HOW this newly created game plan at run succeeded in triggering those from my end safely established New York guards to slowly crumble down by substituting these vanishing elements with a LOT more lightness and inner peace. AHHH. Again. Yay! And this *"Cause and eFFecT"* truth therefore quickly let my *Self* to conclude, that whatever I kept on practicing, within this magical City filled with so many wonderful Angels, certainly must have been resonating with the beloved Universe inside out as well. Strike! *"Coo-coo-cool. Yeah, yeah. This is so cool."* Some of the next two provided and as key shifting interpreted *"Life Toolbox"* ingredients, soon presented themselves to my awareness in the form of the already unraveled *"Change the way you Look At Things and the Things you Look At Change"* perspective game changer and with Tony Robbins' eye-opening and mirror reflecting *"Like Attracts Like"* shared equation truth. That's right. As how genius the latter eventually started to hit my *"Self-*awareness" button, once I successfully completed this from his soul recommended exercise, in which mine got asked to write down all the many criteria that my ideal dream love partner should be carrying along, which list actually ended up including all the many wonderful qualities that I honor about my precious *"little Linda"* the MOST. Ha! Hmmm!? How interesting, right?! Furthermore, Tony then kept underlining, that in order for any soul to attract THiS person, including ANY other desired and compatible relationships or situations into one's reality, that the sender FiRST must become "iT", as a soul always will "only" be able to attract whoever and whatever happens to be vibrating in the same own *"Now Moment"* created frequency range. What?! Yes, and therefore this information flow right away let my*Self* to compare this rather eye-opening tuning in phenomena with this interesting, very old school invention called *Radio*. Ha! WOW. CLiCK. HOW GENiUS. And. LOGiCAL. Abracadabra. And this just rather powerful occurred inner shift, accompanied with the newly provided *"Change the way you Look At Things and the Things you Look At Change"* guideline recommendation, therefore instantly succeeded in providing my soul with the required amount of clarity in order for me to start "understanding", as of WHY *"little Linda's"*, until thus far created *"Living on Earth Game"* production, unraveled itself the way it did and as of WHY this from a few months ago pulled *"You must be my Lucky Star" "Positivity Card"*, kept on blessing my reality creation with all these many magical and to my soul *"Dream come True"* like materialization outcomes. Again. YEEHA. Way to Go. And this absolute wonderful disclosed *"Like Attracts Like"* secret, therefore as a next step triggered my *"inner ARTreyu Warrioress'"* determination and curiosity to find out 1) As of HOW HiGH this vibrational *"Growth and Expansion"* level actually can get raised to, if 2) The *"Not even the Sky is the Limit"* formula would also apply for this kind of SpeCial eFFecT achievement and 3) WHAT exactly I would be able to create with this rather "attractive" resonating *Law of Attraction* "truth". HA. Well, and as *"One Only Knows the Outcome of Anything by Giving it its Fair Shot"*, I therefore instantly jUMPed aboard onto this enticing appeared *"Let's Go All the way"* opportunity at hand, and find my*Self* ever since *"ongRowingly"* enjoying MANY absolute fascinating, satisfying and at times further mind-blowing experience creations, and therefore remain FULL hearted grateful for having opened this with magic filled *"EdgyBlackWombBox"* puzzle "peace". LOVE. One of my next undertaken *"Stepping-Stone"* steps then resulted in my inner voices' guidance to review all the many, especially over the course of this brilliant *"PandoraWombBox" Boot Camp* metamorphosis created chapter adapted US-Swiss Linda's *Thoughts, Believes, Behaviors* and *Action Steps* inventory patterns and to call in the required adjusting choices, that would vibrate more towards *"little Linda's"* so called *"Super Happy Comfort Zone"* reality preference. For starters. Certainly, this new challenging taken on *"The ONLY Person standing in Your Way is YOU"* exercise once again sounded so much easier in theory than in the "real" world experience, especially when one's soul meanwhile so much got accustomed to whatever felt more "comfortable" at that arisen created *"Now Moment"*. Ufff. Driven by the realty "truth", that *"Wherever there is a Way iN, there Always is a Way OUT"*, I therefore *"ongRowingly"* kept on trusting my heart's voiced recommendation steps and the effortless *To Surrender* strategy certainly revealed itself as THE most precious undertaken MUST DO *"Life Toolbox"* ingredient choice. Yup. And this accepted *"Heart over Head"* based *"sHe, who looks iNside AWAKENS"* surrendering journey, eventually ended up leading my soul, alongside with many diverse occurring energy releasing incidents, towards the discovery of this earlier on uncovered loving, healing and transformational *"The Key to your Own inner Happiness lies in your attempt to Bravely Embrace and Look those possibly within yourSelf existing Dragons with LOTS of LOVE and COMPASSiON into the eyes by simultaneously Surrendering yourSelf with all of your Heart and Trust into the whirlwind appearing Chaos, knowing that this is HOW Your beautiful Caterpillar successfully metamorphoses itself into the so-called magical Butterfly. Abracadabra"* formula. Ha! And. Blessings. Alongside with the exploration of these many inward traveling releasing and freeing opportunities, my *"inner ARTreyu Warrioress"* certainly even more so found herself being encouraged in her physical, including mental strengths building quest by the *"ongRowing"* hands on provided guidance of my thriving Gemini's curiosity, who parallel kept my *Self* happily UP to speed with all the many, on that matter gathered *"Stepping-Stone"* guideline suggestions, which UPdates I mainly collected from all the via Tony Robbins' newsletter subscription provided inspirational video clips and from this free and very resourceful detected webpage called *The School Of Coaching Mastery*. Now, as my friendly inner voice on top of it all meanwhile decided to share these rather as thrilling vibrating *"FuN Fact"* insights with my Linda Wartenweiler soul, that as one of my main developed strength', within this particular entered *"Living on Earth Game"* ride apparently resulted in the ability to effortlessly *iNSPiRE* and *GUiDE* any other soul, that finds itself willing and open for it, towards their OWN neglected and unlived *Wants, Needs, Desires and Dreams* reality fulfillment creation, that it therefore would appear as a nice and wise choice of mine, to 1) Add some of my in Abundance existing *"Wait-a-While" "Time and Energy"* resources wisely towards the preparation of the approaching own Life Coach to be test-ride exercise of mine and that this journey as part of its *"Cause and eFFecT"* truth with guarantee would be providing my *"Finding back Home again"* travels with many more significant and rewarding key CLiCKiNG element insights. Boom. What?! Really?! WOW. *"Coo-coo-cool. Yeah, yeah. This is so cool."* Honored by this shared outlook, of possibly finding my *Self* being able to assist and guide other interested souls with all the many, since my invaluable and life-changing Rock Bottom visit collected *"Life Toolbox"* ingredient experiences towards their own *"wiLD & Free"* reality creation interpretation, certainly for ONE resonated full on with my thus far VERY well developed *Helping Syndrome* gene and SECONDLY caused for my heart and soul to *"jump, jUMP A little HiGHer"*, whenever thought of. AHHH. OK. Let's then. After a diligent and very informative further *"Growth and Expansion"* exploration phase of a few weeks, my inner voice then by mid-March came to inform my soul, that I happened to be in Ready Steady shape and that therefore the *"Now Moment"* just arose for "her", to "officially" start offering my thus far developed skills and "knowledge" resources to some of from "it" at that instant also provided friendly "guinea pig" recommendation list. GO. *"Thy Will is My Command"* and within a short amount of days, those specific invited "lady" souls found themselves, alongside with *"little Linda"*, curiously and Ready Steady to *"Rock 'n Roll"* aboard as well. Yeeha! Yes, and this is HOW this *iNSPiRiNG* and *GUiDiNG Others* chapter started its own wonderful and magical journey upon this *"Finding back Home again"* path of mine, which spectacular adventure eventually led for the two of our souls to "reunite" right here, within our mutually entered *"Living on Earth Game"* spectacle creation, at this VERY, our own SpeCial manifested *"Now Moment"*. ABRACADABRA?! AbracadabrAHHHhugs. Well and who knows, maybe this happens to be one of the reasons WHY the incredible Universe put my *"inner Artist"* on a *"NeverEnding"* being on hold reality check?! HMMM. Maybe. Time certainly will reveal its true "purpose" at its perfect arising instant. One day. Until then. Let's keep on *"Rock 'n Rollin'"*. LOVE. Now, the probably MOST precious and awareness changing gathered puzzle "peace" that my soul found "herself" able to gain out of this over a total duration of 4 months practiced exercise, resulted in the rather quick observation "truth", that each of our souls happened to be floating within a similar tiring and unsatisfying *"Get the Balance Right. Get the Balance Right."* juggling contest of all the many, from my end meanwhile as fundamental *"Living on Earth Game"* declared vibration essentials, known as *TatAAA!* *"Self*-love", *"Self*-worth", *"Self*-respect", *"Self*-esteem" and *"Self*-confidence". Boom. What?! YUP. That's right. And your own soul, my beloved *Co-Traveler*, with certainty connects to a 100% with what mine is underlining here right NOW. Right?! Right. Been there. Done that. *"On and On and On and On."* OH YEAH. Welcome, to the wonderful earthly "human being" experience. LOL. And in this just appeared second, I am feeling a new impulse to SHOUT OUT a warm THANXOXO to all of these wonderful involved guinea pig friends, who supported this Life Coaching test-ride adventure of "ours" with their generous and invaluable offered *Time, Honesty, Trust, Openness* and *Commitment* resources, by furthermore "unknowingly" providing my *"inner ARTreyu Warrioress"* with many more essential and precious *"Life Toolbox"* ingredient insights, upon her then still *"ongRowing"* Adjusting, Healing and reBooting LA-LA-Hollywood-Land mission at run. Blessings.

"Time to say Goodbye"
Now, whilst I *"ongRowingly"* kept my*Self* busy with the as most efficient and rewarding perceived investment choices, of directing all the in Abundance gifted Time resources towards my *Own Wants, Needs, Desires and Dreams* reality creation, June nevertheless of course kept on

approaching on the calendar as well, by simultaneously carrying along the pre-set *"Truth or Dare"* exercise that would allow for my soul to experience a further BiG *"Growth and Expansion"* breakthrough within her thus far undertaken *"Living on Earth Game"* adventures. Ha. Yes, which *"Home Sweet Home"* base sphere shall be THE ONE for *"little Linda"* to "keep on" marching upon in regards of her still very heart desired and somewhat aching *"Don't Dream your Life. Live your THE Ultimate Childhood Dream"* quest at hand. The City filled with Angels or The Jungle built with Concrete?! Hmmm. Who shall be THE ONE? *"The Choice is Yours"*, my precious *"little True Self"*. That's right. Well, and THE answer certainly already happened to be known to my heart, ever since that day that my *"Head Cinema"* creation started its very first recording file, which result yours meanwhile with "No Doubt" finds itself matching with mine for sure. Ha! Right, my lovely *Co-Traveler*?! Oh yeah. And therefore this UPcoming and further essential from *Madam ProCrastination* well-guarded *"Letting go of Something that No Longer Serves One's Growth and Expansion"* exercise right away succeeded, in calling in some more of those as rather as uncomfortable and saddening considered emotions, as three of my next action steps resulted in UPdating my all-time supporting Williamsburg located roommate, including landlord about my definite "disappearance" decision game plan at hand and in finding out, if my vessel still happened to remain a welcomed guest in this, throughout the past almost 5 months wonderfully established LA-LA-Hollywood-Land roommate situation creation. Boom. About 2 weeks prior to the end of this absolutely as satisfying, transforming and as elevating developed *"wiLD wiLD West"* Coast "test ride" of mine, my soul therefore came to decide to start with the latter task first in order to find myself instantly in the clear, of where my vessel would be residing after the return of the by then in its official history switched *"Don't Dream your Life. Live your Dream."* chapter. Thankfully, both of my lovely roommates, the baby "on board", including my dear furry paw friends still considered themselves as Happy Campers of being able to host *"little Linda"* on our *"ongRowing"* created win-win couch deal at run for as long as desired. YAY. And this, within a SNAP manifested *"Home Sweet Home"* base reality success, thereafter excited, relieved and somewhat saddened led for my soul to officially set those rather overdue Concrete Jungle closing wheels into motion as well. Finally. Uiii. Yes, and saddened out of the awareness reason, that I found my*Self* about to "truly" step outside of everything, that *"little Linda"*, alongside with this *"ongRowing"* US-Swiss Linda emerged identity, ended up creating and achieving, since my vessels *"NeverEnding"* reconnection moment with this *"The Other Planet"* sphere, on June 2nd 2006. Ufff. Alrighty, let's get it over with. Then, once my soul found "herself" being connected with my very understanding and well-wishing soon "ex" considered roommate to be, my, by the end of July moving-out announcement, to my surprise suddenly found itself being orchestrated by an unexpected SpeCial eFFecT of many teardrops. Wow. What?! Somewhat puzzled about this emotional appeared reaction choice, over this just significant and "everything" changing *"I NOW just Broke*

Free" executed *"Stepping-Stone"* at hand, I immediately, after the phone separation incidence, found my *Self* wondering as of WHY my soul decided to pick this form of vibration releasing tool, instead of the from my end as "logical" expected *"YEEHA"* sounding choice. Hmmm. Yeah, what's up with that, my lovely inner voice?! Based on the *"Thy Wish is My Command"* truth, my curious *"inner ARTreyu Warrioress"* then instantly got UPdated on the "facts", that this just a 100% commitment choice, to the for *"little Linda"* as healthier, more thrilling and as a LOT more suitable interpreted *"Finding back Home again" "Cali Dreamin' Catchin'"* path, for that reason successfully found itself getting encouraged to release many more of these over the past few years accumulated emotions, which based on my at this very appeared *"Now Moment"* adapted own believe system, found themselves representing sensations like *Failure, Relieve, Giving up, Letting Go, Exhaustion, Joy* and the uncomfortable by *Miss Fear* led "official" *"Starting Over Again" Uncertainty "truth"*. Hmmm. OK. Got it. As soon as this interesting rollercoaster ride found itself slowing down again, I then, as the last required action step, furthermore informed my always loyal and supportive landlord slash neighbor of almost 5 years about what's to come, who's soul instantly as expected blessed my decision with his best wishes as well. Strike. Mission Completed. LA-LA-Hollywood-Land. *"We Come 1"*. At last. WooHOO. After those newly achieved reality transformation creations, I then with LOTS of joy directed all my focus back to this thus far rather rewarding experienced *"Self*-love" discovery journey and towards the preparation of my soul for the on the other rope of things as uncomfortable perceived Big Apple reconnection ride approach. BooOaaHH. Thankfully, the always supportive Universe meanwhile already wonderfully took care for the latter to be able to take its proper course, by providing my dutiful marching *"inner ARTreyu Warrioress"* with two VERY exciting and as *"Super Happy Comfort Zone"* interpreted NYC hiGHlighting treats. YEEHA. Ready? *TatAAA!* Number ONE introduced itself a couple of months earlier with the 5th seamless set villain collaboration opportunity of *"little Linda's"* vessel in the, from my talented Filmmaker friend for mid-July scheduled LGBT Erotic Thriller Short Film creation, called "Taste" and number TWO announced itself in the middle of February with the amazing inflowing newsflash from my precious long-time *"Extended Family Member"* Möne, that 1) All her many own blood and *"Extended Family Members"* just happened to have gifted her the from apparently my dear friend's end "secretly" desired JFK roundtrip airfare green paper resources to her vessels 4th decade milestone celebration occasion and that she therefore 2) Would love to materialize her missed *"little Linda"* hugging mission, as soon as my own vessel would be finding itself safe and sound back on New York City's ground again. *"Coo-coo-cool. Yeah, yeah. This is so cool."* Right?! WooHOO. YES, and these invaluable established second of July week treats, most certainly hit my soul Spot On. Yeeha! Thanks, you wonderful Universe you. LOVE. As far as of my mysterious *"NeverEnding"* OMG *"Wait-a-While"* cruising yellow key situation at hand, I most certainly, alongside with the purchase of a one-way JFK ticket for now, also took the liberty to schedule a LiVE meeting with my newly hired "captain", including his very friendly and helpful assistant aboard in order for our souls to get to know each other in a One-on-One opportunity as well and to furthermore exchange our both experienced whereabouts as *"wiLD & Freely"* as possible. Sweet. Let's Go. With very mixed feelings about this just entered NYC wrapping UP chapter at hand, my vessel then found itself by the end of June Ready Steady to spend one last month in my "old" reality creation embarking the assigned aircraft at the late PM, whilst thoughts like *"HOW would this "home coming" feel like"* or *"WHAT eFFecTs would this meanwhile as rather dark perceived city cause onto my more relaxed and peaceful inner created world"* kept my mind busy throughout those 6 b*zZZ* hours UP, UP in the air. Interestingly, I then, as soon as the pilot successfully docked "our" airplane at its destined JFK terminal on this Monday early morning, instantly came to notice how my entire vessel suddenly started to fill itself with heavy emotions and how the further noisy and hectic approaching welcoming vibes left my awareness check with some rather unpleasant and resisting emerging feelings. WHAT?! Go away. Ufff. After a this time smooth traveling back journey to my Williamsburg *"Home Sweet Home"* base, I then at around 9:05AM with LOTS of curiosity and with a dEEp breath decided to unlock the on Monitor Street located apartment door and the reality check of finding my vessel placed in this suddenly, as rather tiny and narrow perceived residence again, felt EXTREMLEY weird and surreal, all in one. OH YEAH. And let me tell you, my precious *Co-Traveler*, the from then on additional added emotions caused by for instance ONE the expected hugging welcoming gestures from the "out of the blue" appearances of my roomy of 1 ½ years, including the one of my Swiss friend's and by TWO the as rather overwhelming perceived *"Truth or Dare"* action choice, of placing my *"little Linda"* vessel, after a secluded *"sHe, who looks iNside AWAKENS"* excursion of 6 months and this within the as opposite experienced *"Yin and Yang"* sphere, right into the middle of this pulsating, LOUD and with an Abundance of vessels filled Union Square formation, with "No Doubt" even more so succeeded in intensifying whatever my soul *"ongRowingly"* kept on undergoing, ever since our touch down a couple of hours earlier. POW. WOW. *"All or Nothing"*, right? LOL. The adaption process to these "newly" presented energies though thankfully "only" took my meanwhile with this rather familiar *"Empty your Mind and become Water my Friend"* exercise trained *"Self"*, only a couple of days, which reality UPdate therefore parallel allowed this with *"FuN Facts"* filled *"Cause and eFFecT"* delivered mirroring adventure, sides the from my determined and on the Edge marching *"inner ARTreyu Warrioress"* until thus far implemented US-Swiss Linda adjusting and re*Booting* action steps, appear in a very interesting light. Ha. First of all, it very soon came to my attention, that even though my soul found "herself" rather busy with the smoothening out practice of this newly exposed culture shock ride at hand, my inner *"ongRowing"* oak tree as a matter of "truth" presented itself to my thrilling joy with a LOT more gathered lightness and peace, compared to the beginning of that year at run. YAY! Well, and as this throughout the first few days with SpeCial eFFecTs filled *"Self-love"* phenomena still found itself radiating in some hiGHer tunes, three various during that time period encountered cashier souls furthermore suddenly felt prompted to point out, that 1) Each one of them loved my Energy and that 2) My own soul's state of floating apparently appeared rather difFeRent, compared to their "usual" customers. HA. And. Thanks. Joyfully *"little Linda"* then every time quickly would appear and inform them with a BiG SMiLE, that her vessel just happened to have returned from a magical *"Cali Dreamin'"* excursion adventure and that THiS is what WE DO over THERE. Oh yeah. That's right. By the arrival of my first Saturday though, I suddenly came to face the phenomena of how my soul already started to miss the friendlier, UPlifting and with a LOT more nature filled *"wiLD wiLD West"* Coast lifestyle creation, that those crumbled protective walls already felt prompted to slowly rebuild themselves again, that this Concrete Jungle formation simply involved a little bit TOO much unnecessary efforts from my wonderfully charged batteries and that I for these and many moRE reasons actually very much so felt Ready Steady to hit the road again. HA. Though this *"My Wish is My Command"* action step needed to remain with *Madam ProCrastination* unto this very pre-agreed *"Now Moment"*, in which all the goals upon my pre-set NYC closing chapter itinerary would be finding themselves happily ticked off, of which the as MOST important *"Self-loving"* marked task carried my utmost desire to exit this, once as thrilling and magical perceived Big Apple *"Living on Earth Game"* playground, with as much PEACE and LOVE for its soul and for the there still existing accumulated few dragons as possible. OH YEAH. And THiS essential healing *"Stepping-Stone"* element, certainly needed to get attained by my driven *"inner ARTreyu Warrioress"* as powerfully as feasible, as I after all found my *Self* VERY aware of the two facts, that my vessel for One would remain AFAR for quite some years, once UP, UP in the air again and that this for now last organized Making Peace opportunity therefore TWO would enhance my *"ongRowing"* and thus far as SO rewarding experienced *"Finding back Home again"* journey with some many more important key *"Life Toolbox"* puzzle "peace" ingredients. AHHH. And this soothing UPscaling chance, certainly resonated in its very HiGH notes with my soul in regards of my precious discovered *"Like Attracts Like"* quest at hand. That's right. Now, in order for those eagerly set goals to get accomplished as productive as possible, within these remaining almost 4 weeks at run, my lovely inner voice therefore as for its motivational suggestion gesture decided to remind my sparkling soul on this particular Saturday afternoon, of Where my vessel found itself currently vibrating in and that my pleasantly gained *Personal and Precious "Time and Energy"* resources therefore for the time being required a little bit more of my "attention" than usual. Ha! And this important element "truth" I truly almost forgot. *"Oops. I did it Again."* Guided by this helpful *"Thy Will is My Command"* recommendation, I then slowly continued with my already sorting out, eliminating and packing entered mission, whilst *"little Linda"* excitedly counted the nights for this "surprise" announced *"Extended Family Member"* reunion spectacle to occur, on this for the second half of the following week set *"Now Moment"*. YEEHA. Wow, and HOW thrilling this longed for materialized instant felt, of witnessing how my dearly missed Geneva buddy in crime's vessel suddenly, after a prior *"I am almost here"* in beeping heads UP text message, started to appear out of a in front of my Williamsburg *"Home Sweet Home"* base stopped yellow cab. Boah. And this new surreal dream like presented *"Head Cinema"* creation, certainly immediately succeeded in triggering my *"Self"* to check in with my soul if this REALLY WAS my Möne. You know, this FuN girl who ended up missing her train at the very beginning of our delightful Housekeeping School Adventure in 1991. Remember? GiggLE. GiggLE. GiggLE. Or if this experience simply happened to be part of a wiLD dream. Hmmm. Somebody poke me please?! Gina? Wink. Of course it WAS her for "real" and this WAY overdue family reunion experience, which enabled for my still *Patience* practicing and somewhat tired turned soul to for once fully let GO with my "Eyes Wide Shut", whenever in company of this very familiar, from *"little Linda's"* magical teenage reminder days rooted dear one, whilst I furthermore allowed for my *"Self"*, to simply dive into this extraordinary, soothing and MUCH needed quality time emerged "getaway" opportunity, that with "No Doubt" ended up unraveling itself as the perfectly from the wonderful Universe this time around orchestrated, "closing" Act gesture. HAHHH. And Gratitude. Those way too *FAST* speeding precious 4 granted days, within this, our second mutually entered Big Apple *"Living on Earth Game"* excursion, the two of our souls happily ended up filling with LOTS of *Giggling, Relaxing, Walking, Exchanging, Reflecting, Enjoying, Floating, Nature Seeking, Sweating* and with many new and with *"FuN Facts"* filled memory creations for our *"ongRowing"* MonikaLinda repertoire collection, before my beloved Geneva buddy's vessel thereafter merrily returned back into the arms of her meanwhile own cute and blood produced family members, located upon our wonderful *"Home Sweet Home"* Confederates started out planet. LOVE. Alongside with the closure of this first NYC undertaken *"Super Happy Comfort Zone"* hiGHlighted treat, my with *Patience* cruising still on hold put *"inner Artist"*, then with bitter-sweet accompanied emotions kept on preparing herself for her last thus far in front of a moving picture camera recorded speaking performance part, which casting call found itself getting set two days after Möne's departure. Sweet! Wait. What?! Last Performance? WHAT? YUP. That's right. And that for these surprisingly, sides my newly hired "captain's" one day prior to my Geneva buddy's appearance disclosed recommendation UPdate, to 1) Instantaneously refrain from ANY Acting interactions, until this mysterious *"NeverEnding"* security check stated yellow key case would be finding itself in its being solved mode, as based on the lawful "truth" 2) Any in the magical world of the internet exposed Linda Wartenweiler related Art material dating 2013 and younger, potentially could "harm" our *"ongRowing"* visa journey at b*zZZ* and this for the WAY for it TOO late arriving reason, that 3) All the many from my end, since then primarily FREE entered *"Dream come True"* adventure creations, actually in the eyes of an immigration officer would indicate, that my being on hold set vessel No Matter what "illegally" continued to "work". BOOM. WHAT?! Excuse me? Well, and THiS "minor" just revealed detail truly would have been rather helpful to have been aware off a few years prior, as the magical Universe nevertheless resumed supporting *"little Linda's"* all-time beloved *"SwiMMing AGAiNST the Stream"* hobby dream desire by sending a various amount of Acting treats my *Patience* practicing and grateful for it *"inner Artist's"* way, which as its *"Cause and eFFecT"* truth to my excitement *"ongRowingly"* kept on feeding Linda Wartenweiler's flourishing iMDB page with many, especially during that time frame collected credits. Oo-WAH! SNAP. Into what a messy whirlwind mess this entire FREE *"Nothing to Worry About" "Acting Dream"* Piece of Cake melting away disaster simply continued transforming itself into. What else will we both be "learning", right, my dear *Co-Traveler*? UiUiUi. And this granted reality UPdate, certainly led my dutiful and law following Swiss originating soul instantly pray that all those many as "illegal" declared online exposed Linda Wartenweiler evidence creations did NOT stand in direct connection with this earlier on unraveled security Easter Egg spectacle and to therefore furthermore decide, that this UPcoming and suddenly as "risky" exposed Acting "Taste" opportunity MUST be iT then, until further notice. SNiFF. Yup. Guided by my in that instant pulled *"Positivity Card"* remedy trick, the then emerged "fact" of at least being able to experience this "last" set performance within this *"The Other Planet"* formation in which everything happily began, caused for my somewhat intimidated turned *"inner Artist"* to accept whatever got asked from her end, as part of this newly welcomed further Risk Avoiding strategy plan upon this *"Don't Dream your Life. Live your THE Ultimate Childhood Dream"* shutting down path of mine. Bummer. Equipped with this shifted outlook, I then on the arrived particular mid-July scheduled morning, made my way filled with a variation of mixed vibrations and Ready Steady to *"Rock 'n Roll!"* towards its in Williamsburg set shooting location. The reconnecting experience with my dear talented Filmmaker friend, including with the many from his end *"ongRowingly"* re-recruited familiar cast and crew member souls, thankfully unraveled itself into another wonderful and with *"FuN Facts"* filled last Concrete Jungle undertaken adventure, of which the stepping into the usual, especially for *"little Linda"* created villain shoes of a this time "dead" French speaking mother character, certainly stood out the MOST. AHHH. Action. Voilà. Ça y est. The wonderful *"Cause and eFFecT"* result out of this latest and with "Taste" filled undertaken *"Soul Acting Dream"* collaboration creation though, to my surprise unto this very arising *"Now Moment"*, unraveled itself with the many sides my dear talented Filmmaker friend's ambitious, throughout the over past 2 years pro-Activity based undertaken promoting *"Stepping-Stone"* action choices, of having ONE won an impressive amount of 31 Awards in various categories resulting from the thus far 33 accepted Film Festival celebrations, that TWO my

"NeverEnding" on hold put Linda Wartenweiler vessel therefore nevertheless unknowingly *"ongRowingly"* continued and still continues its magical journey on the BiG screen and this geographically spread out from New York City to Auckland, Virginia, London, Canada, Washington D.C. and right to my current *"Home Sweet Home"* state *"Californication"* for instance and with the UPdate that THREE this rewarding "fingers crossed" screening cycle should be continuing its magical flow until further notice. BOAH. How amazing. BRAVO everyone. BRAVO. *"Life is Good"* after all. Oh yeah. And this just discovered *"Hip Hop Horray. Ho. Hey. Ho."* storyline redirects my train of thought right back to *"little Linda's"* first ever stared in Music video, which interesting emerging awareness revelation furthermore leads me, as part of our *"ongRowing"* experienced *Dot Connection* exercise, to realize that ONE this in 2007 produced "Circa Survive" video, the in 2012 until thus far unmentioned "Death by Scrabble" Short Film creation and the latest "Taste" performance to my own knowledge appear as THE three MOST popular and still out there exposed Art pieces of my Linda Wartenweiler vessel, which "facts" on a closer look even mark a rather fascinating Beginning, Middle and End milestone loop cycle upon this closing *"Don't Dream your Life. Live your Dream."* chapter at hand. Ha! Hmmm. LOVE iT. Gratitude. The third, very spontaneous created highlight, that immediately succeeded in convincing my *"inner ARTreyu Warrioress"* to take the fullest advantage of within this entire last NYC wrapping UP month at run, found itself getting triggered during a from my end on the 4th of July weekend *"SURPRiSE!!!"* undertaken visit, at my first dear close Big Apple gained co-Gemini friend's then fairly new opened restaurant called *Maite*, which is located in *Bushwick*, Brooklyn. After some happy reunion catching up celebrations and after some FuN *"Get into the Groove"* shared dance moves to some of our mutually favored Madonna 80ies tracks, her soul then suddenly found "herself" curious about my vessel's availability during the last week of July, as "she" happened to be in the need for an extra pair of managing filling in hands, for a couple of evenings. Well, and as the suggested dates with "No Doubt" ended up fitting into my overall very flexible set NYC game plan at hand, I certainly happily right away jUMPed aboard onto this kind presented trusted offer and this even more so with the reality outlook, of therefore furthermore being enabled to end this "vacation" with the gesture of supporting my first within this *Boot Camp* adventure attracted close friend with her "baby", whom my soul OF COURSE also ended up connecting with during one of these many precious and legendary *"All night long. All night. OOH YEAH."* Deep & Juicy spectacles. *"OOH YEAH."* Wink. Certainly, those few scheduled nights simply ended up being THE further perfectly from the wonderful Universe orchestrated wrapping UP formula and this even more so, as I found myself on top of it all able to create some last exciting *"Living on Earth Game"* adventures with my beloved "red" bike companion *"Miss Rusty"*, while doing so. Yeeha! This Maite owner slash chef co-Gemini friend and *"little Linda"* actually do share a rather incredible *Dot Connecting* incidence that MUST be revealed here as well, which storyline finds its

origin placed within those magical Herr Keller grade school years. What?! That far back? YUP. That far back, my curious *Co-Traveler.* LOL. Ready? Steady? zoOM. During every attended school day, starting from our first 4th grade on in 1985 until Spring 1987, the vessels of my dear "NYC" Katja friend's and my own always used to be sitting right next to the, earlier on mentioned Alexandra one, that found its roots half way in Switzerland and the rest in Colombia. Now, as this Alexandra's and my soul ended up getting along rather well, we therefore quickly became good friends and decided to create some further with *"Fun Facts"* filled *"Living on Earth Game"* adventures outside of the school environment as well, of which results *TatAAA!?* Yes, in the invention of the still as a secret remaining "Stingi/Stinky" nickname reason for Herrn Carl Gustav Jung's once *"Home Sweet Home"* chosen birth village. Ha! That's right. Then, by the time that the end of our mutual 5th grade entered journey slowly started to approach, this dear classmate of ours suddenly came to inform everyone, that 1) Her mother decided to relocate their *"Home Sweet Home"* base to a place called *Miami*, that happens to be located on this thrilling sounding *"The Other Planet"* and that for that reason 2) A *"Time to say Goodbye"* moment would be arising for us all shortly. Ok. Sniff. Ufff. Certainly, the two of our souls for quite some time succeeded in staying in touch within these pre-rEvolutionary electronic pan and paper days, by keeping each other posted with occasional letter and postcard exchanges, before time eventually disconnected us. For good. Bye-Bye. Then, as soon as my *"little Linda Wait-a-While"* vessel 22 years later on a regular basis started to hang out with this "randomly" on the dance floor encountered, extremely *"wiLD & Free"* spirited co-Gemini one's, I therefore soon came to learn that her with Hispanic and Germanic "equipped" soul's *"Home Sweet Home"* base roots all the way to South Colombia and that based on an inner reoccurring Miami relocation urge, her soul at its vessel's 19th years count came to decide, to continue "her" many *"Living on Earth Game"* adventures UP north, before the Big Apple called my new friend over, a couple of years later. Based on these revealed "facts", my reliable *"Head Cinema"* library for that reason instantly got triggered to reproduce some of my own thus far ColombiaMiami experienced recordings onto its screen, which *"Cause and eFFecT"* reflection thereafter instantly prompted for *"little Linda"* to 1) Recite the storyline of my then to this *"The Other Planet"* FuN "lost" Alexandra classmate and to for this newly *"wiLD & Free"* gained co-Gemini friend to further let me in on the interesting "truth", that 2) In Miami, she herself for three years straight, became rather tight with a Colombian rooted Alexandra, who's vessel prior used to be residing somewhere in Switzerland. Wow. What a cool "coincidence", right?! As amazed and driven by this arisen "maybe" mutual Alexandra vessel interaction experience, our both souls then curiously started to dive into a picture organizing hunting quest of our each own Alexandra version in order to find out more about this just discovered and with similarities filled storyline. Now, even though our both first attempts ended up leaving us empty handed, my own Gemini's curiosity nevertheless *"ongRowingly"* felt triggered to check this incredible Facebook invention in the hopes, to at some point come across of a from my ex-classmate opened account, including picture, which efforts a few months later finally paid themselves off. Yay! *"Gotch Ya'."* HA. And most certainly, you all along already kept on sensing to where this story is leading itself UP to, right, my precious *Co-Traveler*? That's right. And. BiNGO. As crazy and incredible this may sound, the two of our souls truly ended up attracting THE EXACT same "Stingi/Stinky" Alexandra vessel into our own previous *"Living on Earth Game"* adventure creations. Boah! RiGHT?! And this almost unbelievable and super "random" *"I'mPOSSiBLE"* encountered "True Snapple Fact" *"Like Attracts Like"* "coincidence", accompanied by the additional gained awareness realization, that this storyline on top of it all even finds itself being connected to my, in July 2013 after-Rock Bottom encountered *"sHe, who looks OUTside DREAMS. sHe, who looks iNside AWAKENS."* recommendation discovery, to this very second keeps holding its power in leaving *"little Linda"* with rather mind-blowing sensations. BAOHWOWOW. HMMM. The magical Universe. The all-time surprising magical Universe. LOVE. Now, since this in June 2006 entered *Artistic and "Self-*developing" *Boot Camp* spectacle with certainty found itself running towards its *"Final Countdown"*, I therefore, as part of my Fare *Well* present ended up getting exposed to some additional rather interesting and mind-blowing puzzle piece *"Life Toolbox"* ingredients, which succeeded in providing my awareness with an overall very important eye-opening A-HA CLiCKiNG realization experience, as of WHAT caused this entire with magic filled *"little Linda"* abandonment joyride to occur and as of WHY it took my *Patience* practicing soul SO many years, to at last close this within *"The Other Planet"* opened and with thrills and chills packed *"PandoraWombBox"* with an *"Enough is Enough"* attitude. Ha! Ready? ABRACADABRA. Sometime towards the end of the 3rd week at run, I, after a "friendly" conversation, suddenly found my*Self* getting triggered to start a YouTube researching mission on this very enticing vibrating and prior psychological heard of *CoDependency* term, which immediate entered *"Living on Earth Game"* adventure from the get-go successfully caused for *"little Linda"* to *"ongRowingly"* narrate each with "truth" packed CLiCKed on reality check video spectacle with comments like *"OMG. What?! No way. No. FrEaKiNG. Way! WHAT?! Really? Oh My God. Really? Ohhh. Ohhh. Ohhh! What? O.M.G. NOOOooo. "Seriously?!?" pOops. UFFF."* Yup. Something like that it must have sounded like, whenever another "peace" of my *"ongRowing"* awakening revelation journey successfully found itself getting unlocked by its perfectly targeted *"Boom. BoOm. BOOM."* shots, whilst I simultaneously AWfully started to notice that all these many disclosed *CoDependency* symptoms actually precisely matched my very own throughout this *"Acting. Uncertainty. Complete Life Change."* invented US-Swiss Linda behavior and pattern mechanism, which I on top of it all diligently and successfully more and MORE started to nurture throughout this entire Concrete Jungle adventure of 8 ½ years. Boah! And this discovery about my OWN *"Self"*, certainly hit me about as well, as two fists probably would have, once slowed down by the appearance of my face. SLAM. BANG. OUCH. After some further detail digging on this newly introduced subject, my soul then soon came to realize, that "she" for sure must have skipped another rather important MUST KNOW fine print, within this almost 4 decades ago presented *"Living on Earth Game"* introduction manual, whilst I shockingly came to learn that *One CAN get Addicted to Another Human Being*. WOAW. What? One *CAN* get Addicted to Another Human Being?! Well, and this train of thought certainly with "No Doubt" NEVER would have crossed my own mind by itself, even though I found my*Self* "unknowingly" floating within this own reality created experience on a "daily", with duality filled basis, for quite some years. What?! YUP. Hmmm. The irony of this entire "just" detected "addiction" behavior of mine though actually ended up being that my soul for ONE always consistently made triple sure that my mind and willpower would remain in control over the whatever as potentially addictive "risky" declared substances I did expose *"little Linda"* to in the past, which behavior mannerism certainly leads back to my very much so appreciated dear Urs' fatherly provided *"Life Toolbox"* ingredients, and that I therefore UP to that very arisen *"Now Moment"*, TWO *"ongRowingly"* proudly kept on considering myself *"A Soul with a Non-Addictive Personality."* pOops. LOL. Ok, besides my early on within this *"Don't Dream your Life. Live your Dream."* chapter established On and Off relationship with that wonderfully soothing and "emPowering" black water brewed liquid called *Coffee*. HA. Yes, and as everyone at least should "own" ONE vise, my *"Visely"* choice therefore devotedly continues on sticking to Black Coffee's *"Turn me On"* recommendation, as it after all reliably succeeds in doing so. Oh YEAH. *"I'm sO. I'm sO. I'm sO. I'm sOOO. Addicted. No Drugs. No Alcohol. BUT Caffeine and Rock 'n Roll."* is how my talented high school classmate friend Christa Müller confesses it within her own *"Self*-created" *"Caffeine"* recorded addiction confession, which lyrics with "No Doubt" find themselves spot on mirroring *"little Linda's"* own daily morning experienced cat and mouse dance ritual. Ha! I'm right there with ya' my friend. *"I'm sOOO. Addicted."* Prost. And this *CoDependency* definition is THE ONE, that instantaneously resonated with my soul from head to toe, once spotted *"Codependency is a Psychological Condition or a Relationship, in which a Person Manifesting LOW "Self*-esteem" *and a STRONG Desire for Approval has an Unhealthy Attachment to Another Person and places the Needs of that Person BEFORE his or her Own. In Codependency, a Person tries to Satisfy the Needs of ANOTHER, who is often Controlling or Manipulative and who may have an Addictive or Emotionally Unstable Personality. Broadly: Dependence on the Needs Of or Control By anOther."* BOOM. Wow. There you Go. And so much instantaneously makes a LOT moRE sense, correct, my wonderful *Co-Traveler*? Ha! Yes, and with this newly gained *"Change the way you Look At Things and the Things you Look At Change"* puzzle "peace" perspective, it as a next step soon dawned on me, that this with magic filled anti *"wiLD & Free"* vibrating *CoDependency* symptom with guarantee stood in direct correlation with those early on with *Mister*

Loneliness and *Miss Fear* undertaken Big Apple adventure creations, which practiced *"Cause and eFFecT"* choices therefore on one hand wonderfully ended up nurturing and developing my *Being Nice, Pleasing* and *Helping Syndrome* behaviors for 8 ½ years straight, by furthermore blessing this *"Living on Earth Game"* ride of mine with the complete abandonment experience of my precious, FuN and with giggles filled *"little Linda"* and with the in retro perspective ultimate inner and outer world gained reflection "understanding", based on the oh so eye-opening and "logical" *"Like Attracts Like"* formula, on the other. Abracadabra. Gratitude. LOVE. Interestingly, the many further, by my curious Gemini on that topic attempted researching action choices, actually a few months later, gradually guided my attention successfully all the way back to its origin, which to my surprise revealed itself as the very *"Now Moment"*, during which my soul after a *"NeverEnding"* and boring Developing, Growing and Floating Around journey of a total amount of 8 months came to the conclusion, that *"Enough was Enough"* and that therefore it officially was at the time, to finally get this *"Living on Earth Game"* adventure started. Anew. Boah. WHAT?! Yup. And this further valuable and with SpeCial eFFecTs delivered A-HA CLiCKiNG "fact" about my *"True little Self"*, I came to experience, whilst in one of my dear mom's and my vessel's usual *"NeverEnding"* Skype meetings, during which her soul suddenly felt prompted to mention, that as part of *"little Linda's"* instant vessel removal into her first and without any physical contact yet granted Temporary Incubator home base and with the further genius Inguinal Hernia copycat request choice of mine, the bonding process between my parents' and my soul therefore ultimately needed to get postponed until this very day, on which they finally were able to keep her baby girl in Sulgen TG. For good. Boom. Which meant, about these 4 weeks later. Hmmm. Well and this overall with twists and turns provided reality UPdate combination, eventually even more so succeeded in feeding my awareness with a LOT more additional *"Growth and Expansionary"* ingredients for my precious developing *"Life Toolbox"* collection and to furthermore provide my*Self* with an even clearer "understanding" for this back then embarked Linda Wartenweiler *"Living on Earth Game"* "character" at hand. Abracadabra. Got it! Driven by the *"Where there is a Way iN, there Always is a Way OUT"* equation, my *"inner on The Edge walking ARTreyu Warrioress"* then very much so felt prompted *"To Find its Remedy. To Find its pulsating rhythmical Remedy"* upon this rather important and essential *"Finding back Home again"* mission completion at run. That's right. Within a snap, Google therefore led my awareness towards this wonderful and emPowering resonating *Recovery Option* suggestion, which further newly provided information flow left my soul with some more rather shocking insights on what To Do. Boah! My lovely *Co-Traveler*, are you Ready for this one? Let's blow your mind a little bit more. Shall we? Ha! OK, the MOST eFFecTive TWO stated Key Elements for a successful recovery journey of ANY *CoDependent* are TatAAA! ONE *"Self*-love" TWO The removal of one's vessel from these addictive and as "unhealthy" experienced vibrations. BOOM. BOAH. WHAT?! How crazy, right?! This is EXACTLY what the beloved Universe, as part of its own "established" master plan I assume, guided my soul towards to, ever since the, a year prior experienced 444% *"Enough WAS Enough"* CLiCKiNG awakening revelation of mine, upon the then soon after provided and entered *"Cali Dreamin'" Adjusting, Healing* and *Rebuilding* journey. WOWOWOW. Well, and this *Law of Attraction* "truth factor" certainly keeps on convincing *"little Linda"*, that ANY as incredible and *"I'mPOSSiBLE"* declared desires can get achieved by every "visible" soul, as soon as one allows one *"Self"* to actually trust all these many *"Heart over Head"* appeared suggestions, by furthermore following through as optimistic as possible, No Matter how "wiLD" or "scary" those proposed action *"Stepping-Stone"* choices might be sounding like. YUP. Been there. Done that. U2. Ha! Thrilled about this just discovered *"Self*-loving" triumph of mine, it as a next step suddenly dawned on me, that whatever my *"inner* on The Edge walking *ARTreyu Warrioress"* decided on practicing, throughout the course of this about 3 weeks ago exited *"wiLD wiLD West"* Coast "test ride" chapter, ended up resulting in the *"ongRowing"* dissolvement success of some of the online stated *CoDependency* symptoms, which invited transformational *"Cause and eFFecT"* SpeCial eFFecTs therefore must have substituted my way of floating with those from some of these "Manhattatian's" picked UP lightness instead. Ha! The from EXACTLY two years ago presented oak tree vision therefore with "No Doubt" found itself getting nourished into the desired direction and all the many from Herrn Albert Schweizer earlier on predicted amazing puzzle "peaces" on top of it all, One-by-One slowly seemed to be falling into place as well. Yay! And. Bingo. Way to Go. Alongside of my further *Recovery Option* entered researching journey, I then soon came to learn, that the STRiCT application of *Clear Boundary Settings, Discipline*, the *Trust* of one's *OWN inner Guidance, Courage*, a *Staying* as *TRUE* to one*Self* as possible attitude, *Allowance, Patience* and the implementation of a LOT of one's own *"FuN Fact"* preferences over the course of 12 months straight, eventually successfully would metamorphose ANY once *CoDependent* practiced soul into a stable and vibrant *interDependent* version. Abracadabra. Meaning, that as soon as this new state of awareness permanently would get ingrained, that this once experienced *"Dependence on the Needs Of or Control By anOther"* desire suddenly would have vanished by instead causing one's soul to be floating within a MORE emPowering, UPlifting and harmonious *"Get the Balance Right. Get the Balance Right."* dance routine of all the many fundamental and essential discovered *"Self*-love", *"Self*-worth", *"Self*-respect", *"Self*-esteem" and *"Self*-confidence" *"Living on Earth Game"* vibrations. Yeeha! And this remedy path certainly instantly resonated in its *"wiLDest and Freest"* notes possible with *"little Linda"* and continued to *"Push"* all my already adapted "doings" forward with an even MORE so specific and clear defined game plan at hand. Boom. Well, and happily and proudly I, at this very arising *"Now Moment"*, am finding my*Self* able to confirm to you, my wonderful *Co-Traveler*, that all those many stated *Recovery* "*Life Toolbox*" ingredient suggestions as predicted revealed themselves to have been SPOT ON and that they ever since, *"ongRowingly"* keep on blessing my soul with an Abundance of rewarding and thrilling inflowing treats again, upon this from the magical Universe once guided into *"The Truth About self-Love"* exercise at run. WooHOO. Gratitude. Meanwhile, this 12 months recommended timeline finds itself placed by more than 21 months in the past and the results, my soul remains certain of, do reflect themselves right here along on our mutually, a while ago embarked *"Living on Earth Game"* adventure excursion. LOVE. Yes, and on that note, I warmly and with all of my heart encourage each "remaining" CoDependent out there to do the same. *"Start living your OWN Lives, Dreams and Truths, if desired, with the attempt to Look all your inner and outer detected Dragons into their Eyes. Remain Strong, Loving, Respectful, Open, Positive, Courageous, Grateful and Determined towards what will appear, whilst your soul slowly and surly WiLL be entering onto a Powerful ReBonding journey with your Beautiful, Happy, Loving, Precious, Unique and Much HiGHER Vibrating "True little Self". YEEHA. Therefore, keep on Remembering that Any LOVE based Action Choices WiLL be blessing Every involved soul with the MOST Powerful and UPlifting outcome possible. Guaranteed. Yay. It works! Been There. Still "Do". And so can YOU. A 100%. You Got this."* Well, and if you happen to be a *Co-soulTraveler*, who currently finds itself still "unconsciously" nurturing all your OWN many possible accumulated CoDependent symptoms, then *"little Linda"* remains VERY positive, that our two souls meanwhile successfully connected on that matter and that your own inner calling, including curiosity about "iT" got ignited as well. So shall be it. Now Go, my dear friend, THiS *"Truth AND Dare"* exercise is SO worth its "disruptive" journey. *"interDependence is the Mutual Reliance between Two or More Groups. In Relationships, interDependence is the degree to which members of the group Are Mutually Dependent on the Others. This Concept Differs from a Dependent Relationship, where Some members Are Dependent and Some Are Not."* Or in other words *"Some People are Very inDependent in Relationships, others are Dependent, and a number of People are CoDependent, which means they Put Aside their OWN Well-Being to maintain a Relationship with anOther. The Healthiest Way we can interact with those Close to Us is by Being TRULY interDependent."* And so it is. Amen. With all these many new *"Living on Earth Game"* experience ingredients stored within my *"Head Cinema"* library, the *"NeverEnding"* seemingly departure out of this with diversity filled NYC wrapping UP chapter at run, slowly started to arrive as well, which reality check therefore for the first time ever, since this delightful Housekeeping School Adventure of mine, triggered my *"ongRowing" Patience* practicing soul on the 9th remaining day, to create one of those *"Final Countdown"* sheets. Snap. Déjà Vu. Möne? Was that you?! Peut être. Ha. Then, alongside with the crossing off gesture of the aimed for number 0, I furthermore felt prompted to take a closer inventory inspection upon my pre-set NYC closing chapter itinerary and found myself rather contented about the inside out appeared achievements. Ticked off too. Yay. Ready Steady. Now let's Go and *"Hit that Road Jack."* That's right. And these activities lastly called in for THE awaited *"Time to say Goodbye"* moment to emerge, accompanied by the official prosecution of this rather utmost important interpreted *"Letting go of Something that No Longer Serves One's Growth and Expansion"* *"Stepping-Stone"* at hand. *"Sniff. Sniff. Horray. Ho. Hey. Ho."* After an emotional Bye-Bye ritual with my dearly grown Monitor Street *"Home Sweet Home"* base of 5 years, including with my skilled pots and pans iPhone juggling roommate of 1 ½ years, my vessel then found itself "key less" and with some bitter-sweet accumulated vibrations stepping inside of a pre-ordered car service vehicle, before it then hit the road towards JFK. Now, as this to my surprise, ever since my roommate's goodbye moment appeared salty teardrops phenomena kept on *"Rock 'n Rollin'"* for quite some time longer, I therefore suddenly felt prompted to check in with my precious *"little Linda"* in order to find out what caused for her to react so saddened. Quickly, I therefore came to learn, that on one hand she felt ABSOLUTELY relieved and thrilled about this materialized reality check of finally officially being able to start "over" anew and this in her all-time favorite *"THE Ultimate Childhood Dream Vision"* home base formation, which *"ongRowing"* experienced action step on the other end though, nevertheless brought along the "truth", that everything wonderful that "we" as a unit found ourselves blessed to create and experience throughout these powerful and with thrills and chills filled *"PandoraWombBox" Boot Camp* years, would remain behind. Ufff. That's right. And this valuable provided *"sHe, who looks iNside AWAKENS"* insight, therefore instantly guided my attention towards *"little Linda's"* magical developed *"Life Toolbox"* collection, which as a next step led me to pick the with duality filled equation that *"One Door Always MUST get closed First, before MANY others thereafter will be able to Burst wide Open by rewarding THE Daring Soul with many UPgrading and more Suitable Blessings instead"* as its soothing *"Change the way you Look At Things and the Things you Look At Change"* *"Positivity Card"* trick remedy. Abracadabra. And, so it is. Fare *Well* New York. Thank you for an unforgettable joyride. PEACE. LOVE. CiAO. For now. zoOM.

"My Way. I'll do iT MY way."
Now, whilst my vessel found itself exactly, 11 weeks and 5 days prior to Marty McFly's legendary, in this from genius Doc Emmett Brown invented DeLorean Time Machine, *SPEED*ing from October 21st 1985 straight to the one set on my own in 2015 in motion ignited *"Cali Dreamin'"* arrival year at run, I myself felt very fortunate, to actually undergo the "exact" opposite with SpeCial eFFecTs filled duality spectacle within my own from the magical Universe orchestrated "Back to the Future" time traveling *"Dream come True"* experience. Yay! Finally, *"little Linda's"* over decades lasting heart desired 80ies throwback wish got "materialized" and this all the way from JFK to Burbank LA. Woohoo! "True Snapple Fact". As "luck" has it, my eyeballs right after our take off happened to be catching the information flow on someone else's seat screen, that the on January 1st 1985 launched MTV "sister" channel

Video Hits One (VH1) just started to air the amazing, on February 17th 1984 released "Footloose" flick, of which *"little Linda"* certainly owns its original Music CD, by rounding this UP, UP in the air ignited *"Cali Dreamin'"* chapter UP with the then following all-time classic and on interestingly February 15th 1985 released "The Breakfast Club" indulgence. Yeeha! One most likely can only imagine, how "Gone with the Wind" and all *"Alive and Kicking"* my soul found itself zoOMing through the heavens. Oh yeah. Then, as soon as my vessel safe and sound arrived in its pre-established Cali *"Home Sweet Home"* base again, my lovely inner voice rather quickly felt the urge to challenge my *"inner ARTreyu Warrioress"* with its famous *"What's Next Linda. What's Next?"* line by furthermore wondering *"Where to would you LOVE to travel from here on? Achieved you have a LOT and you definitely created enough room for your "Self" to jUMP onto some further "Growth and Expansionary" providing new adventures."* Ha! And these words certainly instantly resonated with my curious turned soul in its fullest potential and caused "her", after the creation of an UPdated accomplishment inventory list, to observe, that 1) This magical and with many SpeCial effecTs packed *"PandoraWombBox" Boot Camp* chapter lastly switched itself into a Been there. Done that. *"Life Toolbox"* ingredient *hi*Storyline, that 2) The throughout these days successfully inner and outer *"Self-*produced" whirlwind phenomena for the most part got tamed and replaced again with a LOT more sunshine, that 3) My overall upon this *"ongRowing"* pursued *"The Truth About* self-*Love"* quest attained physical, including mental well-being strengths reflected themselves with the new scale figure of 56kg/125 lbs for instance and with a more radiant inner created stability, that 4) My *"Soul's Childhood Dream"* meanwhile transformed itself into a practically *"NeverEnding"* 100% shut down "accepted" "Status Quo" and that those overall, over the past 8 months obtained *"Cause and eFFecT"* results, therefore as a matter of "fact" 5) Re-invited the almost entire accessibility rate of this "magical", in 2006 delivered *"The Management of a to my soul preciously granted infinite "Abundance of Time" gift, which "she" EXCLUSiVELY gets to share with Linda Wartenweiler on a difFeRent "Planet", FAR away from "her" usual accessible "Comfort Zone" reality exit door opportunity."* into my awareness, which undertaken check-UP in short revealed the "truth", that 6) All the many dusty and rocky turned roads basically found themselves Ready Steady and Clear again for my *"inner ARTreyu Warrioress"* to further explore. If desired. Boom. Well, except for those that for another *"NeverEnding"* amount of cruising days would "allow" for my vessel to for ONE peacefully part with this *"The Other Planet"* formation in order to travel to ANY further beautiful "out there" placed locations, which certainly also included the physical reconnect option with my beloved and missed rooting small apple sphere, or TWO bless *"little Linda"* with ANY further OUTSiDE of her own *"ongRowing"* thrilling *"Head Cinema"* production undertaken ACT, ACt, Act, AcT, act, aCt, acT, aCT, ACTing gigs. *"Hip Hop Horray. Ho. Hey. Ho."* AAh. What?! LOL. Yes, and these magical "truth" factors with "No Doubt" immediately caused for my soul to GiggLE. GiggLE. GiggLE. out aLOUD, as at the end of the day, I truly all along strongly kept on believing that *"little Linda's" "NeverEnding" "Soul Childhood Acting Dream"* realization quest happened to be the MAiN MUST DO discovered reason, as of WHY my heart, my intuition and the magical Universe, after a *"Back, Back, Forth and Forth"* inner *"Should I Stay OR should I Go now" "Buffalo Stance"* of 1 ½ years, guided my vessel onto this thrilling *"Swimming AGAiNST the STdream Catchin'"* adventure, set upon this *"The Other Planet"* formation, MiLES away from its then, throughout three decades safety and *"Comfort Zone"* established Swiss lifestyle empire, by causing my soul to leave all the many of *"little Linda's"* beloved collected blood and *"Extended Family Member's"*, including "her" dear fluffy Gina and this very SpEciAl *"I've had the Time of My Life and I Owe it All to You"* encountered someone behind, to then instead, almost one decade later, basically finding my *Self* "stranded" on the complete opposite end of my original envisioned *"NeverEnding"* LA-LA-Hollywood-Land Story*line*. LOL. What?! And this rather illogical *"Dream come True"* detected outcome certainly instantly stroke my *"inner ARTreyu Warrioress"* as rather sarcastic, which it actually still happens to be doing so right UP onto this VERY emerging *"Now Moment"*. Giggle. GiGGle. GiGGLE. OMG. For real, my dear *Co-Traveler*. What's UP with that?! Right?! LOL. Anyway, with the accumulated knowledge, that *"Everything happens for a Reason"*, I therefore trustingly came to decide to consult my wise inner voice for any further thought-of *"Stepping-Stone"* suggestions, as "iT" after all happened to be the source of getting this entire *"What's Next Linda. What's Next"* exercise into motion. Ha! With the pre-set game plan ingredients of desiring to invest all those additional, throughout this *"NeverEnding"* visa *"Wait-a-While"* race at run gained *"Time and Energy"* resources into a creation, that would include the many of *"little Linda's"* thus far discovered and *"Fun Fact"* collected *Loves, Passions, Skills, Hobbies, Interests, "Life Toolbox" ingredients* plus *Abilities* as *Wise, "Legal", eFFecTive, Productive, Meaningful* and as *"Self*-satisfactory" as possible, this kind inner voice then, after the practice of a few *"sHe, who looks iNside AWAKENS"* practiced TM sessions, including some further undertaken dEEper brainstorming digging excursions, kindly ended up providing my *Patience* practicing *"inner Artist"* with the enticing and somewhat groundbreaking resonating *"Doing Me"* suggestion. Ha! Doing ME?! Well, this idea certainly sounded moRE than intriguing to my, still with this US-Swiss Linda lingering around confused vibrating soul. Oh yeah. The questions of *"HOW exactly this Doing Me preposition would be Presenting and Defining itself as in its True meaning"*, thereafter immediately turned themselves into the next puzzle pieces to figure out. After some additional invested inward traveling and pondering excursions, my lovely inner voice then suddenly presented my awareness with THE required powerful *"Change the way you Look At Things and the Things you Look At Change"* insight "truth", which revealed itself as a *"Ok, according to the magical books of the law it would suit my "NeverEnding" yellow key Storyline better to stay away from ANY* further possible, within this *"The Other Planet"* sphere appearing *"Childhood Acting Dream"* offers. Got it. Though, No One Ever mentioned ANYTHiNG about my Linda Wartenweiler vessel NOT being allowed to Work within my OWN Project and Opportunity creations. Ha. And this solution with Guarantee appears to me as THE MOST legal available existing work environment resource within everyone's own *"Living on Earth Game"* ride." HA! That's more than right. Right, my dear *Co-Traveler?*! Oh yeah. *"I got the Poison and the Remedy. I got the Pulsating Rhythmical remedy."* Abracadabra. *"Gotch Ya'."* Yup and that is HOW this *"ongRowing"*, precious, *"NeverEnding"*, rewarding and with magic filled The Doing Me Project master Plan B strategy found its birthing moment. YeehAHHHH. Here you finally are. Welcome. And how it furthermore fed my awareness with the emPowering and awaking epiphany shift of noticing that this *"What's Next Linda. What's Next"* appeared exercise actually just started to SCREAM out for a new *"Enough was Enough"* reaction attitude step, which dissolved itself with another rather overdue *"Letting go of Something that No Longer Serves One's Growth and Expansion"* execution of *"The iMMEDiATE Reclaiming Procedure over ALL the many, throughout the at LEAST past 2 years, as from Miss Fear sincerely suggested to various strangers GENEROUSLY passed on steering wheel Commands in regards of ESPECiALLY "little Linda's" overall sinking "THE Ultimate Childhood Dream Vision"* and that therefore my dear Marco friend's early picked UP wise *"Always follow your Hearts Desires as Radiant as possible by ensuring to Keep On Pushing Any presented Boundaries with a Living Life to its Fullest possible Approach and to therefore absolutely NEVER take NO for an answer, No Matter what, as Not even the Sky is the Limit" "Life Toolbox"* ingredient, once more needed to get reActivated instead. Right then. SNAP. *"I've Got the Power."* OH YEAH. The more that this rEvolutionary presented outlook started to sink into my awareness, the more it then dawned on me, that this OWN Project and Opportunity creation idea with "No Doubt" introduced itself as The One and Only option left, that would grant my Ready Steady bleeding *"inner Artist"* with a 100% *"All or Nothing"* freedom formulated *"Don't Dream your Life. Live your THE Ultimate Childhood Dream Catchin'"* solution. Boah. How "true". Hmmm! And right then, my wonderful *"Head Cinema"* production all over sudden began to project this very interesting Short Film scenario onto its screen, in which I found myself able to observe HOW the magical and supporting Universe with all its many, throughout those spectacular *"PandoraWombBox"* years undertaken action steps succeeded, in patiently narrowing *"little Linda's"* apparently still *"ongRowing" "Acting. Uncertainty. Complete Life Change."* path down, to this very *"Last Resort"* MUST DO spectacle at hand. BOAH. WHAT?! What? HMMM. And this newly gained outlook then instantaneously caused for my curious inner Gemini to wonder if this manifested OWN Project and Opportunity creation puzzle "peace" possibly even ended up being the lovely Universe's ORiGiNAL, from the get-go intended *"The Owls are NOT what they Seem"* master plan, in regards of my *"NeverEnding"* Linda Wartenweiler *"Soul's Childhood Dream"* and that my vessel therefore actually found itself MORE than Spot On cruising upon its desired track, than all along assumed. HA. BoaOW. Well, this "geniusness" certainly right away would explain a WHOLE LOT and make some rather wonderful sense to my awareness. YUP. *"Step-by-Step. Oh yeah. I really Know it's just a Matter of Time"* as *"You Always Are what you Thinkest."* Hmmm?! Well, let's find out then. Filled with a LOT of enthusiasm, I thereafter continued my brainstorming quest with the gathering task of all the many, within this LA-LA-Hollywood-Land formation available resources and possibilities as of HOW this Doing Me Project could present itself as, which results soon after introduced themselves in the shapes of *Writing, Shooting and Starring within my Own OUTSiDE of my "Head Cinema"* produced Short Films, the creation of a *"Doing Me Project"* YouTube Channel with intervaled own Recorded Video UPloads of some sorts, starting a Blog, sharing *"little Linda's" "NeverEnding"* Story *"One way or Another"* with the world and to simultaneously possibly also start taking some *Acting classes*, at the from my roommates Over and Over hiGHly recommended Ivana Chubbuck studio, so that one of my toes *"ongRowingly"* would remain connected within this magical *"Super Happy Comfort Zone"* of mine, whilst my *"inner Artist"* furthermore also would be enabled to expand her creative City filled with Angels network collection with some UPdated *"Like Attracts Like"* vibrating souls. Sweet. With all these few thrilling and with *"FuN Facts"* packed Doing Me Project ideas at hand, my soul then right away came to the conclusion, that "she" first needed to focus on a *"Stepping-Stone"* venture that would allow for my *"inner Artist"* to 1) Happily keep on moving forward in her fullest *OWN Commanding Pace*, which set strategy therefore "solely" would leave room for this rather interesting existing *"The ONLY Person standing in Your Way is YOU"* phenomena challenge and on something, that on top of it all preferably 2) Would be keeping her as *Productive, iNspired* and *Engaged* as possible. Day in. Day out. Which further discovered details therefore right away left me with the choices, to either create a Blog, an own YouTube Channel or with the sharing approach of this *"ongRowing"* and with magic filled *"NeverEnding" "Wait-a-While"* spectacle at hand, of which the latter instantaneously invited itself as THE strongest and MOST fitting MUST DO requirement to Go with. Hmmm. Here you are AGAiN, I guess. HMMM. Yes, and AGAiN for that reason, as a very dear, in NYC encountered Actress soul Friend of mine, on March 27th 2014, which emerged date also happens to be marking the 2 weeks celebration milestone of my brave *"inner ARTreyu Warrioress'"* first edgy Black Panther confrontation, during a dinner get together conversation within my Williamsburg *"Home Sweet Home"* base kitchen walls out of the blue came to express her urge to write all the many of *"little Linda"* until then experienced *"Living on Earth Game"* adventures down, in the form of a biography. AaHH. What?! Turned out to be my soul's EXACT immediate reaction choice, once "hers", right after my, within those FuN coat checking events discovered VERY tip enhancing *"Just be Nice and they'll Give you Their Money"* shared success formula, with BiG eyes and absolutely well amused decided to interrupt my further train of thought with a LOUD "*LiNDA! What a GREAT line! This should be the title for your biography!*" comment. Boom. Exactly. LOL. Somewhat confused, I then kept on starring at my rather inspired seemingly dear Friend for a few seconds, before my curious inner Gemini felt prompted to wonder as of WHY on heavens earth Linda Wartenweiler should be having her biography written down for. Certainly, my vessel for ONE found itself MORE than FAR away from being "publicly" known, well, besides from my own thus far rather precious, in Abundant and globally spread collected *"Connecting and Belonging"* resources and that therefore TWO the interest in my persona with "No Doubt" would remain as rather small and therefore "senseless". That's right. This delivered information flow though seemed to leave my thrilled Friend rather unimpressed, as Sarah's soul thereafter instantly felt prompted to expand my awareness with a *"Change the way you Look At Things and the Things you Look At Change"* enriching perspective, by furthermore adding that, as THREE *"little Linda's"* thus far shared adventures in general always sounded very interesting and fascinating to "her" auricles, that she therefore FOUR believed that these many with SpeCial eFFecTs filled *hi*Storylines with certainty as well would succeed in triggering a similar reaction out of the remaining American audience's vessel, that her soul actually FiVE would happen to feel the impulse to step in as the author of this hysterical *"Just be Nice and they'll Give you Their Money"* MUST DO titled biography and that she therefore SiX *"ongRowingly"* would be delivering my e-mailbox with various questionnaires. ASAP. Boom. OK?! Hmmm. Still rather unconvinced, though very aFFecTed by my dear Friend's sparkling experienced enthusiasm, I after some more inward traveling pondering moments, happily found myself expressing *"little Linda's"* green light with an *"Ok. So as Steve Jobs most likely would approach this entire "biography" idea with a "Think Outside the Box. Go ONLY after what YOU think is Possible and "right" for Your experience by knowing that this choice therefore WiLL be THE Perfect "Stepping-Stone" for You to take"* attitude, I think that we truly should Go ahead and jUMP onto this "crazy" book sounding venture creation of yours and simply see what will be happening with it. I mean, who knows, maybe one day I truly will be needing it "for sure" and if so, then it actually already would be completed and Ready Steady to Go on sale. Right? Ha. Yeah, I like this idea and as "Everything always happens for a Reason", I'd say LET'S DO iT. I'm in." chosen justification line. That's right. Just like that. And yes, Mister Jobs certainly appears as another wise Hero of mine, as "his" soul's EXTREME remarkable, powerful and rEvolutionary on a global level inflicted *"Living on Earth Game"* vision materialization achieved fingerprints *"ongRowingly"* keep on appearing in basically every human soul's daily experienced routine and this reality "truth" thought with "NO DOUBT" reliably succeeds in filling *"little Linda's"* vessel with MANY mind-blowing and inspirational WOWOWOAHBOAH *"I'mPOSSiBLE"* vibrations. BOOM. "tHinK BiG. thiNk difFeRent. Do YoU." And, so it is. Gratitude. About 2 weeks later, my lovely Sarah Friend then cheerfully found herself Ready to let the ball for this *"Just be Nice and they'll Give you Their Money"* project of ours rolling, by forwarding her first created questionnaire into my e-mailbox, which answers, my still within "her" whirlwind tangled soul later than sooner One-by-One with LOTS of inner appearing resistance heavy hearted started to record on my magical silver black iPhone 5s device. Oh boy. Do you remember those colorful blossoming days, my wonderful *Co-Traveler*? Uiii. LOVE. And. Rest. in. PEACE. Wink. Then, another 6 months and two further completed questionnaire recordings later, the magical Universe for some reason suddenly must have experienced an *"Enough was Enough"* reality check moment, or anything of that matter, as it EXTREME spontaneously decided to relocate my Friendly Sarah's vessel back to her originating sunny Cali *"Home Sweet Home"* Bay Area base by providing her soul with a fantastic desired job opportunity within the magical Silicon Valley formation, based in *Palo Alto*, CA. zoOM. That's right, my lovely *Co-Traveler*. This "job" destination "of course" on top of it all also succeeded in making history with Mister Steve Jobs genius accomplished Apple birthing creation within his parents legendary *"Home Sweet Home"* garage, which newly detected *"Synchronicity par Excellence"* "coincidence" once again leaves me rather baffled and *"little Linda"* as a happy camper, as this presented Two-in-One opportunity allowed for her a year later, to record some additional with *"FuN Facts"* filled Sarah moments, plus some impressive Palo Alto, including *Cupertino* CA footage for her precious *"Head Cinema"* repertoire collection. Yay! Now, since every inner and outer launched caterpillar like shift always produces an *"ongRowing"* ripple eFFecT on its entire environment, the *hi*Storyline of my dear Sarah Friend's case ended up resulting in the reality UPdate, that her overall creative resources instantaneously transmuted themselves into The Nothing, which "fact" on one hand caused for our "embryo" to Rest in Peace for the time being, of which the "reasons" by now with "No Doubt" revealed themselves as rather crystal clear. I guess. HAbracadabra! Got it. And with this newly, from the all-time supportive Universe delivered MUST DO required WiNK in my mind, my soul then right away felt prompted, to as a next step get a first feel and some feedback from my "direct" possible future audience by therefore spreading the word of this *OWN Project and Opportunity creation* intention to my, since 2007 with many precious and in Abundance collected networking souls filled Facebook community, which action step furthermore succeeded in enriching my awareness with some additional invaluable inputs and with the ABSOLUTE convincing *Autobiography, Autobiography, Autobiography, Autobiography!!!* cheering remarks, sides the still rather eager for it sparked *TatAAA!* Yes, Sarah soul. Ha! LOVE. OK, my beloved Universe and Friend. GOT iT. *"Thy Will is My Command."* Thank you. LOL. With this as thrilling acknowledged sharing approach of this *"ongRowing"* and with magic filled *"NeverEnding" "Wait-a-While"* spectacle at hand, my further undertaken definition exploration quest then guided my *"inner Artist"* to furthermore figure out, as of 1) HOW this Autobiography should get approached and present as and 2)

HOW all these desired set puzzle pieces of *"little Linda's"* thus far discovered and *"Fun Fact"* collected Loves, Passions, Skills, Hobbies, interests, *"Life Toolbox"* ingredients plus Abilities could get woven together into ONE magical creation, and this 3) As *eFFecTive, Productive, Meaningful* and as *"Self*-satisfactory" as possible, so that I on one hand would be finding my *Self* able to 4) Actually daily "Do Me" a 100%, whatever that meant at that particular time upon my overall *"Finding back Home again"* oak tree vision mission at run, whilst my *"inner ARTreyu Warrioress"* on the other end 5) *"OngRowingly"* would be finding herself being encouraged to *"wiLDly & Freely"* unravel *"The Truth About* this as amazing experienced Self-*Love"* mystery. Oh yeah. From there on, things then started to *"Rock 'n Roll"* rather quickly and after some more dEEper digging *"sHe, who looks iNside AWAKENS"* undertaken TM, including pondering excursions, my inner voice thereafter soon left my *"inner Artist"* with the instructions to approach this entire *"NeverEnding"* Story sharing adventure out of this rather emPowering *"Change the way you Look At Things and the Things you Look At Change"* provided angle, by furthermore ONE having all the many existing *"little Linda" "FuN Facts"* broken down into her thus far favorite three Entertainment. Human Behavior. The Unseen. discovered *"Super Happy Comfort Zone"* passions, to then TWO instruct my *"inner ARTreyu Warrioress"* with the importance in finding a way to deliver all the many with duality filled *"Living on Earth Game"* spectacles as *UPlifting, Entertaining, Light, Truthful, emPowering, FuN, Adventurous* and *Authentic* as possible and this in its THREE most *"Growth and Expansionary"* providing English challenge first, by lastly, and most essentially making sure, to FOUR inside out staying a 100% true to my own *"little Self"* and to therefore FiVE *"Doing iT My Way"*, which in detail meant *"My Way"* of interpretation, *"My Way"* of writing style, *"My Way"* of "accent", simply *"Doing iT My Way"* from A – Z, à la Frank Sinatra. BOOM. Ok. Sounds cool! This as genius interpreted *OWN Project and Opportunity creation* master Plan B strategy most definitely infused my soul with even more excitement, as it right away dawned on me, that this Autobiography MUST DO requirement simultaneously with "No Doubt" furthermore rather drastically would be impacting my overall *"ongRowing" Adjusting, Healing* and *Rebuilding* journey and therefore reward my *"Finding back Home again"* mission with THE most eFFecTive "Abundance of Time" and *"Energy"* resources invested outcome, even in regards of my *Own Wants, Needs, Desires and Dreams* materialization creation cravings at run. HA! *"The Choice is Yours."* You bet. Thrilled about this new formulated success at hand, I then as a result, once again found my soul completely motivated and driven to continue this quite action filled *"Living on Earth Game"* journey as *"little Linda Wait-a-While"*, now lastly outside and FAR away from this with thrills and chills filled *"PandoraWombBox"* formation, which reality UPdate this time around led me to release a LOUD and clear *"The Key to your Success is to KEEP your Dream in Focus and to have the Courage to do things Other's WON'T do"* scream into my father's "ears". Yeeha! That's right. Now, *"Let's Rock 'n Roll!"*

"Hit Me, baby, One More time."
After some further preparation undertaken gestures, my *"inner ARTreyu Warrioress"* then found "herself" by the end of August 2015, Ready Stead and equipped with everything required, in order to feel comfortable to let the ball for this promising *"All or Nothing"* resonating OWN Project and Opportunity creation ride rolling by thereafter permitting my Patient practicing *"inner Artist"* to finally give birth to the at that *"Now Moment"* for another 11 months untitled very first *"the DOiNG ME PROjECT"* line, known as *"Push"* SWiTZERLAND or *"Let the Games Begin."* HA! GO. This newly entered writing spectacle of reliving *"little Linda's"* entire childhood once anew within my magical *"Head Cinema"* detected Time Machine, and this time even out of the eyes of a more "grownUP" perspective, truly revealed itself from the get-go as one of my initial favorite experiences, my beloved *Co-Traveler*. This much I must share with you. Smile. Whatever and whoever my soul within those with plenty of *"FuN Facts"* infused replayed files, after so many decades allowed to come across and to encounter again, instantly succeeded in filling my heart with even moRE appreciation and LOVE for this rather fantastic, almost forgotten *"wiLD & Free"* re-experienced *"Living on Earth Game"* ride, that I after all chose to explore within this vessel known as Linda Wartenweiler. HA. Oh yeah. And these many soothing and with SpeCial eFFecTs enhanced from afar undertaken small apple temp visits, with "No Doubt" on top of it all made triple sure to throw their magical sparks onto my overall *"Finding back Home again"* journey and to furthermore provide my soul with the wonderful instant opportunity, to reconnect with this somewhat out of sight lost precious *"True little Self"* of mine, on an even dEEper and moRE emPowering level. Yay! And. STRiKE. Speaking of *"little Self"*. The vessel of our per October 1st expected new earthling, including roommate, certainly all along kept on enjoying its own fascinating fruits and vegetables based *"Growth and Expansionary"* journey as well and this, since February for the first time ever on a daily basis witnessed "baby on board" miracle, most definitely supported the process of the *"ongRowing"*, from my on the Edge marching *"inner ARTreyu Warrioress'"* undertaken re*Booting*, *Rebuilding* and *Adjusting* gestures in its very own and unique from the magical Universe orchestrated ways. Ha! That's right. Looking back onto the storyline of my during that LA-LA-Hollywood-Land inner and outer undertaken journeys, my soul once again feels prompted to state that *"Everything* nevertheless *Always happens for a Reason"* and that this from a few months ago, within my beloved *"sHe, who looks iNside AWAKENS"* practiced TM excursion obtained suggestion to check in with my ex-June 2006 NYFA classmate if my *"little Linda"* vessel possibly would be able to rent out his and his wife's on Airbnb posted extra bedroom in their LA condo for a couple of nights, in retro perspective meanwhile makes MORE than sense to my soul, as of WHY I was "sent" there. Yup. THE experience, that a 100% enabled for my soul to basically re-create that "missing" link with my *True little Self"*, to my utmost surprise actually ended up occurring during the "baby on board" soul's

own *"Enough was Enough"* of this floating around epiphany experience, which further from "her" end ignited womb exiting action steps *"ongRowingly"* kept on feeding my awareness with many additional mind-blowing vibrations, whilst I found myself busy capturing this miraculous and with many SpeCial eFFecTs filled provided *"Living on Earth Game"* spectacle with the help of my dear Canon EOS Rebel SL1 camera. *"Push."* CLiCK. CLiCK. *"Push."* CLiCK. *"Push."* BOAH. What?! That's right, my wonderful *Co-Traveler*. As wiLD and crazy as this one may sound, this win-win City filled with Angels guided into *"Home Sweet Home"* base deal, on September 22nd, which Virgo number combination interestingly furthermore happens to be matching the, from the magical Universe very recently via some thrilling with twists and tricks orchestrated internet cruising incidences out of the blue very STRONGLY into my awareness thrown, *"Whoomp! There she is."* appearing milestone of this with LOTS of *Energy, Drive, Passion, Love* and *Willpower* infused Warrioress soul identified as Electrifying, iMpressive and iNspiring *"I Love Rock 'n Roll"* pioneer Queen *Joan Jett*, *"Yeah, Oh Yeah, Oh Yeah"*, who within a CLiCK even instantaneously succeeded in transmuting "herself" into a newly discovered Heroess of mine, on top of it all even ended up providing my Linda Wartenweiler soul with the EXTRAORDiNARY opportunity and honor to attend this "Baby Boom's", from my inner voice's pre-predicted arrival date, One-on-One and this out of the, from "her" parents a few months prior expressed desired birth photographer perspective. BOAH! WHAT?! YEAH. How cool, right?! And this with magic and action packed opportunity, with "No Doubt" still leaves my awareness with many breathtaking AWE vibrations, especially these VERY to my soul marking experiences of witnessing how the baby "girl's" soul, wrapped within her brand new created bluish pale vessel, seconds upon "her" arrival with BiG and vivid eyes safely got placed onto her mother's chest and how it then, as of her own unsafe considered weight, a few minutes after the introduction to her absolute loving, overwhelmed and proud parents, instantaneously got relocated into her new temporary home called *The Incubator*. HA. Here we Go again. Smile. Now, witnessing this entire spectacle from a this time front row seat, of HOW an entire new and unique developed human considered vessel suddenly appears within our sphere, certainly is one of the MOST incredible phenomena's that my eyeballs thus far came to experience. BOAHWOWAH. And. Thank you everyone, for this amazing granted opportunity. Then, whilst I found my *"Self"* somewhat dazzled, uncomfortable and rather baffled capturing everything that stroke my *"inner Artist"* as mesmerizing, my curious inner Gemini on the other end certainly VERY MUCH so would have loved to know WHAT exact thoughts, if any, happened to be speeding through this fresh and untouched appeared "old" soul's mind, throughout its entire zWoOMb exchanging transformation right into our sphere, that presented itself with a variety of difFeRent vessels, lights, machines, sounds, vibrations, shapes, colors and so forth. Yes, as spectacular all those many first few "Baby Boom" minutes hit my soul for sure, especially the unexpected incubator Déjà Vu experience. Oh yeah. Even though the baby girl welcomed our realm within her 39th watermelon supposed to be developed week, her vessel interestingly presented itself with *"little Linda's"* then almost matching 36 week's Romaine lettuce version, which "coincidence" revealed itself, caused by "her" soul's apparent recent decision to give the eFFecTs of a dietary discovered eating break a trial. BoaHA! Yup, and with this rather magical *"When the Student is Ready, the Teacher will Appear"* granted opportunity, of witnessing HOW this baby girl's soul for the first time received the chance to connected with her chosen parents' and HOW her fragile and undiscovered in an incubator placed vessel thereafter, accompanied by her father's, who's count at that very *"Now Moment"* also happened to equal Urs' and Bruce Lee's disappearance amount, carefully got *"Push*ed*"* away from her mother's, definitely succeeded in unlocking some of my, apparently over 4 decades somewhere within "blocked" energies, by additionally feeding my awareness with the eye-opening UPdate that this I'm*Patience* womb escaping action step choice from back then actually ended up leaving some remarkable unthought-of imprints on my "soul". Hmmm. Yes. "Something" certainly must have occurred during those first 4 *"little Linda"* weeks, as at a matter of "fact", I suddenly found myself being caught up on a battlefield of for ONE trying hard to hide all these many salty appearing teardrops from the newly blessed parents, accompanied by my simultaneous TWO juggling attempts in allowing for my *"inner ARTreyu Warrioress"* to fully surrender herself to this rather freeing caterpillar eFFecT granted opportunity. wOOsh. Then, whilst my soul *"ongRowingly"* kept "herself" busy with the adjusting process of this transformational inner and outer *kind*led "Baby Boom" journey, the three vessels of my roommates 2 days later, happily, safe, sound and somewhat exhausted already found themselves walking through our mutually *"Home Sweet Home"* base declared front door again and this "minor" additional, now outside of its mother's womb floating added soul, certainly instantly brought along many expected energy, including rhythm changes. *"Boom. BOOm. BOOM."* Welcome home. "Baby Boom." For which purpose, the "freshly backed" parents gladly accepted the just turned mom's own mother's prior offered helping and supporting hands for 2 weeks straight, so that this rather fragile and brand new *"Living on Earth Game"* created experiment could get launched as *"Smooth* as a *Criminal."* as possible. *"AaoW."* Well, and then I am assuming, that all these many inner and outer occurred changes on top of it all must have called in the perfect *"Now Moment"* for *"little Linda"* to enter onto her own next, from the magical Universe orchestrated *"Growth and Expansionary"* master puzzle "piece" ride, as a few days into this newly established routine to be, my ex-classmate suddenly felt prompted to approach my vessel wondering if I possibly would be able to take over his mother in law's assisting position, once hers would be heading back to *Arizona*, the following week. AAHH. What?! Certainly turned out to be my soul's first inner reaction, which then instantly led me to somewhat startled and taken aback express that 1) His request with "No Doubt" differed rather drastically from my actual *Own Wants, Needs, Desires and Dreams* created materialization plans, that 2) My *"inner Artist"* as of his knowledge happened to be already quite busy with this thus far wonderful recreational flowing Autobiography venture, that 3) I just a few days ago finally succeeded, in finishing reading the, from his end provided Ivana Chubbuck required class preparation book, that my further intended *"Stepping-Stone"* therefore resulted in 4) Slowly throwing *"little Linda"* back into her decades old *"Don't Dream your Life. Live your THE Ultimate Childhood Dream"* within this *"Dream come True"* like LA-LA-Hollywood-Land formation and that for all these many reasons 5) My soul felt quite unsure as of HOW to furthermore reAct. Hmmm. Understanding, my somewhat disappointed and desperate seeming turned friend then certainly acknowledged those many just heard of reasoning's, which sudden, from my end as uncomfortable noticed *"Cause and eFFecT"* shifted reality check succeeded, in triggering my still quite pleasing oriented soul to give my heart a little *"Push"* in order to at least find out more of WHAT this "assisting position" entailed. Happily, my former classmate then continued his train of vision by sharing that my vessel basically would be asked to support his wife with the daily recurring tasks of Washing and Folding the many used Diapers, Blankets, including Baby Cloths and to Provide her with Water, Food and with an overall Helping Hand, whenever needed, whilst his would be busy at work and that both on top of it all would LOVE for my soul to *"ongRowingly"* continue "her" baby taking care services, once his wife would be heading back to her full-time teaching occupation, by mid of December. WOAW. Hold on. WHAT?! Well, and this as EXTREME time consuming voiced second preposition definitely sounded just a tiny tad TOO much of an interference with my overall rather filled schedule at hand, which reality already included the few tasks from our previous win-win set arrangement. Hmmm. Still unsure as of how to reAct to this entire unexpected appeared *"Everything happens for a Reason"* proposition, I thereafter instantly consulted my inner voice for assistance, as the first part of this new game plan at hand with "No Doubt" vibrated in its doable notes, of which the second one though *"ongRowingly"* continued to leave my awareness in its resisting resonating mode. Bummer. What to do. What to do. After some further *"Head vs. Heart"* experienced *"Back, Back, Forth and Forth"* Yes or No moments, my still activated *Being Nice, Pleasing* and *Helping Syndrome* symptoms then finally decided to take over the command by thereafter instantly convincing my *"inner ARTreyu Warrioress"* with the just pulled *"Positivity Card"* trick "facts", that as 1) This thrilling *"NeverEnding"* seemingly *"Wait-a-While"* Easter Egg surprise of mine still found itself for who knows how much longer floating *"Somewhere over the Rainbow"* and as this proposal furthermore included an opportunity for my *"Self"* to 2) Donate some of my extra available "Abundance of Time" gift resources towards this newly picked-UP *"Self*-less" Help and Service to Others in Need *"Life Toolbox"* ingredient insight, it would be an OK choice for me to accepted this *"With our Mind on our Money, with our Money on our Mind"* agreement, with the extended "strings attached" importance though, of finding myself furthermore being enabled to accordingly invest all the for my 3 times per week gym routine, including for the from my end as slightly "more" important considered Autobiography MUST DO project venture required *"Time and Energy"* resources, as a play it by ear trial experience. Deal. Well, and as already assumed, things of course instantaneously even moRE so started to shift, the second that my vessel, after its thrilling and inspiring Palo Alto road trip, stepped into the shoes of the meanwhile vanished mother in law's and within a few days' time, my *"inner Artist"* then suddenly found herself once anew getting challenged with a freshly generated juggling contest between the mastering exercise of her own Creative Flow versus the rather often "Baby Boom" occurred interruption task breaks by furthermore for the first time truly being able to witness, HOW MUCH of a moving forward interference these once upon a time *"Swimming ALONG WiTH the Current"* and *"Swimming AGAiNST the Stream"* discovered duality phenomena's actually happened to be causing to one another, whenever focused upon at the very same *"Now Moment"*. YUP. "Water can Flow or it can Crash." "Boom. Clash." And certainly, this with SpeCial eFFecTs filled manifestation UPdate ended up occurring all in one SPLASH, as soon as my *"inner Artist"* found herself On Duty. Uiii. Somewhat concerned about my overall *"the DOiNG ME PROjECT"* progress, I therefore shortly after decided to consult my lovely inner voice for any further advice in regards of this as distracting perceived revised *"Don't Dream your Life. Live your THE Ultimate Childhood Dream"* game plan at run and found myself rather surprised by its immediate assurance that everything moved along alright, by furthermore underlining, that this current experienced *"Living on Earth Game"* adventure with guarantee would be providing some very beneficial *"Growth and Expansionary"* outcomes for my curious traveling soul. Hmmm. Alright then. *"Thy Will is My Command."* About 1 month prior to my official *"All or Nothing"* "Baby Boom" taking care reality arrival, my *"inner Artist"* as a next step very much so came to the understanding, that this *"ongRowing"* Autobiography venture with "No Doubt" instantaneously would be finding itself endangered, once my vessel would be remaining "Home Alone" and that my overall OWN Project and Opportunity creation game plan strategy therefore urgently required some reviewing as well. Guided by a newly pulled *"Positivity Card"* and by the meanwhile gained knowledge, that basically most of my overall available focus' flow, soon mainly needed to get directed towards the "baby girl on board's" well-being, I decided to consult my once created Doing Me list for a suiting *"Empty your Mind and become Water my Friend"* substitution resolution, which action step quickly drew my attention towards the then Starting a Blog, including The creation of a "Doing Me Project" YouTube Channel with intervaled own Recorded Video UPloads of some sorts received suggestions, as a two birds with one stone fusion idea. Hmmm. After some further pondering undertaken moments, it then suddenly dawned on me that this UPcoming "Home Alone" exercise actually would grant my Patience practicing *"inner Artist"* with the delightful extended Plan B opportunity, to showcase *"little Linda"* and this City filled with Angels formation to all the many mutual Germanic *"Cali Dreamin'"*understanding souls and this in the form of a variation of new *"Living on Earth Game"* adventure creations, whilst the baby girl hopefully quite often would be finding herself having FuN in dreamy b*zZZ* land. Yes, and in doing so, I therefore ASAP could be using all the many weekend hours ahead, in order to head Out There and *Explore, Experience, Collect, Capture* and *Share* whatever information flow *"little Linda"* stroke as non-touristy based LA-LA-Hollywood-Land MUST DO's and MUST KNOW's, so that I would grant myself with the opportunity to furthermore stay creative in a FuN and fulfilling way. Yeah! This wonderful as genius *"Yin and Yang"* resonating Keeping Everyone Happy idea with "No Doubt" instantaneously succeeded in activating every within my vessel with thrills marked existing buttons and to right then transform this UPdated *OWN Project* and "Baby Boom" *Opportunity creation* game plan into its *"Thy Will is My Command"* mode. Great. Let's do this. *"Schweizerin in LA/Swiss Lady in LA"* thereafter then revealed itself as the available and to Go to title and off the preparation quest took, that led my soul to invest all the throughout these 4 weeks ahead available *"Time and Energy"* resources exclusively towards the establishment of the proper for this journey required platform, which included the creation of my Blogs template, its newly linked own YouTube channel and the as more tedious perceived gathering exercise of all the numerous online revealed tips and tricks on how to reach an as BiG of an audience as possible within both medias. Ufff. Then, after the completion of a rather busy and with an enhanced baby holding and mutually adjusting added "Home Alone" hours filled pre-launching phase, my *"Schweizerin in LA"* Blog as desired presented itself, a couple of days prior to my roommates' maternal break's end, with its first few UPloaded LA-LA-Hollywood-Land adventure creation iNsights and Suggestions, hiGHlighted by hopefully many Helpful, Entertaining and iNspiring Word, Video and Picture combinations, of which activity my *"inner ARTreyu Warrioress"* thankfully happily found herself able to implement some of the from her end in May 2015 birthed and with an Abundance of Positive, Encouraging and *"Self*-loving" quotes filled *empowering_kicks* Instagram page gathered A-HA eFFecTs. Ha! And yes, of course the all-time for that magical, since February 2015 undergone journey's "responsible" bright P!NK and white "SCREAMiNG" *"LOVE YOURSELF Love yourSelf FiRST and Everything else Falls into Place"* key postcard, absolutely ended up receiving its own place of honor within the first "opening" week as well. LOVE. Well, and things from then on to my surprise rather drastically started to shift even more so and within a few heartbeat beat beat beat beat beats time, I successfully found my *"Self"* out of nowhere, once anew tangled within a new *"Yeah, let's go ALL the way. Let's give yourSelf away"* created situation, which eventually got caused by 1) The unexpected *"NeverEnding"* "Baby Boom" Holding, Rocking, Soothing, Entertaining, Monitoring and Carrying staying indoors allowed only shifts of 6 to 11 hours in a row, 4 to 5 times per week, by 2) The extra pressure *Pleasing Everyone* feeding three, throughout our apartment installed *"BiG Brother is Watching you"* talk through cameras, by 3) The one handed completion trials of the further "Home Alone" required cleansing tasks, whilst the baby on board's tinny 90 *"ongRowing"* days young vessel safely got strapped around my chest as part of her *"Comfort Zone"* established experience, by 4) The absolute zero *"Time and Energy"* resources availability for *"little Linda's"* Own Wants, Needs, Desires and Dreams fulfilling approaches, which furthermore including any proper meal intake "breaks" and by 5) The short and mostly disturbed resting hours, for my light bzZZ "wired" sleep mask and earplugs wearing "soul", within the meanwhile into the new hangout and office transmuted living room space, whenever the baby girl found herself sound asleep in the parents' bedroom. ABRACADABRA. *"Gotch Ya'. Again."* Yes indeed. Congrats. And this new energy and creativity deflating Déjà Vu UPdate, therefore instantaneously led my sudden, on the Other Edge of things landed lethargic transforming *"inner ARTreyu Warrioress"* with "No Doubt" skip one workout session after the other, followed by the decision to furthermore release all the many, as very *"Time and Energy"* consuming interpreted blogging adventures, after its 4th launched week out of my reality and those many by *Miss Fear* based "easy way out" considered resolution solutions therefore *"ongRowingly"* succeeded, in swinging their doors WiDE open for this dearly missed and completely out of sight lost *Mister Loneliness* friend of mine, who this time around came to decide to comfort *"little Linda"* in an even more extraordinary way than ever before. AHHH. *"My Loneliness is Killing me. Hit Me, baby, One more Time."* Yes, my beloved *Co-Traveler*, *"Oops. I did it again."* is what my soul came to think at some point as well, which train of thought then furthermore led me to realize, that this afresh and still lingering around *CoDependency* symptom chosen *"Putting Aside one's OWN Well-Being to maintain a Relationship with anOther"* performed "glitch", within this "Baby Boom" entered Dream, including *"little Linda"* Fading Away adventure at run, eventually reliably succeeded, in *"Push*ing" my *"Self"* over another undesired Edge and this in its most *FAST SPEED*ing experienced timeframe thus far. zoOM! Crash. Boom. CLASH. oucH. The wonderful news out of this storyline though ended up resulting in the amazing *"Cause and eFFecT"* "truth", that this entire "misinterpreted" *"Self*-less" Help and Service to Others in Need undertaken exercise, either must have unlocked the last needed puzzle "peace" upon this *"Finding back Home again"* journey at play or that the all-time supportive Universe simply guided my soul successfully into THE perfect required state of emotional *"Now Moment"*, in order to LASTLY release *"little Linda"* out of this gnawing *"NeverEnding"* seemingly *"Enjoy the Silence"* *"Wait-a-While"* cycle of 2 ½ years. AHHH, my beloved *Co-Traveler* and this time for real. wOOt WooT. YES! Just in time, with the beginning of this brand new 2016 launched year at count, the kind Universe FiNALLY blessed my awareness with the MORE than freeing *"And there upon a Rainbow is the Answer to a "NeverEnding" Story. Ah. Ah. Ah."* immigration discovery, which TREMENDOUS life-changing appreciated key experience very much so ended up revealing itself to have been THE essential magical needed

"Stepping-Stone" spell, so that my Linda Wartenweiler Doing Me Project mission truly found itself being enabled to take OFF as *"wiLD & Free"* as it most likely all along happened to be meant for it to be. YeehAHHH. And. ThanXoXo. Are you Ready? Alrighty then. Let's lastly let this "grumpy" old cat out of its molded Easter Egg bag. Shall we?! Abracadabra. This very first 2016 business Monday early morning hour, in which I am witnessing my *"Self"* of how my vessel strapped with the baby girl around it, espied an at this point rather unexpected e-mail from my newly hired lawyer aboard in my mailbox app, with "No Doubt" will always remain safe, sound and vivid within *"little Linda's" "ongRowing" "Head Cinema"* library collection and this even more so, as its attached document finally disclosed THE expected. Yup, my *Patience* practicing *Co-Traveler*, possibly you all along already might have intuitively figured out for your*Self*, what exactly ended up occurring behind the scenes of this entire yellow key *"Wait-a-While"* spectacle at hand. TatAAA! *"Whoomp! There it is."* In this attached document, which originated from the immigration department, my soul heavy hearted came to learn that both, for this entire yellow key process required first two Green Light delivered *"Stepping-Stone"* approval papers that were issued by 1) *SAG-AFTRA (Screen Actors Guilt-American Federation of Television and Radio Artists)* in February 2013 and by 2) *AMPTP (The Alliance of Motion Picture and Television Producers)* in April 2013, for ONE happened to differ quite a LOT from their usual exchanged correspondence interactions, which reality check therefore eventually TWO left our assigned immigration officer, after some researching undertaken action steps, with the almost "unbelievable" UPdate, that THREE neither of them ever issued any paper work in behalf of my Linda Wartenweiler identity during that time frame and that these from my old lawyer handed in "approval" notices consequently got declared as *TatAAA!* Fraudulent. SLAM! BAM! Here is the rest of your cake and now you better eat it too. OUCH. Yup, my wonderful *Co-Traveler*, this is what ended up happening with *"little Linda's"* first precious *"Don't Dream your Life. Live your THE Ultimate Childhood Dream Vision"* materialization attempt and believe me when I say, that this information flow with "No Doubt" welcomed my reality with the LEAST surprise and yours probably neither. Sniff. Now, even though my soul rather likely found "herself" already during my Rock Bottom visit excursion quite aware of such an outcome, this unbelievable Movie like Dream crashing "truth" revelation, nevertheless instantaneously succeeded, in 1) Pulling the rug from under my feet in one light *speed*ed paced SWOOSH, in 2) *"Push*ing" and twisting this within my heart placed dagger all the way to its maximum possible position and in lastly 3) Assisting my *"inner ARTreyu Warrioress"* with the relieving releasing task, of all the many, in this regards throughout those colorful years accumulated salty healing teardrops. AAAH. NO! NO. No. no. HOW on heavens earth was this "deadening" outcome simply possible and WHY in the magical Universe's name would this lawyer take his liberty to nonchalantly Go ahead and gamble MY precious *"Soul Childhood Dream"*, as if it literally happened to be "just" a Piece of Cake object. OMG. What a disaster after all. Then, as

soon as I caught my breath again and a moment in which the baby girl kept on happily smiling at my soul, I then led by many *"ongRowing"* flowing tears quickly went ahead and dialed my new lawyer's office number with the objective, to discuss my *"inner Artist's"* further Dream realization options. From his end, my soul then quickly came to learn, that as those defrauding discoveries with certainty reflected the "truth", that a reaching out to my old lawyer would remain a dead end and that therefore my vessel once anew got presented with two options at play. *Number ONE* resulted in the withdrawal action step of this first case in motion before its end of January "proofing different" set deadline, in order to avoid a "declined" status UPdate within my Linda Wartenweiler records. Then, as this overall Easter Egg surprise brought along the inevitable "fact" that *"little Linda's"* overall legal welcome within this *"The Other Planet"* formation No Matter what found itself about to expire, my vessel therefore nevertheless would be required to exit its *"Home Sweet Home"* base of almost a decade for "good" and that my only chance of a possible reentry trial would remain in the master plan, of building a new *"Childhood Acting Dream"* resume somewhere else by thereafter led by a freshly *"You must be my Lucky Star"* pulled *"Positivity Card"*, give a new yellow O1 Artist visa key application quest another trial. In about 4 years-time or so. LOL. What? In about 4 years?! LOLOL. This *"NeverEnding"* Story*line* truly is getting better and better by the month. For real. LMAO. And *Number TWO* once anew called in for the, at that *"Now Moment"* considered *"FAST*est way out" solution *TatAAA!* The legal and truthful knot tying action step to an American citizen declared vessel. Unless the still silently slumbering second case miraculously would be finding itself getting approved at some point, which outcome based on our, with thrills and chills packed reality UPdate though very much so seemed to be unlikely. *"The Choice is Yours."* Ufff. With this revealed UPdate, including with my already chosen MUST DO path in mind, my soul then furthermore desired to find out more about the "whereabouts" in regards of this "magical" lawyer's secretly sparkly chosen tricks and treats tactic steps. After all, "his" soul remained as the Rebel with a Cause, within this entire *"Don't Dream your Life. Live your THE Ultimate Childhood Dream Vision"* ignited clashing "True Snapple Fact" disaster at hand and therefore the law certainly should be directing their focus on his behalf, instead of taking it out on the costs of the all along legally and on rather thin ice walked *"little Linda"* persona. Sniff. Quickly, my soul then came to learn, that there surely might exist a way in having an investigation started towards this Rebel with a Cause at play, though as my new lawyer's soul's expertise solely remained in the immigration field, I therefore would be finding my *"Self"* being forced in hiring a for that matter claimed specialist. Bummer. Alright then. Got it. After some further *"Back, Back, Forth and Forth"* Q and A exchanged details, we then ended our phone conversation with the mutually set agreement to allow this entire whirlwind a 1 week settling down phase, during which my *"inner ARTreyu Warrioress"* simultaneously furthermore would be finding herself able to spend some additional time with the meanwhile chosen voiced path desire. Just to make sure. Smile. Well, and as you most likely can imagine for yourself, my supportive *Co-Traveler*, the *"Cause and eFFecT"* reaction outcome of this rather eye-opening conversation certainly for the most part found themselves resonating as rather "illogical" *"Stepping-Stone"* suggestions in regards of *"little Linda's"* overall own *"NeverEnding" "Dream Catchin'"* experienced *Wants, Needs, Desires and Dreams* materialization quest. Oh yeah. First of all, this granted UPdate that my vessel found itself about to get "forced" to exit out of this, after all from the kind Universe in 2005 guided into *"Acting. Uncertainty. Complete Life Change."* path and this reasoned upon someone else's "inappropriate" action choices, who on top of it all even seemed to be able to get away with the practice of some as unlawful declared "magical" deeds, with "NO DOUBT" made zero sense to my VERY justice oriented soul and therefore hit "her" as an absolute *"I'mPOSSiBLE"* doorway option. Boom. That's right. Then, furthermore the idea of throwing my *"Self"* into this even more *"Time and Energy"* consuming dating jungle as a desperate and still undesired getting married action plan move, even more so succeeded in sparkling the least enthusiasm within any of my existing cells. *"Oh GOD NO"* is all that my inner voice had to comment on that matter, as *"Like* after all *Attracts Like"* and I most definitely found my *"Self"* in that very *"Now Moment"*, once again rather FAR off from my desired *"True little Linda Self"* version experience track. Ufff. YUP. With this newly gathered outlook, including with the from ambitious *"little Linda"* in 2006 defined *"Soul Childhood Dream come True"* materialization rule, that the ONLY acceptable track upon this *"Acting Dream"* s-Express train joyride at end would remain in the honest *"Step-by-Step. Oh* Heidi Klum *baby."* recommended approach, which strategy therefore called in the disallowance of any short cuts or cheating attempts so that my curious inner Gemini soul eventually would be presented with the ACTUAL, from the magical Universe foreseen Linda Wartenweiler *"Don't Dream your Life. Live your THE Ultimate Childhood Dream"* unfolding outcome in view, my unimpressed on the Edge walking *"inner ARTreyu Warrioress"* therefore within a SNAP came to decide to determinedly *"Keep on Movin'* forward *my Darling. Ooh ooh-ooh ooh."* on this as "distracting" perceived, from *Miss Fear* organized visa battlefield at play, by instead simply handing over all my trust into this "Universal", dependable, adventurous and thrilling *"Always follow your Hearts Desires as Radiant as possible by ensuring to Keep On Pushing Any presented Boundaries with a Living Life to its Fullest possible Approach and to therefore absolutely NEVER take NO for an answer, NO MATTER what, as Not even the Sky is the Limit"* ingrained *"Self-loving"* philosophy. That's right. *"Don't stop Believin'. Hold on to YOUR Dreamin'."* NO MATTER what. Let's GO. With this UPdated New York style gathered attitude, including with this as rather freeing One and Only interpreted to got-to path in my perspective, my friendly inner voice then brought to my attention, that the course of my soul's overall *"Living on Earth Game"* reality creation required some according adjusting as well and that the evaluation and *"Letting go of Anything that No Longer Serves One's*

Growth and Expansion"* execution *"Stepping-Stone"* appeared as the following essential requirement to focus upon. Aye aye, Sir. After some recommended undertaken inward traveling and reflecting excursions, my *"inner ARTreyu Warrioress"* then came to the realization that sneaky *Miss Fear* anew succeeded in convincing my *"Self"* to pass the steering wheel command, upon *"little Linda's"* overall own *"NeverEnding"* unfolding Story*line* wish, fully and generously over to strangers and that based on this UPcoming planed *"Truth or Dare"* exercise of leading my vessel towards the overstaying its "welcome" reality check choice, it would appear as a mighty glorious idea, to ASAP redirect my entire available *"Time and Energy"* resources back onto my soul's OWN Wants, Needs, Desires and Dreams materialization goals, which included the respectful nurturing approach of the tremendously neglected *"Self*-love", *"Self*-care", *"Self*-worth", *"Self*-respect" and *"Self*-confidence" elements, within this Doing Me entered *"Self*-realization" oak tree journey at run. Abracadabra. *"The Choice is Yours."* Well, and this train of thought then furthermore guided my awareness into this *"Growth and Expansionary"* A-HA CLiCKiNG *"Now Moment"*, in which it suddenly dawned on me that the wonderful Universe's possible *"Life Toolbox"* ingredient providing intent with this entire "misinterpreted" *"Self*-less" Help and Service to Others in Need undertaken task could have resulted in the rather eye-opening reality "truth", that *"One Foremost NEEDS to take CARE of one's OWN precious "Self's" Well-Being and Happiness, before it THEN Freely and "Self*-lessly" *can be of valuable Help and Service to Others in Need."* Oh boy! That actually very much so made sense. DAH. And this minor *"Change the way you Look At Things and the Things you Look At Change"* received wisdom input surely right away succeeded, in leading my *"Head Cinema"* production ALL the way back to the initial, in July 2013 provided *"Self*-loving" guidelines, in which this friendly voice continued explaining, that if I decided to follow through with this quite and *Patience* required *"The ONLY Person standing in Your Way is YOU"* liberating game changer at hand, that the next *Vital* step therefore would appear of UTMOST importance, which revealed itself as the TOP ONE responsibility for me to *Nurture* and *Protect* this newly planted treasure *"ongRowingly"* with LOTS of *LOVE, CARE* and *RESPECT* in order for it to be able to grow and *"grOW and Expand"* and GROW stronger by the day, just about as *"little Linda"* instinctively used to practice it with her *"Acting. Uncertainty. Complete Life Change."* hobby desired dream seed, and replenish my entire vessel this time around with *"little Linda's"* beloved *"NeverEnding"* love and light stream *"Comfort Zone"* experience, so that I eventually would be finding my *Self* swimming within an Abundance puddle of LOVE and LiGHT, which remains I THEN happily could be sharing with other soul travelers, if desired. PhewwW. This "truth" factor truly once again slipped my mind. pOops. Oh boy. *"Thy Will is My Command."* Equipped with this newly gained reality check, including with many more shaded emotions within my backpack, my rather saddened, vicTiMized and rebellious vibrating soul then as promised UPdated the newly hired lawyer's about my *"inner ARTreyu Warrioress'" "ongRowing"* and final

"Keep on Movin' forward *my Darling. Ooh ooh-ooh ooh."* MUST DO decision path towards the as "illegal immigrant" considered status gates by confidently and with "No Doubt" disregarding ANY further as distracting and intimidating perceived sidetracking elements upon my Linda Wartenweiler soul's ingrained *"I'mPOSSiBLE" "Living on Earth Game"* materialization quest at play. That's right. *"Where there is a Will there ALWAYS is a Way, 'cause wherever there is a Way iN, there ALWAYS MUST exist minimum ONE Way OUT."* Boom. And my soul's *Will*, including its inner "truth" factor knowledge by then very much so found themselves being lit UP brighter than the, in Wolfgang Petersen's "The *NeverEnding* Story" version featured ivory tower. HA. *"Watch and Learn, baby. It's Hot, it Burns, so I Drop it."* And that's exactly what my soul set into motion next. Once this UPdated master game plan successfully and under some further appeared salty teardrops found itself officially in its voiced *Law of Attraction* order status, my soul then furthermore instructed the one on the other side of the line with the last, within our very helpful and satisfying business relationship request, to please ASAP proceed with the somewhat costly announced visa withdrawal recommendation gesture, so that at least *"little Linda's"* records would remain "clean". For now. Ufff. Sniff. Thanks. Bye-Bye. Yes, and within the ending second of this thus far last conversation of ours, my soul then came to experience an even more so tremendous liberating and relieving inner reality transformation, which allowed for those many more accumulated healing indicating emotions to *"wiLD and Freely"* exit out of my system. Hooray! Finally, the wonderful Universe granted my, up for nearly 3 years *Patience* practicing *"inner Artist's"* nerve-wracking wish, of simply getting released out of this gnawing *"NeverEnding"* seemingly *hi*Storyline as its first priority, and this regardless the outcome. Glory hallelujah! THANK YOU SO MUCH. Ahhh! This UPdated accomplishment at hand to my soul's surprise actually truly felt incredibly liberating, my beloved *Co-Traveler*. O.M.G. YES. And this regardless the still open and meanwhile as SO unimportant declared *"ongRowing"* silently slumbering second visa application trial at run or by the additional delivered "truth" factor, that *"little Linda's"* "normal" Acting career materialization path within this *"The Other Planet"* sphere officially found its bitter-sweet End. Oo-WAH! *"I Want to Break Free"* was all that mattered for quite some time and this state of *"Dream come True"* reality creation, my soul therefore within a snap with all of my heart allowed to once again take over the command upon *"little Linda's"* neglected *"Don't Dream your Life. Live your THE Ultimate Childhood Dream"* oak tree quest. Ha! POOF. Ufff. Yup and those many existing emotions then even more so got enhanced by my further with thrills and chills filled awareness check, that this just expressed visa withdrawal *"Stepping-Stone"* choice actually called in for the final required releasing puzzle "peace" outcome, that for ONE still resulted out of my many, within this colorful *Artistic and "Self-*developing" *Boot Camp* accepted *"Living on Earth Game"* joyride chapter and that TWO *"ongRowingly"* succeeded in keeping on inter*Fear*ing and on holding my *"inner ARTreyu Warrioress"* back from her *"Truth AND Dare"* postponed

"True little Linda Self" Doing Me implementation desire. Well hello again, lovely *Madam ProCrastination*. Let's *"Get this Party Started."* *"That's why we have to say Goodbye."* Bye-Bye. Swoosh. And all those many further A-HA CLiCKiNG puzzle "peace" assembled elements upon this chess board at play, then eventually presented themselves with these further mind-blowing and eye-opening realization "truths", of HOW MUCH I actually all along allowed for this entire *"NeverEnding"* seemingly Piece of Cake visa debacle to define my whole Linda Wartenweiler *"Self*-experience" within every in my precious vessel existing cell by simply handing iT the fullest command over my soul's entire *"Living on Earth Game"* unfolding storyline as part of a magical distraction opportunity, of HOW these by sneaky *Miss Fear* orchestrated action step choices then as a matter of "fact" ended up succeeding in shaping the form of those several inner and outer *"Self*-created" whirlwind adventures and of HOW this last chosen and with "No Doubt" required complete *"Swimming AGAiNST my OWN truthful inner "Self-stDream"* "Baby Boom" path at hand, then eventually led my soul to experience this most likely essential prior mentioned *Complete Abandonment of my OWN identity and of my OWN "True little Self"* tipping point instant, so that my soul's once *Red* life purpose and mission chosen path pill would be finding itself enabled to finally take its "actual" destined rabbit hole course within my *"ongRowing"* own "The Matrix" experience at play. Hold on. What?! The *Red* pill? Oh boy. That's right, *"little Linda"* actually once swallowed this "risky" and as unknown considered *Red* pill that brought along its attached lifetime commitment "truth" with NO return ticket on sale ever. Oops. And this "minor" reality creation choice furthermore succeeded, in "somehow" slipping my preoccupied bee*zZZ* mind as well. Hmmm. Though, what if this once with SpeCial eFFecTs provided "The Matrix" *"Head Cinema"* vision possibly truly finds itself being linked to everything thus far experienced? HMMM. Wow. Well, that "truth" factor certainly even more so would blow *"little Linda's"* mind. iF. Boah. Anyway, with this additional "risky" and as unknown reconnected *"Acting. Uncertainty. Complete Life Change."* stepping outside of my *"ComfortWombBoxZone"* chosen *Red* pill reality UPdate at hand, my curious *"inner ARTreyu Warrioress'"* Gemini soul then very much so felt Ready Steady and Thrilled to extend her experimental *"Like Attracts Like"* explorations out of this soon as rather incredibly unthought-of "illegal immigrant" to be resonating perspective and this as *"wiLD & careFreely"* as possible. Outch. Yes, and this *"Der Anfang vom Ende/The Beginning of the End"* declared status "debacle" with "No Doubt" immediately caused for my quite proud Swiss originated soul to for quite some time release a LOT of these as uncomfortable interpreted resistance vibrations. Double OUTCH. Sniff. Oh well. At the end, it is what it is. The past belongs to the past. And with the help of an *"ongRowing"* diligent *"Change the way you Look At Things and the Things you Look At Change"* applied believe rewiring attitude, I eventually thankfully ended up succeeding, in substituting this saddening *"You Always Are what you Thinkest"* experience with its rather encouraging *"The Key to your Success is to KEEP your Dream in*

Focus and to have the Courage to do things Other's WON'T do" green light outlook instead. Yay! *"The Power of Words."* Ha. Lastly, my friendly inner voice then came to point out the importance of having this newly and somewhat limiting adapted "vicTiM" dominating *"Head over Heart"* mindset ASAP getting switched back into its *"The Eye of the Tiger"* soundtrack vibration, so that my brave on the Edge walking *"inner ARTreyu Warrioress"* rapidly would be finding herself enabled again, to *"ongRowingly"* ONE as eFFecTive and efficient as possible keep on swimming forward from a then with *"Self*-love" infused *"I'm Possible"* emerging Moment into the Next instead, which action step decisions then within a snap would TWO be throwing *"little Linda"* right back into her ACTUAL Own heart desired *"Living on Earth Game"* materialization stDream reality puddle. SPLASH. And this then magical and emPowering provided *"Life Toolbox"* ingredient phenomena, in other words found itself matching with my, a few months later "stumbled upon's" first encountered Hero's soul once expressed *"Be like Water making its Way through Cracks. Do NOT be Assertive, but Adjust to the Object, and you SHALL find a Way Around or Through it. If Nothing within you Stays Rigid, Outward Things WiLL Disclose themselves. Empty your Mind, be Formless. Shapeless, like Water. If you put Water into a Cup, it Becomes the Cup. You put Water into a Bottle and it Becomes the Bottle. You put iT in a Teapot, it Becomes the Teapot. Now, Water can Flow or it can Crash. Be Water, my Friend."* wisdom. Oo-WAH. *"Thy Will is My Command."* Gratitude.

"Rising UP, Back on my Feet. Have the Guts, to Chase my Glory."
Alongside with this BiG inner awareness metamorphosis in progress, the wonderful Universe then EXACTLY on time for my 1 year LA-LA-Hollywood-Land *Dreamin'*, including 12 months *CoDependency* recovery milestone celebrations, kindly pre-organized a 10 days "Baby Boom" break for my vessel, of which opportunity I certainly and with "No Doubt" immediately took advantage of in order to *"Hit the Road Jack"* for a couple of days, so that my soul finally would be finding "herself" able to for ONE refill "her" rather used up *"Time and Energy"* resources and to for TWO peacefully and carelessly be enabled to *"Dive Within"*, as Mister David Lynch loves to state it, in order to as truthfully get in touch with the next desired slash required *"Stepping-Stones"* to jUMP onto upon this *"Finding back Home again"* quest of mine. Boom! Oh yeah. Quickly, I therefore decided to consult the, from my by then temp "employer" of a couple of years, great offered Airbnb homepage in the hopes to find a suitable accommodation in beautiful Santa Barbara CA, as this location very much so stood out to *"little Linda"* during "our" past October travels UP north, towards my dear Sarah Friend's house and which destination after all, during the in 2005 chit chat warming up taken place phase with this friendly young men got recommended, in which "his" soul then at some point began to share that "his" brother happened to be studying Film directing in Santa Barbara, that "he" for that reason just returned from a FuN visit a few days prior and that I most certainly should pay this

beautiful city a visit now or someday. Wink! Well, and *someday* finally seemed to have arrived in its entire glory. HA. So here WE go, my curious *Co-Traveler*. Oo-WAH. As soon as my eyes then within a few minutes time, excitedly stumbled over this rather cute, simple and wooden Instant Book available cottage close by the ocean, my heart right away knew that "iT" would serve my tireless on the Edge walking *"inner ARTreyu Warrioress"* as THE perfect retreat facility in order for her to as requested *Rest*, to *Be*, to *Recharge*, to *Dive Within*, to *Feel*, to *Listen*, to *See*, to *Understand*, to *Regain*, to *Create*, to *Plan*, to remain in *Solitude*, to *reConnect* with *Mother Nature*, including with my *Own "Self"* and to eventually *Break Free*. Again. AHHH. Yes! Two days later, I then as planned picked up a car at my favorite rental company *Enterprise* and off my vessel took UP north again, from where it ended up coming from, just before this entire "Baby Boom" spectacle started its own with SpeCial eFFecTs enhanced journey. Yeeha! Into what a powerful and soothing action step choice this entire mini trip gift within seconds revealed itself as. WOW. Thank you, my inner voice and beloved Universe. Y'all simply keep on *"Rock 'n Rollin'"* my world. LOVE. Let me share with you, my dear, dear *Co-Traveler*, this absolute meanwhile as rather unusual *"Self-*created" reality check experience of finding my vessel solely placed within an environment filled with nature, complete privacy and with my own *"Self"* for 4 days straight, and this FAR away from any *"BiG Brother is Watching you"* installed cameras, that on top of it all included this sudden as luxury acknowledged treat of being able to follow *"My Way"* of *Rules*, *"My Way"* of *Wants*, *"My Way"* of *Pace*, *"My Way"* of *Desires*, *"My Way"* of *Habits* and *"My Way"* of *Believe* interpretations only, simply appeared as another form of a HUGE "peace" of heaven "spoiler alert" discovery. WOW. This extraordinary being with my *"Self"* exercise, after especially those rather intense past 3 *"Self-*neglected" Easter Egg newsflash infused "misinterpreted" *"Self-*less" Help and Service to Others in Need committed weeks, that allowed for my *"inner ARTreyu Warrioress"* to dive into this incredible and to her thus far unknown experience of witnessing how every within my vessel vibrating cell instantaneously found itself VERY busy with sucking these many in Abundance available and as blissful identified energy particles in, whilst my *"wiLD & Free"* set loving soul *"ongRowingly"* kept "her" focus on this sensational and liberating with tranquility packed inhaling and exhaling opportunity, I definitely always will be carrying within a SpeCial for it created *"Head Cinema"* box. Wow. WoW. WOW. Those 4 days, I then, besides those pre-set *"sHe, who looks OUTside DREAMS. sHe, who looks iNside AWAKENS."* planned activities, furthermore enhanced with daily undertaken nature seeking excursions, of which the sarcastically matching named "Prisoner Harbor" hiking visit, located on the unpopulated Santa Cruz National Park Island, stood out the most to my solitude seeking soul and would have within a heartbeat been featured on my then oh so slumbering *"Schweizerin in LA"* Blog. Oh yeah. So therefore, if you EVER happen to *someday* be in Santa Barbara, my beloved *Co-Traveler* friend, then make sure to add this Island or any other from the further 4 existing Channel Island options, onto your MUST DO *"Cali Dreamin'" "Living on Earth Game"* adventure To Do list. With "No Doubt", your soul will LOVE it. Yup. Enjoy. After the granted spoiling gesture for my dear *"inner ARTreyu Warrioress"* to inside out relax and reflect for 2 days straight, my soul then on the 3rd day suddenly very much so felt prompted, to finally get the ball rolling in order to allow for the magical Universe to feed my awareness with the UPdated, once upon a time discovered and in a *"NeverEnding"* loop returning *"What's Next"* game plan ingredient preposition. Ha! Good old days. Right? Wink. Well and certainly, it reliably did so by leading my attention right back to all the many, within one of my bags placed precious *"Life Toolbox"* collected note and pocket book ingredients, which contained all the valuable wisdom resources that my curious Gemini's soul *"ongRowingly"* kept on attracting and resonating with the most, since the beginning of this in mid-July 2013 received *"Finding back Home again"* oak tree vision mission at growth. Now, whilst I kept my *"Self"* busy with this rather genius and as emPowering vibrating reconnecting exercise, by furthermore adding the as helpful detected action steps of ONE hiGHlighting every information flow that stroke my senses at that very arisen *"Now Moment"* as valuable MUST focus upon *Next* items and by the then TWO added task of writing everything down on a separate for it created MUST REMEMBER pen and paper list, my amazing inner voice then suddenly "out of the blue" felt triggered, to interrupt this entire inspirational flow of mine with the ultimate *"The Artist's Way"* game changer comment, the second that my eyeballs took in the, during a in October 2014 Soul Imprint reading recorded and noted down received *"So if you do Everything for yourSelf to Grow. And part of that is to Write about your Feelings and about what it is you Care About. A Blog."* statement. Boom. What?! Somewhat perplexed about this unexpected and as rather abstract seemingly interjection, I then immediately stopped my doings, whilst my inner voice nonchalantly continued its own train of thought with a *"The Artist's Way"* Start *"The Artist's Way"* explanation. Hmmm. *"The Artist's Way?"* Ok? HMMM. Now, as this book suggestion, within *"little Linda's"* many thus far magical *"Living on Earth Game"* undertaken travels, already had been brought to her attention three times prior, of which every with raving filled incidences twice resulted from my dear Sarah Friend's own *"inner Artist's"* during her two separately in it dwelled adventures, plus once from my talented MC, Actor, Writer then Bamboo boss's AKA *New York City's Lyrical Giant, Malik Work,* who's soul btw in 2012, in collaboration with one of those thrilling Sweet N' Low DJ's Nickodemus' ended up creating and producing a with LOTS of *"FuN Facts"* filled Music video called *"Let Me See some iD"*, that incidentally also showcases the three of our vessels, wink, my curious inner Gemini therefore finally felt encouraged enough, to first add these three words onto my newly started MUST REMEMBER pen and paper list and to thereafter with the help of this wonderful Google search engine, find out more about this "apparently with magic filled" 12 weeks *"Self"* workshop book for Artists that required an *"ongRowing"*, from my end undesired journaling exercise, each morning. Search. Oh, and how thrilled my tired and listless fallen *"inner Artist"* suddenly started to vibrate, the second that my eyeballs espied these on its *"Red and Golden"* cover printed *"The Artist's Way by Julia Cameron. A Course in Discovering and Recovering Your Creative Self. A Spiritual Path to Higher Creativity."* word combination. OMG. YES. THiS as absolutely promising sounding remedy with "No Doubt" happened to be EXACTLY *What* my Linda Wartenweiler soul needed to explore *Next*, as meanwhile the slightest thought of any Artistic endeavors after all succeeded in evoking a complete disinterested nonsense attitude within this one too many soon as U-Turns identified *"Living on Earth Game"* reality UPdate at run. Ufff. After some further information gathering about this very sympathetic and humble appearing bestselling Author, Teacher, Filmmaker, Playwright, Journalist Julia Cameron, my own *"inner Artist"* then eventually felt more than Ready Steady to as well accept this kind soul's offered helping and guiding hand upon my *"ongRowing"* fading, though oh so dearly kept and further adjusted *"Don't Dream your Life. Live your THE Ultimate Childhood Dreams come True truth"* believe, which sensations therefore immediately prompted my vessel, to order its own *"Truth AND Dare"* screaming copy on this incredible online shopping "mall" invention called *Amazon*. CLiCK. Purchased. Yay! 3 more days to GO, before this newly disclosed *What's Next "TreasureWomBox"* ingredient would be finding itself materialized within my own two palms and a few more to come, before I would be enabled to further equip my brave on the Edge walking *"inner ARTreyu Warrioress"* with hopefully many more enriching *"Life Toolbox"* ingredients, including priceless *"Living on Earth Game"* adventures upon this somewhat interrupted *"Finding back Home again"* journey towards "our" crucial *"True little Self"* set "end" destination goal. Boom. BOOM. Abracadabra. Well, and as you most possibility already might have realized and experienced for your*Self*, my dedicated dear *Co-Traveler*, this literally out of nowhere appeared *"Course in Discovering and Recovering Your Creative Self. A Spiritual Path to Higher Creativity."* inner "calling" suggestion revealed itself thus far to have been of EXTREME unexpected EXTRAORDiNARY and mind-blowing assistance for my meanwhile *"wiLD & Free"* sparkling, *"Growing and Expanding" "inner Artist"*, including for my lost and eventually reanimated *"True little Linda Self"*. WooHOO. And. YAY!! Therefore, the most-grandest THANKS ever to those *"The Artist's Way"* mentioning voices and especially to the all ball game changing genius author Julia Cameron. Gratitude. Blessings. Gratitude. Though before this ultimate "risky" and as unknown identified *Red* life purpose and soul mission ride of mine found itself being enabled to fully take its magical course down the from the wonderful Universe actual destined rabbit hole lane, my soul first needed to lock this from 11 months and 2 weeks ago opened *"EdgyBlackWomBox"* puzzle "peace" experience with this adjusted key master plan at hand, so that *"little Linda"* would be transported right back into her original *"wiLD wiLD West"* Coast LA-LA-Hollywood-Land *"Cali Dreamin'"* entered *"Swimming DOWN ALONG my*

OWN truthful inner *"Self-stDream"* "Mulholland Drive" reality creation flow again. Oh yeah. *"Silencio. No hay Banda."* That's right. And therefore, the as this time as rather uncomfortable perceived *"One Door Always MUST get closed First, before MANY others thereafter will be able to Burst Wide Open by rewarding THE Daring Soul with many UPgrading and more Suitable Blessings instead" "Growth and Expansion"* truth formula, needed to get set into motion as part of its *Next "Self*-loving" *"Stepping-Stone"* requirement, as my kind inner voice furthermore came to reveal that this nurturing loving *"inner Parent"* of mine, lastly found itself equipped with all the wonderful and required *"Life Toolbox"* ingredients in order for her to finally feel Ready Steady and Determined, to accept this apparently, as rather challenging appearing Taking Care of my Abandoned *"little Linda Self"* task, as its first and One and Only *"All or Nothing"* agreed responsibility. Starting from that very emerging *"Now Moment"* on. *"Push."* Deal. *"Thy Will is My Command."* Filled with all those many, throughout these absolute amazing *"wiLD & Free"* 4 days assembled UPdated emotions, experiences and perspectives, I then, after a spontaneous pit stop in beautiful *Ojai* California, somewhat heavy hearted and with the uncomfortable MUST DO *"Truth AND Dare" "Letting go of Something that No Longer Serves One's Growth and Expansion"* knowledge in mind, slowly made my way back towards my LA-LA-Hollywood-Land *"Home Sweet Home"* base of almost 1 year. Ufff. Yes. The reality check of finding my vessel back in its meanwhile as unmatching and *"Self*-created" U-Turn *"Swimming UP AGAiNST my OWN truthful inner "Self-stDream"* detected environment, certainly *"ongRowingly"* caused for many of those resisting vibrations to arise, the second that my hand pressed down that front door handle again. UFFF. Which UPdate therefore right away triggered my *"wiLD & Free"* floating soul to with "No Doubt" first dive into some further with *"FuN Facts"* filled LA-LA-Hollywood-Land *"Living on Earth Game"* adventures throughout the remaining 3 off duty days at run. Yeeha! Then, after an *"ongRowing"* Gwen Stefani like inner "Back, Back, Forth and Forth" "Should I Stay or Should I Go Now" "Buffalo Stance" dance of 2 ½ days and with this meanwhile magical ordered *"TreasureWomBox"* key placed within my reality, my on the Edge walking *"inner ARTreyu Warrioress"* finally felt Ready Steady to heavy hearted let this all destiny changing, from lovely *Miss Fear and Madam ProCrastination* guarded dice rolling by announcing my soul's 2 weeks US standardized notice from this 3 ½ months ago entered play it by ear "Baby Boom" trial experiment to my friendly, surprised and somewhat concerned reacting ex-NYFA class- and roommate transformed friend, followed by my further forged decision information flow to thereafter *"Hit the Road Jack"* for good, so that my *"inner Parent"* would be finding herself able to invest EVERY single element of this once "Abundance of Time" granted gift, EXCLUSiVELY towards privacy seeking *"little Linda's"* countless Own *"I'mPOSSiBLE"* desired *Wants, Needs, Desires and "Dream Catchin'"* materialization adventures, somewhere else in this *"BiG Wide World."* *"Push."* Done. YAY! Well, and the instant *Next* required puzzle "peaces" that this, parallel to my vessel's last day as a "legal" immigrant considered status reality tipping point on January 31st 2016, all-time rewarding, liberating and with duality filled *"Everything you Desire lies on the Other Side of Resistance"* applied Butterfly eFFecT equation ended up unlocking, presented themselves with the wonderful UPdates, that 1) My roommates decided to right away cancel their still on Airbnb offered extra bedroom for my soul's longed for privacy and recharging purposes, with this 2) EmPowering A-HA CLiCKiNG realization "truth" that those days of playing iT "save" officially dissolved themselves into The Nothing, that therefore 3) Practically every road within this *"The Other Planet"* formation "suddenly" found themselves being sprung Wide Open instead for my determined *"Eye of the Tiger"* walking *"inner ARTreyu Warrioress"* to explore, that 4) These continuous, from *Miss Fear* offered *"I Don't wanna Lose You"* recommendation *"Stepping-Stone"* choices, truly NO longer mattered and with a 10 days later, 5) Final absolute unthought-of news flash reaction text message, sides this still slumbering and to my old lawyer's linked second *"NeverEnding" "Wait-a-While"* visa case at hand. Wow. What?! YUP. Glory HallelujaH. And the content of this incoming text message, that my vessel a few months prior found itself able to "alert" set up online, indicated that the immigration office experienced difficulties in delivering an important letter to my lawyer's desk and that therefore some action happened to be required from our end. Boom. Is that right. Right, my lovely *Co-Traveler*? LOL. What's new and yes, this UPdate with "No Doubt" once again made more than complete sense. Certainly, my dutiful Swiss originated soul immediately went ahead and tried to order this "mysterious" letter online and via the phone, though both action step choices to my surprise right away got dismissed sides the immigration office, as their party only happened to be authorized to deliver ANY kind of information flow about MY Linda Wartenweiler *"Acting Dream"* s-Express train ticket case to the hired representative. Oh boy. With this delivered newsflash, including with the sudden somewhat confusing discovery of a to my soul's unknown mentioned lawyer's name and address on the from their end in May 2014 sent second 01 case reception confirmation reaction notice in my pocket, I therefore driven by these once encountered wise *"Your Time is Limited. Don't Waste it Living Someone Else's Life. Don't be Trapped by Dogma, which is Living the Result of Other people's Thinking. Don't let the Noise of Other Opinions Drown your Own inner Voice. And Most Importantly, have the Courage to Follow YOUR Heart and Intuition, they somehow already Know What You TRULY Want to Become. Everything else is Secondary"* collected *"Life Toolbox"* ingredient attitude, came instantly to decide that it was at the time to start dismantling any further visa distracting appearances with this wonderful *"Whatever"* approach and to instead simply determinedly *"Keep on Movin'* forward *my Darling. Ooh ooh-ooh ooh."* as had. HA. That's right. And so my soul even more so did, once this rather annoying *"NeverEnding" hi*Storyline after its colorful run of 3 years lastly arrived at its final denial destination status in April 2016, which reality UPdate absolutely anew succeeded in twisting and turning this within my heart placed dagger even a tiny bit further, though VERY much so got released again, the second that the amazing Universe made sure of to, for one of *"little Linda's"* dear "Imprisoned Souls" encountered "children", who meanwhile furthermore transformed himself into the talented and passionate author of the in 2016 published fictional *"Unattainable, Volume 1"* book, forward a with thrills and chills packed internet page to my a 100% justice believing soul in May 2017, that revealed to my utmost satisfaction that this Rebel with a Cause's vessel very recently got charged for Visa Fraud and aggravated Identity Theft. SLAM. BAM. ABRACADABRA. *"Gotch Ya'. Gotch Ya'."* WOOHOO. Thank you, dear *Frau Karma*. Thanks a million, in my soul's name and in every apparently over 150 other affected ones for this wonderful, kind and reliable deed of yours. WouW. What?! Hold on. That many? Yes, apparently that many. UFFF. Into what a shameless disaster this FREE *"With my Mind on my Money and my Money on my Mind" "Acting Dream"* Piece of Cake ride simply turned itself into. Especially on "his" soul's end. Oh boy. *"I got the Poison and the Remedy. I got the Pulsating Rhythmical remedy."* Oh yeah. Ha! And this as rather thrilling resonating arriving newsflash ABSOLUTELY unraveled itself within the following heartbeat as one of the MOST satisfying and radiating *"Now Moments"*, within this entire *"ongRowing" "NeverEnding"* hiStoryline thus far and therefore right away triggered *"little Linda"* to with a *"Rebel Yell"* SCREAM OUT aLOUD *"Shooting at the Walls of jUstice. BANG. BANG." LalaaAALAAAH! Hooray. Thank you SO MUUUHUCH"*, whilst my soul simultaneously with certainty began to glow even BRiGHTER than the in the URSa Minor constellation placed Northern Star on "her" end. YUP. That's right. Hallo Papi. LOVE. Which scenario therefore leaves my *"I'mPOSSiBLE"* knowing *"inner ARTreyu Warrioress"* ever since with "No Doubt" remain convinced, that this *"Self-*created" and with justice filled *"You must be my Lucky Star"* avalanche at flow, continuously will be delivering many further thrilling A-HA CLiCKiNG *"Everything happens for a Reason"* magic into mine and hopefully into every other denied involved soul's own *"Living on Earth Game"* reality. *"One way or Another."* Oh yeah. Though, in order that these countless Blessing in Disguise phenomena results find themselves being enabled to TRULY appear into one's awareness, it remains of utmost importance, to ALWAYS keep on applying the *"Heart over Head"* orchestrated *"Change the way you Look At Things and the Things you Look At Change"* key attitude formula. Inside. Out. Ha. See it? Abracadabra. BRAVO. Therefore, *"Don't stop Believin'. Hold on to Your Dreamin'."* No Matter what. *"Cuz the ONLY way is UP, my beloved Co-Traveler. For You and Me now."* Peace. LOVE. Gratitude. Now, as far as of the approach for these 14 remaining "Baby Boom" days at count, my inner voice kindly came to suggest for me to enhance this transitional phase with the 1) Preparation exercise for this, for the following Monday set *"The Artist's Way"* Week 1 launching adventure, with the 2) Look out mission of where to relocate *"little Linda's"* vessel *Next* and with the most important defined task, to 3) As consciously as possible enjoy these many "few" invaluable and enlightening, towards its end running One-on-One *"Living on Earth Game"* basic reminder sessions with this sweet Lady Bug's soul, by applying my newly gained awareness, that this absolute amazing and mind-blowing provided giving "birth" to another soul's vessel opportunity, with MOST certainty found itself meanwhile being switched into its THE One and Only status desire within this Linda Wartenweiler *"Living on Earth Game"* experience, which reality UPdate as its powerful *"Cause and eFFecT"* result, lastly I assume, succeeded in triggering my *Being Nice, Pleasing* and with *Helping Syndrome* infused *"inner Parent's"* craving to exclusively start taking care of this precious *"FuN Facts"* loving giggling *"little Linda"* as its fair *Next* priority compromise instead. Oh yeah! And therefore, this once as one of my bucket list last noted *Creating a family by giving birth to another soul and to therefore getting tied down to a possible part time home-stay mom reality or that sort of image* activity "yearning" with "No Doubt" found itself being satisfied, ticked off and instantly CLiCKed into its Been there. Done that. mode. Ufff. And. Hooray! ThanxOxO. Then, one week prior to my vessels *"Time to say Goodbye"* approaching moment, my soon *"wiLD & Free"* set *"inner ARTreyu Warrioress"* to be then happily felt Ready and Steady to invest her weekend available *"Time and Energy"* resources towards the thrilling attraction task of "our" *Next* perfect future *"Home Sweet Home"* base foundation to come. Sweet! Yes. Please. Let's. Well, and this mission from the get-GO succeeded in feeding my awareness with this wonderful eye-opening and somewhat liberating reality "truth", that *"little Linda's"*, once as utmost important Residing close to the Entertainment World defined game plan strategy, as part of all those many *"Don't Dream your Life. Live your THE Ultimate Childhood Dreams come True truth"* collected puzzle "peaces" in play, meanwhile found itself being transmuted into The Nothing as well and that therefore ANY place within this *"BiG Wide The Other Planet"* formation actually would be suiting my lethargic turned *"inner Artist"* just fine in order to put her focus back onto the materialization task of her many *"NeverEnding"* creative *"I'mPOSSiBLE"* appearing *"Living on Earth Game"* endeavors. Boom. That's right. *"All the World's* after all *a Stage"* and this with LOTS of "truth" filled statement of yours, Mister Shakespeare, *"little Linda"* finds herself for once with "No Doubt" agreeing and fully connecting with. Ha! And so it is. Based on my soul's most important two pre-determined *"Like Attracts Like"* longing criteria's of 1) Finding my *"Self"* a 100% able to *"ongRowingly"* as undisturbed and as peacefully as possible *"All or Nothing"* like dive right back into my dearly missed *"Finding back Home again"* oak tree vision mission again, by Doing Me EXCEPTiONALLY and this 2) Preferably somewhere down south in the warmer mid-February appearing *"Cali Dreamin'"* sun rays area for 4 weeks straight for starters in mind, I then once anew opened this way UPgraded "Craigslist" like Airbnb webpage on my genius MacBook Pro gadget and quickly started this exciting ANYTHiNG GOES for this temp *"Home Sweet Home"* hunting quest at hand, by furthermore passing the trust of *"little Linda's"* Next required whereabouts right back over into the hands of the all-knowing Universe's. YUP. It after all happens to obtain the perfect insights of my soul's actual destined rabbit hole master plan route and therefore iT shall remain as THE chosen and most trustworthy guiding force upon this entire *Red* pill unfolding storyline, placed within this Candyland of Spirituality platform. Three. Two. One. GO. *"The Choice is Yours."* With all the required, including desired selected search options at show, my hand then nonchalantly began its scrolling down south journey on the with many options appeared screen map, which undertaken action step then suddenly got interrupted by my inner voice's suggestion to adjust the entered monthly rental amount a "few" dollars UP. With a *"Thy Will is My Command"* attitude, I certainly right away did as told and found my *"Self"* within the following 68 seconds, with thrills and chills filled eying onto THE *Next* MUST DO delivered jackpot solution. Yeeha! Oh yeah, my dear *Co-Traveler*. Let me share with you, HOW mesmerized my soul immediately turned, the second that my eyeballs lay their sights on this rather magical Light & Zen Purple Door Cottage in *Oceanside* CA vibrating description, followed by its various, as absolutely PERFECT espied *"Dream come True"* heaven on earth like pictures. WOW. "Gone with the Wind" my soul once again certainly right away ended up being, by furthermore knowing, that this Instant Book CLiCKiNG undertaken activity with "No Doubt" just ended up bursting open a rather SpeCial doorway into a sphere that would allow for this entire newly opened *"TreasureWomBox"* adventure to take off in its magical, from the wonderful Universe already pre-planned, flow. Abracadabra. *"Gotch Ya'"*. *"Hip Hop Horray. Ho. Hey. Ho."* With this adjusted *"Living on Earth Game"* outlook in view, I then certainly found my impatient and curious fallen inner Gemini counting down the remaining few days, within my once anew soon as old *"Home Sweet Home"* considered base to be and very much so longing for this 2016 Valentine's Day to arrive. Yes. Well, and interestingly, we just happen to be coming across another EXACT on the date 1 year ago fairly important *Dot Connecting* launched key shifting *"Stepping-Stone"* closing cycle, which this time around introduces itself with my *"ongRowing"* Patience practicing soul's out of the blue on this within "her" vessel's then first moving in week for "self-*LOVE*" declared 2015 day, with a *"Rebel Yell"* announced *"ENOUGH was ENOUGH"* epiphany experience in regards of this absolutely disserving and annoying magical *"NeverEnding"* seemingly *"Enjoy the Silence"* *"Wait-a-While"* whatever at hand, followed by its then *"I've Got the Power"* triggered iMMEDiATE COMPLETE change of captain MUST DO undertaken strategy. HMMM. Interesting, right?! Well, and please allow for my soul to deliver you another *WELL* right here, at this very other morning arising story reciting *"Now Moment"* line, as LiTERALLY last night my e-mail inbox got fed with an incredible topic matching information flow, that on top of it all even allows for *"little Linda"* to continue sharing her many thus far experienced adventures with you right where my fingers left off at yesterday's *Interesting, right?!* comment. *WOW*, is all that I am catching my *"Self"* these days stating over all these countless and *"ongRowing"* experienced *"The Power of Words"* attracted "coincidences", ever since the launching journey of this incredible *"the DOiNG ME PROjECT"* Autobiography project on August 26th 2015. WOW. WOw. Wow. This magical, in 2007 first ever heard of "The Secret" *Law of Attraction* phenomena, of which a lovely, from *St. Petersburg* Russia originated NYC soul friend spontaneously decided to gift my vessel a DVD copy of hers as a MUST WATCH exercise, with "No Doubt" *"ongRowingly"* proofs itself to my awareness to, especially within this entire *Dot Connecting* journey at run, literally work truer than at times mind-blowing spot on, and these as almost unbelievable SpeCial eFFecTs interpreted *"Synchronicity par Excellence"* occasions then usually furthermore succeed, as it happens to occur right NOW, in almost convincing *"little Linda"* to actually truly believe that she is being part of her own "The *NeverEnding* Story" Movie reality shooting, just as demonstrated with Bastian in its original 1984 *"But it's Only a Story"* recording. HMMM. Anyway. Let's *"Keep on Movin' my Darling. Ooh ooh-ooh ooh."* This "matching" e-mail, that found its way into my mailbox in the early 12/12/2017 evening, to my surprise originates from my old lawyer's as Help Line indicated address and reveals in its opening sentence, that this Rebel with a Cause's office due to his passing will be closed. BoOM. BOAH. WHAT?! Exactly, my dear *Co-Traveler*. Are you experiencing what my soul is experiencing right now? First of all, the timing in our storyline simply appears as PERFECT in order to lastly wrap this *"NeverEnding"* old lawyer chapter UP with these rather bitter-sweet, almost Hollywood Movie like finishing news at display, and this even more so, as the two of us literally find ourselves about to dive into this *"ongRowing"*, with many soothing AHHH's filled *"TreasureWomBox"* adventure at run. WOW. Certainly, my heart and soul still find themselves rather busy in trying to grasp this, from my intuition ever since his arrested vessel's inflowing May notice eventual *"Cause and eFFecT"* anticipated "truth" factor reality outcome, including its rather shifting *"Everything happens for a Reason and this always at its Perfect time"* master game plan understanding at hand. Hmmm. Wow. Well, what I am finding my *"Self"* with certainty being convinced of is, that "his", once as very good hearted, sensitive and kind encountered "Imprisoned Soul" with "No Doubt" finds itself floating within a much HAPPiER, PEACEFUL and LOViNG space by now and that this *"With my Mind on my Money and my Money on my Mind"* inflicted *"Living on Earth Game"* hiStoryline definitely appears to *"little Linda"* once anew as THE best solution for everyone involved. YUP. And so it is. Which delivered "truth" factor on the bright end of things therefore leaves my soul as usual with the rather exciting knowledge, that this once as Rebel with a Cause identified "persona", instantaneously finds itself enabled to 1) Step back into our in January 2013 forged "Peace" of Cake green key attracting master plan vision, if desired, and to furthermore 2) Assist my *"inner ARTreyu Warrioress"*, alongside with her thus far amazing collected supporting troop of my beloved father's, Sniffy's, Regu's, all my four grand-parent's, the wonderful Universe and all the many other "over there" accumulated energy recourses, on her materializing quest of those various from *"little Linda"* UP onto this very *"Now Moment"* UPdated *"Don't Dream your Life.*

Live your THE Ultimate Childhood Dreams come True truth" itinerary at hand. YUP. Ha! That's right. And therefore, my soul officially invites "his", with meanwhile clarity filled rabbit hole master plan insight infused helping hand, back into our *"Living on Earth Game"* reality creation and this even more so, as "his" soul in our mid-November 2014 held phone conversation came to mention, that the Writing of a Book Plan B exercise once attracted the green key into one of his client's existence. Boah. Alrighty then. Let's keep on *"Rock 'n Rollin'!"* Welcome back dear Jason. Though, *"The Choice is Yours."* Please Rest in Peace. Blessings. Guided by one of *"little Linda's"* favorite, from the many via her daily inspiring Abraham-Hicks inflowing newsletter wisdom collected Law of Attraction *"Life Toolbox"* ingredient suggestions, that formulates itself with the *"Turn your Attention To the Desire. Think about Where you are Going and Never Mind where you have been. It Doesn't Matter"* "truth", the two of our souls now shall be diving right back into our closing *"EdgyBlackWombBox"* chapter, which realty re-creation action step actually furthermore happens to be calling in for another perfectly matching *"Time to say Goodbye"* moment exercise. Ha! Thrilled about this new key transformational Valentine's adventure Day at start, my driven *"inner ARTreyu Warrioress"* happily found herself filled with LOTS of, during her precious twice a day *"sHe, who looks iNside AWAKENS"* practiced TM morning routine gathered energy flow, jUMPing out of her bed knowing, that TODAY would be calling in another quite important with *"Truth AND Dare"* filled Stepping Outside of One's *"ComfortWombBoxZone"* milestone mark, which this time around literally would be leading down this *"wiLD & Free"* infused ultimate "risky" and as unknown identified *"Swimming DOWN ALONG my OWN truthful inner "Self-stDream" Red* life purpose and soul mission "Mulholland Drive" rabbit hole lane. Yeeha! Let's GO. As soon as my vessel found itself, after the packing completion task at around noon, once anew in the possession of a from Enterprise amazing Weekend SpeCial deals offered rental car, the with *"little Linda's"* usual salty water eye drops guided *"Letting go of Something that No Longer Serves One's Growth and Expansion"* instant arose as well and with it the 5 hugging gestures of my dear and generous ex-roommates of exactly 12 months. Bye-Bye. Be well. Thanks so much for everything. LOVE. After a first stop at my close by in August 2015 opened storage box facility, I then quickly made sure to truly gather everything required and desired along into this new *"Living on Earth Game"* chapter at start, so that *"little Linda"* and my *"inner Artist"* happily would be enabled to Do THEM as authentic and carefree as possible. Equipped with all the selected personal missed items, the many thus far valuable collected *"Life Toolbox"* ingredients, with this into my awareness fallen *"The Artist's Way"* treasure, the absolute convincing gained knowledge to ASAP leave any further Charlotte NC and delightful Housekeeping School Adventure related income opportunities to those souls that FULLY and authentically feel aligned with, including with *"little Linda's"* first and in its Been There. Done That. Not for Me. ticked Reality TV Actress trial, I then, with LOTS of curiosity of what's to come

Next started the engine of my car rental anew and off the ride took down south towards *San Diego* CA. Yeeha! *"Here we Go again with total Dedication."*

"So this is What "The Truth About self-Love" Feels Like. 'Cause I'm Feeling it. Oh yeah I'm Feeling it."
After a wonderful and VERY liberating experienced drive, my vessel then finally arrived about 2 ½ hours later, safe and sound in its even more so magical appeared and sent into temp Oceanside *"Home Sweet Home"* base, which *"Self-rEcreated"* *"Don't Dream your Life. Live your Dream."* TKB releasing like emerged key *"Now Moment"* as a matter of "fact" in retrospective ended up bringing along the ever since then *"ongRowingly"* experienced *"Living on Earth Game"* adventure instant, in which I lastly allowed for my soul, to faithfully and completely throw my *"Self"* right back into its once as exciting *"Work equals FuN"* detected *"Working by mySelf as my Own Boss"* placed, within the oh SO fulfilling *"Swimming DOWN ALONG my OWN truthful inner "Self-stDream"* reality creation flow, by additionally entirely honoring the within *"little Linda's"* US itinerary once detected *"The Exploration of this magical "The Other Planet" experience MUST be carried out on Your Own, as being on Your Own after all is part of your current "Living on Earth Game" agreement"* formula, which guidelines I diligently kept on practicing UP onto this very arising *"Now Moment"*. Boom. That's right! Then, whilst the very welcoming and most perfect attracted direct neighbor host found herself busy showing her paradise like created oasis to *"little Linda"*, I *"ongRowingly"* experienced my *"Self"* being absolutely pleased and grateful about the result of my soul's then achieved *"Like Attracts Like"* reflection status. Yay! This *"Dream come True"* like brand new renovated cottage Valentine's Day present to my own *"True little Self"*, that found itself being placed within palm trees, a variation of difFeRent flowers, a Bamboo wall, LOL, welcome back you old work space you, a hammock, two outdoor lounging areas, many bugs, birds, lizards, Buddha statues, succulents, silence and within an all day long vitamin D providing sun rays kissing attack opportunity, truly filled my entire vessel and aura UP with loving vibrations only. SMASH. AHHHH. Thank you, my beloved Universe. Thank you, for this amazing *"Everything you Desire lies on the Other Side of Resistance"* reward. Yeeha! As soon as I thereafter completed the unpacking and settling in task of my newly with an Abundance of privacy claimed and gained environment, the probably first two realization checks that HiT my awareness within a SNAP, introduced themselves with ONE the as incredible weird detected sensation, of suddenly everywhere espying all these various, from *"little Linda"* over time personal collected items, which included pictures of her beloved fluffy *"Red and White"* ex-roommate, THAT *"Dream Catchin'"* enhancing, on October 11th 2002 recorded NENA concert DVD, my in NYC started gemstone collection, including precious miniature Ganesh statue, books, the once gifted *"The Key to your Success is to KEEP your Dream in Focus and to have the Courage to do things Other's WON'T do"*

reminder card and a few more DVD's for instance, and with the observation, that TWO my brave on the Edge walking *"inner ARTreyu Warrioress"* available *"Energy"* resources actually mutated themselves into a much lower availability rate than all along assumed. Wow, my wonderful *Co-Traveler*. Into what an interesting and in a way fascinating *"Growth and Expansionary"* providing exercise this one year couch *"Home Sweet Home"* ride actually suddenly revealed itself as, by furthermore granting my awareness with the enhancing *"Life Toolbox"* ingredients of the actual *"Cause and eFFecT"* understanding, as of HOW much MORE any personal materialistic gathered objects actually are tied to each soul's own *"Living on Earth Game"* created "identity" and of the astounded results of an *"ongRowing"* to Strangers exposed chosen Lifestyle versus the one placed within an Abundance of privacy filled resources. Boah. Boah. BOAH. *"The Choice is Yours"*, right? Wink. *"Yeah, Oh Yeah, Oh Yeah."* With all these newly gathered insights at view, I then decided, to lastly direct all my regained focus on the from my soul's as THE most important declared ASAP reconnecting with my *"True and entirely abandoned little Self"* exercise, which as its MUST DO required success formula called in the further complete retreat practice of this as Linda Wartenweiler identified vessel from this once anew as *"Self*-deconstructive" established outer world reality creation as its very first *"Stepping-Stone"* to take. *"Thy Will is My Command."* OH YEAH. And that action step direction suited my *"Leave Me ALONE. Leave Me AlooHoHone"* screaming soul MORE than simply fine. HA! This immediate into motion put master plan strategy then allowed for my *"inner ARTreyu Warrioress"* to lastly direct all of her focus towards the *Next* pre-defined MUST DO tasks upon these first 4 *"wiLD & Free"* initiated *"TreasureWomBox"* weeks, which contained the 1) Complete dedication exercise of this very much so craved for *"Truth AND Dare"* infused *"Course in Discovering and Recovering Your Creative Self. A Spiritual Path to Higher Creativity"* state of floating experience, the 2) *"OngRowing"* allowance of this soothing, in Santa Barbara started lifestyle sneak peek habit of simply Doing Me from *"Moment-to-Moment"*, by within a SNAP granting my soul ANY appearing *"Heart over Head"* desired wishes, the 3) Proper approach of this still rather as important declared *"Like Attracts Like"* formula at run, which as its immediate adjusted action choice ingredient entitled the permission of SOLELY any as UPlifting identified vibrations into my sphere and to 4) Dedicate all the from my soul required quality *"Time and Energy"* resources with my own *"Self"*, so that this friendly inner voice would receive my fullest attention, during its *"NeverEnding"* and tireless undertaken guiding attempts in regards of the "proper" unfolding route of this from the magical Universe's pre-planned rabbit hole lane. BOOM. And therefore, the from my soul ever since October 11th 2014 desired and via some rather cool with twist and turns attracted *"sHe, who looks iNside AWAKENS"* MUST DO Transcendental Meditation practice, proofed itself UP onto this very arising *"Now Moment"*, to have been THE *Next* PERFECT additional extraordinary and truly unthought-of matching assisting tool, within this entire *"the DOiNG ME PROjECT"* project adventure at run. WOOHOO. Who would have thought. Ha! Well, and as your soul possibly just happened to have noticed for it*Self*, this mentioned October date actually appears to also mark the anniversary milestone of my Heroess' in 2002 recorded comeback concert DVD, plus my iPhone calendar on top of it all furthermore just revealed to my awareness as well, that this EXACT date even ends up representing my dear Sarah Friend's vessel's first waking UP experience, within its the night before sunny Cali *"Home Sweet Home"* originating Bay Area ignited replacing sphere action choice. BOAH. Weird. Though it's the "truth". Hmmm. Anyway, let's keep on *"Growing and Expanding"* with this interesting and to my soul as rather fascinating resonating *Dot Connection* exercise, as this following TM storyline for ONE ended up taking place EXACTLY 1 week after Danny's and Harry's "accidental" stranding appearance, including on the from the amazing Universe's two days later *"wiLD wiLD West"* Coast "test ride" provided *"PandoraWombBox"* escaping opportunity and furthermore TWO happens to be marking the on this wonderful Sarah Friend's vessel's yearly on September 14th celebrated *"Whoomp! There she is."* experience. HA! WOW. AbracadabrAHHH. Well, Let's GO. A few days prior, to this, to "her" soul as WooHOO knotted approaching calendar date, this dear here and there LiVE encountered Friend of *"little Linda's"* to my surprise out of the blue ended up expressing "her" wish to THEN spend a few hours in this book enthusiastic wired *"True inner Self's"* as very favorite stated *Barnes and Noble* store, if available. Absolutely thrilled about this honoring and always with sparkling magic filled catching UP opportunity on this SpeCial occasion of hers, my soul within a SNAP jUMPed aboard with a *"Thy Wish is my Command"* attitude and after some further *"Back, Back, Forth and Forth"* text messaging exchanges, the two of our vessels then on THAT particular day found themselves happily and coffee slurping sitting across one another on a, in the on the 3rd floor available Starbucks table, located at Union Square. HAPPY BiRTHDAY Friend. Then, at some point, during our countless with *"FuN Facts"* filled *"Living on Earth Game"* adventure UPdate exchanges, my brain suddenly felt the urge, to provide *"little Linda"* with the important *"Empty your Water and become Mindful towards your Friend again"* information flow, which valuable delivered hint therefore caused for my vessel to instantaneously excuse itself from the birthday gal for a tiny tad. As soon as this "business meeting" successfully got set in its completion status, I quickly started to make My Way back towards where my vessel just came from, as this intention abruptly got interrupted by some in white appearing *David Lynch* screaming letters, that happened to be printed on a dark blue covered book, placed on one of the many with reading material filled tables. What?? Boah! Trance-like, my vessel certainly instantaneously HAD to make its way straight to this newly espied jewel, found itself a few seconds later excitingly scanning through the many of this *"David Lynch Catching the Big Fish Meditation, Consciousness, And Creativity"* available pages, loved it, purchased it, told dear Sarah about it and started to read it right after the two of our souls parted. Boom. *"Caught Ya'."* Wink. A few days later, *"little Linda"* then found herself busy working on an all-day Monterone catering gig for a commercial shoot that brought along many downtime opportunities in order for my soul to "indulge" this newly delivered treasure, when all over sudden one of the male models approached my vessel with an *"Oh, you are reading David Lynch's new book? It's great. I read it too and actually just happen to have met him 2 weeks ago. He is such a great guy."* introduction line. WoaW! What?! This model for ONE came across this book as well and even more so TWO found himself able to meet *"little Linda's"* all-time Director Hero? WHAT?! OMG. How cool was that. Impressed and amazed about this soul's further shared storyline, "he" then quickly after came to mention, that one of those, to David Lynch's in 2005 "birthed" Foundation linked TRANsCEndental Meditation Centers, happened to be located a two blocks walking distance afar and that I might want to check it out once this work day would be finding its end. Ha! What? WhAT?! That close this prior online heard of *"Diving Within"* facility found itself being placed at? Well, of course the beloved Universe instantly anew succeeded, in catching my curious fallen inner Gemini's fullest attention with this *"Synchronicity par Excellence"* "coincidence" and to right away lead my fingers to ASAP begin their researching quest on this in Mid-Town situated TM Center via my precious silver black iPhone 5s device. Boom. Things from then on started to move fairly quickly and my soul during its the following week free attended introductory talk offer, found "herself" even MORE so convinced that THiS magical Trance term including and as absolute soothing and emPowering resonating *"sHe, who looks iNside AWAKENS"* meditation technique UPgrade, despite its as fairly hiGH interpreted tuition fee, needed to get explored *Next*. That's right. Quality after all always carries its OWN price tag and based on the many of my beloved mom's countless beneficial passed on *"Living on Earth Game"* teaching's, this theory thus far with "No Doubt" reliably kept on proofing its "worth" also with this then guided into *"Stepping-Stone"* at oHm. Yeeha! And. Thanks once again to all the many fantastic forces involved. LOVE. Now, this mentioned October 11th 2014 date therefore called in for ONE the first NYC disappearance day of my dear Sarah Friend's vessel, for which the wonderful Universe, as part of its pre-defined AutoBiography game plan unfolding storyline at run, apparently made sure of to TWO send my soul for "substitution" purposes onto "her" ever since then parallel seamlessly learned, adapted and diligently twice per day practiced TM journey. And this NO MATTER what. YUP. Expect for the, during my curious inner Gemini's on October 12th 2016, 10-days with LOTS of silence, "*Truth AND Dare*" filled Vipassana undertaken meditation retreat challenge at *TwentyNine Palms* CA, which happens to be situated on the northern side of the famous *"With or Without You"* Joshua Tree National Park. Smile. Well, and this additional, as rather mind-blowing perceived *"Growth and Expansionary"* triggered HAD TO *"Diving Within"* attracted experiment, certainly carries its own absolute unique and with SpeCial eFFecTs enhanced *hi*Storyline, within *"little Linda's"* many thus far taken on *"Living on Earth Game"* ventures, by furthermore enriching my awareness with the strong knowledge, that this absolute effortless and peaceful infused, from then EXACTLY 2 years ago "sent into" TRANsCEndental Meditation journey *"ongRowingly"* needed to be "iT". *"Yeah, Oh Yeah, Oh Yeah."* Yes, and these various, since then undertaken TM sessions thus far revealed themselves with "No Doubt" on many levels to have been THE most rewarding daily invested 44 minutes out of *"little Linda's"* precious available "Abundance of Time" gift resources and its countless, from my soul into "her" UP onto this very *"Now Moment"*, favorite four experienced "benefits" introduced themselves in the form of 1) The incredible, as predicted *"Catching the BiG Fish"* "secret" power tool ingredient in regards of my *"inner Artist's"* information gathering flow, within this *"ongRowing"* via *"The Artist's Way"* journey resurrected *"the DOiNG ME PROjECT"* project commitment, with the 2) Overall as radiant and UPlifting perceived metamorphosis phenomena of my UPdated inner and outer *"Self*-crated" existing worlds, with the 3) From the magical Universe's kind WOOHOO orchestrated *"Dream come True"* materialization reality check, that punctually for my soul's 3 years TM anniversary celebration milestone on October 13th 2017, enabled "her", thanks to a via some months prior within a TM session provided action step suggestion, to lastly for about 3 to 5 minutes *"Eye-to-Eye"* connect with the one placed within *"little Linda's"* all-time Director Hero's vessel, during a from "his" end VERY inspiring in Los Angeles organized and with LOTS of "Twin Peaks" filled Festival of Disruption weekend. WOOT. WOOT. And with the 4) From its get-GO very much so well-being enhancing detected *"Cause and eFFecT"* outcome, which my soul shortly into this newly taken on *"sHe, who looks OUTside DREAMS. sHe, who looks iNside AWAKENS."* game changer journey according to an on November 12th 2015 in an unexpected from the TM Social Media Director received e-mail, "Once Upon a Time" happened to have worded as a *"During the past 3 1/2 years I have been having a lot of anxieties, stress and I was all over the place mentally and emotionally. My health (body, mind and spirit) was suffering, I had eating problems and wasn't able to gain any weight. Now, 6 weeks into my TM practice I feel very peaceful, clear, zen-like, simply wonderful and I have noticed that I gained 4 pounds!!! All those results make me so happy and I feel inspired throughout my days. My energy level, focus and my joy in life have increased a lot! I can't wait to experience more and more beautifulness within the upcoming days, weeks, months, years. :)"* experience in its then TM technique undertaken survey, for which lines this friendly Social Media Director kindly found herself wondering if she could be using them for their Facebook and possibly also for their tm.org/blog pages. HA! Yes, of course she could and so did just I. LOVE. Abracadabra. One of the *"ongRowing"* and *"NeverEnding"* detected elements that my soul truly loves about this *Dot Connecting* exercise at play, certainly hiGHlights the "fact", that this kind soul, placed within this dear Sarah Friend's vessel, seems to have "unconsciously" guided my *"inner ARTreyu Warrioress"* towards ALL The Three MOST essential and fundamental required ingredients, which as a matter of "fact", ever since that metamorphosing 2016 Valentine's Day ended up enabling her to full on dive down this thrilling *Red* pill injected rabbit hole Matrix lane. BOOM. BOAH. WOW. And therefore, once again ThanXOXO from the bottom of my HEART for your amazing "divine" help dear Friend. Three definitely carries YOUR delightful charm. LOVE. PEACE. Blessings. One of the first rather powerful *Next* important MUST DO action step, that announced itself into my awareness within the then second *"The Artist's Way"* embarked week at count, ended up being with this rather strong inner desire to extend this *"Live Me ALONE. Live Me AlooHoHone"* retreat exercise of mine with the complete withdrawal gesture, from the overall as impersonal and somewhat as "surreal" perceived World of Social Media sphere and to instead direct these valuable connecting moments " *Visely"* towards those rather many neglected Swiss Confederate rooting souls, resulting from *"little Linda's"* magical SWiTZERLAND or *"Let the Games Begin"* gained ventures. Oh yeah. And from all the meanwhile in Abundance available virtual staying in touch invented options, my soul therefore with "No Doubt" came to pick this thrilling WhatsApp selection as its only "distraction" option aboard, as it for ONE happened to be THE number one choice for all these countless smartphone using vessels, placed within the Germanic speaking realm and as it for TWO simply offers every thus far imaginary way possible in order to *"wiLD & Freely"* stay in touch with one another, by sending text and voice messages, pictures, videos or with the performed action step to even connect in a "LiVE" dialed conversation *"With or Without You"* on the gadget screen. WOW. This current *"ongRowing"* rEvolutionary experienced reality UPdate, certainly differs quite a tad from those "ancient" Charlotte North Carolina pen and paper slash landline phone call days, right, my beloved *Co-Traveler*? LOL. Ufff. And. Thank Goodness. Within a short amount of time into this redirected, adjusted and limited "being social" picked UP habit, my somewhere "Lost in Translation" transmuted soul therefore happily came to experience HOW soothing this guided into reconnecting "doorway" with its rooting and dearly missed *"Home Sweet Home"* planet actually made "her" feel like, HOW all these FuN, supporting, well-meaning and "like-minded" One-on-One undertaken communication interaction "kisses" to my soul's surprise suddenly *"ongRowingly"* kept on resurrecting all these rather essential, apparently throughout the countless *"Self-*destructive" undertaken Big Apple bites into a dEEp slEEp fallen small apple Started Out As memory cells and HOW each virtual Swiss re-anchoring "traveling" adventure on top of it all succeeded in propelling this, on September 22nd 2015 very tight knotted bond with my own *"True little Self"* onto a new and moRE thrilling level. AbracadabrAHHH. STRiKE. Certainly, this newly adapted road map, upon this fantastic What's Next *"TreasureWomBox"* spectacle at run, very much so must have resonated with the all-time supportive Universe in its HiGHest notes, as it within the same first Oceanside settling in week strongly made sure of, to trigger my beloved mother's own Gemini infused soul during one of our *"NeverEnding"* Skype meetings of 6 hours, to offer her lastly giggling, relieved and happy radiating experienced "baby girl" an extended MUST DO 4 weeks recovery ride at this guided into Oasis, if available. BOAH.

What?! HELLOU?! A *"YES, YES, YES, I'd LOVE THAT"*, my soul with "No Doubt" right away started to scream out aLOUD and to further sparkle even moRE so, the second that my eyeballs espied on this so convenient Airbnb page, that these additional dates, besides of already 2 booked weekends, actually still happened to be available. WOOHOO. Strike. Yes. Let's! After a quick *"Back, Back, Forth and Forth"* text messaging interaction session with this super flexible and generous attracted host, I then thrilled, about this magical delivered present from the heavens, ended up being the "key" owner of this *"ongRowing" "You must be my Lucky Star"* materialized "peace" of paradise resident, until April 19th for sure. Boom. And this UPdated Reconnecting with my *"True* and entirely abandoned *little Self"* game plan strategy at hand, therefore right away succeeded, in filling this tired fallen Linda Wartenweiler vessel with many MORE electrifying and UPlifting vibrations and to equip my brave on the Edge walking *"inner ARTreyu Warrioress"* with the knowledge, that this adjusted outlook with guarantee furthermore introduced itself as THE most perfect platform in order for her to as eFFecTively and focused as possible dwell, within those 8 in solitude dedicated *"Course in Discovering and Recovering Your Creative Self. A Spiritual Path to Higher Creativity"* weeks to come. YAY. AHHH. Tausend Dank mein geliebtes Mami! Kisses. Alongside with all these *"Moment-to-Moment"*, from within and via the from kind Julia Cameron's powerful offered tasks and exercise guidance triggered inner adjustment action steps, I then Day in, Day out found my *"Self"* being busy with the then as luxurious perceived opportunity, to lastly and as UNDiSTURBED as it can be, launch the re-creational and authentic to this as Linda Wartenweiler designated soul's re-discovery journey, which magical ignited *"Swimming DOWN ALONG my OWN truthful inner "Self-stDream"* reality flow, soon presented itself with a daily practiced activity routine filled with LOTS of *Resting, Pondering, Reflecting, Being, Recovering, Digging even dEEpEr, Listening, Watching, Feeling, Understanding, Surrendering, Releasing, Adjusting, Creating, Shedding, Breathing, Doing, re-Building, re-Discovering, Becoming, Developing, Singing, Growing, Remembering, Expanding, re-Connecting, Healing, Dancing, Allowing, Laughing, Loving, Nurturing, Playing, Exploring, Forgiving, Rising, Starting, Indulging, Carrying* and, and, and whatever else *"little Linda's"* precious heart desired to experience *Next*. That's right. And just in time for the, in *"The Artist's Way"* week #4 assigned complete Reading Deprivation exercise, I then actually to my utmost satisfaction and surprise suddenly found my *"Self"*, in synchronicity to kind Julia Cameron's soul for this week added re-connecting with my lovely 7 years *"True little Self's"* vessel count intent, happily floating within the for it MOST suitable created reality sphere, which at a closer look rather astoundingly ended up resembling those as absolutely magical perceived *"This is how we did it"* Parkweg gang days. Wow! SNAP. You know, my dear *Co-Traveler*, those days in the 80ies, in which *"little Linda"* used to spend her in Abundance available *"Time and Energy"* resources with activities placed in nature with "real" human and animal vessels in its purest One-on-One interaction form possible and with very little technology distractions at hand. AHHH! How wonderful and alive this form of *"Finding back Home again"* awareness glimpse simply succeeded in making me feel. Jodeliuuuhuuu! This with rather powerful shifting instances packed #4 week, therefore in retrospective with "No Doubt" leaves *"little Linda's" "Head Cinema"* collection as her favorite of them all and with many soothing and with happiness infused *"Living on Earth Game"* adventures, of which the storyline of an unexpected and to my Linda Wartenweiler's soul quite unusual attracted new friend, during the 3rd morning of this, with an Abundance of inner and outer world provided awareness resources week, stands out the most. Oh yeah! As one of my UPdated daily developed morning rituals included the intake of a with various fruits, vegetables, superfoods and with protein powder packed breakfast smoothie, and this right after the completion of my *"sHe, who looks iNside AWAKENS."* TM practice, these meanwhile as amazing interpreted daily morning MUST DO *"The Artist's Way"* pages exercise and right after the pouring gesture of a freshly, from my soul as delicious and emPowering declared *"I'm sO. I'm sO. I'm sO. I'm sOOO. Addicted. No Drugs. No Alcohol. BUT Caffeine and Rock 'n Roll."* brewed *"Vise"* into a cup, I therefore as usual nonchalantly placed my vessel on this particular morning, at around 9am, on one of those to many sunrays exposed in front of this charming Light & Zen Purple Door Cottage wooden available steps and happily started to slurp on either beverage in a *"Back, Back, Forth and Forth"* loop, as suddenly a tinny creature out of nowhere decided to *speed* straight towards my legs. AAAH! Completely taken aback about this unanticipated *Fast* approach of this whatever little "thing" it was, my vessel instinctively reacted with a seated-UP jUMP, which *"Cause and eFFecT"* action step therefore immediately prompted this suddenly, as baby lizard identified object, to within the next arriving breath, swiftly turn around and to escape towards the bush that it happened to have appeared from, a few seconds ago. LOL. YES. And this with SpeCial eFFecTs enhanced spectacle most likely must have looked rather hysterical from the outside, as surely both of our souls almost scared one another to "death" by furthermore leaving each other with a hiGHer beating heart rate than usual. LOL. Accompanied by an awkward feeling over this first time ever baby lizard "attack" experience, I then happily finished these yummy two beverages at hand and as usual continued my travels through this wonderful day from *"Moment-to-Moment"*, though wondering, whether this "attacking" incidence happened to have stirred UP my soul more than this very property protective farmer's dog once did, back in the day. HA. Do you remember that storyline, my dear *Co-Traveler?* LOL. Then, as soon as I once anew placed my vessel on the usual for this breakfast ceremony designated wooden step on the following morning, my eyeballs actually to my surprise came to experience the almost exact same scenario from the day before, with the adjusted difFeRence though, that this baby lizard this time around decided to approach "his" new neighbor more cautiously. Giggle. Giggle. Giggle. That's right. Here "he" was again, which reality check certainly caused for *"little Linda"* to instantaneously notice some as uncomfortable identified vibrations to arise from within. Help?! What do you want?! During this apparently "curious" fallen baby's vessel's choice, in approaching mine in a much slower speed than the day before, "he" then about 6 feet in front of *"little Linda's"*, suddenly performed an abrupt stop, which kind granted halt therefore allowed for the two of our souls to at least for a tiny tad break the ice, before this cute little baby fella then decided, to "bravely" place "his", about 1 foot next to mine on the wooden step. AAAH. WHAT?! *"Hello?! Is it ME you're looking for?!"*, certainly appeared as my initial reaction within this somewhat as awkward perceived reality UPdate, whilst this innocent seemingly baby simply kept on taking my appearance in with a friendly *"Do the Thing that Keeps the Smile on your Faces"* attitude and this orchestrated by some *"ongRowing"* *"Back, Back, Forth and Forth"* head tilting movements, including some here and there loving released winking motions. Hmmm. And yes, this cute little fella by then definitely struck *"little Linda"* as a baby boy, which received information flow therefore within a snap caused for her to decide, that this charming soul simply HAD to be placed within a male considered vessel. Ha. Now, even though this newly discovered neighbor of mine seemed to be rather tame and friendly, my soul still remained feeling quite unsure of as of HOW to react, to behave and as of WHAT to think of this all. The "facts" of which I found my *"Self"* completely positive of though, for ONE turned out to be the awareness "truth", that this "brave" baby definitely dared to enter a little bit too close into my own considered space, that according to my thus far collected lizard information flow they TWO in general were supposed to be scared of human vessels and that THREE, this cute little fella very much so decided to *"All or Nothing"* like disregard this for "his" species programmed behavior trait. HMMM. Then, after a few more minutes into this rather interesting checking out spectacle at play, "he" then quickly jUMPed off the stairs again and disappeared right behind the same bush that his vessel happened to appear from, a few minutes ago. Bye-Bye. Now, since the as magical Three identified number always seems to carry its wonderful Charm, this storyline of course transformed itself into an even moRE spectacular level on the following morning and this the instant, that my hand pulled opened that Purple front door. HA. Ready? Yay! Now, guess what *"little Linda's"* eyeballs espied, the second that this in Abundance fresh outside available Oceanside morning breeze rushed UP her nostrils? YUP. "HiM". This apparently newly gained friend to my utmost surprise already happened to be hanging out on MY designated breakfast step and truly seemed to be quite eager to spend some moRE quality time with this 7 years *"True little Self"* of mine. Wow! Let me tell you, my beloved *Co-Traveler*, HOW flattered, honored and ecstatic "his" presence this time around succeeded in causing my *"wiLD & Free"* animal loving soul to vibrate. AHHH. "Curiously" and cautiously, I then slowly went ahead, placed my vessel right next to "his" on my usual spot, whilst *"little Linda"* *"ongRowingly"* kept on reassuring to this cute little fella's soul, that everything was well and that "he" happened to be welcomed here for as long as "he" wished for. Well, and now guess WHAT, WHAT, my wonderful *Co-Traveling* friend? To my even more so developed amazement, this absolute adorable blinking, head tilting and smiling baby lizard for ONE turned out to be EXTREMLY trusting and always nonchalantly continued remaining on "his" prior selected hanging out spot, whenever my vessel moved inside and back again and for TWO ended up blessing my presence for another 2 hours. BOAHHHH. Yes, and starting from that particular incidence on, this new "mysterious" gained breakfast "date" of mine, basically always already ended up appearing at the same selected spot, whenever my hand pulled open that Purple front door, on a with LOTS of sunrays filled 9am and *"ongRowingly"* kept on giving *"little Linda"* some wonderful company for a couple of hours. And this Day in. Day out. Yay. *"Coo-coo-cool. Yeah, yeah. This was SO cool."* Yes, and as this entire, as rather unusual detected friendship ended up resonating as a true "mystery" to my own *"Self"*, including to those few souls that mine shared this thrilling *"Living on Earth Game"* spectacle with, *"little Linda"* triggered by a further mutual David Lynch fascinated friend, into who's vessel she of course "accidentally" happened to be bumping into on this in 2017 with magic and inspiration filled attended Festival of Disruption event, then one day came to decide, to name this little fella "Mystery", as "he" simply happened to be one. At least to me. LOVE. Then, about 1 week into our bonding adventure, my friendly "date" suddenly decided to introduce my soul to two of his buddies or family members, this "fact" though shall remain in its own "mysterious" mode, which adorable, much larger and more according to their species programmed behavior traits brought along vessels, this 7 years *"True little Self"* of mine soon came to name "Brave" and "Curious", as "Brave" all along truly "bravely" tried hard to step over "his" skeptical mind and as "Curious" with "No Doubt" struck my soul as a REALLY "curious" lady, whenever "she" spotted my presence, starting from that then *"Now Moment"* on. LOL. Well, and since "Mystery" launched this with *"FuN Facts"* filled own species introduction game, my soul then, during a following Skype meeting with my dear and missed mom came to decide to take this bull by its horns as well by truly succeeding in introducing this VERY SpeCial gained friend to her over my MacBook Pro gadget. WHAT?! That's right. This is an absolute "TRUE Snapple Fact". LOL. "Mystery" to our both, within a human vessel wrapped souls Acted as if this once from Mister Jobs genius designed device would be the absolute MOST normal thing on earth for "him" to experience in front of "his" cute tiny face and to our both' amazement nonchalantly remained sitting on its selected spot, whilst lovely Heidi's soul kept on conversing with "his", all the way from her seat placed in Winterthur ZH, to which my always smiling friend decided, to respond with some usual adorable blinking and head tilting movements. BOAH! Right?! What a story indeed. Yes, and this is HOW my dear, on this *"Red and White"* flagged Swiss planet placed mom's vessel came to meet her baby girl's new "mysterious" gained friend from afar as well and HOW my own soul *"ongRowingly"* found it *"Self"* able to rekindle that further out of sight lost LOVE for the animal kingdom, for nature in general and even more so for precious *"little Linda"*. AHHH! Thank you. Thank you. Thank you. Well, and as this absolute fantastic existing *Law of Attraction* "truth" certainly reliably continuous to mirror all the many from my soul from *"Moment-to-Moment" "Self-*created" inner vibrations in its looping *"Like Attracts Like"* materialization reflection equation, I to my surprise OF COURSE about 2 months ago did attract another sweet and rather tame transformed lizard friend into my current inspirational *Encinitas* CA *"Home Sweet Home"* "nest" of exactly 12 months by now and this teenage grown lady "herself" decided at some point, to *"ongRowingly"* support *"little Linda"* with her sweet presence on an almost daily magical Cali sunny basis within this, *"The Artist's Way"* ending *"the DOiNG ME PROjECT"* project at run and therefore meanwhile came to carry its "Lizzie" identification code. Ahhh. One truly gotta love life and its *"NeverEnding"* "mystical" provided *"Now Moments"*, right?! *"Yeah, Oh Yeah, Oh Yeah."* Gratitude. A further, extreme powerful and ballgame changing accepted incidence, within this Reading Deprivation week at run, actually ended up occurring about 11 hours after *"little Linda's"* initial BooO awareness interaction with cute little "Mystery". HA. That's right! Very vividly and easily I do recall this particular with *"FuN Facts"* packed event onto my soul's *"Head Cinema"* screen, which opening Act found itself unfolding right after the intake of a delicious and with LOTS of *"Self-*love" seasoned cooked dinner, at around 8pm. Now, as my blOOming *"inner Artist"* and prospering *"little Linda"* still happened to be eager to create some additional *"Living on Earth Game"* adventures before calling it a night, I therefore found my eyeballs, after some pondering invested seconds of WHAT to experience *Next*, being lead onto THAT on my nightstand placed *"Dream Catchin'"* enhancing, on October 11th 2002 recorded NENA concert DVD, which *"Cause and eFFecT"* ignited discovery thankfully ended up triggering my soul's interest in watching it again. 10 absolute unforgettable, colorful and with chills and thrills packed *"Don't Dream your Life. Live your Dream." "Acting. Uncertainty. Complete Life Change."* years ultimately ended up cruising by my brave on the Edge walking *"inner ARTreyu Warrioress"*, ever since her One and Only in December 2005 in it engaged interaction, which reality check therefore with "No Doubt" let the timing interpretation of this *Next "Swimming DOWN ALONG my OWN truthful inner "Self-stDream"* guided into *"Stepping-Stone"* exercise appear as simply excellent, as its impact last time after all resulted in the magical outcome of getting the ball for *"little Linda's" "NeverEnding" "Childhood Acting Dream"* desire rolling. That's right. And therefore, my curious turned inner Gemini certainly right away felt Ready Steady Go in order to dive into a new reconnecting adventure with this as well out of sight lost first female inspirational encountered soul of mine. What?! U2? pOops. Who and What else?! Hmmm. Though before this action step found itself being set into its materialized *"Rock 'n Rollin'"* mode, my dutiful Swiss rooted soul with "No Doubt" first needed to check in with dear "Julia Cameron" if watching Music happened to be an "allowed" task for *"little Linda"* to perform during this with SpeCial eFFecTs filled week 4 and shortly found my *"Self"* rather excited about "her" green delivered light, stated within the outer storytelling consumption defined guidelines. Yeeha! Alrighty then. Let's have some REAL FuN for a change, as its last memory recoding after all dated a couple of years back. What? A couple of YEARS? OMG. *"Seriously?!?"* Yes, and this incident then furthermore succeeded in feeding my awareness with this rather irritating realization "truth", that basically all those, from my soul "Once Upon A Time" as wonderful and thrilling identified *"Watching Movies and TV shows, enjoying Music, Dancing and Celebrating this "Living on Earth Game" adventure of mine as often as possible"* packed *"Super Happy Comfort Zone"* providing *"FuN Fact"* activities, actually somewhere down this sizzling US-Swiss Linda metamorphosis invention path, gradually transmuted themselves into The Nothing as well. UFFF. Boah! This eager *"All or Nothing" "Swimming UP AGAiNST my OWN truthful inner "Self-stDream"* tactic clearly once anew revealed itself to have taken its magical toll on this topic as well, which reality check therefore within a SNAP caused for my brave on the Edge walking *"inner ARTreyu Warrioress"* to scream out aLOUD *"I want it ALL. I want it BACK. And I want it NOW!"* YEAH. With this newly infused attitude, my vessel then quickly made its way to the nightstand, grabbed this "dusty" turned DVD out of its cover, slipped it into the for it designated slot on my reliable MacBook Pro companion, connected the brought along with external *"Boom. BOOm. BOOM."* LOUDspeakers to it, lit UP some candles, switched off all the lights within this cozy transmuted cottage, released some water, took a DEEP breath, hit the Play button and off my soul took within this recreational The Red Room and The Dark Room rocket, towards its *"Not even the Sky is the Limit"* destination. Yeeha! That's right! *"Hilfe. Rette mich. Bitte Hilf mir so wie früher. Rette mich./Help. Rescue me. Please Assist me as you did prior. Rescue me."* LOL. After a hilarious opening Act of two rather FuNNy German standUP comedians, followed by a short and crisp introduction speech of NENA's loving sister, the LONG overdue reconnecting *"Now Moment"*, with *"little Linda's"* thus far MOST influential experienced soul upon her *"Don't Dream your Life. Live your THE Ultimate Childhood Dream Catchin'"* quest at run, then finally arose. WOW. And let me share with you, my delightful *Co-Traveler*, this experienced second, in which my recovering Linda Wartenweiler soul found "herself" so unexpectedly, after a break of 9 looong years, being exposed to 1) This, in its then 42 years count recorded and always with pure LOVE and LiGHT filled AKA Gabriele Susanne Kerner vessel, which number as part of our *Dot Connecting* exercise btw as an OF COURSE identified awareness "truth" fact, meanwhile magically happens to be matching my own measured traveling duration timeline right NOW. What?! YUP. *"Synchronicity par Excellence."* LOL. Including to 2) *"little Linda's"* own *"NeverEnding"* to this DVD knotted *"Dream Catchin'" "Living on Earth Game"* hiStoryline recordings, truly seemed to have been all that it needed in order for this further dEEp slumbering and in retrospective as rather essential required *"Finding back Home again"* rewiring puzzle "peace" button, to immediately switch itself back into its thriving ON mode again. CLiCK. WOOHOO. Ha. This from the magical Universe and from kind Julia Cameron's soul mutually orchestrated reconnecting exercise, truly transformed itself into a new *"Hit me with your Best Shot"* adventure, though with the this time experienced outcome of finding my *"Self"* directly thrown onto a wonderful and with thrills and chills filled emotional *"Super Happy Comfort Zone"* rollercoaster ride, which undertaken action step then *"ongRowingly"* rewarded *"little Linda"* with this spectacular opportunity to, for the first time within this *"wiLD wiLD West"* Coast formation at run, from *"Moment-to-Moment"* capture a sudden from within emerged avalanche attack, packed with solely HiGH vibrating *"Now Moments"* for her *"ongRowing" "Living on Earth Game"* memoir collection. BOOM. AHHH. LOVE. Once the DVD recording, after a spectacular interaction adventure, filled with *Dancing, Singing, Weeping, Laughing, Sparkling, Remembering* and LOTS of *Nose Blowing* activities of over 2 hours straight, once again found its magical and emPowering end, I then to my utmost satisfaction came to notice, that my soul for ONE found "herself" floating within this as OH SO incredible peaceful, lovely, *"wiLD & Free"* perceived state of being, that TWO *"little Linda's"* entire vessel kept on vibrating in its HiGHEST *"Super Happy Comfort Zone"* tunes possible and that THREE my LOVE for these neglected and with FuN packed *"Enjoying Music, Dancing and Celebrating this "Living on Earth Game" adventure of mine as often as possible"* activities successfully got unlocked as well. Yay! *"Sesame Opened."* Mission *"I'M POSSiBLE"* completed. *"Hip Hop Horray. Ho. Hey. Ho."* Absolutely ecstatic about all these spontaneous soothing *"Self-created" "Cause and eFFecT"* achievements, resulting out of this Next *"Swimming DOWN ALONG my OWN truthful inner "Self-stDream"* guided into *"Stepping-Stone"* exercise, I then happily found my *"Self"* more than Ready to end this glorious and with "Mystery" filled Wednesday and therefore shortly after allowed for my soul to fall ab*zZZ* in heavenly peace. Nite. Nite. As soon as the first few bright, from the rising sun released rays succeeded in causing for my soul to open its "windows" again, I happily right away came to notice, that this NENA infusion from a few hours ago, reliably succeeded in refilling my cup *"ongRowingly"* with LOTS of *Love, Joy, Confidence, iNspiration, Courage* and *Determination*, that my brave on the Edge walking *"inner ARTreyu Warrioress"* suddenly felt an even stronger urge to discover moRE about this with SpeCial eFFecTs packed *"Course in Discovering and Recovering Your Creative Self. A Spiritual Path to Higher Creativity"* session at run and that this rather pleasant reality shift left *"little Linda"* to with a *"Rebel Yell, Cry For more, More, MORE. AaoW!"* Oh my. LOL. That's right. Driven by this newly injected NENA virus, I then quickly started this very promising day ahead with my soul's sacred established MUST DO morning ritual and found my *"Self"*, right after *"little Linda's"* second "mysterious" interaction spectacle, excitedly Ready Steady to lastly jUMP onto a catching UP adventure session in regards of all the many, from this out of sight lost Heroess' own, within these past with whirlwind infused years created *"Living on Earth Game"* Doings. YAY. Let's GO.

YouTube therefore right away invited itself as The One and Only Reading Deprivation based solution at hand, which absolute as comfortable perceived rEvolutionary information gathering tool within a SNAP even more so succeeded, in feeding my *"ongRowing"* HiGH vibrating vessel with further thrills and chills filled *"Now Moments"*. Jodeliuuuhuuu! Yes, this iNspiring attracted Remedy with "No Doubt" hit my soul's spot within a further SLAP and hooked *"little Linda"* once anew was. HA. *"Gotch Ya'."* Yeeha! As soon as I found my *"Self"* equipped with a first UPdated impression, of this meanwhile into a mid-50ies transmuted with LOVE and LiGHT radiating *"99 Red Balloons"* chick's vessel, I then as a *Next* step happily decided to follow through with the further genius, from my inner voice provided *"All or Nothing"* game plan move, that required for *"little Linda"* to One-by-One listen to EVERY, within her iTunes over those many decades passionately No Matter What UPdated, almost 180 collected and entirely neglected wisely composed NENA tunes. Boom. *"Thy Will is My Command."* After an even further powerful re-bonding adventure ride of another 2 days straight with this to my soul as wonderful, UPlifting and as extremely iNspiring resonating friend-like individual, I to my utmost satisfaction, found my brave on the Edge walking *"inner ARTreyu Warrioress"* happily equipped with all the from her end *Next* required How to *Start Anew*. How to *Step Over One's Fears*. How to *Stay Positive*. And with some further exciting How to *Do Me* gathered *"Life Toolbox"* tips and tricks ingredients, that allowed for her to *"Swim DOWN ALONG my OWN truthful inner "Self-stDream"* path with even more *Passion, Clarity* and *Determination*. Yeeha! *"When the Student is Ready, the Teacher will Appear."* And so it is. ALWAYS. ThanXOXO, once again liebste NENA! LOVE. And. Blessings. With all those many delightful and encouraging shifted vibrations within my outlook, I then diligently continued my travels with the set intention, to for ONE direct my entire focus on the proper and truthful to my Linda Wartenweiler soul vibrating own inner and outer world implementation interpretation action steps, in regards of these countless useful from my Heroess' gathered *"Living on Earth Game"* enhancing remedy reminders and on the rekindled *"Cause and eFFecT"* equation desire of my to its re*Booting* *"True little Self"* traveling soul to for TWO as a *Next* defined MUST DO quest get these once so passionately developed and meanwhile disappeared *"hiStorical"* HiGH vibrating and *"NeverEnding"* GiggIE GiGgle GiGGLE attack trademark back into the game plan as well. Ha! That's right. Well, and in doing so, *"little Linda"* then *"ongRowingly"* kept on deciding, to trustingly set all the inflowing inner voice's suggestions into motion, which *"Heart over Head"* undertaken *"Stepping-Stone"* choices then, especially during this incredible week #4 at play, succeeded in launching this with SpeCial eFFecTs and *"FuN Facts"* loaded Time Machine right *"Back to the 80ies"*, in which sphere she with LOTS of jOY instantaneously came across the many of those in Aqua's in 2009 further "sung" *"You will Always be our Superstars"* reality check, which spectacular journey then eventually led my way back to Master Bruce Lee's many still as mind-blowing and as mesmerizing resonating *"Oo-WAH"* vessel movement skill recordings and to the creation of some further new thrilling and suddenly with enormous *"Life Toolbox"* wisdom detected "The *NeverEnding* Story" adventures with *"little Linda's"* beloved "playmates", known as *Fearless Atreyu, Luck Dragon Fuchur/Falkor, Bastian* and with heart beat beat riSiNG *LimahAhAhAhl*. ABRACADABRA. Yup. And as the amazing Universe with certainty must have found itself once anew rather satisfied with the unfolding course of this thus far fully committed *"wiLD & Free"* infused ultimate "risky" and as unknown identified *"Swimming DOWN ALONG my OWN truthful inner "Self-stDream" Red* life purpose and soul mission "Mulholland Drive" rabbit hole lane at play, it therefore EXACTLY 8 days after the completion of the from "iT" guided into *"This Is What The Truth Feels Like"* Gwen reconnection exercise at the Channel 933 Summer Kick Off 2016 Music Festival and/or 1 week prior to my vessel's yearly *"Whoomp! There she is"* celebrations, decided to bless my overall *"The Artist's Way"* Doing Me committed achievements with THE to my soul as absolute most ULTiMATE *"Ask and You shall Receive at its PERFCT Time"* infused *Law of Attraction* newsflash possible. Yeeha! Are you Ready for this last *"Synchronicity par Excellence"* "miracle" to come, my wonderful *Co-Traveler*? Let's *"Simply safe THE BEST"* for last. HA. WOOHOO. Alrighty. *"Here we Go again with total Dedication."* On this particular further game change shifting May 21st 2016 early PM Saturday afternoon, I remember how my still quite high on *"Coo-coo-cool. Yeah, yeah.* Gwen Stefani *SHE truly is SO cool"* vibrating soul, during one of "her" here and there screen checking undertaken action choices on this incredible invented silver black iPhone 5s device came to detect a rather as rare considered WhatsApp notification alert, resulting from this dear, WAY earlier introduced first Monterone-Industria ex-coworker, NYFA and air mattress offering LA-LA-Hollywood-Land residing friend. With LOTS of curiosity, my inner Gemini therefore swiftly went ahead, nonchalantly opened its content and found herself within a SNAP being exposed to the, as complete surreal and as mind-blowing resonating *"Hallo Linda, wie geht es Dir?!? Still happy where you're at?!? I have a message from Winten Jo, you know the French guy, who knows your hometown: Nena will be in concert October 2nd in LA (Regent Theater)!! Hope you are well well well!!!! Miss you!!!"* composed information flow. *"WHAM. BAM." "Gotch Ya'."* Again. Boom. Indeed. And this newly attracted spontaneous *"Now Moment"* mirroring reflection inventory exercise of my soul's thus far entire inner and outer, throughout this *"ongRowing"* spectacular developing *What's Next "TreasureWomBox"* chapter at run undertaken metamorphosis achievements, then right away caused for my disbelieving *"Self"* to release a LOUD *"Oo-WAHHHwHAT?!?! My NENA will be appearing in the City filled with Angels in October? NO FREAKiN' WAY!! That's "I'mPOSSiBLE"!"* vibrating reaction in public. That's right, my beloved *Co-Traveler*. LOL. That's right. Well, and as this with *"Dream come True"* loaded message succeeded in *"Hitting"* my awareness with another perfectly placed *"Best Shot"*, I therefore for "security" reasons instantaneously went ahead, re-read its content one more time, in order to truly ensure that my brain cells translated these letters accordingly, which activity then to my excitement once again ended up leaving my reality with the EXACT same *"Nena will be in concert October 2nd in LA (Regent Theater)"* outcome. O.M.G!!! This is iNCREDiBLE. This iS iNCREDiBLE. THiS iS FREAKiN' iNCREDiBLE! Oh. My. GOD!!! Within the following second, I then immediately performed an abrupt HALT on everything that *"little Linda"* happened to be enjoying in that very appeared *Solana Beach* CA *"Now Moment"* and instead allowed for my nervously turned thumbs to as quick as a bunny dance over the entire screen of my precious Apple gadget, in order to ASAP secure MY oh SOOOOOO longed for *Next* on the horizon glowing NENA LiVE interaction *"Open Sesame"* key. LET'S GO. As soon as my eyeballs shortly after successfully came to espy the on this amazing Google web browser exposed Find Tickets option, I then as part of the *"One Thing ALWAYS leads to Another in its magical Cause and eFFecT unfolding truth"* equation, furthermore came to witness HOW my right-hand thumb quickly decided to Trance-like HiT this sizzling discovered "button" and HOW *"little Linda"* whilst doing so, instantaneously found herself over the "fact", that she had been given an unusual selection of 3 Various Ticket Choices, being transported into an even moRE with thrills and chills infused Fata Morgana resembling state of awareness check. WOAW. Wait! What?! They are giving me 3 options? Wow. Well, that's truly something new. Yes, and this as EXTREME uncommon detected offer for ONE certainly right away succeeded, in filling my entire vessel with even many *"more, More, MORE. AaoW!"* curious appeared vibrations, as *"little Linda"* for those prior 7 with LOVE, FuN and iNspiration packed NENA attended events, happened to be blessed with the General Admission opportunity as its One and Only Way In selection and to then TWO shoot my entire soul right UP towards this *"Not even the Sky is the Limit"* existing realm, the second that I came across, the from the incredible Universe extended ViP and ViP Meet & Greet cherry on top delivered *"The Choice is Yours"* SURPRiSE. WOWOWOWOAH. HOLD on. WHAT?! Did I just read Meet & Greet?!? WoAoW. Do they mean, Meet & Greet in the sense of finding my *"Self"* being enabled to encounter *"little Linda's"* all-time and recently re-bonded Heroess on an actual REAL time One-on-One close UP experience? NO WAY. HOLLY MOLLY! You've GOT to be KiDDiN' ME!! This entire *"Don't Dream your Life. Live your THE Ultimate Childhood Dreams come True truth"* storyline truly is getting better and better by the millisecond. BAOH! Yes, indeed. And as you most possibly can imagine for your*Self*, my wonderful *Co-Traveler*, my entire Linda Wartenweiler identified soul by then with "No Doubt" entirely LOST iT and therefore first felt the urge to invest some further emerging *"Now Moments"* with the grasping task of this ULTiMATE out of the blue from the heavens provided *"Dream come True"* materialization opportunity at CLiCK, before this absolute precious and with MaGiC sparkling ViP Meet & Greet key found itself safe and sound being placed within my online pocket. YEEHA! Dear NENA, here I come! *"Coo-coo-cool. Yeah, yeah. This is SO COOL."* That's right. And that newly *"Self-*created" *"Living on Earth Game"* reality SLAP then as its *Next* action step furthermore succeeded in welcoming my eager *"Truth AND Dare"* walking *"inner ARTreyu Warrioress"* with the inflowing awareness UPdate, that 1) This LONG, dry and *"NeverEnding"* NENA re-encounter *"Wait-a-While"* experienced period of 9 colorful years, lastly in 4 ½ months, would be facing its oh so dearly aimed for Happy Ending ceremony as well, which occasion then 2) Finally would allow for my *"wiLD & Free"* vibrating soul, to enjoy "her" thus far BiGGEST influential *"Don't Dream your Life. Live your Dream."* MUST DO iNspiration out of my meanwhile own *"inner The Artist's Way"* resurrected perspective and this all during this *"99 Red Balloons"* chick's vessel's FiRST, within this *"The Other Planet"* formation EVER announced mini-tour appearance, which with SpeCial eFFecTs loaded *"Living on Earth Game"* adventure then magically would be finding its closing Act with *"little Linda's"* second, over one decade ago strongly sent out "spell", that 3) ONE DAY in the future, my Linda Wartenweiler vessel would be granted the opportunity to thank this even MORE influential Germanic considered soul *"Eye-to-Eye"* for "her" unconscious kind *Help, Guidance* and *iNspiration* as well. WOOHOO. TatAAA! And *"Whoomp! There it is."* YAY! Once this crisp *"Self-*created", with LOTS of ecstatic mind-blowing *"Thoughts become Things"* vibrations packed *"Ask and You shall Receive at its PERFCT Time"* avalanche attack found itself throughout the following few days slowly and thrillingly sinking *"more, More, MORE. AaoW!"* into my awareness, it then suddenly dawned on me, that my vessel actually found itself EXACTLY being placed, where it all-along was supposed to be and that this incredible in January, from my unimpressed and determined *"Keep on Movin'* forward my Darling. Ooh ooh-ooh ooh."* on the Edge walking *"inner ARTreyu Warrioress'"* chosen *"Follow your Hearts Desires. It will Lead you Towards your Destiny"* trusted MUST DO *"Stepping-Stone"* direction, therefore clearly led my travels straight towards *"little Linda's"* at that particular *"Now Moment"*, as MOST rewarding and emPowering interpreted *"Everything you Desire lies on the Other Side of Resistance" "TreasureWomBox"* jackpot possible. YUP. Which "truth" factor then, as its *Next* move on this spectacular chess board at play succeeded, in triggering this, from my inner voice a few weeks prior provided MUST DO suggestion into my *"Head Cinema"* screen, in which I witnessed, how my recovering *"inner Artist"* noted down the from "iT" kindly genius provided *"Send Copy to NENA!!"* advice into her by then reanimated *"the DOiNG ME PROjECT"* booklet. BOOM. WOW. Yes. WOW. And with all these thus far ULTiMATE ECSTATiC and with sizzling twists and turns spiked collected *Dot Connecting* puzzle "peaces" at view, I then instantaneously came to experience a further incredible awareness shift, in which this precious *"Dream come True"* materialization opportunity at reach, within a SLAP transformed itself into THE *Next "The Eye of the Tiger"* MUST DO urgency mission to focus upon. ASAP. That's right. Almost 4 months my on the Edge walking *"inner ARTreyu Warrioress"* therefore had available to get this meanwhile, slowly picked up, very *"Last Resort"* MUST DO *OWN Project and Opportunity* Autobiography *creation* back on its committed track, so that my thriving *"inner Artist"* and exhilarated *"little Linda"* on October 2nd 2016, as happy as a bunny would be finding them*Selves* being enabled, to actually HAND this with NENA infused Doing Me "baby", as part of the envisioned *"Danke Schön"* gesture, into the palms of this with LOVE and LiGHT glowing Germanic vessel. *"WHAM. BAM."* YEAH. LET'S. Certainly, this meanwhile new *"Whatever the Mind can Conceive and Believe it can Achieve"* collected *"Life Toolbox"* ingredient at play, then right away convinced my soul to ONE fire this tedious and still bzZZ lingering around *"Self-sabotaging"* Queen *Madam ProCrastination* a few seconds ago already from her marvelous tricky DOiNGS and to TWO instead grab this with *"Own Opportunity Creating"* screaming bull by its serious horns. Ha! And so I naturally did. *"Yeah, Oh Yeah, Oh Yeah."* And that is HOW this emPowering Heroess of mine in retrospective once anew unknowingly succeeded, in fueling my soul's engine with the EXACT required *Will-Power, Thrive, Determination* and *Urgency* mixture, upon this to "her" as SO essential *"Don't Dream your Life. Live your THE Ultimate Childhood Dreams come True truth"* path linked *"Where there is a Will there ALWAYS is a Way. 'Cause wherever there is a Way iN, there ALWAYS MUST exist minimum ONE Way OUT"* vibrating proActivity key resolution, which result meanwhile finds itself being safe and sound placed within your own two palms right NOW. HA. And HOW my *"little Linda"* soul with this unique, throughout magical NENA's *"ongRowing"*, almost 4 decades ago entered *"Swimming DOWN ALONG her OWN truthful inner "Self-stDream"* chosen path FiRST EVER planned SF, LA and NYC "99 Luftballons Over America" mini-tour, accompanied by its incredible *"Timing per Excellence"* matching orchestrated reality check upon my own spectacular entered What's Next *"TreasureWomBox"* *"Living on Earth Game"* adventure creations timeline at run, came to decipher the SO encouraging, from the wonderful Universe this time delivered message with a crystal clear *"All is Good. All is Well. Keep on Doing what you have been Doing. You are SO on YOUR way."* translation. STRiKE! Yeeha! *"Wunder Gescheh'n. Ich hab's soeben auch Geseh'n./Miracles DO happen. I've just witnessed it for mySelf."* And so it is. *"Moment-to-Moment"*. Day in. Day out. LOVE. Well, and as you most certainly can imagine for your*Self*, my delightful *Co-Traveling Soul*, this *"NeverEnding"* *"Self*-created" surreal *"Now Moment"* materialization duration over approximately 3 to 4 minutes, in which my soul as envisioned found "herself" being enabled to lastly *"Eye-to-Eye"* express all "her" gratitude to this dearly and oh SO influential gained Heroess's guidance upon *"little Linda's"* own *"Don't Dream your Life. Live your THE Ultimate Childhood Dreams come True truth"* chosen path at run, followed by its as ultimate marvelous perceived HANDiNG Over gesture, of this then in its *"ongRowing"* baby shoes expanding, almost completed 2nd *"the DOiNG ME PROjECT"* SpeCial NENA Edition labeled project, into the palms of this VERY appreciative and with LOTS of LOVE, jOY, CURiOSiTY and LiGHT dazzling vessel, transformed itself into one of *"little Linda's"* MOST precious and with many *"more, More, MORE. AaoW!"* infused experienced *"Living on Earth Game"* adventure recordings thus far. OH YEAH! And therefore, my soul once anew feels a tremendous urge

to SHOUT OUT a HUGE *"DANKE SCHöN"* to everyone involved in this EXTRAORDiNARY encountered *"Like Attracts Like" hi*Storyline materialization jackpot, as this incredible experience on top of it all even allowed for my then still rather battling *"inner Artist"*, to for the first time actually get in touch with many appreciative vibrations towards this FREE, in 2013 undertaken *"Acting Dream"* Piece of Cake melting away "disaster", as *"Without"* it, this marvelous Blessing in Disguise wrapped ViP Meet & Greet interAction package would have taken its course in a MUCH LESS impActing and in a more "ordinary" considered manner. OH YEAH! A 100%. And so my soul actually happened to once anew have come across the EXACT same with SpeCial eFFecTs enhanced Déjà Vu realization phenomena, during *"little Linda's"* latest, from the wonderful Universe absolute smoothly guided into *"The Owls are NOT what they Seem" "Dream come True"* proActivity venture. BooM. *"Change the way you Look At Things and the Things you Look At Change."* Always. Abracadabra. LOVE. BLESSiNGS. YEEHA. Now, as the magical Universe must have found itself rather pleased about the overall progress of my, on *"The Artist's Way"* traveling soul, it therefore right after my vessel's essential and remarkable *"sHe, who looks OUTside DREAMS. sHe, who looks iNside AWAKENS."* completed Vipassana retreat journey decided, to lead my attention during one of *"little Linda's"* beloved *"Growth and Expansion"* providing Google researching undertaken action steps onto this further with magic infused information flow, that the in the City filled with Angels situated Microsoft Theater on January 28th 2017, would be hosting a as "80's Weekend #3" titled LiVE Music event, for which occasion the organizers therefore succeeded in booking some of those Entertaining vessels that *"little Linda"* "Once Upon a Time" first came across throughout her then countless as sacred MUST DO declared entered Formel Eins, BRAVO and Hitparade interAction sessions. HA! *"Do you Remember the Time"*, when I first embarked onto this with my own Music Taste infused discovery quest? Smile. Well, my lovely *Co-Traveler*, now once anew guess, WHO my *"inner Artist"*, besides ABC, Howard Jones and Spandau Ballet's Tony Hadley, came to enjoy during this further spectacular with thrills and chills embarked Time Machine zoOMing excursion? HA. That's right. Missiz NENA. For the third time. Within 11 months. BOAH. What?! Exactly. *"All or Nothing"*, right? LOL. And certainly, this *"You will Always be our Superstars"* guided into *"Super Happy Comfort Zone"* transmuting Microsoft Theater event, reliably ended up working its magical spell onto my soul, as this wonderful with *"FuN Facts"* filled *"Enjoying Music, Dancing and Celebrating this "Living on Earth Game" adventure of mine as often as possible"* "bug" with "No Doubt" found itself thereafter being UP to *spEED* again, of which newly detected *"Finding back Home again"* recovery symptom the incredible Universe swiftly made sure of, that my brave on the Edge walking *"inner ARTreyu Warrioress" "ongRowingly"* found herself being enabled to nurture this essential achieved reanimation *"Stepping-Stone"* into an even hiGHER vibrating level, by therefore instantaneously providing exhilarated *"little Linda"* with many *"more,*

More, MORE. AaoW!" rewarding *"Back to the 80ies"* beaming *"inner Artist Date"* opportunities throughout the course of the following 9, with LOTS of *"the DOiNG ME PROjECT"* project invested *"Time and Energy"* resources filled months. Yeeha! *"Yeah, Oh Yeah, Oh Yeah."* And this incredible motivating, iNspiring and with TONS of *"Work* equals *FuN"* infused accepted What's Next *"TreasureWomBox"* 2017 itinerary, ended up containing a spectacular lineUP packed with sizzling and from *"little Linda"* as oh so *"You must be my Lucky Star"* declared retro tunes infusion, resulting from souls identified as 1) *Lisa Lisa, Stevie B, Arrested Development* and *"Hip Hop Horray. Ho. Hey. Ho." Naughty by Nature* at a in *Long Beach* CA organized Freestyle Festival for starters, followed by 2) *Bryan Adams*, 3) *"little Linda's"*, throughout her teenage days third collected star love *Jordan Knight*, whose still quite attractive vessel possibly might be better known to you as the leading voice of this then from my *"Self"* SOOO MUCH adored *"Step-by-Step. Oh baby." New Kids On The Block* boy band formation, which evening on top of it all even offered this fantastic opportunity, to also enjoy *Boyz ll Men* and *Paula Abdul* as their *"Hangin' Tough"* opening Acts, 4) *Poison*, followed by main Act *"Let's Get really ROCKED. Yeah. Let's go ALL the way." Def Leppard*, 5) *TLC* in their amazing duo comeback appearance after 15 years, R.i.P. *Left Eye* *"'Cause We go Way Back, Way Back, Way Back"*, 6) *Cheap Trick*, followed by main Act *Foreigner*, 7) *Melissa Etheridge*, 8) *"The Truth About* self-Love" spreading *P!NK* who truly understands how to *"Get the Party started"*, *Garbage, Red Hot "Californication" Chili Peppers* and *Alanis Morissette* at the phenomenal, in *Del Mar* CA hosted, 3 days lasting KAABOO Festival location, 9) *U2*, whilst *"With or Without You"* celebrating their 30y years *"The Joshua Tree"* anniversary milestone, 10) *"Get the Balance Right. Get the Balance Right."* and *"Enjoy the Silence"* teaching *Depeche Mode* and with the closing Act of a vessel, that *"little Linda"* remembers to have enjoyed as her second ever attended LiVE Music event choice in 1995, recognized as *TatAAA!* Miss *"Black Cat" Janet Jackson.* Gr*AaoW*L. *"One way or Another, it's gonna Find Ya' and Give Ya'. Watch Out."* That's right, my dear *Co-Traveler*. And if you happen to be interested in experiencing some of these magical created *"Now Moments"* alongside with me, then please know that *"little Linda"* meanwhile with LOTS of jOY decided to UPload her many, during those time traveling spectacles with her reliable silver black iPhone 5s device recorded footage, in the form of Medley's onto her lindaswizz YouTube channel. HA. Enjoy! Then, as soon as these various occasions *"ongRowingly"* succeeded in transporting my *"True little Linda Self"* back to those further with LOTS of *"FuN Facts"* linked *Teenage, delightful Housekeeping School Adventure, Charlotte North Carolina*, first *"Dream come True" "Cali Dreamin'"* visit, *TKB Erlen, WUBA* and to her *"Don't Dream your Life. Live your Dream."* Preparation *"Head Cinema"* recordings, the amazing Universe then swiftly made sure, to seal this spectacular and with plenty of flashback infused SWiTZERLAND or *"Let the Games Begin"* provided journey, by treating my sparkling *"inner Artist"* with many *"MORE. AaoW!"* thrilling and this time from Mister Lynch's soul hand-picked LiVE Act vibrations, throughout the entire course of this magical 2 ½ days lasting Festival of Disruption event of his. Boom. That's right. Yeeha! Which wonderful attended occasion therefore furthermore granted *"little Linda"* with the splendid opportunities, to for ONE enhance her thus far own collected Music taste repertoire with various newly attracted and as fine acknowledged Entertainers, that introduced themselves as wooHOO *"Rock 'n Rollin'" The Kills, with Bon Iver, TV On The Radio, Sharon Van Etten, Laura Marling* and as complete hilarious *Reggie Watts*, to for TWO finally materialize my *"inner Artist's" Desire* to No Matter What being part of the mystical and surreal "Twin Peaks" reality creation, whilst have given the fantastic opportunity, to place my Linda Wartenweiler vessel on the, in the recreational The Red Room formation placed couch, CLiCK, to for THREE witness "Mulholland Drive's" legendary and incredible talented *Rebekah Del Rio's* voice perform her, within one Episode of the "just in time" 25 years later picked UP and aired "Twin Peaks: The Return" 2017 introduced new song twice, and this first on a, within a ViP venue located balcony perspective, and once again in front of the famous "Lynchian" GiANT Red curtain wall scenery 2 nights later, to for FOUR Take in *Moby's* complete genius, in November 1990 released and into an instant smash HiT metamorphosed own interpretation recording of "Twin Peaks'" renowned *"Laura Palmer's Theme"* song, titled *"GO"* as part of his LiVE DJ Act appearance and to for FiVE enjoy two with thrills and chills packed *"Dream come True"* like Q&A's from a very close by provided perspective of first "Laura Palmer's" borrowed vessel, also known as *Sheryl Lee*, followed by THE perfect last cherry on top delivered gift of the one, that inhabits the soul of *"little Linda's"* the night before *"Eye-to-Eye"* encountered *"Catching the Big Fish"* Hero's, David Lynch. YEEHA. And. Jodeliuuuhuuu! YUP. And with this additional, with LOTS of *"WHAM. BAM."* and with plenty further SpeCial eFFecTs loaded avalanche collected puzzle "peace" at view, it out of my, within this very *"Now Moment"* emerging *Dot Connecting* perspective, actually happens to dawn on me, that the amazing Universe's genius master game plan fusion of all these many thus far, within this SO REWARDiNG experienced *What's Next "The Artist's Way" "TreasureWomBox"* chapter *"Heart over Head"* guided into *"Swimming DOWN ALONG my OWN truthful inner "Self-stDream" "Stepping-Stone"* action choices, in collaboration with my soul's in mid 2017 ignited desire, to *"All or Nothing"* like implement this rather powerful, within a new *"Catching the Big Fish"* reading undertaken venture re-encountered *"Living The Art Life means a Dedication to it, a COMPLETE Dedication, and therefore Anything that Distracts from that Path is NOT part of The Art Life" "Life Toolbox"* ingredient philosophy into "her" daily Doing Me doings, to my UTMOST excitement actually seemed to lastly successfully have led my determined and *"The Eye of the Tiger"* whistling on the Edge walking *"inner ARTreyu Warrioress"* at some point, during the course of this previous *"Rising UP, Back on my Feet. Have the Guts, to Chase my Glory."* embraced chapter creation, towards "our" in 2013 set *"Finding back Home Again"* oak tree road trip arrival spot. Which is *TatAAA!* That's right. Destination *"True little*

Linda Wait-a-While Self". "Welcome back ho*ME again, my dear ME."* BOAH!!! Wait. WHAT?! Really?! WE FiNALLY MADE iT BACK?! O.M.G.! That is SO AWESOME! WOOHOO! YAY. YAY. YAY. OH.MMHH.G. UFFF. Ufff. ufff. GRATiTUDE. And. *"AaoW!"* YES, and this wonderful discovery surely finds it selves in this very *"Now Moment"* resonating in about the EXACT same *"My body's raiSiNG and flying in the HiGHER Place in Space"* experience manner, just as Meck and Dino's soul express it in their UPlifting *"Feels like* ho*ME"* sensation description. That's right my beloved *Co-Traveler.* YEEHA. Which newly gathered perspective actually on top of it all even HiTs my awareness with this quite interesting A-HA CLiCKiNG reality UPdate, of making it seem as if all these past, especially throughout this as rather powerful resonating 2017 undertaken *"Living on Earth Game"* adventure *"Stepping-Stone"* creations, eventually just in time ended up for my vessel's *"Now* appearing 3rd *"Cali Dream Catchin'"* anniversary relocation celebration *Moment"*, lining themselves UP in order to lead this then entered *Adjusting, Healing* and *Rebuilding* journey into its Three's A Charm "Mission *I'mPOSSiBLE"* full circle status mode. WOAH. WHAT?! That's so *"Coo-coo-cool. Yeah, yeah. This is so cool."* YEAH. Well, and this reality check therefore lastly finds itself wonderfully succeeding, in revealing to my at times SO tried fallen *Patience* practicing *"Push*ing" on the Edge walking *"inner ARTreyu Warrioress"*, as of WHY this *"NeverEnding"* seemingly *"the DOiNG ME PROjECT"* project metamorphosis ended up demanding SO many resources out of my *"ongRowing"* available precious "Abundance of Time" gift at hand. BOOM. CLiCK. A-HA. *"Eventually all Things Fall into Place. Until then Laugh at the Confusion. Live for the Moments. And Know that Everything happens for a Reason."* HA! That's right Herr Einstein. Your bequeathed wisdom surely once anew finds itself resonating with my SO delighted soul in its HiGHEST notes available. YEEHA. Danke schön. Though, before this entire *"Self-*r*Ecreational" "Spread your Wings my Child and Fly HiGH." "Butterfly eFFecT"* found itself fully being enabled to embark onto its magical journey down *"little Linda's"* destined *"I'mPOSSiBLE"* Red life purpose and soul mission "Mulholland Drive" rabbit hole *hi*Story lane, and this as *"wiLD & Free"* as possible, my brave on the Edge walking *"inner ARTreyu Warrioress"* first needed to execute ONE last for it essential with *"Truth AND Dare"* infused key *"Stepping-Stone"* action jUMP. ABRACADABRA. Let's GO.

"WOW. I truly was re-Born in the U.S.A. Yeah."
Now, as one of my MOST important, within the first 5 inward traveling *"The Artist's Way"* filled weeks detected discoveries came to introduce itself with the awareness "fact", that all these many additional, throughout this past *"Head over Heart"* accepted U-Turn chapter accumulated *"Cause and eFFecT"* practiced choices, actually ended up leading my entire US-Swiss Linda created existence into a with The Nothing disclosed inner reality UPdate experience, the all-time supportive Universe therefore immediately, after its successful *"Back to the 80ies"* launched reconnection rocket, swiftly continued its magical supporting Doings by informing my

soul, that all the many thus far achieved transformations just happened to have unlocked a new *"Letting go of Something that No Longer Serves One's Growth and Expansion"* exercise and that the execution of this action step thereafter VERY much so would enabling my *"Self"* to even MORE so efficiently *"Keep on Movin'* forward *my Darling. Ooh ooh-ooh ooh."* towards this *"True little Linda Self"* destination of mine. Sweet! Sounds great. What is it? What is it? Well, and the *Next* delivered MUST DO *"Stepping-Stone"* suggestion this time around ended up presenting itself in the form of an as EXTREMLY crazy vibrating *"Not even the Sky is the Limit"* skydiving equation. Boom. WOAAAAH! What?! Are you insane? Are you *"Seriously?!?"* asking me to throw my vessel out of an actual flying airplane?! Why on heavens earth would I want to do that for!? NO WAY! Yup. Something like that happened to appear as my instant by *Miss Fear* conducted reaction choice, which information flow therefore right away led my *"Leave Me ALONE. Leave Me AlooHoHone"* screaming *"Self"* to disregard the just heard of by furthermore deciding, to simply direct my available *"Time and Energy"* resources on activities, that with guarantee would be continuing to enhance this wonderful *"Living on Earth Game"* experience of mine, from *"Moment-to-Moment"*. That's right. Certainly, the wonderful Universe found itself as usual the least impressed with my soul's initial developed defense mechanism attitude and therefore simply continued its own Doings by sending my brave on the Edge walking *"inner ARTreyu Warrioress"* with some further get Ready Steady for what's to come filled reminders. UFFF. Oh boy. Yes. And this "iT" instantaneously did, by first having *"little Linda"* "stumble" over a, within this cozy cottage mounted TV screen set espied "Baywatch" episode, which for ONE happened to air her teenage flame's vessel David Hasselhoff placed within a small aircraft, that of course TWO showed his "Mitch Buchannon" character hesitantly and doubtfully getting Ready for his own skydiving adventure. AAhh. What?! Yup. What's new right, my dearest *Co-Traveler*? LOL. Exactly. Followed by "iT's" Getting through to Me gesture, of presenting my eyeballs, a few days later, with an on the horizon appearing hawk and this literally the instant after my curious inner Gemini released her *"Where Should I Go from Here on"* question. Hmmm. Certainly, my animal loving soul happily started to follow its flight route from her outdoors situated lounge area seat and found "herself" rather taken aback, the second that it's diving down ignited vessel a few heart beats later decided, to as quick as a bunny disappear behind the many below it rooted trees and placed buildings. WOAHW. WHAT just happened?! That's right. And this entire out of the blue appeared spectacle then even more so succeeded, in catching my brave on the Edge walking *"inner ARTreyu Warrioress'"* attention, the moment that my *"Head Cinema"* got triggered, to project a, from a few days prior recorded tape, onto its screen which to my amazement ended up showcasing some actual, from the heavens gliding down towards mother earth again, observed skydiving vessels and this at the EXACT matching horizon spot. Holly Molly! Really?! NO WAY. OMG. Oh man. Yup. And that is HOW the wonderful Universe lastly got through to my meanwhile with Giggle. Giggle. Giggles transmuted *"Self"* and HOW I thereafter declared my willingness, to take a look into this as life-threatening resonating game plan suggestion at hand. For starters. Guided by a *"Thy Wish is my Command"* adapted attitude, I therefore instantly walked my vessel back towards this inside of my oh SO magical experienced Light & Zen Purple Door Cottage *"Home Sweet Home"* base formation placed MacBook Pro device and found my *"Self"* once anew rather astounded and somewhat freaked out about the swiftly, from this genius Google search machine delivered skydiving results. UiiiUiiiUiii. That's right. At first, my awareness found itself getting fed with the information flow, that the closest falling from the heavens opportunity found itself being situated "only" a 5 minutes car ride from my Oasis away, followed by its then as rather sarcastic interpreted *GoJump Oceanside Inc.* enforcing picked suggestion. Boom. OMG. Right?! LOL. Yes, and all these many UP onto that arisen *"Now Moment"* accumulated *"Synchronicity par Excellence"* "coincidences" at play, then with "No Doubt" succeeded in stirring my entire inner world UP to its wiLDest, which newly *"Self-created"* reality UPdate therefore right away caused for my soul to within a SLAP call in a much-needed *"Help! I need Somebody"* Breath-in Breath-out related time out. Throughout the following 10 to 15 minutes or so, I then, guided by a newly pulled *"Positivity Card"*, found my *"Self"* anxiously being busy in directing all my available focus on the gathering exercise of the possible reasons, as of WHY this crazy MUST DO proposal would disclose itself to be of "SUCH" tremendous help upon my soul's hopefully *"ongRowing"*, as Linda Wartenweiler identified *"Living on Earth Game"* experience. UFFF. After some various inflowing collected insights, that to my surprise also happened to include a sudden flashback journey to my vessel's approximately 7 years counted "matching" *"Growth and Expansion"* state, in which my soul came to re-witness, how *"little Linda"* during one of those many with *"FuN Facts"* infused Parkweg gang play dates came to express her skydiving interest as a "grownUP", *"AAAH. WHAT?! Oh boy. Yes, that's actually true. I DiD send this "The Power of Words" materialization request out back then. Oh NO!"*, my awareness then at some point got left with the as rather iNspirational and as "logical" resonating insight, that this entire with *"Truth AND Dare"* filled package actually would be offering an extraordinary opportunity for my re*Booting* ho*ME* cruising soul, to with one clean eFFecTive SLAM strip away ALL the remains of this meanwhile "Gone Baby Gone" transmuted, once so diligently US-Swiss Linda *"Self-*established" identity. BOOM. *"Gotch Ya'."* Well, and this explanation certainly hit my auricles in its sweetest tunes, as it on top of it all caused for my brave on the Edge walking *"inner ARTreyu Warrioress"* to realize, that this shedding exercise with guarantee would be shooting this OH SO annoying, especially throughout this as after all quite rewarding unraveled *Artistic and "Self-*developing" *Boot Camp* chapter bonded *Miss Fear* "friend", straight away back to *ScarEcity*. To where she actually belonged to. HA! Sounds GREAT. With these UPdated inner shifts, I then quickly dived back into this rEvolutionary world of Internet in order to find out more about the actual costs of this UPcoming *"Living on Earth Game"* adventure proposal and found my *"Self"*, right after the disclosure of a very affordable Groupon offer, thrown into about the same out of excuses and "exit doors" reality sphere, as back then, when *"little Linda"* found herself with the help of this kind Albert's soul suddenly faced with being only one more action step away from embarking onto the then just at its station reappeared personal *"Acting Dream come True"* s-Express train opportunity. AAAH. HELP. Anybody? Gina?! UFFF. Alrighty then. Let's do this! Let's *"Push"* this OLD invented *"Self"* entirely out of my system, so that there ONLY will be room left for this "NEW", AUTHENTiC and with Giggles filled *"True little Linda Self"* of mine. Whenever she feels Ready Steady to move back hoME again. YEAH. *"I Want to Break Free."* CLiCK. And just like that, this with thrills and chills packed *"The Choice is Yours"* dated *"One Door Always MUST get closed First, before MANY others thereafter will be able to Burst Wide Open by rewarding THE Daring Soul with many UPgrading and more Suitable Blessings instead"* first ever purchased tandem skydiving key found itself being save and sound zoOMed into my possession, which ticket most likely even ended up being tied to the "then" bluntly sent out *"Ask and You shall Receive at its PERFCT Time"* request. HA! Then, after another 2 days lasting *"Back, Back, Forth and Forth"* prep talk ride with these alluring *"Head over Heart"* praising Madam ProCrastination, including hopefully soon *"Live Me ALONE. Live Me AlooHoHone."* altered Miss Fear "companions" to be, my brave on the Edge walking *"inner ARTreyu Warrioress"* lastly felt Ready Steady, to as a Next *"Stepping-Stone"* proceed with the reservation definition of this essential MUST DO *"Now Moment"* exercise at view, which re-birthing date therefore soon set itself in stone with the wonderful *Sunday March 20th 2016, 11:00am* resonating time slot availability. Which date on top of it all furthermore happens to be placed 4 days away from Missiz NENA's own *"Whoomp! There she is."* festivities. HA. BOOM. *"Gotch Ya'."* The remaining 7 days, within this soon as OLD to be declared *"Living on Earth Game"* creation reality chapter at hand, I then decided to acknowledge even mORE so from an enhanced applied awareness perspective than usual and to furthermore use wisely in regards of the proper preparation approach of What's to come Next, which ignited *"I'mPOSSiBLE"* reflection process therefore certainly also left enough room for my *"Self"*, to also dwell upon a possible GAME OVER outcome. Yup. After some further inward traveling undertaken excursions, my soul then at some point found "herself" floating even more so in peace, the instant that my awareness came across the as rather emPowering *"Change the way you Look At Things and the Things you Look At Change"* resonating believe formula, that iF this incredible, genius and absolute precious, once from beloved Heidi and Urs gifted *"Not even the Sky is the Limit"* *"Home Sweet Home"* base of "hers", after this CRAZY assigned jUMPing outside of an airplane exercise as Desired truly would be stepping safe and sound back onto mother earth's ground again, that this as miraculous acknowledged reunion moment, therefore simultaneously also would be ringing in a, as mind-blowing and as VERY appreciated vibrating NEW *"Living on Earth Game"* cycle, identified as THE OTHER PLANET or *"Let the Games Begin"*, in which reality formation my Linda Wartenweiler soul therefore furthermore would be granted with the, as ABSOLUTELY as *Privileged* and *Honored* interpreted opportunities, to 1) *"OngRowingly"* proceed with the creation materialization process of many MORE from *"little Linda's"* so beloved thrilling and with *"FuN Facts"* infused *"Enjoying Movies, TV shows, Music, Dancing and Celebrating this "Living on Earth Game" adventure of mine as often as possible" "Super Happy Comfort Zone"* experiences, upon this once *"wiLD & Free"* chosen ultimate "risky" and as unknown identified *"Swimming DOWN ALONG my OWN truthful inner "Self-stDream" Red* life purpose and soul mission "Mulholland Drive" rabbit hole lane and to 2) Approach my *"Don't Dream your Life. Live your THE Ultimate Childhood Dreams come True truth"* travels once anew about as *FREE, "ALiVE and KiCKiN'"* as back then, during my *Patience* practicing soul's *"NeverEnding"* and as boring perceived *Developing, Growing* and *Floating* around journey over a total duration of 8 months. ABRACADABRA. Yeeha! YEAH. *"Let's Rock 'n Roll!"* As soon as THE day appeared on the calendar, my brave on the Edge walking *"inner ARTreyu Warrioress"* therefore even more so came to decide to AS awake as possible *"Keep on Movin' forward my Darling. Ooh ooh-ooh ooh."* from one Moment into the *Next*, as I with "No Doubt" found my *"Self"* very aware of the "truth", that EVERYTHiNG Inside Out, would be getting experienced differently after my vessel's touch down. And this No Matter what. BOOM. With many further NENA infused preparation and supporting molecules dancing within my system, I then still rather nervously parked my car rental at the given meeting minute at an available spot at the in Oceanside located mini airport facility, where *"little Linda"* shortly after to her utmost amusement came to learn, that the owner of this provoking GoJump invention actually happened to be considered a *SURPRiSE!* Swiss Confederate himself. *"Grüezi"*. HA! Of Course! Right, my dearest *Co-Traveler?!* Giggle. Giggle. Giggle. OMG. Certainly, this newly gained information flow thereafter within a SLAP succeeded, in calming my *"Self"* down to its fullest and that with SpeCial eFFecTs infused *"All is Good. All is Well."* appeared inner cognition then even more so got enforced, the second that my soul, approximately 45 minutes later, lastly came in touch with the one of "her" as kindly acknowledged assigned tandem guide's, who introduced "himself" as *Wilox. "Hello? Is it me you're looking for?"* Aahh. Yes. I guess. Hello. After a short and crisp introduction and instruction period, this *"ongRowing"* soothing inner knowing then lastly developed itself into this fantastic awareness check, in which I came to feel, that this originally in England started out falling from the heavens expert with "No Doubt" happened to be THE perfect sent along "midwife" and that *"little Linda's"* vessel with guarantee found itself being guided into VERY safe hands and laps. HA. Then, as soon as the *"Now Moment"* arose, in which the tinny airplane, equipped with some further "CRAZY" embarked *"wiLD & Free"* loving souls, found itself Ready Steady Go rolling fastER, *faSTER* and *FASTER*, it at some point very much so HiT my awareness, that my OLD *"Self's"* time was UP and that the ONLY way out from there on remained THE Door leading into The Nothing. WOAHHHH. Or in other words, straight back into the sphere, in which *"Not even the Sky is the Limit."* WOOHOO. YES. YES. YES. And this thrilling, from the with magic filled Universe's disclosed *"Living on Earth Game"* master key plan UPdate at grasp, certainly within a SLAP succeeded, in resonating in the HiGHEST notes available with all the many *"NeverEnding"* from *"little Linda's"* thus far sent out *Own Wants, Needs, Desires and Dreams* orders at "catch" and to furthermore leave my reflecting and ecstatic turned soul with this wonderful inner certainty, that this with countless opportunities packed *"Action holds the Key to your Freedom"* launched *"Everything you Desire lies on the Other Side of Resistance"* rocket, truly revealed itself as THE last essential puzzle "peace" needed, within this chess game at play and that my *"Self"* thereafter lastly in its fullest capacity would be enabled to Do Me as authentically as I *DARED* for it to be. *"Yeah, Oh Yeah, Oh Yeah." "Let's Get really ROCKED. Yeah. Let's go ALL the way."* LOVE. And. GRATiTUDE. Then, as soon as this friendly Wilox's interesting wristwatch *"more, More, MORE. AaoW!"* started to indicate, that the airplane almost found itself cruising within the recommended safe zone altitude so that everyone lastly could get dismissed, I therefore as rehearsed quickly began to relocate my, with trust, thrills and chills filled vessel onto my guide's laps, which executed motion then immediately caused for my assigned "midwife" to proceed with the pre-instructed Strapping onto his Gesture action SNAP. *"Gotcha. Where I wanted Ya'."* Uiiii! In our sudden, into a Siamese twins transmuted set up, Wilox then slowly began to move this EnglishSwiss converted package towards the for us as *Next* aimed for Edge at view, to where our ecstatic radiating souls full hearted found themselves embracing this magical arisen *"Time to say Goodbye"* moment, with some liberating *"Get Ready Steady to Jump my Darling. Just take my hand. jUMP!"* sound*zZZ*. AHHHH! Bye-Bye. CLiCK.

* * *

"Der Anfang vom Ende/The Beginning of the End"

*

Hello and welcome again, my dearest *Co-Traveler*, NOW being placed on the Other Side of this magical and "transformational" umbilical cord sphere. Wink. Very much so, my Heart, *"little Linda"* and my Soul would LOVE to congratulate You and Your *"True little Self"* for successfully having arrived at The End of this mutually undertaken "little" *"Growth and Expansionary"* excursion of ours as a glorious *"Dream Catchin'"* TEAM and also Thank YOU for your valuable and MUCH appreciated gifted *Attention, Support, "Time and Energy"* resources. It truly means a LOT to me. Hugs. Now, even though that another *"Time to say Goodbye" "Now Moment"* is about to hit our senses, my soul very much so remains ABSOLUTELY thrilled for this arising The Beginning chapter of your OWN *"ongRowing" "Living on Earth Game"* reality *"Self*-aware" creations ahead, which with the help of your personal UPdated collected *"Life Toolbox"* ingredients hopefully will be blessing your many adventures with an Abundance of your precious soul's EXACT *"Heart over Head"* picked Wants, Needs, Desires and Dreams *"Stepping-Stone"* materialization outcomes. *"The Choice is Yours."* After all. Always. HA. Please, also feel free to share ANY of your *"True little Self's"* inner and/or outer achieved *Successes, Breakthroughs, Experiences, Shifts* or *Anything Else* that you feel triggered to express, with *"little Linda"* that stand in direct *"Cause and eFFecT"* collaboration with this *"the DOiNG ME PROjECT"* project at End. Excitedly, I thereafter would LOVE to spread your own UPlifting and iNspiring *"Truth AND Dare"* infused Word, Picture and/or Video combinations to all the many further brave *Co-Traveling* souls out there on the, eSpeCially for iT in this rEvolutionary "www." world created *www.theDoingMeProject.com* BLOG section. Let's be a Light for One Another and Let's *"Heal the World"* together as a Unit by first *"Starting to make That CHANGE with the Soul in the Mirror"*, as carrying and talented Michael Jackson's "Once Upon a Time" very wisely worded it in these two precious Art "peaces" of "his". ThanXoxo Michael for everything. Please R.i.P. And therefore, *"Let's Go Crazy."* Let's Do iT. Let's Make That Change. *"ongRowingly"*. Together. As in The End, *"WE ARE ALL EXACTLY THE SAME"*, No Matter one's appearance, "position" or preferences, remember? HA. Which magical *"Truth Fact"* equation therefore with No Doubt keeps us all swimming in this rather incredible miraculous and mysterious *"Living on Earth Game"* spectacle as ONE Team, and this in its earlier discovered *"NeverEnding"* loop phenomenon. *"Gotcha, where I want Ya'?"* Ok then, *"Get UP my Darling and Get Your Dreamin' before your Chance is over." "NOW, take my hand. jUMP!"* YeehAHHHH! CLiCK.

* * *

<u>Mark Twain</u>
"Twenty Years from Now You Will Be moRE Disappointed by the Things you Didn't DO thAn by the Ones you DiD DO. So throw OFF the Bowlines. Sail Away from the Safe Harbor. Catch the Trade Winds in YOUR Sail. Explore. Dream. Discover."

* * *

<u>Mark Twain</u>
"Life is Short. Break the Rules. Forgive Quickly. Kiss Slowly. Love Truly. Laugh UNcontrollably and NEVER Regret ANYTHiNG that makes YOU Smile."

* * *

<u>Mark Twain</u>
"When you find yourSelf on the Side Of the Majority, you should Pause and Reflect."

* * *

<u>Mark Twain</u>
"Give EVERY day The Chance to Become THE MOST beautiful of YOUR Life."

* * *

<u>Henry David Thoreau</u>
"I learned this, at least, by My Experiment, that iF One Advances Confidently in the Direction of "HiS/HER" Dreams, and Endeavors to Live THE Life which "sHe" has iMagined, "sHe" WiLL meet with a Success unexpected in Common Hours."

* * *

<u>Mark Twain</u>
"I've had a LOT of Worries in my Life, mOST of which NEVER happened."

* * *

<u>Mark Twain</u>
"Don't wait. The Time will Never be just "right"."
...and tomorrow might Never arrive...

* * *

SO
tHinK BiG
thiNk difFeRent
Do YoU
ALWAYS
thanXOXO

**

P.S. And if you happen to be UP for one very last *emPowering, iNspiring* and *A-HA CLiCKiNG* adventure KiCK, my beloved *Co-Traveler*, then please make sure to take a look at the on *www.TheDoingMeProject.com* from *"little Linda"* as BONUS UPloaded and for our purposes slightly adjusted Movie script of the recently with enormous *"Life Toolbox"* wisdom filled and as rather iNcredibly to our excursion "matching" detected last sceneS, of this magical in 1984 "The *NeverEnding* Story" production. See it for your *"True little Self"*. *sHE* definitely will be loving to find out what *Fearless Atreyu, Luck Dragon Fuchur/Falkor, Bastian, Gmork and the Childlike Empress* have to say about this mysterious *"Living on Earth Game"* spectacle of ours. *"Yeah, Oh Yeah, Oh Yeah."* Wink. Alrighty then,

*

eNjOy
saFe traVels
kEEp having FuN
ByE-bYe
LOVE

*

www.ingramcontent.com/pod-product-compliance
Lightning Source LLC
Chambersburg PA
CBHW071700160426
43195CB00012B/1525